Financial Strategy

Financial Strategy: Adding Stakeholder Value brings together some of the best articles from leading writers in the field of financial strategy. The increased emphasis on adding value for organisations is reflected in the writings in this book, each of which looks at a particular aspect of how to add value: through investment, financing, and risk management. This volume also covers the debate on corporate governance and performance measurement and reflects both the coming together of issues in accounting and finance as well as the application of financial strategy to organisations in the private and public sectors worldwide.

Financial Strategy: Adding Stakeholder Value is the prescribed MBA Course Reader for the Financial Strategy module of the Open University Business School MBA course. Designed to meet the needs of students studying at advanced undergraduate and postgraduate levels, it will also appeal to practitioners wishing to keep abreast of the latest thinking in the field of financial strategy.

The editor is Janette Rutterford, Professor of Financial Management at The Open University Business School.

Opinions expressed in this Course Reader are not necessarily those of the Course Team nor of The Open University.

If you are interested in studying the MBA course, Financial Strategy, or other related courses, please write to the Course Reservations and Sales Centre, PO Box 724, Milton Keynes, MK7 6ZS, or visit The Open University Business School website at http://oubs.open.ac.uk for more information.

Financial Strategy
Adding Stakeholder Value

Edited by

Janette Rutterford
The Open University Business School

JOHN WILEY & SONS
Chichester · New York · Weinheim · Brisbane · Singapore · Toronto

in association with

Selection, editorial material and article 21 Copyright © The Open University 1998

Published 1998 by John Wiley & Sons Ltd,
Baffins Lane, Chichester,
West Sussex PO19 1UD, England

National   01243 779777
International (+44) 1243 779777
e-mail (for orders and customer service enquiries): cs-books@wiley.co.uk
Visit our Home Page on http://www.wiley.co.uk
    or http://www.wiley.com

Other Wiley Editorial Offices

John Wiley & Sons, Inc., 605 Third Avenue,
New York, NY 10158–0012, USA

WILEY-VCH Verlag GmbH, Pappelallee 3,
D-69469 Weinheim, Germany

Jacaranda Wiley Ltd, 33 Park Road, Milton,
Queensland 4064, Australia

John Wiley & Sons (Asia) Pte Ltd, 2 Clementi Loop #02–01
Jin Xing Distripark, Singapore 129809

John Wiley & Sons (Canada) Ltd, 22 Worcester Road,
Rexdale, Ontario M9W 1L1, Canada

British Library Cataloguing in Publication Data

A catalogue record for this book is available from the British Library

ISBN 0–471–98348–9 (cloth)
ISBN 0–471–98349–7 (paperback)

Typeset in Times 11/12pt
Printed and bound in Great Britain by Biddles Ltd, Guildford and Kings Lynn
This book is printed on acid-free paper responsibly manufactured from sustainable forestry, in which at least two trees are planted for each one used for paper manufacture.

Contents

Introduction

Janette Rutterford

It has long been acknowledged that finance plays a vital role within the organisation, with accounting systems designed to help organisational decision making and control and financial techniques such as discounted cash flow providing tools for valuing projects and investments.

However, in recent years, it has become clear that financial strategy on its own can have a major impact on organisations. Choosing the correct financial strategy can add value and make the stakeholders of the organisation better off, independent of production or marketing decisions. This book will outline the major ways in which this can be done, looking in particular at adding value through investment decisions, financing decisions, and risk management decisions. Most texts concentrate on accounting or on finance and fail to recognise the dilemma facing managers in practice – how to ensure that the decisions taken within the organisation using accounting measures feed through into financial valuation based on cash flows. This collection of articles will show how this split between accounting – which has traditionally been historic in emphasis – and finance – which is viewed as forward looking – is being broken down through the use of such measures as economic value added.

Indeed, advances have been made in performance measurement in a number of areas. First, the traditional split between analysts concentrating on earnings and corporate financiers concentrating on cash flows has been eroded, with analysts now valuing companies using cash flows, and financiers aware of the impact of earnings announcements on share prices. In fact, accounting regulators, particularly in the UK, are moving towards a discounted cash flow valuation of assets approach and away from the historic cost approach in an attempt to reduce the gap between financial market value and accounting book value.

Second, as globalisation of capital markets has taken place, the need for common accounting standards to ensure comparability of financial reporting has been recognised and investors are no longer so confused by the differences between, say, Japanese, German and US differences in accounting methods. Investors have also become more aware, through publications such as Terry Smith's *Accounting for Growth*, of the ability of management to be creative in their reporting of profits and assets, and accounting regulators have moved to stamp out the worst practices. As a result of these changes, there is a trend towards a common international accounting standard to which multinationals seeking finance in international capital markets will be required to adhere.

Third, the use of financial performance measures has become more widespread, particularly in the light of the massive privatisation programme which took place in the UK in the 1980s and is still taking place around the world. Newly privatised organisations whose objectives and performance measures had been stated in non-financial terms were suddenly required to report to creditors and investors and sometimes regulators who assessed performance in financial terms. But this trend has also taken place within the public sector, with public services required to compare their performance with that of equivalent private sector enterprises. The notion of *value for money* has become commonplace. Public sector projects are now being evaluated, financed and judged on hitherto exclusively private sector performance measures.

Internationalisation has also widened the financial strategy debate in terms of financial objectives. The traditional dominance of the US in finance theory is being eroded. Although Jensen and Meckling's 1976 paper on agency theory pointed out that managers may not all be trying singlemindedly to maximise shareholder value, the emphasis until recently was on how best to make sure that managers did adopt that approach, through appropriate covenants in loan agreements, say, or well-structured incentive schemes. However, other countries have different cultural histories and expressing corporate objectives only in terms of shareholders has come to be viewed as too narrow by some commentators who prefer the stakeholder approach of Continental European countries or who are concerned with the consumer in public sector service organisations.

Finally, a major development in the theory of finance has been that of options, both as risk management instruments and as ways of valuing contingent liabilities such as are embedded in convertible bonds or even equities. The ability to hedge or take on risk in the light of the volatility of future returns has been one of the major advantages of options and an activity known as financial engineering has developed to help companies and financial institutions to manage their risk and return effectively and even to add value through exploiting capital market inefficiencies.

More recently, attention has been turned on what are known as real options, options which are not traded on financial markets but which are linked to projects or investment decisions by firms. These include, for example, the option to delay an investment until more detailed information is available, the option to abandon an investment once it has been started, or the option to keep a plant in mothballs until demand increases sufficiently to warrant opening it again. This is one of the most exciting developments in financial strategy, as it explains management actions which appeared incomprehensible under the more simplistic discounted cash flow approach.

TRENDS IN FINANCE THEORY

The first section of the book includes articles which look at recent developments in the key theories underpinning the study of financial strategy of organisations, namely the efficient markets hypothesis, portfolio theory and the capital asset pricing model.

The efficient markets hypothesis is key to an understanding of capital markets and is expressed in three versions, weak, semi-strong and strong, in terms of the efficiency in which certain types of information are incorporated into market prices. If information is included into market prices in an efficient way, so that no investor can make excess returns by using that information, this means that managers can use share prices as fair value measures, not needing to worry about, say, when to make a rights issue or when to launch a takeover bid. In the 1970s and 1980s, a large number of studies were published which provided evidence, for a particular type of information on a particular sample of share prices, that markets were indeed efficient in so far as publicly available information such as earnings and past share prices were concerned. However, more recently, academics have suggested that the tests were flawed, either in the models they used or in the quality of data tested, and that even the largest stock markets such as in the US are in some cases inefficient. Lee and Verbrugge, in their article, 'The Efficient Market Theory Thrives on Criticism', discuss these criticisms of the theory but argue that the concept is still valid in many contexts.

The Economist article, entitled 'Risk and Return', summarises both portfolio theory and the capital asset pricing model (CAPM). The latter offers a pricing model for shares, suggesting that returns on individual shares can be estimated from the expected return on shares as a whole, the risk-free rate, and the share's Beta, which is a measure of its cyclicality with respect to the market. First put forward in the 1960s, the CAPM as it is known has also come under attack both for the assumptions which it makes and the failure of empirical evidence to support the model. The Fischer Black article, 'Estimating Expected Return', critiques the latest attempts to develop a more complex multi-factor model, such as the Fama-French suggestion that individual share returns are determined by size and price earnings (PE) ratios as well as by the market as a whole. As you will see, consensus has not yet emerged on a replacement for the CAPM which, although flawed, does have the advantage of simplicity and is used by most firms when determining the rate of return on equity their investors expect.

ADDING VALUE THROUGH INVESTMENT

The use of discounted cash flow techniques and the theoretical dominance of the net present value rule as a decision tool for project appraisal have long been part of finance textbooks. In this section of the book, we look at the investment decision from a different perspective, first by exploring what

happens in the real world and why managers do not always follow the theoretically optimal model and, second, by exploring how option valuation and
the concept of real options can be applied to investment decision making.

The Wardlow article, 'Investment Appraisal Criteria and the Impact of
Low Inflation', looks at firms' hurdle rates for projects and reports on an
informal survey of UK companies conducted by the Bank of England. It
finds that hurdle rates for UK companies are higher than expected and do
not seem to have come down in line with lower inflation rates. It reports on
how firms do not just use the net present value decision rule but also place
emphasis on measures such as the internal rate of return and payback.

Lumijärvi, in 'Selling of Capital Investments to Top Management', describes
in detail how managers in a major Scandinavian corporation managed their
project appraisal process and how political processes and non-financial factors influenced decision making and how financial techniques such as discounted cash flow were seen as screening devices. The inclusion of this
article is designed to highlight an innovation in finance and accounting
research, namely a willingness to go into organisations to explore how financial decisions are taken in order to be able to identify flaws in the fairly
limited theoretical models of financial behaviour.

In the third article, by Dixit and Pindyck, 'The Options Approach to
Capital Investment', the authors describe in detail how options can be used
to better understand the investment decision. They explore such issues as
the option to abandon and to delay, and suggest examples of companies for
whom this approach might be valid. They also go on to explore how options
might explain why managers do not follow the NPV rule, recommended by
the academic literature, to the letter. The oil company and electricity gener-
ator case studies are extracted from an article by Leslie and Michaels, first
published in the *McKinsey Quarterly*, and show how, even though real options
are difficult to value in practice, thinking through investments decisions in
an options framework is a vital tool in financial strategy and in adding value
to the organisation.

The remaining article and case study in this section are concerned with
equity valuation, and hence in investment in companies rather than capital
projects. If markets are efficient, one would expect shares to be correctly
priced and any premium paid by an acquirer would have to be paid for by
synergistic benefits or cost savings achievable by the merged entity. There
is a substantial literature on how, in the main, takeovers do not add value for
the acquirer, but do add value for the acquirees who sell their shares. Until
recently, however, there was little understanding of the valuation process
inherent in new issues of shares on stock markets nor of the role of analysts
in their valuation. The article by Dechow, Hutton and Sloan, 'Solving the
New Equity Puzzle', covers this fascinating area and points out that many
primary and secondary issues of new shares are overpriced and that analysts
consistently overestimate the earnings achievable by these firms, reassess-
ing their forecasts downwards as time goes on. This calls into question the
efficiency of the new issue process and the independence of market analysts.

The final case study in this section is a collection of press cuttings concerning a major privatisation, that of Deutsche Telekom in 1996. The first article highlights the trend away from PE ratios towards such measures as enterprise value to earnings before interest, tax, depreciation and amortisation (EBITDA), and even towards discounted cash flow. The latter cuttings show that the issue was a success and that the post-issue price rose well above the issue price, even though the various valuation techniques pointed to an intrinsic value per share lower than the issue price.

ADDING VALUE THROUGH FINANCING

There has been much interest of late in optimal capital structure in the sense of how best the firm can finance itself, particularly the choice between debt and equity. The article by Myers, 'The Search for Optimal Capital Structure', discusses how the theory of optimal capital structure has developed, taking into account corporate taxes, personal taxes, bankruptcy costs and agency costs. The corporate sector has recently begun to concentrate quite heavily on the this area, trying to find the capital structure which minimises the weighted average cost of capital or WACC.

This concentration on the financing as well as the investment decision began in the 1980s with the leveraged buyout. In the 1990s, financing began to be dealt with separately from investment in the form of share repurchases (replacement of equity by debt which is more tax efficient) and repayment of excess equity in the form of special dividends. The article from *Corporate Finance*, 'Brand Owners and Capital Structure', is a case study of the branded goods sector, examining how those firms wishing to add value can do so through improvements in capital structure.

The Carapiet article, 'Making the Right Connections for Melbourne', reports on a funding exercise carried out for an infrastructure investment in Melbourne, Australia and is an example of how secured lending and judicious use of the capital markets can reduce funding costs for a project and hence add value.

The final case study of this section, by Soter and Evanson, 'Dividend Cut: The Case of FPL', reports on what happened when the dividend policy of a firm, in this case a US utility, FPL, was radically altered. After an initial downturn in the share price, the share price then more than recovered, showing that dividend policy is also an important financing decision which can affect value.

ADDING VALUE THROUGH RISK MANAGEMENT

All organisations, whether public or private sector, need to assess the different types of risk facing them and to carry out, whether formally or informally, some kind of risk audit. This has historically been most developed in the context of investment appraisal as the article by Ho and Pike, 'The Use of Risk Analysis Techniques', shows.

Foreign exchange risk, in terms of potential losses from changes in exchange rates, is also relatively well understood, although the impact of operating (or economic) exposure, outlined in the article by Lessard and Lightstone, 'Operating Exposure', is less well understood than the more obvious transaction and translation exposures to currency movements.

Organisations are exposed to a number of financial risks, including foreign exchange risk, interest rate risk, and credit risk, and the advent of futures and options linked to foreign exchange, interest rate and credit products have allowed treasurers a much greater say in how much risk they are prepared to take on and how much they wish to hedge through the use of these derivatives. The problem has been that the mathematics of derivatives, and particularly of portfolios of derivatives, is highly complex and has led to a lack of understanding between treasury departments and senior management. In some cases, treasurers have run their departments to increase returns rather than reduce risk (both approaches theoretically add value!) but in a few cases, this approach has led to substantial losses giving derivatives a bad name.

The trend therefore is to try to develop a strict risk management framework for treasury departments and the application of systematic risk analysis techniques is now routinely applied. The article by Steyn and Boessenkool, 'Modules for Standardising the Process', sets out a four-module process for managing treasury risk which tries to explain to senior management the more complex mathematical risk management tools available to treasurers today.

Tufano, in 'How Financial Engineering can Advance Corporate Strategy', looks at how, to achieve strategic objectives, firms can use financial engineering techniques to fix prices in a certain currency, link costs to revenues, or develop human resource strategies where employees have a financial interest in the firm's performance. He concentrates on derivatives as the means by which particular financial strategies can be enhanced. Brady, in 'New Ways with Derivatives', shows how particular financial derivatives can be used to hedge interest rate risk, exchange risk, commodity risk, and credit risk with what are known as over the counter or OTC options, namely derivatives sold directly by investment banks and specifically tailored to the organisation's needs rather than traded on financial markets.

Stultz, however, in his article, 'Rethinking Risk Management', explores possible reasons why the theoretical advantages of risk management tools such as derivatives, which can clearly add value through an optimal risk/return profile for the organisation, are not used in practice as the theory would suggest. A short case study on how Colgate-Palmolive manages its financial risks in practice, entitled 'Ring of Confidence', concludes this section.

MEASURING PERFORMANCE

We now turn to financial measures of performance – how to assess whether the organisation has delivered or will deliver what it has promised and how it compares with its peers either in the public or private sectors.

We start by looking at the impact of measuring performance through earnings, the traditional accountant's approach, or through cash flows, the financier's preferred method. The article by Sloan, 'Using Earnings and Free Cash Flow to Evaluate Corporate Performance', concludes that earnings do have an impact on share returns but additional information on performance is gained by also looking at cash flows. Both accounting and corporate finance measures of performance are relevant.

The next two articles cover what has become known as creative accounting. This was much discussed in the early 1990s, when firms such as Polly Peck and Queens Moat went into liquidation or had to be restructured and their financial accounts had given no indication of the disasters to come. It emerged that the flexibility allowed by the UK accounting authorities had led to managers being able to give a misleading picture of the financial performance of the firms under their management. The article by Shah, 'Creative Compliance in Financial Reporting', discusses a particular example of creative accounting used by a number of UK firms – they issued what was effectively debt in the financial sense which was treated as equity by the accounting profession. Shah highlights the game by which bankers and advisers sought to outwit the regulators to enable firms to report more conservative measures of financial gearing. The second case study is simply an extract from the 1992 Annual Report and Accounts of Queens Moat, a UK company which had used a number of accounting methods to appear more profitable than it actually was. The 1992 accounts show how, by creative accounting, a 1991 *loss* of £56 million appeared as a *profit* of £90 million.

Ball, in his article, 'Making Accounting more International: Why, How, and How Far Will It Go?', documents the pressures for convergence in accounting standards worldwide as capital markets become more global and as multinationals access funding in a number of markets. Hawkins, in his paper, 'Daimler Benz: A US GAAP Based Stock', describes how when Daimler Benz went to the US capital markets to raise funds, it reported under US GAAP as well as under German accounting rules. Investors were surprised to discover that the figures were much less attractive under US GAAP than under what had previously been considered conservative German accounting rules. Hawkins argues that this is because German accounts were not designed to be used by equity investors. The case highlights the fact that no national set of accounting rules dominates in the sense of providing 'better' measures of performance; it all depends on user needs.

Kaplan and Norton's article, 'The Balanced Scorecard – Measures that Drive Performance', introduces the idea of a wider set of performance measures than simply financial ones. It describes how firms should integrate non-financial measures into their strategy and performance measurement process to ensure that strategic objectives are achieved. This idea is clearly of relevance in the public sector where performance indicators such as length of waiting lists in hospitals reflect customer objectives which are not just financial. Likierman, in 'Performance Indicators: 20 Early Lessons from Managerial Use', reports on the success of using a wide range of performance indicators in a number of public sector organisations.

Finally, in this section, *The Economist* article, 'Valuing Companies: A Star to Sail By', looks at financial measures such as ratios and the up-and-coming economic value added, as a means of assessing organisational performance. Economic value added measures the difference between the return on capital employed (operating profits after tax) and the cost of capital – all multiplied by the money value of capital employed. Such a measure will be high for firms which have good profits *or* a low WACC, and so forces them to concentrate on adding value both through investment and through financing. It can be and is used at the divisional level to measure management performance and to design incentive schemes. *The Economist* article also refers to the balanced scorecard approach. Measures such as this and economic value added are evidence of a trend towards convergence of internal and external measures and of accounting and financial measures of organisational performance.

WHO SHOULD BENEFIT?

This section covers issues of what is known as corporate governance. This term refers to how organisations should best be managed in order to achieve their objectives. In the US, for example, with the model of managers managing firms primarily owned by outside investors, including institutional investors, the debate has been concerned with how managers can be made to act in the shareholders' best interests and whether the problem lies with the passivity of institutional investors, who are only now beginning to use their voting power to change management behaviour.

In other countries, such as the UK which has a similar organisational structure to the US, this model has been criticised. Authors such as Hutton, in his best-selling book, *The State We're In*, of which an extract is included here, have argued for a stakeholder approach, where customers, bankers, employees, and others with an interest in the organisation are considered when determining financial objectives. Hutton argues that the stakeholder approach, which is the model for organisations in Germany and France, for example, has advantages, although the increasing importance of the capital markets in these countries is leading to emphasis on shareholder and not stakeholder value.

The final article in the book offers a salutary reminder that not all finance theory can be based on adding value for shareholders or even stakeholders. Arar, in an article written specifically for this book, 'Islamic Banking: An Overview', offers an insight into an organisational entity for which religious principles and not the welfare of customers or shareholders, dictate financial strategy.

Section 1

Trends in Finance Theory

1

The Efficient Market Theory Thrives on Criticism

D. R. Lee and J. A. Verbrugge

The efficient market theory applied to financial markets has been an unquestionable success. It has provided the theoretical basis for "event studies," given rise to an extensive empirical literature on the ability of the stock market to transmit and price information, and played a supporting role in other major theoretical advances in financial economics such as the capital asset pricing model (CAPM) and arbitrage pricing models.[1] But, like all successful theories, the efficient market theory has come under attack. An academic cottage industry has grown up around attempts to discover efficient market "anomalies" – that is, observations that are inconsistent with the operation of efficient markets.

By efficient markets in a financial market context we mean financial markets in which prices reflect information to the point where the marginal benefits of acting on information do not exceed the marginal costs.[2] By efficient market theory we mean the theory that financial markets are indeed efficient and do not have inconsistent anomalies. The question we ask is, will the efficient market theory eventually collapse under the weight of these anomalous findings and be replaced by a more powerful theory? Will the Kuhnian dynamic that describes scientific progress in terms of the rise and fall of successive theories overtake the theory of efficient markets as it has so many others?[3] The answer we provide in this article is an emphatic 'No'.

In Kuhn's view of scientific progress, a theory is typically discarded only when a better theory is available. Even a largely discredited theory can remain dominant unless, or until, a more robust theory comes along. And even then, according to Kuhn, elevation of the more robust theory typically requires the assistance of a few funerals. But we believe even Kuhn's view of the persistence of theories understates the tenacity of the efficient market theory. As we will argue, the theory seems nearly impregnable, unlikely to be dislodged by either anomalies or a better theory.

DISAPPEARING ANOMALIES

No theoretical abstraction is likely to be entirely consistent with the complexity of the real world it attempts to explain, and the theory of efficient markets is no exception to this rule. Quite apart from the problems of accurately testing the efficient market theory, and determining just how anomalous an identified anomaly really is, there are no doubt real anomalies out there. But the efficient market theory is practically alone among theories in that it becomes more powerful when people discover serious inconsistencies between it and the real world. If a clear efficient market anomaly is discovered, the behavior (or lack of behavior) that gives rise to it will tend to be eliminated by competition among investors for higher returns.

If, for example, it becomes clear that investors in general overreact to new information, as some studies suggest, such overreaction presents other investors with clear opportunities for profitable behavior – and such behavior will in turn reduce, if not eliminate, the overreaction. Similarly, if stock prices are found to follow predictable seasonal patterns unrelated to financially relevant considerations, this knowledge will elicit responses that have the effect of eliminating the very patterns they were designed to exploit. We survey evidence on these and related issues below.

The implication here is rather striking. The more empirical flaws that are discovered in the efficient market theory, the more robust the theory becomes. Actual behavior, when discovered to be incongruous with what is predicted by the theory, then adjusts to conform more closely to the theory. In the case of efficient market theory, the Heisenberg principle – the idea that to study something is to change it – rather than confounding attempts to understand the world, has the effect of bringing the real world more in line with our understanding. Those who do the most to ensure that the efficient market theory (EMT) remains fundamental to our understanding of financial economics are not its intellectual defenders, but those mounting the most serious empirical assault against it. Attempting to destroy the efficient market theory by uncovering anomalies is no less difficult than attempting to destroy a hydra-headed monster by chopping off its heads. For every head that falls, two more grow back.

In the rest of this article, we make our point by discussing three questions addressed by the EMT:

1. Are returns predictable?
2. Do investment managers earn consistently superior investment returns?
3. Do stock prices react quickly to new information about individual companies?[4]

For managers of publicly-traded firms, the last area may well be the most important.

PREDICTABILITY OF RETURNS

Financial academics have been especially interested in the issue of the predictability of returns. If a pattern in returns does exist, it suggests that some investment strategy or trading rule may produce excess returns on a risk-adjusted basis and so cast serious doubt on the efficient market theory.

One such anomaly is the *small-firm effect*, which suggests that investing in firms with small market capitalization can produce excess risk-adjusted returns. Originally proposed in 1981, the effect was quickly identified as a *small-firm-in-January effect* – that is, virtually all of the excess returns from investing in small firms were shown to be obtainable by buying portfolios of such firms in December and selling them in January.[5]

There are several reasons why this anomaly cannot be used to generate excess returns. First, more recent evidence suggests that the abnormal return to small stocks in January is really attributable to a *neglected firm effect*.[6] That is, once a company begins to acquire a larger institutional investor following, January excess returns tend to disappear quickly; they are "arbitraged away," in effect, by market forces. Second, expected returns may be higher for small firms that are less liquid and involve higher trading costs, and trading costs alone could easily wipe out any apparent short-term profit opportunities. Third and finally, had you acted on the small-firm effect upon its discovery in 1981 by buying a portfolio of small-cap stocks and then holding for the decade, you would not have earned excess returns. As things turned out, small stocks (as measured by the Wilshire 4500 index) underperformed the S&P 500 by about 2% points per year.[7]

Another much-cited anomaly is the *mean reversion* hypothesis, which suggests that markets overreact to new information and then revert toward some mean value. Put somewhat differently, losing performance is followed in more or less predictable fashion by winning performance, and winning performance is followed by losing. Published in a study by Werner DeBondt and Richard Thaler in 1985,[8] this finding suggests that investing in recent winners will produce losses while investing in losers will generate above-average performance – in short, a contrarian strategy.

However, this apparent anomaly has been discredited on several fronts. First, it has been shown that the evidence of mean reversion comes mainly from the periods of the Great Depression and World War II, suggesting that it too may have been arbitraged away.[9] Second, recent evidence suggests that the apparent anomaly is sensitive to how portfolios are formed by researchers; more specifically, the new evidence suggests that the alleged mean reversion effect is concentrated in low-price stocks (those with prices as low as 1/16th), where return measures are extremely volatile and an illiquidity effect may generate higher expected returns.[10] Third, there is recent evidence of persistence of returns (or "momentum"), in which good or bad short-term performance persists rather than reverses. And, if mean reversion sets in only after an episode of initial persistence, then how will investors reliably know when to buy? The persistence of returns implies that the costs of implementing a mean reversion strategy may quickly outpace marginal benefits.[11]

One intriguing anomaly was identified by the late Fischer Black,[12] who suggested that the *value-line* recommendations have predictive value in that the "buy" portfolio showed excess returns of 10% while the sell portfolio exhibited abnormal negative returns of 10%. However, subsequent re-investigations of active trading strategies based on *value-line* recommendations found such strategies to be unprofitable when transaction costs were included in the analysis.[13]

DO FUND MANAGERS OUTPERFORM THE MARKET?

It is, of course, one thing to "find" evidence of inefficiency using sophisticated econometric tools on past data with cadres of graduate students, unlimited computer time, and the leisure to pursue such research projects without serious time constraints. It is quite another matter to find evidence of such inefficiency in markets by identifying actual trading strategies or particular "money managers" who have outperformed the market consistently over long periods.

Certainly there is no evidence of a trading rule that has generated above-average returns for a sustained period. At the same time, there is scant if any evidence supporting the view that presumably well-informed investors such as mutual fund managers and pension or endowment fund managers consistently achieve returns large enough (when compared with a passive investment strategy, like indexing) to warrant their management fees and charges. With the exception of Warren Buffett, Peter Lynch, and John Templeton, the world of fund managers is strikingly devoid of individuals, groups or strategies that consistently achieve a better-than-market return. And, while intending no disrespect for Buffett, Lynch and Templeton, one could argue that in a world of thousands of fund managers (more than 5,000 mutual funds alone at latest count), one would expect the performance of a few to be "positive outliers."

Interestingly, one study of mutual fund performance over the period 1965–1982 that finds evidence of superior performance by mutual fund managers does not view this as discrediting efficient markets. Rather, the author argues that such consistently above-market returns represent an expected economic return to the activities of gathering and processing relevant information. Nevertheless, even this mild evidence of superior fund performance has been sharply criticized by another study re-interpreting the same portfolio evidence.[14]

Perhaps the most interesting evidence on fund performance is that produced by the "hot hand" vs "icy hand" research. Two recent studies of mutual fund performance over the 1974–1988 period suggest that "winners" tend to repeat their success in following periods. Indeed, one study suggested that an investment strategy based on identifying funds with hot (icy) hands improved risk-adjusted returns by 6% per year.[15]

In the most recent and complete study of mutual fund returns, however, Burton Malkiel debunks much of the evidence of excess returns from choosing hot mutual funds.[16] First, most of the evidence of return predictability (i.e. persistence or "hot handedness") in the 1970s breaks down in the 1980s. After simulating a host of reasonable strategies, Malkiel concludes:

> A large number of strategies based on the persistence of returns would have produced excess returns during the 1970s. The results are not robust, however. None of a variety of reasonable persistence strategies would have allowed an investor to beat the market during the 1980s, even assuming away the existence of sales fees and load charges.

This is especially true after 1986, when winners fare particularly poorly. This is powerful support for our premise that anomalies, once identified, quickly disappear.

Additional evidence supporting our point is provided by Malkiel's investigation of the *Forbes* Honor Roll investment strategy. Since 1975, *Forbes* has published a list of funds that have presumably provided superior long-run performance. Had one followed a strategy of investing in the honor roll funds, the returns would have exceeded the S&P 500 for the first eight years. In subsequent years, however, the returns from such a strategy fall below the market averages. Again, this is evidence that while superior performance based on an investment strategy may be observed for a time, it does not persist indefinitely.

Meanwhile, the search goes on and investigations of investment strategies continue. Recently, evidence has been presented suggesting that mutual funds that invest using a momentum strategy outperform other funds.[17] Unfortunately, however, the momentum study ends with 1984 data, which is the point in time that Malkiel's extensive mutual fund study identifies as the beginning of the period when the predictability of returns breaks down.

Skeptics of efficient markets also point to the finding of some studies that so-called "value" strategies – those that focus on stocks with low market-to-book and price-to-earnings ratios – have produced superior long-period returns. Indeed, some variations of such strategies have outperformed the market over the entire 1968–1990 period. Is this a long-term anomaly not yet arbitraged away? Or are such returns better explained by other factors, such as a failure to adjust for the potentially greater risk associated with such stocks?

Although many academics lean toward the last explanation,[18] two other studies have proposed alternative explanations for the superior performance of value stocks.[19] First, investors may systematically underestimate the future earnings prospects of value stocks and overestimate the prospects of "glamor" stocks. Second, investors may have shorter time horizons than those required for value strategies to realize their full potential. Finally, institutional investors may have a bias toward glamor stocks because they are easier to justify to sponsors and managers as prudent investments. Moreover, such a bias toward glamor stocks may help explain why most fund managers underperform the broad market over time.

In sum, if one is exceptionally generous, one might say that the evidence on fund manager performance is ambiguous. However, since an investor can earn the market return with a passive strategy (and minimal transactions costs), fund managers should consistently beat the market in order to justify their fees and charges for acquiring information. Perhaps the most important function of money managers is to make the market efficient in their efforts to establish that it is not. For, in their efforts to outperform the market, the net result is an efficient market. Without such active investment strategies, markets would be less efficient. Put another way, the more investors believe that market inefficiencies exist, the more efficient markets will be.

RESPONDING TO NEW INFORMATION IN EFFICIENT MARKETS

The efficient market theory has provided the profession with a powerful research tool called the "event study." Use of event studies is based on the premise that stock prices reflect all currently available public information, and thus any new information should produce immediate and generally correct price changes in affected assets. It is in this area that the evidence supporting the efficient market theory is especially striking.

Using event study methodology, researchers have concluded that the market prices of individual securities, and portfolios of securities, respond quickly and in the expected direction to changes in various corporate policies and to economic, legal and regulatory changes that affect individual firms or industries. For corporate managers, this powerful evidence of efficiency means that all major corporate decisions are "priced" virtually instantaneously upon announcement. For example, it is now quite clear that significant capital structure changes have predictable effects on firm value. And the same can be said for various kinds of corporate investment decisions, securities offerings, changes in dividend policy, and changes in corporate ownership.[20]

The research has also furnished evidence of the market's ability to see through the form or cosmetics of corporate transactions to the underlying economic substance. For example, whether a merger is accounted for as a purchase or a pooling of interests will affect reported earnings but not actual after-tax cash flows. And, consistent with market efficiency, the most creditable research on this issue suggests that investors do not penalize corporate buyers for choosing purchase accounting (which reduces reported earnings). Indeed, there is some evidence that the market actually looks more favorably on acquisitions that are structured as purchases rather than poolings.

Given the impressive accumulation of evidence in support of market efficiency, it seems ironic that so many corporate executives are among those who most firmly believe that markets are not efficient. Their most common complaint is that the market simply does not understand their company and, as a result, consistently undervalues the stock. Of course, if this is really true, then corporate executives should be spending more time with analysts and fund managers explaining what there is about the company that the market does not understand.

In any event (pun intended), managers should be increasingly aware that it is in their world of corporate decision-making that evidence favoring market efficiency seems most incontrovertible. Markets do price firm-specific information quickly and in the correct direction. Executives of publicly-traded companies who ignore efficient market theory and its implications do so at their peril.

CONCLUSION

Despite the sometimes biting and vituperative discussions in academic circles about market efficiency, there is little dispute over the most basic premise – that markets price information quickly and with reasonable accuracy, and that it is difficult if not impossible to identify any particular strategy that will reliably beat the market. Also, evidence suggests that when anomalies are identified, they quickly disappear, or at least cease to provide opportunities to generate above-normal returns.

None of this, of course, means we can expect an end to continuous efforts to find anomalies and profitable trading strategies. More powerful computing capability at lower cost, together with rocket-scientist brainpower and software, has produced a new generation of anomaly explorers. Chaos theory, neural networking, artificial intelligence, and genetic algorithms are only some of the weapons the "quants" bring to the battleground in their efforts to find complex, albeit predictable, patterns in security prices.[21]

But, like the Energizer bunny, the efficient market theory keeps on going and going, and its basic premise is likely to become stronger over time. As technology becomes cheaper and more available, as information costs decline, and as information is disseminated more quickly on a truly global basis, efficiency will only be increased. At the same time, those who firmly believe in the efficient market theory and its supporting evidence should always be thankful for those who do not. Indeed, one may well offer (with apologies to St Matthew) the following beatitude of efficient markets: blessed are those who believe in the predictability of prices and inefficiency of financial markets, for it is through their efforts to prove markets inefficient that we are truly blessed with efficiency.

NOTES

1. For a more complete discussion of the contribution of the efficient market theory, see Ray Ball, "The Theory of Stock Market Efficiency: Accomplishments and Limitations," *Journal of Applied Corporate Finance*, Spring 1995, 4–17. For further explanation of the capital asset pricing model (CAPM) and arbitrage pricing models, see Janette Rutterford "Introduction to Stock Exchange Investment", 2nd edn Macmillan Press, 1993.

2. See Eugene Fama "Efficient Capital Markets: II", *Journal of Finance* 46, December 1991, 1575–1617 and Michael C. Jensen "Some Anomalous Evidence Regarding Market Efficiency", *Journal of Financial Economics* 6, June/September 1978, 95–101.

3. See Thomas S. Kuhn, *The Structure of Scientific Revolutions*, Chicago: University of Chicago Press, 1962.

4. This grouping follows the format followed in two extensive recent summaries of efficient markets; Fama (1991), cited in note 2: and William I. Megginson, *Corporate Finance Theory*, New York: Harper Collins, 1996.

5. Donald Keim, "Size Related Anomalies and Stock Return Seasonality: Further Empirical Evidence," *Journal of Financial Economics* 12, June 1983, 13–32. Issues and evidence on the small firm effects are summarized in Zvi Bodie. Alex Kane and Alan J. Marcus, *Investments* 3rd ed., Irwin, 1996.

6. The neglected firm effect is discussed in Avner Arbel, "Generic Stocks: An Old Product in a New Package," *Journal of Portfolio Management* 17, December 1985, 979–90.

7. This point is made by Burton Malkiel, "Returns From Investing in Equity Market Funds 1971 to 1991," *Journal of Finance* 50, June 1995, 549–572.

8. See Werner F. M. DeBondt and Richard Thaler, "Does the Stock Market Overreact?," *Journal of Finance* 40, July 1985, 793–805.

9. This point is made by Steven L. Jones, "Another Look at Time-Varying Risk and Return in a Long-Run Contrarian Strategy," *Journal of Financial Economics* 33, February 1993, 119–144.

10. This argument is made by Ray Ball, S. P. Kothari and Jan Shanken, "Problems in Measuring Portfolio Performance: An Application to Contrarian Investment Strategies," *Journal of Financial Economics*, May 1995, Vol. 38, 79–107.

11. See Narasimhan Jegadeesh and Sheridan Titman, "Returns to Buying Winners and Selling Losers: Implications for Stock Market Efficiency," *Journal of Finance* 48, March 1993, 881–898.

12. Fischer Black, "Yes Virginia, There is Hope: Tests of the Value Line Ranking System." *Financial Analysts Journal* 29, September/October 1973, 10–14.

13. See Clark Holloway, "A Note on Testing an Aggressive Investment Strategy Using Value Line Ranks," *Journal of Finance* 36, June 1981, 711–719, and Gur Huberman and Shmuel Kandel, "Market Efficiency and the Value Line Record," *Journal of Business* 63, April 1990, 187–191.

14. See Richard A. Ippolito, "Efficiency With Costly Information: A Study of Mutual Fund Performance, 1965–1982," *Quarterly Journal of Economics* 104, February 1989, 1–23. Criticism of the findings are found in Edwin J. Elton, Martin J. Gruber, Sanjiv Das and Matthew Hlavka, "Efficiency with Costly Information: A Re-interpretation of Evidence From Managed Portfolios," *Review of Financial Studies* 6, 1993, 1–22.

15. See Darryll Hendricks, Jayendu Patel and Richard Zeckhauser, "Hot Hands in Mutual Funds: Short-Run Persistence of Relative Performance, 1974–1988," *Journal of Finance* 48, March 1993, 93–130. For additional evidence along these lines, see William N. Goetzmann and Roger G. Ibbotson, "Do Winners Repeat?," *Journal of Portfolio Management* 20, Winter 1994, 9–18.

16. See Burton Malkiel, "Returns From Investing in Equity Market Funds 1971 to 1991," *Journal of Finance* 50, June 1995, 549–572.
17. See Mark Grinblatt, Sheridan Titman and Russ Werners, "Momentum Investment Strategies, Portfolio Performance and Herding: A Study of Mutual Fund Behavior," *American Economic Review* 85, December 1995, 1088–1105.
18. See Eugene Fama and Kenneth French, "The Cross-Section of Expected Returns," *Journal of Finance* 46 (June, 1992). Fama and French, while providing evidence of superior performance by such value strategies, also argue that such portfolios are likely to be more risky than use of the CAPM would suggest.
19. See Josef Lakonishok, Andrei Shleifer and Robert W. Vishny, "Contrarian Investment, Extrapolation, and Risk," *Journal of Finance* 49, December 1994, 1541–1578 and Rafael LaPorta, Josef Lakonishok, Andrei Schleifer and Robert Vishny, "Good News for Value Stocks: Further Evidence on Market Efficiency," Working Paper 424, Graduate School of Business, University of Chicago, October 1995.
20. Some of this evidence has been summarized in Clifford W. Smith Jr., "Investment Banking and the Capital Acquisition Process," *Journal of Financial Economics* 15, March, 1986, 3–29, and in Gregg A. Jarrell, James A. Brickley and Jeffry M. Netter, "The Market for Corporate Control: The Empirical Evidence Since 1980," *Journal of Economic Perspectives* 2, Winter 1988, 49–68.
21. See James Aley, "Way Off Wall Street," *Fortune*, February 5, 1996, 114–120.

2

Risk and Return

The Economist

Modern portfolio theory has changed the way investors think about equities – though most investors would consider its starting-point other-worldly. The theory assumes that financial markets are "efficient", meaning that the price of any stock incorporates all publicly available information about that stock. The main task of the theory is to say what determines the stock's rate of return. (If it can do that, it will be allowed its assumptions.)

According to the theory's most famous offspring, the capital-asset pricing model (CAPM, pronounced CAP-M), the return on a stock depends on whether the stock's price follows prices in the market as a whole: the more closely a stock follows the market, the greater will be its expected return. This theory has stood up to the facts quite well.

The correlation between the price of an individual stock and the price of the market as a whole is known by a Greek letter; by the late 1960s hardly a securities house in London or New York did not use, or know about, beta.

SAFETY IN NUMBERS

The difficult road to beta and CAPM starts with Harry Markowitz, now a professor at the City University of New York. In 1952 Mr Markowitz published a path-breaking article called "Portfolio Selection". This paper (like many before) argued that investors demand a high return from risky investments. A risky stock, or a risky portfolio, is simply one whose returns tend to vary a lot.

Before Mr Markowitz, economists had been aware that a portfolio with lots of stocks was less risky than one with only a few. Stocks that perform badly tend to be offset by stocks that perform well, so the return on the portfolio as a whole varies less than the return on smaller lots of individual stocks. But Mr Markowitz also saw that the key to diversifying a portfolio lay not simply in the number of stocks it contained, but in the correlation of their returns.

If returns are highly correlated, then the portfolio, in effect, will not be diversified. If the correlation is low, the portfolio will be highly diversified and the risk much less.

An investor can easily calculate the past correlations – or co-variances, to be precise – among the stocks in a portfolio, and the average return on each individual stock. With this information, Mr Markowitz showed that a technique called mean-variance analysis could be used to construct a series of portfolios that were "efficient" – yet another use for that over-used word. Efficient portfolios are those which, in the past, yielded the highest return for any given risk.

Figure 2.1(a) should make the idea clearer. Risk is measured on the horizontal axis, and returns on the vertical axis. The crosses represent combinations of risk and return for individual stocks. The tinted area represents combinations of risk and return that can be achieved by mixing different stocks together in portfolios. The curved line represents the set of efficient portfolios. Any portfolio below and to the right of the line is "inefficient" because it offers a lower return for any given risk.

From this set of efficient portfolios, the investor would pick his preferred portfolio according to his appetite for risk. If the investor wanted a high return, no matter the risk, he might pick portfolio A in Figure 2.1(a). If he preferred a middling amount of risk, he might choose portfolio B; if he was risk-averse he would pick portfolio C.

It turns out, however, that much more can be said about the desirability of these different portfolios – even though all of them may be efficient. In 1958 James Tobin, of Yale University, extended the Markowitz model. He asked what happens if all investors can lend or borrow at the same rate of interest. The answer was surprising: all investors ought to choose the same portfolio of assets, regardless of their attitude to risk.

To see why Mr Tobin reached this startling conclusion, turn to Figure 2.1(b), and imagine that an investor prefers the level of risk given by point C. He could simply buy the portfolio at C. Or, instead, he could put some of his money in B, and spend the rest on a safe, interest-bearing asset (treasury bills, say). But this would enable him to reach point D in Figure 2.1(b) – an investment as safe as C, but paying a higher return. So that is what he will do.

Equally, if he preferred the riskiness of A, he could borrow at the market rate of interest to buy B. By "leveraging" (borrowing against) his investment, the investor's risk would rise, but so would the return – to point E. Just as D was unambiguously better than C, so E is unambiguously better than A.

The chosen investments all lie on a straight line that cuts the vertical axis at the market rate of interest – the return on a riskless asset. And it touches the efficient-portfolio line, in this example, at B. If the investor prefers no risk, he can choose the fixed rate of interest and buy no shares; otherwise, he will buy portfolio B and either lend or borrow. The investor's job has two parts: first, find the point of tangency that defines the best portfolio; second, borrow or lend to adjust the balance between risk and return.

Evidently, investors behave like this only in models. But theorists were unwilling to abandon the trail – and rightly so. There is no such thing as

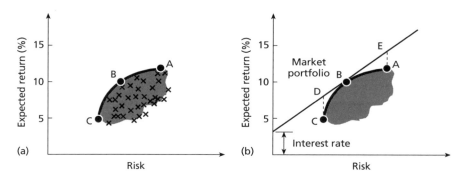

Figure 2.1 A gambler's choice (*Source: Principles of Corporate Finance*, R. A. Brealey and S. C. Myers, McGraw-Hill)

perfect competition, but in many ways market economies behave as if firms are perfectly competitive: the model is a revealing simplification. In the same way, investors do not all choose the same efficient portfolio – but perhaps, in some respects, financial markets behave as if they do.

Before the model in Figure 2.1(b) can be put to the test, it needs to be calibrated. The market rate of interest (where the straight line in Figure 2.1(b) cuts the vertical axis) is known. But how to measure risk? And how to find B, the chosen portfolio? This is where the CAPM – developed independently by William Sharpe of Stanford University, and by the late James Lintner of Harvard University – comes in.

Instead of looking at covariances among stocks in a portfolio, the CAPM takes an ingenious short-cut. It divides a stock's risk into two parts: systematic and unsystematic. Systematic risk, or market risk, is the extent to which the share price is correlated with the market as a whole; it is measured by beta. A stock with a beta of one tends to rise by 10% for every 10% rise in the stockmarket; a stock with a beta of two tends to rise by 20% for every 10% rise in the stockmarket, and so on. A stock's unsystematic risk is the variation that is left after stripping out the systematic risk.

This distinction is extremely fruitful. In a diversified portfolio, unsystematic risks cancel each other out. Since investors can eliminate this sort of risk, it ought to have no bearing on a stock's return. But investors cannot eliminate systematic risk merely by diversifying: a fully diversified portfolio (e.g., the stockmarket as a whole) has a beta of one. So the CAPM focuses on the relationship between systematic risk – the beta of a stock or a portfolio – and returns.

Since betas can be calculated, the model has a usable measure of risk to place on the horizontal axis in Figure 2.1(b). What about B, the chosen portfolio? The CAPM assumes, among other things, that no investor has better information than another. It also accepts the framework of Figure 2.1(b), which concluded that investors will all choose the same portfolio. Together these imply that the chosen portfolio is none other than the market itself.

From this comes a way to price stocks. The straight line in Figure 2.1(b) passes through the so-called market portfolio, which, by definition, has a beta of one. As the discussion above showed, that straight line also reveals the returns that will be required of stocks (or portfolios) with higher or lower betas. Nobody will hold a stock that is below the line; such stocks will fall in price until the expected return rises to the line. Stocks above the line will be in great demand; they will rise in price.

In equilibrium, all stocks will lie on the line. Individual investors need not worry about the market portfolio: they need only decide how much systematic risk they wish to take on. Market forces then ensure that any stock can be expected to yield the appropriate return for its beta.

DOES IT FIT?

The CAPM says that if you know a stock's beta, you can predict its long-run return. It is a model – a simplification. Some of its assumptions are questionable; but instead of asking whether the model is "true", ask whether it works. Most tests of the CAPM have concluded that it does: as predicted, stocks with high betas yield high returns.

In 1972 three researchers (Fischer Black, Michael Jensen and Myrton Scholes) divided the stocks listed on the New York Stock Exchange into ten portfolios. The first portfolio contained 10% of the securities with the lowest betas, the second the 10% with the next lowest betas, and so on. The study found that over 35 years there was an almost exactly straight-line relationship between a portfolio's beta and its average return, just as predicted by the CAPM (see Figure 2.2).

However, niggling doubts remain. Stocks with a beta of zero tended to have a higher return than treasury bills, contrary to the CAPM's predictions. This suggests that investors do expect to be compensated for taking on unsystematic risk. Also, stocks with high betas tended to do slightly worse than predicted by the CAPM.

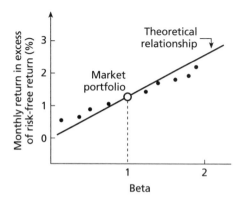

Figure 2.2 Almost (*Source:* Black, Jensen and Scholes)

Efficiency: the search goes on

The CAPM assumes that stockmarkets are efficient. Is this true? The belief that a stock's price takes into account all information (about dividends, earnings and so on) as soon as this information becomes publicly available was once the bedrock of financial economics. Recently, it has begun to be challenged.

- If markets are efficient, no investors would look for new information, because they would not profit from acquiring it. So some inefficiency in a stockmarket is necessary to encourage investors to look for information.

- When assets have no close substitutes (a whole stockmarket, for instance, may have no substitute), investors may be unable to spot when they are under- or over-valued.

- Stock prices tend to move about much more than changes in their dividend payments would suggest.

- Big movements in share prices often fail to happen when there are major public announcements, or big changes in information.

- There are many smaller anomalies. Small stocks tend to do well in January; all stocks do well at the beginning of the month; most do badly on Monday mornings. Stock returns tend to be mean-reverting – i.e., bad days, and even bad years, are more often than not followed by good days, or good years.

Does this mean economists are abandoning clever models to explain how markets move? Not a bit of it. They are using their new mathematical techniques to explore sentiments, fashions, fads and speculative bubbles.

The CAPM works only in the long run. As Burton Malkiel of Princeton University shows in his excellent book, *A Random Walk Down Wall Street*, the returns of America's mutual funds in the 1980s bore no relation to their betas; if anything, in fact, there was a slight tendency for low-beta funds to outperform high-beta ones. And the betas of individual stocks vary a good deal over time. (The beta of a portfolio of stocks is more stable, though, because changes in the betas of individual stocks tend to cancel each other out.)

ROLL'S ROCKET

Despite these doubts, the CAPM passed most of its early tests with honours. Then in 1977 it was dealt a more serious blow, by Richard Roll of the University of California at Los Angeles.

Recall that, according to the original CAPM, all investors choose to hold the market portfolio. Taking this idea literally, the market portfolio would include every financial asset in the world. The trouble with tests of the CAPM, suggested Mr Roll, is that they use a bad proxy for this market portfolio – e.g., the 500 biggest companies listed on the New York Stock Exchange.

Mr Roll showed that the CAPM will always look true if the market proxy (such as the S&P 500) is "efficient" in the sense defined by Mr Markowitz – i.e., if no combination of the shares would give a higher return for the same risk. But this does not prove that each share's expected return is affected only by its correlation with the true market portfolio. Conversely, even if share returns were unrelated to betas derived from the S&P 500, shares might still be correctly priced in relation to the true market portfolio.

This objection might look like a quibble. But Mr Roll showed that a small change in the market proxy (e.g., from the S&P 500 to the Wilshire list of 5,000 listed stocks) can completely alter the expected returns of a stock as predicted by the CAPM. Since nobody knows what the true market portfolio is, nobody can say whether the CAPM holds.

This attack on the CAPM sat comfortably with an alternative model of asset prices, developed by Stephen Ross of Yale University. Known as arbitrage pricing theory (APT), it now demands a chapter in just about every finance textbook.

Unlike the CAPM, the APT divides systematic risk into smaller component risks. It does not specify in advance what these are. In principle, any factor that might affect the return from a group of assets qualifies. An unexpected change in interest rates, for instance, might affect lots of companies' share prices – not to mention bond prices, commodity prices and so on.

In practice, Mr Ross found that returns depend on: (a) inflation; (b) industrial production; (c) the investor's appetite for risk; and (d) interest rates. The APT says that the expected return on a stock is directly proportional to its sensitivity to each of these factors.

Recent research has suggested that the four-factor version of the APT is better at predicting the return on a stock than the simplest version of the CAPM. The model has the further advantage of explaining the pricing of assets in relation to each other, rather than in relation to an unidentifiable market portfolio. Also, the APT can be used to eliminate any specific risks that may worry a particular investor. For instance, a pension fund may want a portfolio that is immune to the inflation rate.

In some of its basic ideas, though not in its details, the APT builds on rather than replaces the CAPM. It may be a "truer" model and in many ways a more fruitful one – but it is far harder to grasp and use, not least because it requires lots of complicated mathematics. If for no other reason, the CAPM will remain every investor's introduction to portfolio theory for many years to come.

3

Estimating Expected Return

F. Black

The key issue in investments is *estimating* expected return. It is neither explaining return nor, as Fama and French suggest, explaining average return.[1] These topics combine estimating expected return with explaining variance, which is a completely different matter.

For example, the capital asset pricing model (CAPM) is a model of expected return. The "market model," which says that the market residuals of all stocks are independent, is a model of variance. The CAPM and the market model are almost wholly unrelated. One helps in estimating expected return, while the other helps in explaining variance.

Similarly, the Sharpe-Lintner-Black (SLB) model that Fama and French cite is a model of expected return. It says that expected return is a linear function of beta with a positive slope, and that only beta matters in explaining expected return.

In contrast, arbitrage pricing theory (APT) is a model of variance. It says that the number of independent factors influencing return is limited, but it is silent on the pricing of these factors, so it is silent on expected return.

Explaining variance is easy. We can use daily (or more frequent) data to estimate covariances. Our estimates are accurate enough that we can see the covariances change through time. Explaining return or average return is easy too, because that's just a way of explaining variance.

Estimating expected return is hard. Daily data hardly help at all. Only longer time periods help. We need decades of data for accurate estimates of average expected return. We need such a long period to estimate the average that we have little hope of seeing changes in expected return.

THEORY AND DATA

Fama and French do not seem to believe much in theory when they estimate expected return. They (and many others) rely heavily on data. They look at average returns on certain factors as evidence of expected returns for those factors.

Similarly, people who use the APT framework in estimating expected return usually use past average return as an estimate. When we have no theory for how a factor should be priced, past average return can give the best estimate, but it's normally a highly inaccurate estimate.

People who rely on data sometimes assume that factor expected returns (or expected returns in excess of the riskless interest rate) are constant, but they often condition expected returns on various observables. In that case, they are using conditional average return to estimate conditional expected return. Using a complex multivariate analysis does not change the essence of the approach. Estimates of conditional expected return are about as inaccurate as estimates of ordinary expected return.

The people who use data often think of the factors as rationally priced, because the factors represent risks that people care about, as in Merton's intertemporal asset pricing model.[2] But they rarely tell us *how* the factors should be priced; they usually don't even predict the *signs* of the factor expected excess returns.

Sometimes (but less commonly in the academic world), people speak of the factors as "irrationally priced" or "mispriced." Factor mispricing can be consistent, as when "institutions" matter a lot to asset prices, or it can shift rapidly, as when "noise" matters a lot.

One version of the "noise" theory predicts that ratios of price to accounting estimates of value can help predict expected return. That's a possible reason for the good performance of Fama and French's price-to-book factor. But Fama and French hardly mention this explanation. They don't want to hear about theory, especially theory suggesting that certain factors and securities are mispriced.

"Investor psychology," which I feel is important, can give various kinds of irrational pricing. Mispricing may be consistent, as when a desire for yield causes people to bid up the prices of high-dividend stocks, or inconsistent, as when fads (like the belief that stocks of small firms are underpriced) sweep the market.

If we are willing to use theory (and data other than past returns), we can estimate expected return without even looking at past returns. We can explain why people may care about long or short exposures to particular factors, and we can explain how investor psychology or institutional behavior may affect factor pricing.

DATA MINING

We have two ways to estimate a factor's expected return – *theory* and *data*. Both have problems.

Theory has problems because, for example, we may not know what portfolio to use to represent a factor. We don't even know what to use for the first factor.

In the U.S., the problem of not knowing what portfolio to use is not too severe (except, as I note later, it tends to flatten the line relating expected return and beta). In my view, all the candidates for the U.S. market portfolio are highly correlated.

The world market portfolio and the U.S. domestic market portfolio are highly correlated. Broader and narrower market indexes are highly correlated. Equally weighted and value-weighted portfolios are highly correlated. Even human capital and real estate are highly correlated (in my view) with portfolios of traded assets.

The problems with data, though, are severe, both because the high ratio of risk to expected return means we need decades of data to estimate the pricing of most factors, and because of *data mining*. We often don't have the decades of data we need. Even when we do, we can only estimate the average pricing of a factor over the whole period; if factor prices are changing, today's price may be far from that average.

In principle, conditioning factor prices on various observables can help. But unless we have strong theory to guide us, we need many more decades to estimate conditional factor prices than to estimate unconditional ones. Each new observable we add tends to weaken our estimates.

It's ironic. We seem to have so much data, with monthly and daily returns on thousands of securities. That does help in analyzing variance; for expected returns, however, it gives us false security and makes us think we're better off than we are. Normally, the best we can do with data alone is to create a portfolio out of traded securities that captures each factor and use the average return on that portfolio as an estimate of the expected return on the factor.

When people use Fama and MacBeth's methods instead of constructing a single portfolio that represents a factor, I think it's out of hope that so many cross-sectional regressions, with so many data points each, will somehow add precision to the estimates.[3] It's similar when people use elaborate multivariate tests. Normally, the loss of degrees of freedom offsets any potential gains, and we end up with worse estimates than the ones that simple portfolio tests give us.

And as if these problems weren't bad enough, we have the data mining problem. (Data mining is also known as "data snooping," "data dredging" or just "hindsight.")

The simplest kind of data mining is when a researcher gives a table filled with t-statistics and labels the big ones "significant" at the 5% level, when only 5% of the ones he gives fall in that range. Another kind is when a researcher fails to report everything he tried in analyzing his data. I'm thankful we have that kind. Without it, the "overpublication problem" would be even worse than it is now.

Yet another kind is when a researcher chooses what to do and how to do it in the light of what others have done using similar data. In a less formal version of this, a researcher designs his studies with the knowledge of past patterns of security returns. He knows these patterns because he reads newspapers and magazines, or because he invests.

All these forms of data mining are made worse by the huge number of miners, both academic and nonacademic. "There's gold in them thar hills," since people who find good ways to estimate expected returns can make a lot of money.

Moreover, all these kinds of data mining are worse when we try to estimate conditional means than when we estimate unconditional ones. We are mining when we choose the observables to condition on. So multivariate tests are especially suspect. (Even time is a suspicious variable.)

The result is that conventional tests of statistical significance are almost completely invalid (and multivariate tests are more invalid than simple ones). We don't know what area was mined, or what mining tools were used.

As I have done more theoretical work than empirical work, you may have anticipated my conclusion: I find theory to be far more powerful than data when we're trying to estimate expected return. When I read an empirical paper, I usually seek out the theory section and ignore the tables.

This means that most so-called "anomalies" don't seem anomalous to me at all. They seem like nuggets from a gold mine, found by one of the thousands of miners all over the world.

The "small-firm effect" or "size effect" may be the best example. There's actually some theory suggesting that such firms may be consistently underpriced, because not many analysts or investors follow them. But most academic researchers downplay this theory, because it implies mispricing rather than a rationally priced factor.

Still, it's a curious fact that just after the small-firm effect was announced, it seems to have vanished. What this sounds like is that people searched over thousands of rules until they found one that worked in the past. Then they reported it, as if past performance were indicative of future performance. As we might expect, in real-life, out-of-sample data, the rule didn't work any more.

WHAT THEORY SAYS

Now let's leave the messy world of data and return to the almost-clear waters of theory.

The strongest prediction of theory is that there is at least one priced factor. It's something like the market portfolio, though we don't know whether to use the world market portfolio or a domestic portfolio, or exactly what assets to include with what weights.

Even Fama and French agree that the market's expected excess return is positive. It's positive enough to make people willing to bear the risk of the first factor.

Can theory tell us what to use for the second factor? One theory can. What Fama and French call the "SLB model" identifies the "beta factor" as a second factor that should be priced. We can define the beta factor as the minimum-variance, zero-beta portfolio of risky assets, where beta is defined using whatever market portfolio we use to represent the first factor.

Curiously, Fama and French don't mention this factor at all. They talk only about a small-firm factor and a price-to-book factor. I think of these as less important in explaining variance than the beta factor and refer to them as the Fama-French "third" and "fourth" factors.

When Fama and French say that the line relating expected return and beta is flat, they are just saying that the expected excess return on the second factor is large. If we believe it's as large as they say, we won't fool around with their third and fourth factors, for which they give no theory. We'll go for the gold in the second factor!

A rational investor who believes the line is flat today should switch out of bonds (if he has any) and move toward low-beta stocks. If he doesn't have bonds, he should borrow (if he can) and do the same thing.

Moreover, a corporation that believes the line is flat can increase its stock price by emphasizing low-beta corporate assets and using lots of leverage. (This can also have tax advantages.)

If beta had been dead, the Fama–French results would have revived it!

But is the line flat today? Is it flatter than the CAPM suggests? Or is the flat line just another offering from the worldwide data mine?

I first wrote on this subject (with Jensen and Scholes) in 1972.[4] We found that the line relating average return (up to that time) and beta was flatter than the CAPM would predict, and we discussed some possible explanations for this result. But we were aware of certain patterns in stock market returns when we started our work, so we may have been mining the data ourselves, at least in part.

The years since 1972 have been "out of sample" in a sense. But I would not be writing this if the average excess return on the second factor had been zero over this 20-year period. Again, I may be mining the data by highlighting the return on the second factor over the last 20 years. So I think we must rely on theory.

THREE THEORIES

Mismeasuring the market portfolio (like using the domestic market when we should be using the world market) tends naturally to give stocks with low measured betas high alphas.

Imagine, for example, an extreme case where all stocks in our universe have true betas of 1.0 and have positive but varying amounts of a "noise factor" that's independent of the true market. (This also works if they all have negative amounts of the independent factor.) Imagine that we use the portfolio of all stocks in this universe for our measured market portfolio.

In this case, the true line is flat. A stock's alpha is proportional to the difference between 1.0 and its beta. Moreover, it pays for an investor to emphasize low-beta stocks from this universe, because that gives him less of the unpriced noise factor. And it pays for a corporation to use high leverage and emphasize low-beta assets, if it is restricted to assets in the same universe.

Another reason for a flatter line is restricted borrowing. Margin requirements, borrowing rates that are higher than lending rates, and limited deductibility of interest costs all tend to make the line flatter. Those who can't borrow at good rates bid up the prices of high-beta stocks instead.

Yet another reason for a flatter line, I believe, is investor psychology, in particular "reluctance to borrow" even when the rules allow it and the rates are good. Many people seem to dislike the idea of borrowing or the trading needed to adjust borrowing amounts to the values of their securities portfolios.

That makes three theoretical reasons for a flatter line in the future – "mismeasurement," "restrictions" and "reluctance." Plus we have some data, for anyone who thinks the data haven't been mined too much.

What do *you* think? That the line will be flat in the future? That it will be as steep as the CAPM says it should be? That it will be flatter, but not completely flat?[5]

NOTES

1. E. F. Fama and K. R. French, "The Cross-Section of Expected Stock Returns," *Journal of Financial Studies* 47 (1992): 427–65. In this article, they find a relationship between share returns and factors related to the price to book ratio and company size.
2. R. C. Merton, "An Intertemporal Capital Asset Pricing Model," *Econometrica* 41 (1973): 867–87.
3. E. F. Fama and J. D. MacBeth, "Risk, Return and Equilibrium: Empirical Tests," *Journal of Political Economy* 81 (1973): 607–36.
4. F. Black, M. Jensen, and M. Scholes, "The Capital Asset Pricing Model: Some Empirical Tests," in *Studies in the Theory of Capital Markets*, M. C. Jensen, ed. (New York: Praeger, 1972): 79–121.
5. This article is based on a talk prepared for the September 1992 Berkeley Program in Finance, *Are Betas Irrelevant? Evidence and Implications for Asset Management*. I am grateful for comments by participants in that program.

Section 2

Adding Value Through Investment

4

Investment Appraisal Criteria and the Impact of Low Inflation

A. Wardlow

The prospect of sustained lower inflation and lower nominal interest rates has implications for all areas of economic decision-making. This article is concerned with just one area – corporate investment decisions – and focuses in particular on firms' adaptation of the appraisal criteria that they use to guide these decisions to reflect the return to low inflation.

Businesses are obviously concerned with the real returns generated by their investments. But the relationship between real and nominal rates of return is often distorted by volatility and uncertainty – both in periods of significant inflation and in the period of transition to a more stable economic environment. It is appropriate to consider how low and stable inflation might affect investment appraisal criteria.

Investment decisions involve the assessment of a great many interrelated variables – and judgments about the future course of these variables – often many years ahead. The decision-making is complex, both in the assessment of particular projects and in the management of the process; and it is therefore sensible to have rules and systems to guide the process. But a rule about the required rate of return from an investment that is appropriate in a world of unpredictable and significantly positive inflation may not be appropriate in a world where prices are generally stable. Clearly, there is a need for firms to ensure that the systems they use for appraisal are responsive to changes in their economic environment. In considering the process of adjustment to an environment of sustained lower inflation, this article considers the use that firms make of investment appraisal criteria. It draws on an informal inquiry undertaken in 1994 by the Bank of England (the Bank) – Table 4.1 summarises its main findings – which offers some preliminary indications and insights into the adjustment process.

INVESTMENT AND HIGH INFLATION

By their nature, investment decisions involve uncertainty. In the recent past, however, there has often been the additional uncertainty stemming from unexpected changes in the general level of prices. High and variable

Table 4.1 Summary of the Bank's inquiry

Through its network of regional agents, in early March the Bank of England conducted an informal inquiry involving around 250 of its industrial contacts. The firms contacted were mainly large and medium-sized companies, including a number of large plcs and foreign-owned enterprises, but smaller firms were also represented. Some 65% of respondents were in the manufacturing sector.

Firms were asked to comment on a number of questions concerning the investment appraisal criteria they used, the role given to these criteria in their investment decisions, and the impact of lower inflation and interest rates to date on their use. The Bank is grateful to all the firms that took part in the inquiry and who continue to inform it on a range of issues.

It should be stressed that the inquiry was an informal one; there was no attempt to structure the sample or to trial the questions. The detail of the findings summarised in the table below should therefore be treated with caution, and the results viewed as indicative, rather than representative. The aim was simply to gain some early indications about the process of adjusting investment criteria to the new inflation environment and to deepen our understanding of the way that firms use appraisal criteria in practice, in order to judge the significance of such an adjustment.

Summary of inquiry findings

1. **Investment criteria: percentage of firms using:**

Target required *real* rate of return	Target required *nominal* rate of return	Payback criterion only	Payback plus a required rate of return
29%	32%	8%	32%

2. **Net present value (NPV): percentage of firms:**
   Making some use of NPV
   70%

3. **Thresholds: approximate average post-tax threshold rate[a]**
   15% real   20% nominal

4. **Adjustment to date: percentage of firms that had:[b]**

Reduced required rates of return (or lengthened payback)	Increased required rates of return (or shortened payback)	Left required rates of return (or payback period) unchanged
26%	2%	72%

a Some firms used more than one threshold rate, depending on the type of investment.
b Among firms using *nominal* required rates of return, 27% had lowered their targets. Among firms using *real* required rates of return, 34% had lowered their targets. Among firms using *payback rules and a required return*, 27% had lowered their thresholds.

inflation makes it more difficult to determine the discount rate that should be applied in order to calculate expected real returns on investment. If the level of future inflation is likely to be different from that seen in the past, past returns are a less reliable guide to what is currently appropriate, complicating judgments about what level of returns to require. And uncertainty about inflation may affect not only the allocation of investment among different projects, but also the overall level of investment and saving. Savers may require higher average expected real returns. Such a risk premium will affect the real cost of funds, and so affect investment decisions.

Over much of the last three decades, it would have been inappropriate for companies deciding how to allocate their resources to have assumed generally stable prices. Both average inflation and inflation volatility were high in the 1970s and 1980s, much higher than in the 1950s and the early 1960s. Between 1945 and 1965, average annual retail price inflation was around 3.75%. Between 1965 and 1990, it was close to 9% and its variance was about four times higher than in the earlier period. Similarly, the real cost of funds has been more variable in recent decades, adding to the difficulties in making investment calculations. It is not surprising in such an environment that companies – and households – not only try to allow effectively for inflation in their calculations, but require a higher return because of the additional uncertainty and risk that accompanies unpredictable monetary conditions.

A RETURN TO LOW AND STABLE INFLATION

One benefit of a return to an environment of lower and more stable inflation, in addition to a lower cost of capital, should be that uncertainty about the value and cost of money is a less critical factor in investment decisions. In such circumstances, the assumptions used in past investment decisions may need to be amended. But the process of transition may be problematical if companies have become accustomed to high and variable inflation.

With the benefit of hindsight, it is clear that at times during the 1970s and 1980s it would have been reasonable for companies considering investment projects with five or ten year horizons to have incorporated nominal discount rates of 20% or more into their appraisal criteria. Between 1970 and 1990, the average annual rate of increase in producer prices was just over 9.5%. Taking 3.5% as a *rough* estimate of the required real rate of return on risk-free debt – the real yield on index-linked gilts since the first issue in the early 1980s has usually been between 3% and 4% – and adding a risk premium of about 6% (based on the average excess return on equities over debt) suggests a required real return on a typical project financed by equity of around 10%.[1] So, allowing for inflation at the average rate between 1970 and 1990 produces a required nominal return of around 20% for the period. Making some allowance for tax raises the figure still higher. These rough calculations illustrate that nominal discount rates of 20% would not have been unreasonable in past high inflation years, and explain why companies may have come to use factors of 20% or more to discount future cash flows.

Firms may be cautious about changing their required rates of return, given both the past history of uncertainty and the relatively short period of low and stable inflation to date; it may take a considerable period for them to become confident about making this kind of adjustment. But if inflation is expected to remain lower over a long period, it would be rational for firms to consider lowering their nominal target rates of return. There would also be reason to reconsider their required real rates of return, if the real cost of capital has fallen or if less variable inflation and lower interest rates have reduced the relevant investment risks. Clearly, if firms require excessive rates of return, they are likely to reject good investment opportunities with the consequent risks for their future earnings and competitiveness.

THE APPRAISAL CRITERIA USED BY FIRMS

This section considers some of the underlying practical issues raised by the adjustment of investment criteria. To understand the process of adaptation to an environment of stable prices, it is necessary to consider both the kinds of investment appraisal criteria firms use and the role they give them in their investment decision-making.

Firms use a wide variety of criteria in their appraisal of investment opportunities. The Bank's inquiry revealed significant differences in appraisal techniques and in the rates of return that firms seek. Those using required real rates generally reported targets in the range of 7%–20%, and those using nominal rates targets in the range of 10%–25%. The average among firms targeting a real rate of return was around 15% after tax; nominal targets averaged around 20%. (Given the nature of the inquiry, it would be inappropriate to draw any conclusions from the differential between these average nominal and real target rates of return.) Larger firms tended generally to employ lower target rates than smaller firms.

Other differences – for example, in the cost of capital faced by large and small firms – may partly explain the width of these ranges; the ranges may also reflect differences in the nature of the investments that firms tend to undertake. Nevertheless, the wide variance is an area that warrants further investigation. It would be interesting to assess the significance to the threshold level of firm size, status (eg whether the company is public or private) and other variables.

Within individual companies, target rates of return varied according to the nature of the investment project: its risk, its necessity for the firm and its size. For example, investment in manufacturing operations – where the returns are largely in the form of known cost savings – attracted lower target rates of return than 'riskier' investment in new product development. The difference in the threshold rates within a single company was as much as 10%. Some multinationals distinguished between investments undertaken in different countries, notably between those in Europe and the United States (where the required rates of return are often lower). In addition, a number of firms noted that a significant part of their recent capital expenditure had been on projects which offered no direct commercial return, such as compliance with environmental, and health and safety legislation.

Table 4.2 Investment appraisal techniques

The Bank's inquiry confirmed that the main investment appraisal techniques used by companies are:

■ *Net present value (NPV)*
The economic value of a project is calculated by estimating its future cash flows over the projected life of the investment, which will depend on a series of assumptions about demand, prices etc. The cash flows are then discounted at a compound rate reflecting the opportunity cost of capital, which – in turn – will reflect the risk and timescale of the investment. The discounted present value of the cash flows is compared with the initial cost of the investment.

Financial theory stresses the superiority of the net present value method of investment appraisal and that, as a rule, projects with a positive NPV should be undertaken.

■ *Internal rate of return*
Formally, the internal rate of return is that rate at which expected future cash flows must be discounted to equate them with the initial project cost – ie to produce a net present value of zero. Once calculated, the internal rate of return is then compared with a specified threshold rate reflecting the firm's cost of capital. The technique can generate the same decisions as NPV, but has a number of potential pitfalls – for example, when ranking competing projects or accommodating variable rates of risk through the life of a project – which are more easily avoided with the NPV method.

■ *Payback period*
The criterion used is the length of the period before the initial investment cost is recovered. Payback rules require that the cost of an investment should be recovered within a specified timescale. Discounted cash flows may be used in the calculation.

■ *Accounting rate of return*
Accounting rates of return are based on the average annual forecast profits of a project (after depreciation and tax) divided by the average annual book value of the investment. This ratio may then be compared with the existing book rate of return for either the firm as a whole or, in some cases, an industry average.

The Bank's inquiry also showed that many firms used more than one criterion when assessing investment opportunities as shown in Table 4.2. The criteria used included: net present values; internal rates of return; accounting rates of return; payback periods and broader measures such as the return on capital employed. Many used accountancy-based measures together with other techniques; this is not surprising given the importance accorded to accountancy practices in many areas of corporate decision-making. It is also not surprising to observe that larger firms tend to employ more sophisticated appraisal and capital-budgeting techniques.

70% of inquiry respondents reported that they made some use of net present values, but other techniques are also common, even in larger firms. Some 40% of firms surveyed used a payback criterion in one form or another; this kind of criterion was used mainly – but not exclusively – by the smaller companies in the sample. It was also notable that many of the firms that used payback criteria alongside other measures stressed the importance of payback rules at that time, ie they sought a target rate of return within a specified period.

The use of payback criteria

The Bank's inquiry drew attention to the prevalence of payback criteria; a number of advantages and limitations of their use can be suggested.

Among the limitations, payback rules give no weight to the timing of cash flows within the period specified; they also do not take account of cash flows beyond the chosen cut-off point. In addition, the payback period that companies use is often short – the inquiry indicated a normal period of around two to three years. And in a period of transition to low inflation, use of a payback criterion may make it more likely that projects will be rejected, if firms do not increase the threshold period: since, when inflation in high, the nominal outlay on a project will be covered more quickly by incoming cash flows.

There are a number of reasons which may explain why firms, particularly smaller firms, feel that the use of payback criteria is justified – or at least that more sophisticated methods are not appropriate. Future cash flows can only be estimated after assumptions about the productive and market possibilities of an investment have been made; for investments relating to export sales, exchange rate assumptions will in addition be a central consideration. Assumptions about, for example, the benefits of new process technology or larger-scale production will be more important than the choice of appraisal technique. Even with reasonable assumptions, it may be difficult to estimate the cash flows over the life of an investment project, particularly if the way that the new project fits into the existing business is complex. This uncertainty and complexity may encourage smaller firms to adopt simpler investment criteria, and to base their investment decisions on more general considerations, often governed by an assessment of 'what needs to be done'.

But perhaps the main reason, for the widespread use of payback criteria – at least recently – has been the financial constraint that firms have faced or imposed on themselves to improve their financial condition. Credit restrictions clearly make it sensible to be concerned about the time-horizon over which investment projects generate returns. Although in larger companies with fairly unrestricted access to capital markets, financing decisions can be relatively easily separated from investment decisions, in smaller firms managers may have to consider the impact of individual projects on the wider corporate position. The impact of a project on the overall financial condition of the company may be the prime concern, and if capital expenditure is being tightly controlled, investment decisions will have to be made on a priority basis. This is, however, less of a justification if the capital rationing is self-imposed as a means of financial planning and control. It will be interesting to see to what extent this kind of criterion is modified as the corporate sector's financial position continues to improve.

None of these points, however, is an argument against discounted cash flow techniques. If used in an appropriate way, they are widely agreed to offer a better basis for firms to formulate their business plans, though this is not to suggest that such criteria should be used uncritically or in isolation.

THE ROLE OF APPRAISAL CRITERIA

The Bank's inquiry indicated that appraisal criteria – in the form of threshold rates of return – are a critical hurdle when there are many competing claims on corporate resources, most frequently in larger groups. Formal appraisal criteria act to limit the number of projects that are brought forward – operating as a kind of feasibility test prior to a more qualitative consideration. Large companies often have to decide between a number of competing claims from different business areas or subsidiaries. Although offering the required rate of return may not guarantee a project success, it may be used to rank it among similar projects.

Broader observation suggests, however, that rate of return criteria tend to be used in a flexible way, depending on wider commercial considerations. Although important, a rate of return criterion appears rarely to be the sole determinant of investment decisions. Many firms in the Bank's inquiry underlined the importance of overall corporate strategy and of 'strategic fit' in investment decision-taking. In some cases, lower target rates of return are applied to projects considered important (or essential) for corporate strategy than to more marginal operational investment decisions. In the case of acquisitions in particular, the usual criteria may be overlooked or relaxed.

These findings might be seen as more coherent with the tenets of strategic analysis than with financial theory. Of course, it is possible that investments that fit well within a company's overall strategy – and so concentrate on areas where the company has a relative expertise or competitive advantage – are more likely to be profitable. But what such observations emphasise is that firms do not tend to use formal appraisal techniques in an uncritical or mechanical fashion.

THE SHORT-RUN IMPACT OF LOWER INFLATION

Having considered both the nature and the role of rates of return criteria, this section looks at the adjustment of them that firms have so far made in the light of lower inflation and interest rates.

Responses to the Bank's inquiry in March 1994 showed that over 70% of firms questioned had yet to adjust their target rates of return, around a quarter had already made a reduction and a number said that they were currently considering revising their criteria.

Of those firms that employed a target real rate of return, around a third reported that they had reduced their threshold rate; this may have reflected either a lower cost of capital or a reduction in the risk premium being included as a result of lower inflation and interest rate expectations. Just over a quarter of respondents using nominal required rates had made an adjustment by the time of the survey.

Firms reported that their current tendency was to leave their target rates of return – and nominal discount rates – unchanged over long periods. Their arguments for this were usually that investments are affected by longer-term considerations and that there was little reason yet to adjust their longer-term expectations of inflation rates and the cost of capital.

Overall, the findings in this area suggested that, by 1994, the process of adjustment was not very advanced. The transition to an environment of stable prices is, however, unlikely to be rapid or smooth, particularly if many firms continue to face fairly difficult trading conditions. The findings in relation to firms using nominal required rates of return would, though, be of some concern if they persisted over a longer period. And it would be of particular concern if firms had implicitly reduced their expectations of inflation in their expected future nominal revenue streams, but had not similarly reduced their nominal discount rates.

One important question arising from the inquiry's results is whether the lack of adjustment by March 1994 had had significant impact on investment decisions. Growth in investment has played only a small part in the economic recovery to date: investment has risen by less in this recovery than it did between 1982–84 (though its share of GDP remained higher throughout the last recession and it may now be picking up). By the time of the survey, however, firms' slowness to adjust their investment criteria may not have implied that they were failing to identify profitable investment opportunities. It has been suggested above that formal appraisal criteria are often given a flexible role in companies' investment decisions; firms may have considered other factors to have been more central to their decisions at the time.

Some firms have even suggested that lower inflation may have a negative impact on investment, arguing that higher inflation makes it easier to widen margins slightly following investment, for example, to improve product quality. Inflation's impact on the real burden of debt and on the real value of assets placed as security have also been cited. But although such considerations need to be borne in mind, the notion that inflation is good for investment needs firmly to be refuted. First, higher inflation and nominal interest rates reduce the income available for investment. In 1993, lower interest rates reduced industrial and commercial companies' interest payments by £11 billion compared with a year earlier; to the extent that cash flow is important as a determinant of investment, lower nominal interest rates will have a positive impact on investment.

More fundamentally, as suggested above, higher inflation is correlated with greater inflation volatility and so greater uncertainty. A stable monetary environment allows investment decisions to be taken more efficiently, on the basis of real returns.

SUMMARY

The Bank's 1994 inquiry emphasised the extent to which many companies remained to be convinced that inflation and interest rates would remain low and stable over the long term. Many firms continued to seek rates of return which partly reflected past higher and more variable inflation and interest rates. In view of the role that many firms seem to give to formal appraisal criteria, this slowness to adjust may not at that stage have been critical to investment. Other factors, such as cash flow and expectations of demand, are likely to have been more important. But, if excessively high target rates of return continue to be used as the recovery progresses and as the financial constraints on investment are further relaxed, there is a risk that they will limit the level and type of investment undertaken by UK firms.

A further period of monetary stability may, however, be needed before a more fundamental adjustment in behaviour becomes widespread. The Bank's inquiry has offered some useful insights into the process of adjustment, but it is an issue that clearly warrants further investigation.

NOTES

1. In fact, the average real yield on index-linked gilts has been less than $3^1/2\%$ and the return on a diversified portfolio of UK equities has exceeded the yield on government bonds by about 8%. The latter, however, overestimates the risk premium on an all-equity financed project, because the 8% reflects the risk of claims upon geared corporations. Gearing increases the riskiness of returns to shareholders; shares are more risky than the firm's other liabilities. Making a rough adjustment for the effect of debt suggests an appropriate risk premium for an average all-equity project of about 6%.

'Investment Appraisal Criteria and the Impact of Low Inflation', reprinted with permission from *Quarterly Bulletin*, August 1994, 34(3). Copyright 1994 Bank of England.

5

Selling of Capital Investments to Top Management

O. P. Lumijärvi

INTRODUCTION

The importance of capital investments and capital budgeting cannot be over-emphasized. Investments affect operations and cash flows of firms for long periods of time, making investment success extremely important. However, an investment *per se* does not improve results but the success of companies depends upon how efficiently and effectively capital resources are utilized. Companies frequently spend large sums of money for capital investments which may give returns only after a long period of time. Moreover, a corporation's capital resources are typically limited. Consequently, the resource allocation decision is often critical to firm success.

Capital investment processes of companies have been under study in the accounting literature for a long time (for example, Dean (1951), Mao (1970) and Pike and Dobbins (1986)). However, a large number of empirical studies in capital budgeting have been surveys and most of them have concentrated on the techniques used in evaluation. In fact, the popularity of different capital investment techniques in large U.K. and U.S. companies has been extensively investigated, as in Scapens and Sale (1985) and Mills (1988). These studies have revealed, for example, that capital budgeting techniques have become more and more popular during the past decades and that the DCF methods – net present value (NPV) and internal rate of return (IRR) – and the payback period are the most popular techniques. Surveys such as in Mukherjee (1987) have also discovered that the capital investment process is normally a bottom-up procedure and investment ideas are screened before the proposals are prepared.

Although surveys have contributed to the capital budgeting literature, they can be criticized in many ways. For example, surveys are fairly superficial. Normally only the results of the questionnaires are presented and the findings are seldom interpreted. Further, surveys may also give too favourable and rational a picture of the company's capital budgeting practices. For instance, although DCF techniques are applied, it does not mean that decision-makers use them, and the role of profitability calculations in the decision-making process is not known. In fact, it is not even obvious who makes the capital investment decisions and what is the role of top management in a capital budgeting process. Casual observations indicate that because typically units compete with each other for the limited amount of funds to be used for capital investments and lower-level operating managers propose capital investments and senior managers approve or reject these investments, the lower-level managers are seeking means for ensuring that the decision-maker – the person who has formal power to make the investment decision – will approve their proposals. Nevertheless, surveys have not uncovered how lower-level managers attempt to have their projects approved. Consequently, the surveys have not completely revealed how companies' capital resource allocation processes work. The purpose of this article is to describe and report a field study, which was conducted within one large organization, of how a subordinate attempts to influence decision-makers so that he or she receives the desired funds for fixed capital investments.

The remainder of the paper is organized as follows. The next section presents findings of earlier studies in the field and states the propositions. Then the research methods are presented. The third section describes the target company, and is followed by the findings section. Finally, the study is summarized and the conclusions outlined.

LITERATURE REVIEW

During the past few decades several scholars have studied capital budgeting from a social process viewpoint. The purpose of this approach, which can be regarded as an opposite perspective to the traditional normative and wealth-maximizing approach of the finance theory, has been to observe and explain the actual behaviour of people in capital budgeting processes. A major study in this social process approach was by Bower (1970) who showed that projects passed through different hierarchical phases and capital investment decisions were made by managers at various levels, not only by the top management of the organization. With the concept of impetus he also demonstrated the importance of the superiors' commitment in the acceptance of capital investments. Impetus refers to the willingness of a (division) manager to commit himself to sponsor a project before his superiors. In practice this means that when an investment is approved at the division and the division managers are committed to the project, it will also be accepted at the higher level of the organization. In fact, Clancy et al. (1982) noted that once a project is set into motion, it becomes increasingly more difficult to stop:

> ...after a project has received approval (or should one say, blessing) at several lower levels, upper-level decision makers are usually loathe to reject it.... It will usually be approved since by this time numerous lower-level managers and analysts have indicated their personal approval and commitment to the project.... Upper-level managers will usually reject a project only if there are overwhelming reasons for doing so (p. 30).

Consequently, from a subordinate's point of view, it is crucial that a superior commits him or herself to a project as early as possible. However, on the basis of the Bower study, it is not totally clear how this commitment can be achieved and whether there exist distinctions between different kind of investments.

Studies have discovered that a superior supports those projects which are in his or her interest to support. For example, Ackerman (1970) studied four companies in a field setting and found that in one of the companies some projects were funded while others had to wait for years. The explanation, according to Ackerman, is the force of backing: such as the supporter's organizational power and how strongly he or she feels about the project. Therefore Ackerman concludes that the capital budgeting process is influenced less by financial than other factors. In effect, there is some evidence in the literature that companies do not always use discounted methods for capital investment decisions.

It has been suggested by, amongst others, Hopwood (1974) that the capital budgeting process may be a mere ritual. This means that lower-level managers submit only such projects which will very likely be approved. If a project is rejected, a subordinate faces embarrassment and loss of face. A similar interpretation can be made on the basis of the findings of Mills and Herbert (1987) who discovered that informal communications between subordinates and superiors are used in order to prevent rejection of investment proposals. Carter (1971) also notes in his empirical study that investment decisions are the result of sequential bargaining at different organizational levels. More precisely, between the initiation and final approval of an investment, different people and groups – for example, first a profit centre manager and a division manager and later the division manager and the president – bargain. During bargaining, people commit themselves to the projects, making it increasingly more difficult to cancel or reject the proposals.

Marsh et al. (1988) argue that the capital budgeting process cannot be regarded purely as a political process. Rather, they stress the importance of formal control systems. Marsh et al. discovered that decision-makers commit themselves to a project via various meetings during the project's acceptance process. In addition, they noticed that typically only one capital investment option is presented to top management. Therefore, top managers can make only yes or no decisions and, according to the findings of Marsh et al., the top management at the corporate level approves the presented projects much more often than it rejects them.

The preceding discussion can be summarized with the following propositions:

P1.   Subordinates attempt to induce decision-makers to become committed to a project because otherwise the investment is not accepted.
P2.   Subordinates try to gain decision-makers' commitment through meetings and informal communications.
P3.   Capital investment calculation is not the most important determinant in decision-making.

P4.   When a subordinate submits a proposal it will very likely be approved.

The present study was designed to gather empirical evidence on these propositions.

RESEARCH METHODS

A field study methodology was chosen for this research in order to provide an in-depth understanding of the subject matter. It was assumed that more accurate and relevant data could be gathered using field research methods such as interviews and observations than through surveys or experimental studies.

The search for a potential research site started in winter 1988. From the beginning it was clear that the study would concentrate on one large company with a vast number of subunits. Two factors were important in this choice. First, numerous organizational levels exist in a large company, and in such a corporation capital investments are typically done on a regular basis. Second, a detailed study of company wide competition for the funds could not be possible in a reasonable period of time if several companies were studied.

By investigating business magazines, annual reports, and newspapers the researcher made a ranking of candidate firms. The most desirable company was approached in April 1988 when a research proposal and a covering letter was sent to the senior executive vice president of Scandinavia Corp (the name of the company is disguised). A phone call was made to this manager in May, during which he gave a preliminary approval for Scandinavia Corp to serve as the target firm.

The field research was carried out at three of Scandinavia Corp's five divisions in 1988–1989. The sources of information were:

- interviews at several organizational levels;
- informal discussions with the interview participants during coffee breaks, lunches, and tours of the unit facilities; and
- historical as well as up-to-date materials obtained from the company (e.g. investment proposals and ex post audit reports of implemented investments).

The primary source of information was interviews, and the objective was to interview people who played an important role in the company's or units' capital budgeting processes – the people who generate, co-ordinate, review, approve and reject proposals. The managers were normally interviewed once each. The duration of the interviews varied between 1 and 3.5 hours, and a typical meeting was 1.5 hours in length. Between September 1988 and June 1989 a total of 71 interviews with 69 different people, totalling 110 meeting hours, were conducted.

All of the meetings were semistructured interviews following 'question-naires' developed in advance. For each interview, the questionnaire was tailored separately because individual characteristics and the setting had to be taken into consideration. The interviews were documented in writing and the notes were transcribed immediately after the meeting to create a per-manent record. Follow-up contacts were sometimes made in order to check the accuracy of the data or supplement the facts and figures. Follow-up calls were also made in order to track some of the investment projects as they progressed during the research project. All in all, the use of various forms of information and interviews with several people within same units as well as at different organizational levels allowed verification of the accuracy of the researcher's observations and helped overcome gameplaying by interviewees.

THE TARGET FIRM

Scandinavia Corp is a publicly traded Fortune International 500 company and one of the largest enterprises in Finland. By means of its subsidiaries, sales offices, and representatives, Scandinavia Corp operates throughout the world. The company has always been a diversified industrial firm with a variety of businesses and today, Scandinavia Corp's organization includes five divisions which are decentralized into business units and further into profit centres.

The profitability of the divisions and business units varies and the profit-ability of the whole company has fluctuated between poor and satisfactory during the 1980s, although the company has shown a profit every year. However, the company's profit increased significantly in 1988 and 1989. Scandinavia Corp is fairly capital intensive and uses a lot of funds for investments. The amount of annual capital investments, excluding company acquisitions, has been lately nearly FIM 1000 million (approximately £143 million).

The study concentrated on three divisions, hereafter Pulp and Paper Divi-sion, Metal Division, and Packing and Service Division. The units studied normally account for 90 per cent of Scandinavia Corps' capital investments and 70 per cent of its net sales. The investigated units offer variation in many ways, for example, capital intensive vs labour intensive production processes, advanced vs standard manufacturing technology, large vs small units, rapidly growing vs stable units, and profitable vs unprofitable units. As a result, the sample provides a good cross-section of sizes and types of investments as well as activities within Scandinavia Corp. A summary of the divisions studied is given in Table 5.1.

During the strategic planning phase the business units announce their preliminary capital investments needs. The investment potential is allocated to the units on the basis of the company's strategy, result projections of the business units, and their investment needs.[1] The investment potential for each unit is determined before the annual budgeting process starts.

Table 5.1 Summary of the divisions studied

	Pulp and paper division	Metal division	Packing and service division
1. Net sales (FIM million)	2500	3000	1400
2. Number of employees	1900	6100	4200
3. Number of business units	4	6	4
4. Profitability of the units	Excellent: 1 unit Good: 2 units Satisfactory: 1 unit	Excellent: 1 unit Good: 2 units Satisfactory: 1 unit Poor: 2 units	Excellent: 1 unit Good: 1 unit Satisfactory: 1 unit Poor: 1 unit
5. Amount of annual capital investments (approximately FIM million)	500	200	150

Although a unit's investment framework is approved during the budgeting phase, each investment proposal has to be accepted separately. For investments of under 1 million marks, the business unit's internal board – which operates as a unit's Board of Directors – releases reserves to the disposal of the general manager two or more times during a year based on current operating results. Before approval of investments over 1 million marks, a detailed investment proposal is required. If an investment falls below FIM 5 million, the proposal can be approved by the internal board of a unit. On the other hand, investments which exceed FIM 5 million are accepted by the company's Executive Committee and projects over FIM 20 million by Scandinavia Corp's Board of Directors.[2]

An investment project's profitability is calculated using the internal rate of return (IRR) and payback criteria. There are no strict IRR or payback targets in the company. Nevertheless, interviews suggest that some informal return targets do exist. For instance, a project that is over FIM 5 million must have an IRR of at least 15–20%.

RESULTS

Observations in Scandinavia Corp indicated that subordinates attempt to 'sell' their investments to a decision-maker in order to have their projects approved. Selling was related to every major capital investment of Scandinavia Corp in one form or another. On the average nine interviewees out of ten said that investments have to be sold. Selling refers to an activity by which a proposer attempts to obtain the decision-maker's commitment to

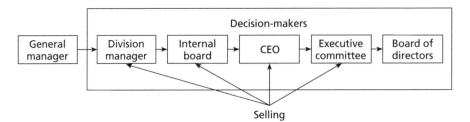

Figure 5.1 The progress of a capital investment and the targets of selling in Scandinavia Corp

the investment. When a person to whom an investment is sold has committed him or herself to the investment, he or she is ready to support the project, to promote it, and to contribute to the investment's approval.[3] More precisely, it was observed in Scandinavia Corp that an investment of over FIM 5 million, no matter how promising, is not accepted purely on the basis of an official proposal or calculations. For example, a member of the Executive Committee said:

> People should consider from the very beginning how an investment will be sold. The truth is that one or two ideas out of a hundred are carried out. This is because everybody doesn't see that an investment has to be packaged properly. You can call it a kind of lobbying but it belongs to the process. ...Investments are considered for a long time...but they [proposers] have to know how to sell so that they'll [investments] be implemented.

Selling can also be understood as a form of persuasion – the proposer of a capital investment attempts to induce the desired person to support the investment.

Depending on the size of a project there can be numerous sellers and decision-makers. However, in the projects of over FIM 1 million the initial seller is usually a general manager of a business unit. In these cases critical to an investment's approval is the commitment of the head of the division (see Figure 5.1). If the division manager does not approve the project, it has no possibility of being accepted. One of the subordinates emphasized the importance of selling to the head of division by saying:

> If you want to ensure that a proposal is going to be accepted you have to know the supervisor [the head of the division] and sell the idea first to him.

Several other interviewees revealed that the division head's cooperation is an essential pre-requisite for investment approval.

Proposers then try to sell the investment to the members of the internal board (see Figure 5.1). If the investment advances to the Executive Committee, attempts are then made to obtain the support of the CEO.[4] It was observed that if the CEO does not approve the project it will not get through the Executive Committee. If, on the other hand, the CEO does not reject the investment attempts are also made to sell the investment to the other members of the Executive Committee.

Typically, efforts to sell the project to the CEO and to the other members of the Executive Committee have been made before an official investment proposal is submitted. In effect, so much has been discussed about proposals in advance that the acceptance of the investment is ensured before the project is even considered by the Executive Committee. Therefore investments are hardly ever rejected by the Executive Committee. The CEO gave the following description:

> The Executive Committee has discussed the project at some point before the proposal comes there. When the proposal comes up for consideration, the decision has already been made. The decision was made at a very early stage when the head of the division informed [the members of the committee] about the investment in advance. But the decision can be delayed at the Executive Committee, so that the investment is studied carefully. If the final decision was made at an early stage, the investment would not be examined properly and planning could be started only after the decision. The Executive Committee's decision at a meeting is just a formality; it's just dotting the i.

Many interviewees made similar points. For example, one of the general managers said:

> Usually an investment has already been discussed in advance and the proposal is just a formality. The investment is simply blessed at the Executive Committee's meeting. It has been accepted earlier.

Investments are not usually sold to the Board of Directors (see Figure 5.1). The Executive Committee is the most important forum of the decision-making which also applies to large investments. Further, the Board of the Directors of Scandinavia Corp does not, in general, reject investment proposals. Up to the present all of the projects which the Executive Committee has accepted have been approved by the Board (in which the CEO is a member).

Selling arguments

Birnberg *et al.* (1983) presented a framework that can be used to study selling of capital investments. Using their terminology, selling investments incorporates the focusing and filtering of information. For example, a proposer of an investment can enhance or focus the significance of the technology. Or the proposer may not reveal the drawbacks of the investment, i.e., information is filtered. It is worth noting that the line between filtering and focusing is not clear because some aspects of an investment may be focused while, at the same time, some other aspects are filtered. In this study the emphasizing of information includes both focusing and filtering.

The observations gave evidence that the different arguments which are used to sell investments to decision-makers, i.e., in attempting to influence decision-makers in order to obtain the desired funds, can be classified as follows:

1. Economic arguments, e.g., profitability of an investment.
2. Strategic arguments, e.g., an investment's strategic applicability.
3. Non-economic arguments, e.g., social factors pertaining to an investment.
4. Production technology arguments, e.g., new manufacturing system.

Next, each of these categories is studied closer.

The basic argument in selling investments is to maintain that the investment is profitable. It was observed that in almost every investment case profitability of the project was emphasized. Especially, if the unit's profitability was poor it stressed the project's return. In fact, the study did not find any proposal where IRR was under 15%. Scandinavia Corp's manager of financial control confirmed this by saying:

> I've never seen an investment proposal where the return is under 20%. And the payback period is normally 2–3 years.

However, the effectiveness of economic arguments was low. Most of the decision-makers saw little value in figures. For example, a member of the Executive Committee disclosed:

> I don't pay attention to calculations but to the description of the investment and what we are going to get out of it. What's written in the investment's description and what's between the lines matter.

A member of an internal board has a similar view:

> They [general managers] are selling investments with percentages. Well, maybe they think that we can't say anything when the return is 20% and payback period 2–3 years. Too may people try to sell like this.

Several decision-makers emphasized that it is demanding to analyse and criticize the proposed calculations and figures. They do not pay much attention to numbers. In fact, it was observed that if a lower-level manager presents calculations convincingly superiors are unable to criticize the figures. One of the general managers gave his opinion:

> If the IRR is, for example, 30% it's difficult for the head of the division to object. He can ask questions, but, to a great extent, he has to rely on what is proposed to him.

As a result, the presented return figures have a minor role in the final decision-making. Nevertheless, it was observed that the return of an investment has to be sufficient, with an IRR of at least 15%, because otherwise the investment would not even be considered. In fact, the study discovered that investments for which returns are insufficient are either presented as profitable or they are not submitted from the units. The CEO confirmed these arguments by saying:

> An investment's estimated return is important for a proposal to even be taken into consideration. . . . The return is about on the same level for all the investments which come to the Executive Committee.

Within Scandinavia Corp, it is essential that an investment fits into a unit's strategy. Consequently, most proposals now state that the investment is part of a strategy or that the investment will allow the planned strategy to be implemented. For example, a controller of a division said that the most typical cliché nowadays is that 'the strategy requires the investment'. Although the efficiency of the strategy argument varied, it appeared in the interviews that for most of the decision-makers it was essential. For example, one of the division managers conceded:

> Large investments, especially, are based on the fact that a good strategy exists. That is the most important criterion.

A member of an internal board explained why it is good to justify and buy an investment with a strategy argument:

> You can frame a strategy and you can understand it.

In addition, all kinds of non-economic reasons are employed to sell investments although it appeared they are rarely used in Scandinavia Corp. An example of a non-economic argument is employment. It was observed that in the investment cases where social factors were emphasized forcefully, the arguments had a significant effect and those investments were finally accepted. For example, in one of the cases social factors were the real reasons for carrying out a large investment of over FIM 130 million. An alternative was the shutdown of the factory. The CEO commented on this project.

> There are several things that matter, [for example] employment of the unit. ...If there weren't any social factors the factory would have already been cemented closed!

Finally, capital investments can also be sold by using production engineering arguments. On the basis of the observations, these arguments are not employed as often as economic and strategic arguments, but more often than non-economic arguments. This is because the production technology arguments are typically applied when the project represents new technology in the company, such as FMS (Flexible Manufacturing Systems). Observations also indicate that the effect of these arguments is good, i.e., an investment can gain acceptance by emphasizing technological details of the project.

These distinct types of arguments are each related to particular information because the persons selling an investment state their arguments using focusing and filtering. The preceding discussion is summarized in Table 5.2.[5] In Scandinavia Corp, economic arguments were emphasized extremely frequently although they did not seem to have much influence on the decision-makers. Strategic arguments were also often employed and they had more effect on the superiors than economic arguments. Non-economic arguments were applied rarely, but when employed they were effective. Finally, proposers emphasized production technology arguments frequently and the decision-makers seemed to value them very highly.

Table 5.2 Frequency and effectiveness of different arguments

	Economic arguments	Strategic arguments	Non-economic arguments	Production technology arguments
1. Frequency of selling arguments[a]	Very frequently	Very frequently	Rarely	Frequently
2. Effectiveness of selling arguments[b]	Ineffective	Effective	Effective	Very effective

a Scale: rarely, frequently, very frequently.
b Scale: ineffective, effective, very effective.

In Scandinavia Corp, some characteristics of the project as well as of the unit submitting the investment were prevalent when certain selling arguments were employed. For example, units with poor profitability emphasize economic arguments when they attempt to promote their projects. More precisely, they stress to the decision-makers that an investment is exceptionally profitable. In contrast, business units with good profitability do not seem to emphasize economic arguments, rather they use strategic and production technology arguments. For example, a well-performing unit in Pulp and Paper Division made an investment of over FIM 300 million. All of the interviewees said that the acceptance of this investment did not depend on the costs. Strategy proved to be more important than the initial outlay. One of the business unit managers said:

> In this case there was a vision that we have to produce [certain] product or otherwise we are going to be out of the market, and this was the major issue.

The decision-makers agreed and one of them stated:

> The investment was sold [with the argument] that new products would result, and this argument was very easy to buy.

An example of production technology arguments is a well-performing unit in Metal Division which was planning a FMS investment of over FIM 55 million. Calculations indicated that the project would be extremely profitable. But the real selling arguments were FMS and its benefits. In fact, the approval of the investment was influenced more by the general appreciation of FMS than by the project's profitability.

This FMS investment also indicated that when an investment represents new technology in the company production technology arguments are emphasized. A similar case emerged in another unit of Metal Division where a FMS investment of FIM 15 million was considered. Also in this case the FMS was emphasized and the fact that the investment included new technology advanced the project in the company.

In addition, for extremely large investments of several hundred million marks, strategic arguments are emphasized more than any others. For example, one unit in Pulp and Paper Division was considering a machine investment of over FIM 900 million. The general manager of the business unit emphasized that strategy is much more important in such a large investment than profitability:

> The most important issue isn't, or, in my opinion it shouldn't be, the return. There should be a vision of the desired market. This means that where we are going is more important than the return. . . . The most important thing is what's the faith in this business. This kind of a large business shouldn't be justified only by a calculation.

Similar comments were also received from other managers who had large investments under consideration or implementation. In fact, the company's top decision-makers agreed and, among others, the senior executive vice president of Scandinavia Corp said:

> In large investments several other things are considered, not just profitability and other calculations. A decision regarding this kind of investment is more a decision of strategy than of calculation or profitability.

These two cases give partial evidence for the observation that if an investment represents standard technology, such that already exits in the company, proposers may emphasize strategic arguments. In addition, if the investment is small, typically under FIM 5 million, the proposers emphasize economic arguments. All in all, if a project is small and represents standard technology, proposers stress more economic and strategic arguments than any others. The final and a natural observation was that if an investment is not based on economic factors but, for example, on the guarantee of employment, proposers emphasize non-economic arguments.

Table 5.3 summarizes the preceding discussion. The figure presents factors which were observed to link a business unit and a capital investment when proposers employed different arguments.

Selling occasions

When selling investments was investigated further it appeared that selling takes place in different situations in Scandinavia Corp. More precisely, the interviews and observations indicated that selling occasions can be categorized as follows:

1. Formal selling occasions, e.g., meetings and negotiations where strategic plans, budgets, and capital investments are considered.

2. Informal selling occasions, e.g., arranged trips, audiences with decision-makers, accidental appointments, and phone calls.

Table 5.3 Characteristics that were dominantly prevalent with different selling arguments

	Economic arguments	Strategic arguments	Non-economic arguments	Production technology arguments
Unit:				
Unit's poor profitability	X			
Unit's good profitability		X		X
Investment:				
Investment represents new technology in the company				X
Investment is extremely large (comparing to average projects)		X		
Investment represents standard technology in the company	X	X		
Investment is small	X			
Investment's real reasons are not economic factors			X	

Examples of both of these selling occasions are provided below.

In some respects, an investment is first sold when a business unit's strategic plan is considered. To illustrate this point, a member of the Executive Committee said:

> During the strategy phase a lot of discussions are held. At that stage people try to sell their ideas to others. They try to convince others that it is worthwhile to put money in this [investment].

After this phase, investments are reconsidered at several later meetings. In fact, it appeared that one of the basic means for selling is that an investment is discussed at numerous meetings over a long period of time. This was exemplified in all large investments, those of several million marks or more. When a project is reviewed several times over a long period of time, decision-makers gradually commit themselves to the investment. Each time the project is considered decision-makers give their approval to promote the project. Finally, when an official proposal is submitted, a commitment has already been made to the project and it is accepted. One of the general managers revealed:

> Decision-making on an investment is a long process and requires several discussions. But it is important that the idea for the investment is generated by a decision-maker so that he notices that this investment should be done and that there is something in it. . . . You can't just bring an investment to a decision-maker and say 'Here it is.' The decision-makers have to be committed to the investment before the decision is made.

If an investment is put before an internal board, the Executive Committee, or the Board of Directors, a general manager or head of the division gives a presentation on the project. This presentation can include the strategy of emphasizing arguments. In fact, according to the interviewees, the presentation is an effective means of selling an investment and of obtaining the decision-makers' commitment to the project. One of the decision-makers regarded the presentation as essential to the acceptance of an investment:

> If poor investment papers [proposal] exist and a person can't present his issue properly, you get the feeling that everything is not in order, even though the idea may be good. Nevertheless, the investment will not be accepted. On the other hand, if the idea is lousy but the person has good papers and can present his stuff clearly and sell it, it's absolutely sure that the project will be accepted.

When the role of a presentation was raised during the interview where a general manager and the unit's vice manager were present at the same time, the following dialogue ensued:

The vice manager:	One important factor when you go to present a proposal is that you are prepared for questions. Many times managers test the idea by anticipating questions, and if you have prepared yourself for this and you can give reasoned answers, everything is going to be ok.
The general manager:	A good, logical presentation is very important because it can have a great influence.
The vice manager:	It's very important that at the end of the presentation you get somebody to say how good this idea is as soon as possible because the Executive Committee members actually know very little about the issue and are watching other members to see what they think about it. When one person says that this is a good idea then, normally, the others follow. But if you get a tough opponent, then it's more difficult because now the others may follow his opinion.

The interviews indicated that selling occurs frequently in informal selling occasions. More precisely, investments are sold, for example, when proposers unexpectedly meet a decision-maker. To illustrate this point, one of the operating managers said:

> There exist so many decision-makers in this large company that you have to sell your own [investment] to the decision-makers every time you meet one of them.

Another manager had a similar opinion:

> If you [unexpectedly] run into a decision-maker then of course you start to sell your investments and you make it clear that we really have to get the funds.

Table 5.4 Frequency and effectiveness of different selling occasions

	Formal selling occasions	Informal selling occasions
1. Frequency of selling occasions[a]	Very frequently	Frequently
2. Effectiveness of selling occasions[b]	Effective	Very effective

a Scale: rarely, frequently, very frequently.
b Scale: ineffective, effective, very effective.

Informal selling occasions often take place during phone calls. Also, investments are frequently presented to the decision-makers during personal visits. Especially, if an investment is large, proposers pay visits to decision-makers. One of the operating managers said:

> One good method [to sell] is visiting one of so called experts [i.e. top managers] and asking his opinion on the idea. This is important because this expert may [otherwise] feel that he was passed by when the idea then officially appears.

A member of the Executive Committee confirmed that often people try to sell investments to him by visiting and asking his advice. He continued:

> People come to discuss. They want to know what is lacking in the proposal and what else should be done. . . . On the other hand, I'm also trying to push this by saying, for example, that you still have to think about this and that. It's a consulting discussion about what is needed so that the proposal can move to the next stage. And in this way the investment comes known in the company, and it just doesn't appear on an agenda.

In addition, one way of selling an investment is to have decision-makers visit a site where a machine similar to the proposed one exists. It was observed that this occurs in Scandinavia Corp especially when a project includes new technology.

Table 5.4 summarizes the above discussion. Selling occurs more frequently in formal than in informal occasions. However, on the basis of the observations, it can be said that an informal selling occasion is more effective than formal occasions. Especially observations indicated that such an informal occasion where a personal visit is made to a decision-maker has a great influence.

DISCUSSION AND CONCLUSIONS

The preceding arguments are summarized in Figure 5.2 where selling capital investment to a decision-maker is illustrated. As the figure demonstrates, the purpose of selling is to induce a desired decision-maker to become

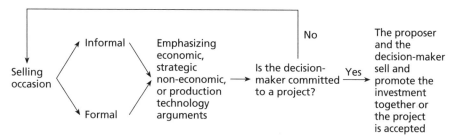

Figure 5.2 Selling a capital investment to a decision-maker

committed to a capital investment. There can be several selling occasions before the commitment is received but when the selling succeeds the decision-maker supports the project, puts it forward with the proposer, and contributes to the investment's approval.[6]

The findings support the first and second propositions which argued that subordinates attempt to induce decision-makers to become committed to a project because otherwise the investment is not accepted, and that subordinates try to gain decision-makers' commitment through meetings and informal communications. In Scandinavia Corp, for every capital investment of over FIM 1 million, lower-level operating managers sold their projects to superiors and this way they tried to receive superiors' commitment and to get investments accepted. In fact, a capital investment, no matter how promising, is not approved purely on the basis of its official proposal or calculations but proposers have to obtain decision-makers' commitment to projects. People carry out selling capital investments by emphasizing (i.e. focusing and filtering) economic, strategic, non-economic and production technology arguments. By using such grounds a proposer attempts to convince his or her superior that the project is sound and worth implementing. In addition, selling occurs in different situations; not only in formal meetings but also in informal occasions such as personal visits and phone calls. Although the study discovered that selling takes place more often in formal than informal occasions, it emerged that an informal selling occasion is the most effective. In particular, a decision-maker's commitment to a project is more easily obtained if a proposer visits him or her.

The results also support the third proposition; a capital investment calculation is not the most important determinant in the final decision-making. The study discovered that decision-makers regard economic arguments as almost useless. On the other hand, proposers often stress profitability figures when selling. However, a project's profitability has to be sufficient for the investment to be taken into consideration. Moreover, observations indicate that the most effective arguments are those associated with production technology. In general, decision-makers consider issues linked to strategy and production engineering relevant and important, but proposers use economic and strategic arguments more frequently in selling than non-economic and production technology arguments.

Observations gave evidence that in general proposers use economic arguments when their units' profitability is poor, an investment is small, or the project represents standard technology in the company. Strategic arguments are prevalent in situations characterized by a unit's good profitability, a large investment project, or an investment in standard technology. On the other hand, non-economic arguments are used when the project is not based on economic factors. Finally, production technology arguments are dominant when a unit's profitability is good and a project represent new technology in the company.

The findings also support the fourth proposition which argued that when a subordinate submits a proposal it will very likely be approved. The study discovered that after an idea has been sold to the division manager, efforts are made to sell the project to the members of the internal board, and in large investment cases also to the CEO and the members of the Executive Committee. If the decision-makers give their commitments to the investment, or at least do not reject it, an official investment proposal is submitted. Expressed differently, efforts to sell the project to the decision-makers have been made before an official investment proposal is submitted. Moreover, the official proposal is presented after it is known that the investment will likely be accepted. In effect, so much has been discussed about the project in advance that the acceptance of the investment is insured before the project is even considered, for example, by the Executive Committee. Therefore investments are hardly ever rejected although it is possible. No rejected investment case emerged in the interviews.

This research, of which results apply only to the target firm, has offered a perspective for understanding how lower-level managers attempt to have their capital investment approved in a large company. Nevertheless, there are still several questions to be answered. Does selling occur in other companies? If it does, how is it carried out? How do different capital budgeting systems affect selling? Finally, it could be studied whether selling is associated with other investments such as company acquisitions.

NOTES

1. Investment potential is based on the projects' expected contribution to the company's asset to equity ratio (AER). Capital investments are made within the limits within which the desired AER can be reached.
2. The 'divisional' level of management is exercised at the internal boards. In all of the other cases except one, a head of the division is the chairman of a business unit's internal board. The other members of an internal board are typically top managers of a division as well as central management.
3. According to Brunsson (1990), 'Commitment links the actor to the action in advance, it is a kind of promise of personal support to an action (p. 48).'
4. The Executive Committee consists of the CEO, the senior executive vice president, and six vice presidents of whom five are division managers.

5. Subordinates and superiors were asked to reveal the way of selling investments as well as employed arguments and their effectiveness.
6. It is also possible that the capital investment is rejected.

REFERENCES

Ackerman, R. W. Influence of integration and diversity on the investment process, *Administrative Science Quarterly*, September, 341–351, 1970.

Birnberg, J. G., Turopolec, L. and Young, S. M. The organizational context of accounting, *Accounting, Organizations and Society, 8*, 111–129, 1983.

Bower, J. L. *Managing the Resource Allocation Process: A Study of Corporate Planning and Investment*, Boston, MA, Harvard Business School Press, 1970.

Brunsson, N. Deciding for responsibility and legitimation: alternative interpretations of organizational decision-making, *Accounting, Organizations and Society, 15*, 47–59, 1990.

Carter, E. E. The behavioral theory of the firm and top-level corporate decisions, *Administrative Science Quarterly*, December, 413–428, 1971.

Clancy, D. K., Collins, F. and Chatfield, R. Capital budgeting: the behavioural factors, *Cost and Management*, September–October, 28–32, 1982.

Dean, J. *Capital Budgeting: Top-Management Policy on Plant, Equipment, and Product Development*, New York, Columbia University Press, 1951.

Hopwood, A. *Accounting and Human Behaviour*, London, Haymarket Publishing Limited, 1974.

Mao, J. C. T. Survey of capital budgeting: theory and practice, *Journal of Finance*, May, 349–360, 1970.

Marsh, P., Barwise, P., Thomas, K. and Wensley, R. Managing strategic investment decisions. In Pettigrew, A. M. (ed.), *Competitiveness and the Management Process*, Oxford, Basil Blackwell, 1988.

Mills, R. W. Capital budgeting techniques used in the UK and USA. *Management Accounting*, January, 26–27, 1988.

Mills, R. W. and Herbert, P. J. A. *Corporate and Divisional Influence in Capital Budgeting, A Study of Corporate and Divisional Capital Budgeting Practice in Large UK Companies*, London, CIMA, 1987.

Mukherjee, T. K. Capital-budgeting surveys: the past and the future, *Review of Business and Economic Research*, Spring, 37–56, 1987.

Pike, R. and Dobbins, R. *Investment Decisions and Financial Strategy*, Oxford, Philip Allan. 1986.

Scapens, R. W. and Sale, T. J. An international study of accounting practices in divisionalized companies and their associations with organizational variables, *The Accounting Review*, April, 231–247, 1985.

6

The Options Approach to Capital Investment

A. K. Dixit and R. S. Pindyck

Companies make capital investments in order to create and exploit profit opportunities. Investments in research and development, for example, can lead to patents and new technologies that open up those opportunities. The commercialization of patents and technologies through construction of new plants and expenditures for marketing can allow companies to take advantage of profit opportunities. Somewhat less obviously, companies that shut down money-losing operations are also investing: The payments they make to extract themselves from contractual agreements, such as severance pay for employees, are the initial expenditure. The payoff is the reduction of future losses.

Opportunities are *options* – rights but not obligations to take some action in the future. Capital investments, then, are essentially about options. Over the past several years, economists including ourselves have explored that basic insight and found that thinking of investments as options substantially changes the theory and practice of decision making about capital investment. Traditionally, business schools have taught managers to operate on the premise that investment decisions can be reversed if conditions change or, if they cannot be reversed, that they are now-or-never propositions. But as soon as you begin thinking of investment opportunities as options, the premise changes. Irreversibility, uncertainty, and the choice of timing alter the investment decision in critical ways.

The purpose of our article is to examine the shortcomings of the conventional approaches to decision making about investment and to present a better framework for thinking about capital investment decisions. Any theory of investment needs to address the following question: How should a corporate manager facing uncertainty over future market conditions decide whether to invest in a new project? Most business schools teach future managers a simple rule to apply to such problems. First, calculate the present value of the expected stream of cash that the investment will generate. Then, calculate the present value of the stream of expenditures required to undertake the project. And, finally, determine the difference between the two – the net present value (NPV) of the investment. If it's greater than zero, the rule tells the manager to go ahead and invest.

Of course, putting NPV into practice requires managers to resolve some key issues early on. How should you estimate the expected stream of operating profits from the investment? How do you factor in taxes and inflation? And, perhaps most critical, what discount rate or rates should you use? In working out those issues, managers sometimes run into complications. But the basic approach is fairly straightforward: calculating the net present value of an investment project and determining whether it is positive or negative.

Unfortunately, this basic principle is often wrong. Although the NPV rule is relatively easy to apply, it is built on faulty assumptions. It assumes one of two things: either that the investment is reversible (in other words, that it can somehow be undone and the expenditures recovered should market conditions turn out to be worse than anticipated); or that, if the investment is *ir*reversible, it is a now-or-never proposition (if the company does not make the investment now, it will lose the opportunity forever).

Although it is true that some investment decisions fall into those categories, most don't. In most cases, investments are irreversible and, in reality, capable of being delayed. A growing body of research shows that the ability to delay an irreversible investment expenditure can profoundly affect the decision to invest. Ability to delay also undermines the validity of the net present value rule. Thus, for analyzing investment decisions, we need to establish a richer framework, one that enables managers to address the issues of irreversibility, uncertainty, and timing more directly.

Instead of assuming that investments are either reversible or that they cannot be delayed, the recent research on investment stresses the fact that companies have *opportunities* to invest and that they must decide how to exploit those opportunities most effectively. The research is based on an important analogy with financial options. A company with an opportunity to invest is holding something much like a financial call option: It has the right but not the obligation to buy an asset (namely, the entitlement to the stream of profits from the project) at a future time of its choosing. When a company makes an irreversible investment expenditure, it "exercises," in effect, its call option. So the problem of how to exploit an investment opportunity boils down to this: How does the company exercise that option optimally? Academics and financial professionals have been studying the valuation and optimal exercising of financial options for the past two decades.[1] Thus we can draw from a large body of knowledge about financial options.

The recent research on investment offers a number of valuable insights into how managers can evaluate opportunities, and it highlights a basic weakness of the NPV rule. When a company exercises its option by making an irreversible investment, it effectively "kills" the option. In other words, by deciding to go ahead with an expenditure, the company gives up the possibility of waiting for new information that might affect the desirability or timing of the investment; it cannot disinvest should market conditions change adversely. The lost option value is an opportunity cost that must be included as part of the cost of the investment. Thus the simple NPV rule needs to be modified: Instead of just being positive, the present value of the expected stream of cash from a project must exceed the cost of the project by an amount equal to the value of keeping the investment option alive.[2]

Numerous studies have shown that the cost of investing in an opportunity can be large and that investment rules that ignore the expense can lead the investor astray. The opportunity cost is highly sensitive to uncertainty over the future value of the project; as a result, new economic conditions that may affect the perceived riskiness of future cash flows can have a large impact on investment spending – much larger than, say, a change in interest rates. Viewing investment as an option puts greater emphasis on the role of risk and less emphasis on interest rates and other financial variables.

Another problem with the conventional NPV rule is that it ignores the value of creating options. Sometimes an investment that appears uneconomical when viewed in isolation may, in fact, create options that enable the company to undertake other investments in the future should market conditions turn favorable. An example is research and development. By not accounting properly for the options that R&D investments may yield, naïve NPV analyses lead companies to invest too little.

Option value has important implications for managers as they think about their investment decisions. For example, it is often highly desirable to delay an investment decision and wait for more information about market conditions, even though a standard analysis indicates that the investment is economical right now. On the other hand, there may be situations in which uncertainty over future market conditions should prompt a company to speed up certain investments. Such is the case when the investments create additional options that give a company the ability (although not the obligation) to do additional future investing. R&D could lead to patents, for example; land purchases could lead to development of mineral reserves. A company might also choose to speed up investments that would yield information and thereby reduce uncertainty.

THE NPV RULE

As a practical matter, many managers seem to understand already that there is something wrong with the simple NPV rule as it is taught – that there is a value to waiting for more information and that this value is not reflected in the standard calculation. In fact, managers often require that an NPV be more than merely positive. In many cases, they insist that it be positive even when it is calculated using a discount rate that is much higher than their company's cost of capital. Some people have argued that when managers insist on extremely high rates of return they are being myopic. But we think there is another explanation. It may be that managers understand a company's options are valuable and that it is often desirable to keep those options open.

In order to understand the thought processes such managers may be using, it is useful to step back and examine the NPV rule and how it is used. For anyone analyzing an investment decision using NPV, two basic issues need to be addressed: first, how to determine the expected stream of profits that the proposed project will generate and the expected stream of costs required to implement the project; and, second, how to choose the discount rate for the purpose of calculating net present value. Textbooks don't have a lot to say about the best way to calculate the profit and cost streams. In practice, managers often seek a *consensus* projection or use an average of high, medium, and low estimates. But however they determine the expected streams of profits and costs, managers are often unaware of making an implicit faulty assumption. The assumption is that the construction or development will begin at a fixed point in time, usually the present. In effect, the NPV rule assumes a fixed scenario in which a company starts and completes a project, which then generates a cash flow during some expected lifetime – without *any* contingencies. Most important, the rule anticipates no contingency for delaying the project or abandoning it if market conditions turn sour. Instead, the NPV rule compares investing today with *never* investing. A more useful comparison, however, would examine a range of possibilities: investing today, or waiting and perhaps investing next year, or waiting longer and perhaps investing in two years, and so on.

As for selecting the discount rate, a low discount rate gives more weight to cash flows that a project is expected to earn in the distant future. On the other hand, a high discount rate gives distant cash flows much less weight and hence makes the company appear more myopic in its evaluation of potential investment projects.

Introductory corporate-finance courses give the subject of selecting discount rates considerable attention. Students are generally taught that the correct discount rate is simply the opportunity cost of capital for the particular project – that is, the expected rate of return that could be earned from an investment of similar risk. In principle, the opportunity cost would reflect the nondiversifiable, or *systematic*, risk that is associated with the particular project. That risk might have characteristics that differ from those of the company's other individual projects or from its average investment activity. In practice, however, the opportunity cost of a specific project may be hard to measure. As a result, students learn that a company's weighted average cost of capital (WACC) is a reasonable substitute. The WACC offers a good approximation as long as the company's projects do not differ greatly from one another in their nondiversifiable risk.[3]

Most students leave business school with what appears to be a simple and powerful tool for making investment decisions: Estimate the expected cash flows for a project; use the company's weighted average cost of capital (perhaps adjusted up or down to reflect the risk characteristics of the particular project) to calculate the project's NPV; and then, if the result is positive, proceed with the investment.

But both academic research and anecdotal evidence bear out time and again the hesitancy of managers to apply NPV in the manner they have been taught. For example, in a 1987 study, Harvard economist Lawrence Summers found that companies were using hurdle rates ranging from 8% to 30%, with a median of 15% and a mean of 17%. Allowing for the deductibility of interest expenses, the nominal interest rate during the period in question was only 4%, and the real rate was close to zero. Although the hurdle rate appropriate for investment with a nondiversifiable risk usually exceeds the riskless rate, it is not enough to justify the large discrepancies found. More recent studies have confirmed that managers regularly and consciously set hurdle rates that are often three or four times their weighted average cost of capital.[4]

Evidence from corporate *dis*investment decisions is also consistent with that analysis. In many industries, companies stay in business and absorb large operating losses for long periods, even though a conventional NPV analysis would indicate that it makes sense to close down a factory or go out of business. Prices can fall far below average variable cost without inducing significant disinvestment or exit from the business. In the mid-1980s, for example, many U.S. farmers saw prices drop drastically, as did producers of copper, aluminum, and other metals. Most did not disinvest, and their behavior can be explained easily once irreversibility and option value are taken into account. Closing a plant or going out of business would have meant an irreversible loss of tangible and intangible capital: The specialized skills that workers had developed would have disappeared as they dispersed to different industries and localities, brand name recognition would have faded, and so on. If market conditions had improved soon after and operations could have resumed profitably, the cost of reassembling the capital would have been high. Continuing to operate keeps the capital intact and preserves the option to resume profitable production later. The option is valuable, and, therefore, companies may quite rationally choose to retain it, even at the cost of losing money in the meantime.

The slow response of U.S. imports to changes in the exchange rate during the early 1980s is another example of how managers deviate from the NPV rule. From mid-1980 to the end of 1984, the real value of the U.S. dollar increased by about 50%. As a result, the ability of foreign companies to compete in the U.S. market soared. But the volume of imports did not begin to rise substantially until the beginning of 1983, when the stronger dollar was already well established. In the first quarter of 1985, the dollar began to weaken; by the end of 1987, it had almost declined to its 1978 level. However, import volume did not decline for another two years; in fact, it rose a little. Once established in the U.S. market, foreign companies were slow to scale back or close their export operations when the exchange rate moved unfavorably. That behavior might seem inconsistent with traditional investment theory, but it is easy to understand in the light of irreversibility and option value: The companies were willing to suffer temporary losses to

retain their foothold in the U.S. market and keep alive their option to operate profitably in the future if the value of the dollar rose.

So far, we have focused on managers who seem shortsighted when they
make investment decisions, and we have offered an explanation based on
the value of the option for waiting and investing later. But some managers
appear to override the NPV rule in the opposite direction. For example,
entrepreneurs sometimes invest in seemingly risky projects that would be
difficult to justify by a conventional NPV calculation using an appropriately
risk-adjusted cost of capital. Such projects generally involve R&D or some
other type of exploratory investment. Again, we suggest that option theory
provides a helpful explanation because the goal of the investments is to
reveal information about technological possibilities, production costs, or market potential. Armed with this new information, entrepreneurs can decide
whether to proceed with production. In other words, the exploratory investment creates a valuable option. Once the value of the option is reflected
in the returns from the initial investment, it may turn out to have been
justified, even though a conventional NPV calculation would not have found
it attractive.

OPTIONS TO DELAY OR INVEST

Before proceeding, we should elaborate on what we mean by the notions of
irreversibility, ability to delay an investment, and option to invest. What
makes an investment expenditure irreversible? And how do companies
obtain their options to invest?

Investment expenditures are irreversible when they are specific to a company or to an industry. For example, most investments in marketing and
advertising are company specific and cannot be recovered. They are sunk
costs. A steel plant, on the other hand, is industry specific in that it cannot
be used to produce anything but steel. One might think that, because in
principle the plant could be sold to another steel producer, investment in a
plant is recoverable and is not a sunk cost. But that is not necessarily true.
If the industry is reasonably competitive, then the value of the plant will be
approximately the same for all steel companies, so there is little to be
gained from selling it. The potential purchaser of the steel plant will realize
that the seller has been unable to make money at current prices and considers the plant a bad investment. If the potential buyer agrees that it's a bad
investment, the owner's ability to sell the plant will not be worth much.
Therefore, an investment in a steel plant (or any other industry-specific
capital project) should be viewed largely as a sunk cost: that is, irreversible.

Even investments that are not company or industry specific are often
partly irreversible because buyers of used equipment, unable to evaluate the
quality of an item, will generally offer to pay a price that corresponds to
the average quality in the market. Sellers who know the quality of the item

they are selling will resist unloading above-average merchandise at a reduced price. The average quality of used equipment available in the market will go down and, therefore, so will the market price. Thus cars, trucks, office equipment, and computers (items that are not industry specific and can be sold to buyers in other industries) are apt to have resale values that are well below their original purchase costs, even if they are almost new.

Irreversibility can also arise because of government regulations, institutional arrangements, or differences in corporate culture. For example, capital controls may make it impossible for foreign (or domestic) investors to sell their assets and reallocate their funds. By the same token, investments in new workers may be partly irreversible because of the high costs of hiring, training, and firing. Hence most major investments are to a large extent irreversible.

The recognition that capital investment decisions can be irreversible gives the ability to delay investments added significance. In reality, companies do not always have the opportunity to delay their investments. For example, strategic considerations can make it imperative for a business to invest quickly in order to preempt investment by existing or potential competitors. In most cases, though, it is at least feasible to delay. There may be a cost – the risk of entry by other companies or the loss of cash flows – but the cost can be weighed against the benefits of waiting for new information. And those benefits are often substantial.

We have argued that an irreversible investment opportunity is like a financial call option. The holder of the call option has the right, for a specified period, to pay an exercise price and to receive in return an asset – for example, a share of stock – that has some value. Exercising the option is irreversible; although the asset can be sold to another investor, one cannot retrieve the option or the money that was paid to exercise it. Similarly, a company with an investment opportunity has the option to spend money now or in the future (the exercise price) in return for an asset of some value (the project). Again, the asset can be sold to another company, but the investment itself is irreversible. As with the financial call option, the option to make a capital investment is valuable in part because it is impossible to know the future value of the asset obtained by investing. If the asset rises in value, the net payoff from investing increases. If the value declines, the company can decide not to invest and will lose only what it has spent to obtain the investment opportunity. As long as there are *some* contingencies under which the company would prefer not to invest, that is, when there is some probability that the investment would result in a loss, the opportunity to delay the decision – and thus to keep the option alive – has value. The question, then, is when to exercise the option. The choice of the most appropriate time is the essence of the optimal investment decision.

Recognizing that an investment opportunity is like a financial call option can help managers understand the crucial role uncertainty plays in the timing of capital investment decisions. With a financial call option, the more volatile the price of the stock on which the option is written, the more valuable the option and the greater the incentive to wait and keep the option alive rather than exercise it. This is true because of the asymmetry in the option's net payoffs: The higher the stock price rises, the greater the net payoff from exercising the option; however, if the stock price falls, one can lose only what one paid for the option.

The same goes for capital investment opportunities. The greater the uncertainty over the potential profitability of the investment, the greater the value of the opportunity and the greater the incentive to wait and to keep the opportunity alive rather than exercise it by investing at once. Of course, uncertainty also plays a role in the conventional NPV rule – the fact that a risk is nondiversifiable creates an uncertainty that is added on to the discount rate used to compute present values. But in the option view of investment, uncertainty is far more important and fundamental. A small increase in uncertainty (nondiversifiable or otherwise) can lead managers to delay some investments (those that involve the exercising of options, such as the construction of a factory). At the same time, uncertainty can prompt managers to accelerate other investments (those that generate options or reveal information, such as R&D programs).

In addition to understanding the role of irreversibility and uncertainty, it is also important to understand how companies obtain their investment opportunities (their options to invest) in the first place. Sometimes investment opportunities result from patents or from ownership of land or natural resources. In such cases, the opportunities are probably the result of earlier investments. Generally, however, investment opportunities flow from a company's managerial resources, technological knowledge, reputation, market position, and possible scale, each of which may have been built up gradually. Such resources enable the company to undertake in a productive way investments that individuals or other companies cannot undertake.

Regardless of where a company gets its options to invest, the options are valuable. Indeed, a substantial part of the market value of most companies can be attributed to their options to invest and grow in the future, as opposed to the capital they already have in place. That is particularly true for companies in very volatile and unpredictable industries, such as electronics, telecommunications, and biotechnology. Most of the economic and financial theory of investment has focused on how companies should (and do) exercise their options to invest. But managers also need to understand how their companies can obtain investment opportunities in the first place. The knowledge will help them devise better long-term competitive strategies to determine how to focus and direct their R&D, how much to bid for mineral rights, how early to stake out competitive positions, and so on.

R&D OPTION EXAMPLE

To illustrate the implications of the option theory of investment and the problems inherent in the traditional net present value rule, let us work through the process of making a capital investment decision at a hypothetical pharmaceutical company.

Suppose that you are the CEO of a company considering the development and production of a new drug. Both the costs and the revenues from the venture are highly uncertain. The costs will depend on, among other things, the purity of the output of the chemical process and the compound's overall effectiveness. The revenues will depend on the company's ability to find a principal market for the compound (and for whatever secondary uses might be discovered) and the time frame within which rival companies are able to introduce similar products.

Suppose that you must decide whether to make an initial investment of $15 million in R&D. You realize that later, if you decide to continue the project, additional money will have to be invested in a production facility. There are three possible scenarios for the cost of production: low ($40 million), middle ($80 million), and high ($120 million). To keep matters simple, we will assume that each of the scenarios is equally likely (in other words, that each has a $\frac{1}{3}$ probability of occurring). Let us also assume that there are two equally likely cases for the revenue (probability $\frac{1}{2}$ each): low ($50 million) and high ($130 million). To focus on the question of how uncertainty and option values modify the usual NPV analysis and to keep the example simple, we will also assume that the time frame is short enough that the usual discounting to reflect the time value of money can be ignored.

Should you make the $15 million investment in R&D? First, let us analyze the problem by using a simple NPV approach. The expected value (i.e., the probability-weighted average) of the cost of the production facility is ($\frac{1}{3}$ × $40 million) + ($\frac{1}{3}$ × $80 million) + ($\frac{1}{3}$ × $120 million) = $80 million. Likewise, the expected value of the revenue is ($\frac{1}{2}$ × $50 million) + ($\frac{1}{2}$ × $130 million) = $90 million. Therefore, the expected value of the operating profit is $10 million, which does not justify the expenditure of $15 million on R&D. So the conventional thinking would kill the project at the outset.

However, suppose that by doing the R&D, you are able to narrow the uncertainty by finding out which of the three possibilities for the cost of the production facility is closest to reality. After learning about the cost, you would be able to make a decision to go ahead and continue the project or to drop it. Thus the $15 million you invest in R&D creates an option – a right with no obligation to proceed with the actual production and marketing.

For a moment, we will put aside the market uncertainty and suppose that the revenue will always be $90 million. If the high-cost ($120 million) scenario is the one that materializes, you will decide not to proceed with the production, and your operating profit will be zero. In the other two cases, however, you will proceed. The operating profit is $90 million − $80 million = $10 million in the middle-cost case and $90 million − $40 million = $50 million in the low-cost case. The probability-weighted average of your operating profit across all three possible outcomes is ($\frac{1}{3}$ × 0) + ($\frac{1}{3}$ × $10 million) + ($\frac{1}{3}$ × $50 million) = $20 million. That exceeds your research and development cost of $15 million, and, therefore, the investment in R&D would be justified.

The logic shows that an action to *create* an option should be valued more highly than a naïve NPV approach would suggest. The gap between the naïve calculation and the correct one arises because the option itself is valuable. You can exercise it selectively when doing so is to your advantage, and you can let it lapse when exercising it would be unprofitable. The amount that an option should be valued over and above the $10 million expected profit (calculated on the assumption of immediate go-ahead) depends on the sizes and the probabilities of the losses that you are able to avoid.

Now let us reintroduce the notion of uncertainty with regard to the expected revenue. Suppose that you have found out that the middle-cost scenario ($80 million) is the reality. If you need to make a go-or-no-go decision about production at this point, you will choose to proceed because the expected revenue of $(\frac{1}{2} \times \$130 \text{ million}) + (\frac{1}{2} \times \$50 \text{ million}) = \$90$ million exceeds the production cost of $80 million, resulting in an operating profit of $10 million. But suppose you can postpone the production decision until you have found out the true market potential. By waiting, you can choose to go ahead only if the revenue is high, and you can avoid the loss-making case where the revenue turns out to be low. If revenue is high (which occurs with probability $\frac{1}{2}$), you will earn an operating profit of $130 million − $80 million = $50 million, and if revenue is low (also probability $\frac{1}{2}$), you will earn zero, for an average or expected value of $25 million, which is more than the $10 million you would get if you went ahead at once.

Here the opportunity to proceed with production is like a call option. Making a go-or-no-go decision amounts to exercising that option. If you can identify some eventualities that would cause you to rethink a go-ahead decision (such as a drop in market demand for your product), then the ability to wait and avoid those eventualities is valuable: The option has a time value or a holding premium. The fact that the option is "in the money" (going ahead would yield a positive NPV) does not necessarily mean that you should exercise the option (in this case, proceeding with production). Instead, you should wait until the option is deeper in the money − that is, until the net present value of going ahead is large enough to offset the loss of the value of the option.

In this example, we have intentionally left out any explicit cost of waiting. But you can easily include potential waiting costs in the calculation. Suppose that while you wait to gauge the market potential, a rival will grab $20 million worth of your anticipated revenues. The revenues under your most favorable scenario will be only $110 million and under the unfavorable one only $30 million. Now, if you wait, you can expect an outcome of $110 million − $80 million = $30 million with probability $\frac{1}{2}$ and an outcome of zero with probability $\frac{1}{2}$, for an expected value of $15 million. That is still better than the $10 million you get if you go ahead at once.

There's an important lesson here: Just as an action that creates an option needs to be valued more than the NPV analysis would indicate, an action that *exercises* or *uses up* an option should be valued *less* than a simple NPV approach would suggest. The reason is that the option itself is valuable. You can exercise an option selectively when the action is to your advantage, or you can let it lapse when such a course would be unprofitable. Again, the extra value gain depends on the sizes and the probabilities of the losses you are able to avoid.

It is even possible to put the revenue uncertainty and the cost uncertainty together. Thus if the R&D investment reveals that costs will be at the high end, you should again wait for the resolution of the revenue uncertainty before you proceed, earning $\frac{1}{2} \times$ ($130 million − $120 million) = $5 million. If the costs fall in the middle, it is best to wait, as we saw above; the expected operating profit will be $25 million. If the cost is at the low end ($40 million), however, the operating profit is positive at both revenue levels. In that case, it is best to proceed with production at once because the expected profit is ($\frac{1}{2} \times$ $130 million) + ($\frac{1}{2} \times$ $50 million) − $40 million = $50 million. The proper calculation for NPV that results from the $15 million R&D investment is ($\frac{1}{3} \times$ $5 million) + ($\frac{1}{3} \times$ $25 million) + ($\frac{1}{3} \times$ $50 million) = $26.7 million, which is even bigger than the $20 million we calculated when we left out the revenue uncertainty. We are now valuing the production options correctly, whereas earlier we assumed, in effect, that those options would be exercised immediately; in the high-cost and middle-cost scenarios, exercising the options wouldn't have been optimal.

All of the numbers in this pharmaceutical example were chosen to facilitate simple calculations. But the basic ideas represented in the case can be applied in a variety of real-life situations. As long as there are contingencies under which the company would not wish to proceed to production, the R&D that conveys information about which contingency will materialize creates an option. And insofar as there is a positive probability that production would be unprofitable, building the plant (rather than waiting) exercises an option.

The option theory of investing also has clear implications for companies attempting to raise capital. If financial market participants understand the nature of the options correctly, they will place greater value on the investments that *create* options, and they will be more hesitant to finance those that *exercise* options. Therefore, as the pharmaceutical company proceeds from exploratory R&D (which creates options) to production and marketing (which exercises them), it will find the hurdle rate rising and sources of eager venture capital drying up. It is interesting to note that this is exactly what has been going on recently in the biotechnology industry as it has progressed from searching for several new products to trying to exploit the few it has found.[5] The increased difficulty of finding venture capital for biotechnology can be explained in other ways – disappointments over earlier biotechnology products, problems securing and enforcing patents, the risk of a health care cost crunch, to name a few. But we believe that, to a large

extent, the market is making an astute differentiation between the creation
of options and the exercising of options.

CASE STUDIES

As companies in a broad range of industries are learning, opportunities to
apply option theory to investments are numerous. Below are a few examples
to illustrate the kinds of insight that the options theory of investment can
provide.

Investments in Oil Reserves

Nowhere is the idea of investments as options better illustrated than in the
context of decisions to acquire and exploit deposits of natural resources. A
company that buys deposits is buying an asset that it can develop immediately or later, depending on market conditions. The asset, then, is an option
– an opportunity to choose the future development timetable of the deposit.
A company can speed up production when the price is high, and it can slow
it down or suspend it altogether when the price is low. Ignoring the option
and valuing the entire reserve at today's price (or at future prices following
a present rate of output) can lead to a significant underestimation of the
value of the asset.

The U.S. government regularly auctions off leases for offshore tracts of
land, and oil companies perform valuations as part of their bidding process.
The sums involved are huge – an individual oil company can easily bid hundreds of millions of dollars. It should not be surprising, then, that unless a
company understands how to value an undeveloped oil reserve as an option,
it may overpay, or it may lose some very valuable tracts to rival bidders.[6]

Consider what would happen if an oil company manager tried to value
an undeveloped oil reserve using the standard NPV approach. Depending
on the current price of oil, the expected rate of change of the price, and the
cost of developing the reserve, he might construct a scenario for the timing
of development and hence the timing (and size) of the future cash flows
from production. He would then value the reserve by discounting these
numbers and adding them together. Because oil price uncertainty is not
completely diversifiable, the greater the perceived volatility of oil prices, the
higher the discount rate that he would use; the higher the discount rate, the
lower the estimated value of the undeveloped reserve.

But that would grossly underestimate the value of the reserve. It completely ignores the flexibility that the company has regarding when to
develop the reserve – that is, when to exercise the reserve's option value.
And note that, just as options are more valuable when there is more uncertainty about future contingencies, the oil reserve is more valuable when the
price of oil is more volatile. The result would be just the opposite of what

a standard NPV calculation would tell us: In contrast to the standard calculation, which says that greater uncertainty over oil prices should lead to *less* investment in undeveloped oil reserves, option theory tells us it should lead to *more*.

By treating an undeveloped oil reserve as an option, we can value it correctly, and we can also determine when is the best time to invest in the development of the reserve. Developing the reserve is like exercising a call option, and the exercise price is the cost of development. The greater the uncertainty over oil prices, the longer an oil company should hold undeveloped reserves and keep alive its option to develop them.

Scale Versus Flexibility in Utility Planning

The option view of investment can also help companies value flexibility in their capacity expansion plans. Should a company commit itself to a large amount of production capacity, or should it retain flexibility by investing slowly and keeping its options for growth open? Although many businesses confront the problem, it is particularly important for electric utilities, whose expansion plans must balance the advantages of building large-scale plants with the advantages of investing slowly and maintaining flexibility.

Economies of scale can be an important source of cost savings for companies. By building one large plant instead of two or three smaller ones, companies might be able to reduce their average unit cost while increasing profitability. Perhaps companies should respond to growth opportunities by bunching their investments – that is, investing in new capacity only infrequently but adding large and efficient plants each time. But what should managers do when demand growth is uncertain, as it often is? If the company makes an irreversible investment in a large addition to capacity and then demand grows slowly or even shrinks, it will find itself burdened with capital it doesn't need. When the growth of demand is uncertain, there is a trade-off between scale economies and the flexibility that is gained by investing more frequently in small additions to capacity as they are needed.

Electric utilities typically find that it is much cheaper per unit of capacity to build large coal-fired power plants than it is to add capacity in small amounts. But at the same time, utilities face considerable uncertainty about how fast demand will grow and what the fuel to generate the electricity will cost. Adding capacity in small amounts gives the utility flexibility, but it is also more costly. As a result, knowing how to value the flexibility becomes very important. The options approach is well suited to the purpose.

For example, suppose a utility is choosing between a large coal-fired plant that will provide enough capacity for demand growth over the next 10 to 15 years or adding small oil-fired generators, each of which will provide for about a year's worth of demand growth as needed. The utility faces uncertainty over demand growth and over the relative prices of coal and oil in the future. Even if a straightforward NPV calculation favors the large coal-fired plant, that does not mean that it is the more economical alternative. The reason is that if it were to invest in the coal-fired plant, the utility would commit itself to a large amount of capacity and to a particular fuel. In so doing, it would give up its options to grow more slowly (should demand grow more slowly than expected) or to grow with at least some of the added capacity fueled by oil (should oil prices, at some future date, fall relative to coal prices). By valuing the options using option-pricing techniques, the utility can assess the importance of the flexibility that small oil-fired generators would provide.

Utilities are finding that the value of flexibility can be large and that standard NPV methods that ignore flexibility can be extremely misleading. A number of utilities have begun to use option-pricing techniques for long-term capacity planning. The New England Electric System (NEES), for example, has been especially innovative in applying the approach to investment planning. Among other things, the company has used option-pricing techniques to show that an investment in the repowering of a hydroelectric plant should be delayed, even though the conventional NPV calculation for the project is positive. It has also used the approach to value contract provisions for the purchase of electric capacity and to determine when to retire a generating unit.[7]

Price Volatility in Commodities

Commodity prices are notorious for their volatility. Copper prices, for example, have been known to double or drop by half in the space of several months. Why are copper prices so volatile, and how should producers decide whether to open new mines and refineries or to close old ones in response to price changes? The options approach to investment helps provide answers to such questions.

Investment and disinvestment in the copper industry involve large sunk costs. Building a new copper mine, smelter, or refinery involves a large-scale commitment of financial resources. Given the volatility of copper prices, managers understand that there is value to waiting for more information before committing resources, even if the current price of copper is relatively high. As we showed in the earlier pharmaceutical example, a positive NPV is not sufficient to justify investment. The price of copper and, correspondingly, the NPV of a new copper mine must be high enough to cover the opportunity cost of giving up the option to wait. The same is true with disinvestment. Once a mine, smelter, or refinery is closed, it cannot be reopened easily. As a result, managers will keep these facilities open even if they are losing money at current prices. They recognize that by closing a facility, they incur an opportunity cost of giving up the option to wait for higher future prices. Thus many copper mines built during the 1970s, when copper prices were high, were kept open during the mid-1980s, when copper prices fell to their lowest levels in real terms since the Great Depression.

Given the large sunk costs involved in building or closing copper-producing facilities and given the volatility of copper prices, it is essential to account for option value when making investment decisions. In reality, copper prices must rise far above the point of positive NPV to justify building new facilities and fall far below average variable cost to justify closing down existing facilities. Outside observes might see that approach as a form of myopia. We believe, however, that it reflects a rational response to option value.

Understanding option value and its implications for irreversible investment in the copper industry can also help us understand why copper prices are so volatile in the first place. Corporate inertia in building and closing down facilities feeds back into prices. Suppose that the demand for copper rises in response to higher-than-average GNP growth, causing the price of copper to rise. Knowing that the price might fall later, producers typically wait rather than respond immediately with new additions to capacity. Since greater supply is not readily forthcoming, the pressure of demand translates into rapid increases in price. Similarly, during downturns in demand, as mines remain open to preserve their options, the price collapses. Recent history has illustrated this phenomenon: The reluctance of producers to close mines during the mid-1980s, when demand was weak, allowed the price to fall even more than it would have otherwise. Thus the reaction of producers to price volatility in turn sustains the magnitude of price volatility, and any underlying fluctuations of demands or costs will appear in an exaggerated way as price fluctuations.

SUMMARY

The economic environment in which most companies must now operate is far more volatile and unpredictable than it was 20 years ago – in part because of growing globalization of markets coupled with increases in exchange-rate fluctuations, in part because of more rapid technology-induced changes in the marketplace. Whatever its cause, however, uncertainty requires that managers become much more sophisticated in the ways they assess and account for risk. It's important for managers to get a better understanding of the options that their companies have or that they are able to create. Ultimately, options create flexibility, and, in an uncertain world, the ability to value and use flexibility is critical.

Decisions that enhance a company's flexibility by creating and preserving options (decisions, for example, about R&D and test marketing) have value that transcends a naïve calculation of NPV. More readily than conventional calculations suggest, managers should make decisions that increase flexibility. Choices that reduce flexibility by exercising options and committing resources to irreversible uses (construction of specific plants and equipment, advertising of particular products) will be valued less than their conventional NPV. Such choices should be made more hesitantly – and subjected to stiffer hurdle rates than the cost of capital – or delayed until circumstances are exceptionally favorable.

The bottom line for managers is that learning how to apply the net present value rule is not sufficient. To make intelligent investment choices, managers need to consider the value of keeping their options open. In this case, we don't think there is any option.

NOTES

1. For an overview of financial options and their valuation, see John C. Cox and Mark Rubinstein, *Options Markets* (Englewood Cliffs, N.J.: Prentice-Hall, 1985); John C. Hull, *Options, Futures, and Other Derivative Securities* (Englewood, Cliffs, N.J.: Prentice-Hall, 1989); or Hans R. Stoll and Robert E. Whaley, *Futures and Options: Theory and Applications* (Cincinnati, Ohio: South-Western Publishing Co., 1993).

2. Of course, one can always redefine NPV by subtracting from the conventional calculation the opportunity cost of exercising the option to invest and then saying that the rule "invest if NPV is positive" holds. But to do so is to accept our criticism. To highlight the importance of valuing the option, we prefer to keep it separate from the conventional NPV. But if others prefer to continue to use positive NPV terminology, they should be careful to include all relevant option values in their definition of NPV.

3. For a more comprehensive discussion of the standard techniques of capital budgeting, see a corporate finance textbook such as Richard A. Brealey and Stewart C. Myers, *Principles of Corporate Finance* (New York: McGraw-Hill, 1991).

4. See Lawrence H. Summers, "Investment Incentives and the Discounting of Depreciation Allowances," in *The Effects of Taxation on Capital Accumulation*, ed. Martin Feldstein (University of Chicago Press, 1987) p. 300; James M. Poterba and Lawrence H. Summers, "Time Horizons of American Firms: New Evidence from a Survey of CEOs" (MIT Working Paper, October 1991); Michael L. Dertouzos, Richard K. Lester, Robert M. Solow, and the MIT Commission on Industrial Productivity, *Made in America* (Harper Paperback, 1990) p. 61; and Robert H. Hayes and David A. Garvin, "Managing As If Tomorrow Mattered," HBR May–June 1982, pp. 70–9.

5. See "Panic in the petri dish," *The Economist*, July 23, 1994, pp. 61–2.

6. The application of option theory to offshore petroleum reserves was pioneered by James L. Paddock, Daniel R. Siegel, and James L. Smith, "Option Valuation of Claims on Real Assets: The Case of Offshore Petroleum Leases," *Quarterly Journal of Economics* 103, August 1988, pp. 479–508.

7. For a more detailed discussion of utility industry applications and NEES's experience in this area, see Thomas Kaslow and Robert S. Pindyck, "Valuing Flexibility in Utility Planning," *The Electricity Journal* 7, March 1994, pp. 60–5.

CASE STUDY 1

Real Options

K. Leslie and M. Michaels

BEST PRACTICE IN MANAGING REAL OPTIONS

Two UK companies, BP and PowerGen, exemplify the benefits of real-options thinking. Between 1990 and 1996, BP increased its market value from $18 billion to $30 billion, representing a total return to shareholders of 167%. Over the same period, PowerGen raised its market value from $1.4 billion to $3.8 billion, a return of almost 300%.

In both cases, most assets and earnings were in mature industries. BP's exploitation of North Sea oil and gas field development options took place against a background of falling reservoir sizes and volatile oil and gas prices – quite unlike the boom days of the 1970s and early 1980s. Power-Gen, for its part, has had to deal with barely rising demand, a saturated market and increasing competition to build new capacity.

Both companies managed to earn extraordinary returns in unfavourable environments because they followed a strategy of making incremental investments to secure the upside while insuring against the downside. They also delayed committing to investment until they had confirmed that it would be worth while, usually by acting on the six levers of option value.

Extending the Field of Vision

The application of real options steers management towards maximizing opportunity while minimizing obligation, encouraging it to think of every situation as an initial investment against future possibility. As a result, management's field of vision is extended beyond long-term plans too rarely properly reexamined, to encompass the full range of opportunities available to it at any moment. Real-options thinking achieves this through its most basic contribution and its most striking departure from the dicta of net present value: the attitude it fosters to uncertainty.

For BP, the economics of a prospective oil or gas field are highly uncertain in terms of margins (oil prices fluctuate, operating costs are unpredictable) and volume (recoverable reserves are difficult to estimate at the start of the licensing, exploration, appraisal and development process). The company has responded by embracing uncertainty. It has increased its exposure to volatile undeveloped prospects by accumulating licences that exploit the flexibility to respond to new technology and operating practices in order to make currently uneconomic prospects profitable. It is a strategy that has transformed BP's view of the North Sea's potential.

For PowerGen, the electricity pool is uncertain in terms of price and volume. The company's strategy evolved from "secure baseload with minimal uncertainty" to "explore opportunistic operating strategies." The outcome was a shift from a net present value approach that would have maximized the baseload volume of a few plants and closed all the others, to a policy of increasing operational flexibilities to respond to the market – and capturing marginal volumes at high prices.

In an increasingly uncertain world, real options have broad application as a management tool. They will change the way you value opportunities. They will change the way you create value – both reactively and proactively. And they will change the way you think.

HOW BP MAXIMIZES THE VALUE OF ITS OILFIELDS

As noted earlier, the sequence of spending decisions that leads to the development of an oil or gas field constitutes a classic real option. First, a company acquires a licence to explore; then it engages in low-cost seismic exploration. If the results are promising, exploratory drilling is undertaken.

If the exploratory well is positive, appraisal drilling takes place. Full development – and most expenditure – goes ahead only if these preliminary stages are completed satisfactorily.

While correct, this description captures no more than the value of the real option's reactive flexibility. Had BP acted on reactive flexibilities alone, it would probably not be earning superior returns in mature provinces like the North Sea, where profitable low-risk investment opportunities were exhausted long ago. By the same token, new opportunities such as those west of Shetland and in certain high-pressure/high-temperature areas of the UK continental shelf require heavy capital investment and carry geological and technical risks, so they usually appear uneconomic under net present value analysis. But because cumulative holding costs are so low and the payoff can be huge if the geological, technical and partnership uncertainties are resolved, almost any option value justifies holding on to such leases.

BP paid the penalty for taking a limited, reactive flexibility approach when it developed the giant Magnus field in the early 1980s. It took an over-cautious view of the forecast production plan and built too small a platform. Had proactive flexibilities been considered, higher production might have been achieved. As it was, production was constrained, and Magnus was obliged to pump for an expensive extended period, rather than following the optimal path of build-up, brief peak and long decline.

When the company has taken proactive flexibilities into account, however, the results have been remarkable.[1] Its handling of the Andrew Field is an example. The field was discovered in the mid-1970s but not developed at the time because it was small and, given the drilling technology of those days, required huge investment. The oil price collapse of the mid-1980s and subsequent market volatility made the prospect of development even dimmer.

Yet by the mid-1990s, through the application of so-called breakthrough thinking, experimentation, the creation of learning networks and benchmarking, BP had developed radical approaches to drilling, field development, project management, and the sharing of benefits with the contracting industry. What the company did, in effect, was to buy an out-of-the-money option to develop the Andrew Field, defer exercising the option until it had proactively driven down the exercise price (that is, the investment in development), and then exercise an option that it had turned into an in-the-money one.

Exploiting proactive flexibility in the case of oilfield development licences involves all the steps to reduce capital costs that BP took in the case of the Andrew Field, along with measures to minimize the cost of the real option. The licence bid and its holding cost are the option price – as critical a part of the management equation as the six levers of option value (the same is true in financial options). The holding cost can be reduced by renegotiating spending obligations such as a commitment to a government to drill exploration wells, or a commitment to a partner.

As always, it is worth comparing real-options thinking, reactive and proactive, with net present value along the six levers of the options model. The most sensitive levers are increasing the present value of expected cash inflows and reducing the present value of expected fixed costs.

The means to pull both these levers is the application of new technology to obtain more reliable profiles of an oilfield's value, better total oil recovery, and more efficient production facilities (fewer wells, lighter platforms). The next most sensitive lever, increased uncertainty and hence price volatility, makes an option more attractive, but management cannot influence oil prices. At the less sensitive end of the spectrum, the option's duration should be managed to trade off potential improvements in cash inflow and outflow against the cost of holding the option and the risk of losing "dividends".

NPV analysis could allow for some of this potential through different scenarios. The danger, however, is that a classic net present value "go/no go", all-or-nothing decision would underestimate the value of expected cash inflows, which could result in a production facility incapable of handling higher-than-expected volume, as in the case of the Magnus Field. Net present value analysis would seriously undervalue volatility, accentuating the risk-averse behaviour already skewing forecasts and budgeting. Go/no go thinking also implicitly assumes (usually incorrectly) that the investment opportunity will be unaffected by competitor behaviour.

It should be clear by now that the lessons of real-options thinking apply as much to existing assets as they do to new areas of exploration and development, where they are much more often applied. Declining or exhausted oilfields are a case in point. Net present value analysis would probably suggest they be closed down. But keeping them running not only effectively defers new investment and saves the cost of removing redundant facilities (sometimes much higher than anticipated, as the enormously expensive Brent Spar incident two years ago showed)[2], it also keeps open the option of benefiting from the development of new technologies.

For instance, satellite unmanned gas platforms in the southern North

Sea, extended-reach drilling (enabling wells to be bored into a reservoir tens of kilometres from a platform originally installed to service a nearby reservoir), and sub-sea templates that pump oil back to far-off platforms all make it possible to use processing capacity that would otherwise have become surplus as soon as the original reservoirs were exhausted. Such developments have greatly increased the option value of fields originally exploited with no thought of such possibilities.

In these circumstances, the importance of options thinking lies less in the way the present values of cash inflows and outflows are managed, and more in the recognition of the value of the option's duration. By exercising options to extend the life of existing infrastructure (thus driving down development costs), and by managing competitors' and its own incremental investments – variables that net present value ignores or oversimplifies – BP has managed to commercialize many small oilfields as its original giant fields have declined.

POWER MASTER-STROKE BY POWERGEN

In 1990, the UK government privatized the electricity generating industry. At a stroke, the stable market enjoyed by a state-owned monopoly was replaced by an unpredictable environment of fluctuating prices. A pool (or spot market) was established into which generators had to sell their electricity, and which priced electricity by the half-hour on the basis of bids from power stations. The new market is characterized by hour-to-hour and seasonal volatility – a nightmare for generators in a highly capital-intensive industry.

At the time, most generating stations were coal-fired baseload stations designed to generate more or less continuously. The variable nature of electricity demand and the availability of environmentally and economically attractive supplies of natural gas fuelled the "dash for gas": the development of combined-cycle gas turbine (CCGT) stations that could be switched on or off according to requirements, reaching full capacity without technical problems in 15 minutes. Most coal stations – PowerGen's among them – were forced out of baseload into periodic production, to which they were unsuited. Many were forced to close.

Net present value analysis of the dilemma faced by coal-fired stations would have suggested driving down costs (an insufficient measure, given the superior economics of CCGT); or hedging electricity output (which would have protected against the downside risk of losing market share but only at the price of eliminating the upside potential); or closing the plant to avoid investing against an uncertain cash inflow. Real-options thinking however, enabled PowerGen to exploit three variables ignored in net present value thinking – uncertainty, duration and dividend – to create a profitable business.

Price volatility meant that, for short periods, coal stations could earn large margins and would thus be worth life-extending investment, provided

Table 1 Real-option valuation and strategy versus the net present
value approach

Example	Net present value	Real option valuation (reactive flexibility)	Real-option strategy (reactive and proactive flexibility)
BP: Maximizing the value of Andrew field	Sell/surrender licence blocks immediately	Still sell/surrender because oil price volatility does not increase value sufficiently	Increase present value of future cash inflows by maximizing recoverable reserves; reduce drilling and platform costs
PowerGen: Flexible operation of the power station	Shut coal-fired power stations immediately	Still shut most coal-fired power stations because they are unsuited to to on/off operation	Reduce exercise price by introducing flexible start/stop operation and transforming fixed costs into variable costs

that PowerGen's operating staff rapidly developed the technological and
operational flexibility to acquire two key capabilities (see Table 1):

1. The ability to switch coal plant on and off frequently. New operating
    skills such as managing the chemical balance in the boilers, in com-
    bination with limited investment such as the use of hardened chrome
    headers to prevent boilers cracking as tubes heat and cool, now enable
    some PowerGen stations to start up more than 200 times a year. Typical
    US coal-fired stations start up just eight to 10 times a year.

2. The ability to bid economically for marginal business by converting
    fixed costs into variable costs through the aggressive use of contractors.

Rather like BP, PowerGen raised its aspirations by benchmarking, by
stretching its management to surpass world best practice, and by freeing
business units and teams to find the best route forward. PowerGen ultimately enjoyed a double benefit, in fact, because unpredictable shutdowns of
nuclear plants, combined with volatilities in supply and demand, have
caused periodic shifts to coal production and an increase in prices.

NOTES

1. See "Unleashing the power of learning: An interview with British Petroleum's
    John Browne", *Harvard Business Review*, Sep–Oct 1997, for BP's own account
    of its value-creating strategy since 1992.
2. Shell sought to sink the redundant storage platform Brent Spar in mid-Atlantic,
    arousing a storm of protest.

7

Solving the New Equity Puzzle

P. Dechow, A. Hutton and R. Sloan

When Yahoo!, a company that had developed a well-regarded Internet search-engine, went public last year, its stock at first seemed to live up to its name. The initial public offering (IPO), managed by Goldman Sachs, the US investment bank, did phenomenally well, and Yahoo!'s stock, priced at $13, increased to $43 on the first day of trading. However by August the stock had declined to $18 and in mid-December it was trading in the low $20s and currently trades in the low $30s.

If this kind of stock price volatility for a new issue has a familiar ring, it is because Yahoo! is not the only company to show this kind of performance. Researchers have shown that many IPOs and seasoned equity offerings (SEOs) start out well. Their stock prices rise, but then over the following three to five years they perform far worse than the average stock. In face they under-perform the rest of the market by around 30 per cent.

In academic circles the phenomenon is known as the new equity puzzle. Our study examined the role of such analysts' long-term growth forecasts in the pricing of stock around the launch of new equity offerings.

Sell-side analysts act as valuation intermediaries, providing expertise in processing financial information. They act as investment advisors to their brokerage clients. However, top-rated analysts also play an important role in developing relationships with their employers' investment banking clients. As a result analysts have become instrumental in attracting underwriting business.

These two roles provide conflicting incentives for sell-side analysts. As investment advisors, sell-side analysts have incentives to act in the best interests of their brokerage clients and provide realistic (unbiased) growth forecasts. However, to attract lucrative underwriting business, these same analysts have incentives to provide overly optimistic growth prospects for their current or future investment banking clients.

OVERLY OPTIMISTIC

Our research examines which of these two incentives dominates – do analysts make unbiased growth forecasts to serve their brokerage clients or do they make overly optimistic growth forecasts to assist their employers' investment banking clients? In particular, we look at whether analysts provide realistic or overly optimistic forecasts of earnings growth around the time of new equity offerings.

We investigate whether analysts employed by the investment bank acting as the lead underwriter of the offering provide more overly optimistic forecasts than other unaffiliated analysts. In addition, we look at whether investors naively rely on the growth forecasts made by analysts so that these growth forecasts are reflected in stock prices.

That is, if analysts are overly optimistic and investors believe their forecasts, do companies with the highest growth forecasts at the time of the offering tend to have the poorest stock price performance after the new equity offering?

Such a finding would suggest that investors initially believe analysts' growth forecasts and are subsequently disappointed when the less-than-expected earnings growth is realised.

To summarise, we found that analysts' growth forecasts are systematically overly optimistic around new equity offerings, and the most overly optimistic growth forecasts are issued by analysts employed by the lead underwriters of the offerings. We also found that analysts' overly optimistic growth forecasts are reflected in the stock prices of issuing firms, suggesting that investors naively rely on analysts' growth forecasts. Overall, our results suggest that sell-side analysts compromise their role as investment advisors to increase the stock prices of their investment banking clients and generate greater underwriting fees for their employers.

Other researchers found that, in general, analysts tend to be overly-optimistic in their forecasts of companies' earnings prospects. Some researchers have suggested that the over-optimism observed in analyst forecasts arises because they selectively report. That is, analysts only make forecasts when they have good news to report.

The business press has reported that many analysts will no longer issue negative reports because of fear of retribution. In a survey of members of the 1989 All-American Research Team, *Institutional Investor* reported that 61 per cent of respondents said they had felt pressure to temper a negative opinion at least once in their careers.

Analysts indicated that corporate intimidation is an important force. They fear losing access to management of companies they follow after issuing negative reports. Analysts also indicated that they could not ignore the wishes of their firms' investment banking clients, even prospective ones, since fees from investment banking activities support their research.

Some have argued that as a result of the pressures to suppress negative reports financial resources are being diverted to companies with the most influence, and not those with the best investment opportunities.

It has been argued that the objectivity and independence of the analyst community steadily eroded during the 1980s as analysts abandoned primary research because of declining commission fees to pursue investment banking fees.

SELLING POWER

"When commissions on stock trading fell, investment research (which generated trading) no longer paid the freight. Today, analysts are supported partly by their corporate finance departments. And much of what they do – marketing and preparing IPOs, for instance – has little to do with pure research, and much to do with investment banking. In the US in particular, investment banks have persuaded clients to hire underwriters on the basis of their analysts' selling power. In turn, the analyst's worth is increasingly dependent on his or her ability to bring in deals.

Of course, some money managers complain that the big emphasis on new-issue fees taints research results if the analysts try to avoid saying anything negative about their underwriting clients."[1]

"It is little wonder that we are where we are. What do they expect for six cents a share?"[2]

commented one Wall Streeter, who believes that self-censorship and watered-down research are the inevitable result of years of declining commission rates.

CONTRARIAN STRATEGIES

If investors are not fully aware of the bias in analysts' growth forecasts, then stock prices may reflect overly optimistic growth expectations. Recent research attempts to document whether anomalous stock return behaviour is consistent with stock prices reflecting analysts' long-term growth forecasts, despite the bias in these forecasts. Dechow and Sloan (1997) examine the extent to which the returns to the "contrarian investment strategies" are consistent with security prices reflecting analysts' long-term earnings growth forecasts.

The "contrarian investment strategies" or "relative-value investing" involve buying and selling stocks that are priced low or high relative to various accounting measures of operating performance such as earnings, cash flows and book values.

The innovation in the Dechow and Sloan study is that they directly estimate the earnings growth rates embedded in stock prices and compare them with the expectations implied if investors recognise the bias in analysts' forecasts versus expectations implied if investors naively rely on analysts' forecasts. Stock return behaviour is shown to be consistent with investors naively relying on overly optimistic analysts' forecasts.

More than half of the returns to "contrarian investment strategies" are explained by investors' naive reliance on analysts' long-term growth forecasts.

In this article, we adopted a similar approach to help explain the new equity puzzle. The new equity puzzle is a well documented stock return anomaly – companies systematically experience low stock returns relative to various market indices in the three to five years following new equity offerings (Loughran and Ritter 1995 and Spiess and Affleck-Graves 1995).

We attempted to document whether the unusually low post-offering returns arise because analysts issue overly optimistic growth forecasts at the time of the offerings and investors rely on these forecasts. After documenting that analysts make overly optimistic growth forecasts for companies issuing new equity securities, we examined whether stock prices reflect these forecasts.

PURE AND MIXED DEALS

We directly estimated the earnings growth rates embedded in stock prices and compared them with the expectations implied if investors recognise the over-optimism in analysts' forecasts versus the expectations implied if investors naively rely on analysts' growth forecasts.

We examined a sample of 1,179 new equity offerings, of these 86 are IPOs and the remaining 1,093 are seasoned equity offerings (SEOs). For these offerings there are 7,169 analysts' long-term earnings growth forecasts made in the 12 months (−9 to +3) surrounding the issue dates. We sort the individual analysts making the growth forecasts into two categories: affiliated and unaffiliated.

If an analyst is employed by the lead manager or a related firm (a subsidiary or a parent of the lead manager), then he or she is classified as affiliated with the particular offering. Otherwise the analyst is classified as unaffiliated. We classified 622 analysts' growth forecasts as affiliated and 6,547 as unaffiliated.

We further classified the stock offerings as pure and mixed deals, depending on which analysts follow the deal and make long-term growth forecasts. Deals with only analysts from one category (affiliated or unaffiliated) making growth forecasts are classified as pure deals. Deals where both affiliated and unaffiliated analysts made forecasts are classified as mixed deals.

In Figure 7.1 we compare analysts' forecasts and five-year realised performance. The mean realised growth in earnings for the full sample over the five years following the offering is 5.7 per cent. The corresponding mean analysts' forecast of growth in earnings at the time of the offering is 16.2 per cent. Thus, on average, analysts over-estimate the five-year earnings growth of issuing firms by 10.6 per cent per year.

This indicates that less than half of the growth forecast by analysts is actually realised. Analysts' growth forecasts are overstated by about 65 per cent. This pattern holds for the various classifications of analysts – analysts' predicted growth is not realised. Note that affiliated analysts make the most aggressive predictions of growth for their clients.

Realised growth is 9.7 per cent, while affiliated analysts predicted growth of 23.3 per cent per year. Thus, the affiliated analysts over-estimate the five-year earnings growth by 14.8 per cent per year for their investment banking clients.

Figure 7.2 summarises analysts' forecast errors and the abnormal post-offering stock performance of issuing firms. It is useful to note the correlation

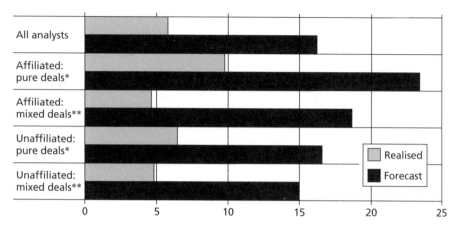

Figure 7.1 Analyst forecasts compared with five-year realised performance
(average annual earning growth (%))

* Pure deals – only analysts from one category (affiliated or unaffiliated) made forecasts.
** Mixed deals – both affiliated and unaffiliated analysts made forecasts on the same
offerings (based on 7,169 analyst forecasts for 1,179 stock offerings between 1981
and 1990).

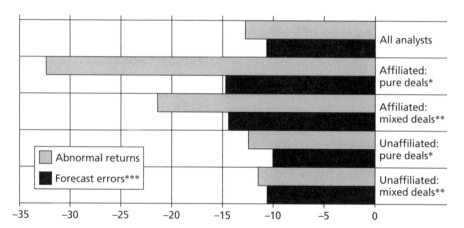

Figure 7.2 Abnormal stock performance compared with forecast errors
following new equity offerings (Variables measured as %)

* Pure deals – only analysts from one category (affiliated or unaffiliated) made forecasts.
** Mixed deals – both affiliated and unaffiliated analysts made forecasts on the
same offerings (based on 7,169 analyst forecasts for 1,179 stock offerings between
1981 and 1990).
*** Forecast error = realised earnings growth – forecast earnings growth.

between the magnitude of the forecast errors and the abnormal returns for
these firms.

The negative abnormal returns in the five years following the offering are
consistent with investors expecting these companies to produce better per-
formances. Measuring post-offering stock price performance using market-
adjusted buy-hold stock returns, the mean abnormal stock return for the

entire sample is −12.7 per cent for the five years following the offering. The mean abnormal return for affiliated: pure deals category is −32.3 per cent. This category has the largest forecast errors and the most negative stock price performance.

These results are consistent with the affiliated analysts issuing more overly optimistic earnings growth forecasts and with investors sharing these earnings expectations. The statistics show a similar pattern for the 491 forecasts in the affiliated: mixed deals category. The mean abnormal return is −21.3 per cent, which is more negative than the average for the entire sample, and the mean forecast error is −14.3 per cent, which is also more negative than the average for the entire sample.

MISTAKEN BELIEFS

Further, the deals followed by unaffiliated analysts have the least negative abnormal returns and the least overly optimistic forecasts.

For the 2,938 forecasts in the unaffiliated: mixed deals category, the mean abnormal return is −12.3 per cent and the mean forecast error is −10.5 per cent. For the 3,609 deals in the unaffiliated: pure deals category, the mean abnormal return is −11.3 per cent and the mean forecast error is −10.0 per cent. This is consistent with the unaffiliated analysts issuing relatively less overly optimistic earnings growth forecasts and with investors sharing these less overly optimistic earnings expectations.

The results of research show that investors believe analysts' overly optimistic forecasts. Further it appears that investors are unaware of the fact that affiliated analysts' forecasts are the most optimistic.

Our results indicate that the poor post-issuing return performance is at least in part driven by investors' mistaken beliefs.

Our results have policy implications in that the analyst's primary responsibility is to provide sound investment advice to brokerage clients. It appears that the co-existence of brokerage services and underwriting services in the same institution leads analysts to compromise their responsibility to brokerage clients to attract underwriting business.

In practice, investment banks claim to have a "Chinese wall" to prevent such conflicts. Our evidence questions the depth of these "Chinese walls".

NOTES

1. From R. Lowenstein: "Today's analyst often wears two hats", *Wall Street Journal*, May 2, 1996.
2. From "The hazards of negative research reports", *Institutional Investor*, July 30, 1990.

REFERENCES

P. M. Dechow and R. G. Sloan, "Return to contrarian investment strategies: tests of naïve expectation hypotheses", *Journal of Financial Economics*, vol. 43, 3–27, 1997.

T. Loughran and J. R. Ritter, "The New Issues Puzzle", *Journal of Finance*, vol. L, no. 1, March, pp. 23–51, 1995.

K. D. Spiess and J. Affleck-Graves, "The long-run performance following seasoned equity offerings", *Journal of Financial Economics*, vol. 38, pp. 243–267, 1995.

CASE STUDY 2

Valuation and New Issue: Deutsche Telekom

VALUATION: FINDING THE RIGHT MEASURE

T. Jackson

Setting a value on Deutsche Telekom presents a considerable challenge on at least three grounds. First, well over half the issue will go to German investors, who use somewhat different valuation criteria from their counterparts in the UK or US.

Second, UK and US analysts are themselves unsure on which yardsticks to use. Third and most fundamental, Telekom is at a turning point in its history. Future earnings, cash flow and dividends are correspondingly hard to predict.

On the first point, the defining characteristic of German investors – who seem likely to buy some 70 per cent of the issue – is their preference for bonds rather than equities. The initial question is therefore how Telekom measures up against the German government bond yield.

This year's dividend is promised by Telekom at DM0.60 per share. Next year, it will double to DM1.20. For German taxpayers, the gross value is some 40 per cent higher again.

The 1997 dividend is plainly the more relevant for valuation purposes, since Telekom says it is the basis from which future payments will be increased in line with results. At DM25, the lower end of the offer range, this gives a gross yield to German taxpayers of 6.8 per cent. At the DM30 end, the yield is 5.7 per cent.

The yield on the 10-year German government bond, meanwhile, is a touch under 6 per cent. This goes a long way towards explaining the enthusiasm of the German public for the offer. Not only is the return more or less in line with bonds, it offers the apparent attraction of earnings and dividend growth.

Non-German investors will prefer to compare Telekom with the German equity market, and to other international telecoms stocks. As for the German market, analysts estimate its average p/e ratio next year at around 14 times.

It appears that Telekom's p/e next year – after an earnings rebound from exceptional charges this year – might be around 13.5 at the lower price of DM25, or 16 at DM30. Given that telecom stocks tend to trade at a slight discount to their home markets, this particular measure would suggest that DM30 is a touch expensive.

When it comes to other telecoms stocks, the picture becomes murkier. There is general agreement that comparing Telekom with non-European telecoms heavyweights, such as AT&T of the US or NTT of Japan, is unhelpful. This is largely because Telekom works within a locally regulated environment, and impending changes in EU regulation will do much to determine its prospects.

The crucial question is which yardstick should be used to compare telecoms companies within Europe. There is general agreement that the old-style price/earnings ratio is unsatisfactory. This is mainly because, in such a distinctively pan-European sector, differences in accounting standards, taxation and the cost of capital make earnings figures inconsistent across national boundaries.

The obvious answer is to concentrate on cash flow. The most popular form is the US-derived EBITDA, or earnings before interest, tax, depreciation and amortisation. This, in turn, is compared not simply with market value – since EBITDA takes no account of the cost of borrowings – but to market value plus debt, less working capital.

This is known as enterprise value, or EV. The EV/EBITDA multiple, it appears, has shown fairly close correlation with earnings growth for European telecoms companies in the past.

But this approach has distinct problems. On the one hand, some analysts argue that comparison with existing EV/EBITDA multiples for other European telecoms companies point to a price range for Telekom so wide as to be meaningless.

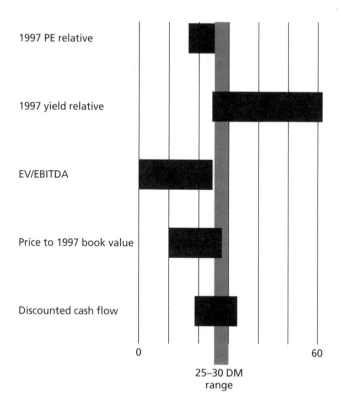

Figure 1 Valuation methods give different prices (DM per share) (*Source*: Analysts estimates)

Table 1 Yield comparisons (%) assuming Deutsche Telekom mid-range price of
DM 27.50

	Local bond	Market net dividend	Stock net dividend
BT	7.8	4.1	5.5
Telecom Italia	8.6	2.0	3.7
Telefónica	8.0	3.9	3.7
KPN	5.0	3.1	4.6
TeleDanmark	7.0	3.5	5.0
Portugal	7.9	3.0	2.9
OTE	13.0	3.5	3.8
Deutsche Telekom	6.0	2.6	4.4

Source: BZW Estimates

In addition, the company forecasts a drop of some 40 per cent in its enormous debt mountain over the next four years. A ratio based on its present debt level is therefore likely to give a misleadingly high multiple.

If the net effect of those valuation methods is confusing, that is perhaps not surprising. Around the world, the profitability of telecoms companies depends at least partly on government action, and almost everywhere government regulation – or deregulation – is in the process of change.

It therefore follows that valuation comparisons with other telecoms companies, inside or outside Europe, are of limited use. The future value of Telekom depends on factors which are beyond the power of investors or the company itself to predict.

The best that can be said is that the average of the various methods produces a price more or less within the proposed DM25–30DM range.

But as the most sophisticated of Telekom's analysts would probably concede, the price performance over the next few years remains hard to guess, even by normal stock market standards.

DEUTSCHE TELEKOM SHARES GET CAUTIOUS PRICING

W. Münchau

Deutsche Telekom, the German group that is headed for a stock market listing later today, has priced its shares at DM28.50 (£11.50), well below the previously indicated ceiling of DM30.

The price underlines the cautious stance taken by the company and the three global co-ordinators – Deutsche Bank, Goldman Sachs and Dresdner Bank – which were keen to avoid the embarrassment of a market backlash in the aftermath of the flotation.

The shares are due to start trading in Frankfurt just after 11am London time. Trading will begin in New York a few hours later after shares have been placed with US investors at $18.89.

With total sales proceeds of DM20bn. Deutsche Telekom's initial public offering is the largest in European history. Two-thirds of the 600m shares in the issue have been allocated to German investors. About 14 per cent go to US investors and 8 per cent to British investors.

Mr Ron Sommer, the chairman of Deutsche Telekom, said at a news conference that he deliberately avoided "pushing the limit" on pricing, and added that he hoped to "seek a long-term stable relationship between Deutsche Telekom and its shareholders".

The issue originally consisted of 500m new shares, a fifth of the enlarged capital, but was raised last week in response to demand. There are a further 90m shares held in a so-called greenshoe – an over-allotment facility to stabilise the market if the price rises above a critical level in the immediate period after launch. The issue was subscribed more than five times.

The pricing decision was taken on Saturday in a meeting attended by Mr Sommer, Mr Joachim Kröske, the finance director, and representatives of the advisers. The price range was set previously at DM25 to DM30.

Bankers closely involved with the deal said the meeting formally confirmed a decision that had emerged through feedback from investors at presentations in financial capitals. One banker said US institutions had been more price-sensitive than German retail investors, who were interested mainly in gross dividend yield. On the basis of the issue price and previously announced dividend rate, the yield will be 6 per cent next year.

Senior management of Deutsche Telekom had initially favoured a price closer to DM30 while the advisers sought a more modest price.

The share sale shifts about 26 per cent of the group into private ownership. German bankers hope the offering will help consolidate the fledgling equity culture in a country where investors have traditionally favoured bond and real estate markets.

Many bids from German retail investors will be scaled down, bids for 1,000 shares will be scaled down to 300.

TELEKOM SHARES SURGE IN BUYING FRENZY

W. Münchau and A. Fisher

Germany yesterday took a big step towards becoming a nation of shareholders as the shares of Deutsche Telekom got off to a racing start on the Frankfurt and New York stock markets.

In Frankfurt, the shares of the giant telecoms utility closed at DM33.90 (£13.70), almost 19 per cent above the issue price of DM28.50. On Wall Street, they closed at $21.50, up just over $2^{19}/₃₂ on the official price of $18.89.

Some 60m shares were exchanged in the first few hours of hectic trading. More than 2m German private investors bought Telekom shares – roughly half the previous total number of registered shareholders in the country.

Mr Theo Waigel, the country's finance minister, said the Telekom issue showed Germans were no longer "anti-share" and that a considerable potential existed for equity investment. He praised the DM20bn flotation – the largest in the world after Japan's 1987 sale of Nippon Telegraph and Telephone – as the "high point of German privatisation history".

Mr Ron Sommer, Telekom's chairman, said the flotation "was also necessary to give Deutsche Telekom a more international outlook, which is critical for a global player".

German ministers and bankers stressed that further stock market issues were needed to keep up the share-buying momentum unleashed by the Telekom issue.

Analysts and financial advisers yesterday urged the public to hold on to the shares and resist the temptation of a quick profit.

Mr Werner Seifert, chairman of Deutsche Börse, which runs the Frankfurt Stock Exchange, said there was scope for more privatisations by the federal government, as well as state and local authorities.

The total market capitalisation of quoted companies as a proportion of Germany's gross domestic product is only 27 per cent. In the US it is 78 per cent; in the UK, 124. "This leaves a gaping space to be filled," Mr Seifert said.

He cautioned, however, against government moves to tax all capital gains as part of its plans to cut income tax rates while removing special allowances.

At present, capital gains are exempt from tax if shares are held longer than six months. Mr Seifert said taxing capital gains would "drive capital away from shares".

Proceeds from the sale of the shares will be used for the reduction of Telekom's net debts of about DM95bn.

The three global co-ordinators of the issue were Deutsche Bank, Dresdner Bank and Goldman Sachs. One banker said the fees earned by banks participating in the distribution would amount to about 2.5 per cent of the roughly DM20bn gross receipts.

Section 3

Adding Value Through Financing

8

The Search for Optimal Capital Structure

S. C. Myers

The search for optimal capital structure is like the search for Truth or Wisdom: you will never completely attain either goal. However, there has been progress.

No one has found the formula for optimal capital structure, but we have learned where *not* to look for it. We have accumulated several useful facts and insights. We can identify some of the costs and benefits of debt vs. equity financing. We can say, with reasonable confidence, what kinds of firms ought to borrow relatively more, and what kinds less.

In this article, I will sketch some of what we know and don't know about firms' choice of capital structure.

First, I will argue that there is no magic in leverage – nothing supporting a *presumption* that more debt is better. Debt may be better than equity in some cases, worse in others. Or it may be no better and no worse. Sometimes all financing choices are equally good.

The case for or against debt financing must therefore be built up from a more detailed look at the firm and capital markets. The smart financial manager ends up asking not general, but specific questions, such as:

1. Is there a net tax advantage to borrowing for my firm?

2. What are the odds that a given capital structure will bring financial embarrassment or distress? What would be the cost of such financial trouble?

3. Is subsidized financing available? If so, are strings attached?

4. Should my firm's existing dividend policy constrain its financing choices? (For example, sticking to a generous dividend payout might force use of debt or new common stock issues.)

5. What are the costs of issuing securities under alternative financing plans?

In this article, I address the first two questions only – which leaves out lots of fascinating practical and conceptual questions. However, it's worth taking the time to review the main ideas on taxes and financial distress with some care. I conclude below that there is a moderate tax advantage to corporate borrowing, at least for companies that are reasonably sure they can use the interest tax shields. Of course the costs of possible financial distress should limit borrowing. These costs are most important for risky firms – no surprise there – *and* for firms whose value depends on intangible assets. Growth firms should borrow less, other things equal.

I end up proposing a three-dimensional checklist for financial managers. The dimensions are taxes, risk, and asset type. This checklist, and the reasoning underlying it, should help financial managers think more clearly about the problem of optimal capital structure.

ASSUMPTIONS AND OBJECTIVES

A warning is necessary before plunging in. The warning is implicit in Brealey and Myers's Fourth Law:[1]

> You can make a lot more money by smart investment decisions than by smart financing decisions.

The Law does not say financing is irrelevant, only that investment has priority. Financing decisions should be shaped to support the firm's investment strategy, not vice versa.

I will therefore assume the firm's *investment* decision has already been set. I will fix the left hand side of the balance sheet and consider changes only on the right.

Another important preliminary point is to ask what the firm is trying to achieve by its financing decision. The standard objective is this: given the firm's assets and investment plan, find the capital structure that maximizes firm value. Thus, if the only choices are "debt" and "equity," we set up a market value balance sheet and try to find the debt *proportion* that makes the market value of the firm as large as possible:

Market Value Balance Sheet

Assets, tangible and intangible, including growth opportunities	Debt (D) Equity (E)
	Market Value of Firm (V = D + E)

NO MAGIC IN FINANCIAL LEVERAGE

The entries on the right hand side of the balance sheet are financial assets – paper claims that have value only because of the real assets (including intangibles and growth opportunities) on the left. Think of the balance sheet this way:

Market Value Balance Sheet

Real assets	Paper assets

The idea is to create value by shuffling the paper assets – by dividing, recasting or recombining the *paper* claims on the firm's *real* assets.

Yet creating true value out of paper sounds like alchemy. Since firm value rests on real asset value, we would not expect purely financial (paper) transactions to change the overall value of the firm.

Of course there could be an effect if the financial transactions were costly, if they affected the firm's tax liability, or if they weakened the firm's incentives to pursue valuable investment opportunities. But set these possible imperfections aside for just a moment. If we ignore the imperfections and reject alchemy, then we must conclude that firm value should not depend on the debt ratio.

PROPOSITION I

In general, if capital markets are doing their job, all efforts to increase value by tinkering with capital structure are fruitless. This is Modigliani and Miller's (MM's) famous Proposition I.

When a firm chooses its' capital structure, it sells its real assets to investors as a package of financial claims. Think of the design of the package as a marketing problem. Then you will see plenty of everyday analogies to MM's Proposition. Imagine going to the supermarket with their proposition in mind. You would predict that "The price of a pie does not depend on how it is sliced," or "It costs no more to assemble a chicken – from wings, drumsticks, breasts, etc. – than to buy one whole."

MM's theorem does *not* hold in the supermarket. The slices cost more than the whole pie. An assembled chicken costs more than a chicken bought whole. Whole milk mixed at home from skim milk and cream costs more than whole milk bought at the store.

There are two reasons why the parts cost more than the whole. In the case of chickens, these are:

1. *Costs on the demand side.* Consumers are willing to pay extra to pick and choose the pieces they like. It's costly for them to buy whole chickens, cut them up and sell the pieces they don't want.

2. *Costs on the supply side.* It's costly for supermarkets to cut up the chickens and sell the pieces separately.

Note that *both* conditions are necessary to explain why the pieces sell for more than the whole. Suppose supermarkets found a way to cut and package the pieces at trivial cost. Then competition would drive out any extra charge for the pieces. Consumers would still be *willing* to pay extra, but they would not have to. On the other hand, suppose there are costs on the supply side, but not on the demand side. (That is, suppose consumers could cut up the chickens and trade in the pieces, costlessly.) Then, consumers would not pay any extra for the pieces offered by supermarkets. Supermarkets would sell only whole chickens.

I apologize for bringing poultry into the world of high finance, but the analogy is almost exact. The firm that uses only common equity financing sells its assets whole. The firm that issues a more complex package of securities sells the assets in pieces. Let's assume investors want the complex package. It will sell at a higher price *only* if there are costs on *both* the supply side and the demand side. It must be costly for the firm to create the complex package, and it must be costly for investors to replicate it.

However, in capital markets, the costs are much lower, relative to the sums involved, than in the grocery store. Suppose a whole chicken costs $2.50 and the corresponding pieces $3.00. The valuation error is $.50 – small change. The same percentage valuation error on, say, $250 million of real assets is $50 million, which surely is enough to get managers' and investors' attention.

It's not clear why investors would be willing to pay 20 per cent more for levered firms than for unlevered ones. However, if some market imperfection created a clientele willing to pay that much extra for levered firms, then there would be a big profit opportunity for corporate treasurers. Since it costs relatively little to turn an unlevered firm into a levered one, the *supply* of levered firms would expand until the valuation error was wiped out.

The firm is creating and selling paper assets, not real ones. So long as investors value these paper assets by the real assets underlying them, then changes in capital structure won't affect value. To repeat: there is no magic in financial leverage.

OPPORTUNITIES TO ISSUE SPECIALIZED SECURITIES

Under what conditions is this "no magic" result violated? When the firm, by imaginative design of its capital structure, can offer some *financial service* to investors – a service investors find costly or impossible to provide for themselves. The service must be unique, or the firm must be able to provide it more cheaply than competing firms or financial intermediaries.

Thus, you look for an unsatisfied clientele – a group of investors willing to pay a premium for a particular financial instrument. The trouble is that the needs of the obvious clienteles have already been met.

For example, most investors would have difficulty borrowing with limited liability on personal account. There is a *demand-side* cost facing investors who want to borrow with limited liability. Some investors would like to borrow indirectly, with limited liability, through the corporation. This creates a clientele of investors who would be willing to pay a premium for the shares of a levered firm.

These investors would be willing to pay a premium for levered firms' stock, but they don't have to. The costs on the *supply side* are trivial. Firms can create levered equity just by borrowing. The supply of levered equity will therefore expand until the clientele seeking limited liability is satiated. Competition among firms will eliminate any premium.

It's hard to believe that investors would pay a premium for one more garden variety bond, or for the stock of the firm issuing the bond. The only "magic" in capital structure comes as a reward to financial innovation, when firms find ways to create *new* portfolio opportunities for investors, or new ways to provide old opportunities at lower cost.

Financial innovation does occur, of course. It has been going on for generations. We see the result in today's capital markets, which offer an elaborate infrastructure of financial institutions and a remarkably rich menu of traded securities.

Innovation proves that *some* financing decisions matter. If financing were always totally irrelevant, there would be no incentive to innovate, and the menu of securities would not change.

The rewards for financial innovation go mostly to innovators, however, not to followers. The recent introduction of zero-coupon bonds provides a good example. The first corporations who issued zero-coupon bonds obtained very attractive yields. They uncovered a clientele of domestic investors who wanted to "lock-in" long-term interest rates and who could hold the bonds in tax-sheltered accounts. There was also a clientele of foreign investors who could avoid income tax on these bonds' price appreciation. However, the *supply* of zero-coupon bonds expanded rapidly as soon as these instruments' attractiveness was clear. Competition also came from zero-coupon bonds issued by brokerage houses and backed up by Treasury bonds, e.g., Merrill Lynch's TIGRs (Treasury Income Guarantee Receipts). Some of the tax loopholes that contributed to the bonds' initial attractiveness were subsequently closed.[2]

All these changes have eroded the attractiveness of zero-coupon bonds. Issues will no doubt continue, but at yields much less attractive to the firm.

When a firm tries to create value through financial innovation, it competes *in capital markets* with thousands of other firms and financial institutions. This competition implies that investors do not have to pay a premium for standard securities.

Thus, the choice of capital structure should not matter, except for temporary windows of opportunity, in which the alert firm may gain by issuing a specialized security. Finding a window does not necessarily call for a move to a higher debt ratio, however. The opportunity might be for a new type of equity, or for a hybrid or convertible instrument.

LEVERAGE AND EARNINGS

Here is one immediate payoff from thinking through MM's "no magic in leverage" proposition: it teaches us *not* to worry about the impact of leverage on earnings per share (EPS).

EPS is the most widely used yardstick of management performance. Normally an increase in EPS is good news, because it signals better operating results. However, sometimes management is tempted to manufacture EPS increases through paper transactions – e.g., by borrowing.

Borrowing increases the book rate of return on equity if the after-tax book rate of return on the firm's assets exceeds the after-tax interest rate. Normally a higher book rate of return on equity means higher EPS. However, this does not make stockholders better off and does not increase the real value of the firm.

Suppose a firm issues debt and retires equity, holding its assets and operating income constant. Suppose it is sufficiently profitable that EPS increases. Are investors really better off?

Increased leverage diverts a larger fraction of the firm's operating income to lenders, and a smaller fraction to stockholders. However, the total going to all investors in the firm must be exactly the same. Lenders and stockholders *considered jointly* receive no more and no less than before.

Stockholders do receive more earnings per dollar invested, but they also bear more risk, because they have given lenders first claim on the firm's assets and operating income. Stockholders bear more risk per dollar invested, and the more the firm borrows the more risk they bear. Lenders accept a lower dollar return per dollar invested because they have a safer claim. If they don't *give up* value by accepting a relatively low rate of return, how can stockholders gain on their side of the transaction? Higher return for higher risk, lower return for relative safety – it ought to be a fair trade. In fact MM *prove* it is a fair trade, provided that investors and financial intermediaries are alert and rational.

Managers who borrow *just* to boost EPS can increase firm value only by systematically fooling investors. Perhaps it's possible to fool some investors some of the time. It's more likely that these managers are fooling themselves.

TAXES

If there are any useful generalizations about capital structure, they must rest on issues not yet discussed. The first of these is taxes.

Unfortunately, "debt and taxes" is an exceedingly messy subject, one which tends to drive out other equally interesting issues. I will just list the few things we can say with confidence, and then move on.

First, interest is tax deductible. The tax saving from debt financing is greatest for firms facing a high marginal tax rate.

Second, few firms can be *sure* they will show a taxable profit in the future. If a firm shows a loss, and cannot carry the loss back against past taxes, its interest tax shield must be carried forward with the hope of using it later. The firm loses at least the time value of money while it waits. If its

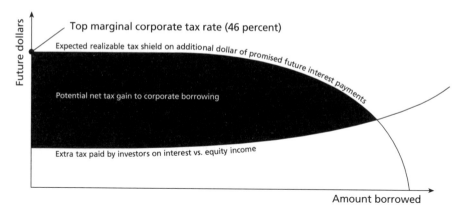

Figure 8.1 The tax benefit of debt financing

difficulties are deep enough, the wait may be permanent, and the interest tax shield is lost forever.

Therefore interest tax shields are worth more to some firms than others. They ought to be worth a great deal to IBM, whose taxable income is relatively high and stable. They ought to be worth very little to Wheeling-Pittsburgh Steel, which has large accumulated tax loss carryforwards and uncertain prospects.

Think of the *expected realizable* value of the tax shield on an extra dollar of promised future interest payments. This amount depends on:

■ the probability that the firm will have taxable income to shield; and

■ its marginal tax rate if it does have taxable income.

This brings us to the third point: the more the firm borrows, the less the expected realizable value of future interest tax shields. I have plotted this relationship as the top line in Figure 8.1.

Fourth, there are other ways to shield income. Firms have accelerated writeoffs for plant and equipment. They have the investment tax credit. Investments in research and many other intangible assets can be expensed immediately. So can contributions to the firm's pension fund.

How soon the top line in Figure 8.1 turns down depends on how profitable it is – i.e., how much income it has to shield – and on how many dollars of *non-interest* tax shields it has. The line *always* turns down if debt is high enough; however, there is some debt burden which would drive even IBM into the bankruptcy courts.

Fifth, and finally, equity investors get a tax break relative to lenders. This partially, perhaps wholly, offsets the corporate interest tax shield.

In the United States, a corporation's income is taxed twice, first at the firm level and again when the income is passed through to lenders and stock-holders. The interest lenders receive is all ordinary income. Stockholders, on the other hand, receive part of their income as capital gains. When a firm borrows in place of equity financing, the Internal Revenue Service loses at the corporate level but usually gains at the investor level (because interest is taxed more heavily than equity income). I have shown the net loss at the investor level as the bottom line in Figure 8.1. The shaded area between the lines is the potential tax gain to corporate borrowing when both levels are considered.

Here is where we hit trouble. We do not know whether the shaded area in Figure 8.1 is big, small, or possibly nonexistent. We cannot know until we can fix the position of the two lines that form the upper and lower boundaries of the shaded area.

The upper boundary is not too much of a problem. Most firms, if they had no debt at all, would pay the full 46 percent marginal rate. That gives the starting point on the vertical axis. We also know the general shape of the declining curve. The only question is when the line starts to bend down sharply, but that could be judged case by case.

The bottom boundary's position is a deep mystery, however. Some believe there is not much difference between the effective tax rates faced by debt and equity investors. That would imply a low bottom line and a correspondingly large tax gain to corporate borrowing, perhaps as much as 46 cents per dollar of interest paid. At the other extreme, Merton Miller has presented an ingenious, appealing, but probably oversimplified model,[3] in which the tax rate faced by the *marginal* investor in bonds is about 46 percent higher than the rate that investor would pay on stocks. If that's the way the world works, the tax gain to the firm from corporate borrowing just balances the tax loss to investors. The firm would have to pay such a high interest rate to bribe investors to hold its bonds that it might as well issue equity. There would be no net tax gain to corporate borrowing.

Each of these positions has extreme implications for debt policy. If the net tax gain is very large, firms that pay taxes at the full 46 percent corporate rate ought to borrow very large amounts – a triple-A debt rating would be an extremely expensive luxury. Yet, such firms as IBM and Eastman Kodak do not seem to suffer from their conservative financing. On the other hand, if the net tax gain is zero for IBM, as Merton Miller's model implies, then it must be strongly *negative* for Wheeling-Pittsburgh. In other words, Wheeling-Pittsburgh should see Big Money in negative debt: it could set up a money machine by issuing equity to buy the debt of other corporations. If you find these recommendations unacceptable, you are more or less forced into an intermediate view, in which there is a modest net tax advantage for IBM, and a modest disadvantage for Wheeling-Pittsburgh, but not so large as to dominate other factors.

I am not brave enough to take either of these extreme positions. Pending further evidence I conclude that there is a moderate tax advantage to corporate borrowing, at least for companies that are reasonably sure they can use the interest tax shields. For companies that cannot use the interest tax shields there is a moderate tax *disadvantage*.

TROUBLE

Every corporate treasurer knows that too much borrowing can lead to financial trouble. That one fact is all many care to know. When they start losing sleep over the firm's bond rating, they stop borrowing.

However, there's a lot going on behind the label "trouble." We need to distinguish among the different *kinds* of trouble and to look carefully at the *costs* of trouble.

Financial trouble has its own extensive literature, usually under a more imposing title such as "Costs of Financial Distress." I will offer just a few examples and observations chosen to show the literature's practical implications.

HEARTBREAK HOTEL

Suppose your firm's only asset is a large downtown hotel, mortgaged to the hilt. The recession hits. Occupancy rates fall, and the mortgage payments cannot be met. The lender takes over and sells the hotel to a new owner and operator. You use your firm's stock certificates for wallpaper.

What are the costs of bankruptcy? In this example, probably very little. The value of the hotel is, of course, much less than you had hoped, but that is due to the lack of guests, not to default on the loan. The costs of bankruptcy are only the costs of the default itself. As Richard Brealey and I wrote elsewhere,[4]

> Bankruptcies are thought of as corporate funerals. The mourners (creditors and especially shareholders) look at their firm's present sad state. They think of how valuable their securities used to be and how little is left. Moreover, they think of the lost value as a cost of bankruptcy. That is the mistake. The decline in the value of assets is what the mourning is really about. That has no necessary connection with financing. The bankruptcy is merely a legal mechanism for allowing creditors to take over when the decline in the value of assets triggers a default. Bankruptcy is not the cause of the decline in value. It is the result.

The direct bankruptcy costs of Heartbreak Hotel are restricted to items such as legal and court fees, real estate commissions, and the time and talent spent by the lender in sorting things out. The costs are proportionally larger for small firms (there are economies of scale in going bankrupt) and larger for firms with complex capital structures.[5]

Who pays the costs? At first glance it seems that the lender does, because the costs diminish the net value of the assets the lender recoups. Lenders of course realize this and charge an insurance premium every time a new loan is made. The size of the premium depends on the probability of trouble and the costs likely in the event of trouble. Your firm paid this premium when it mortgaged the hotel; these premiums cover bankruptcy costs on average.

Thus, *shareholders* end up paying for *expected* bankruptcy costs every time they issue risky debt.

FLEDGLING ELECTRONICS GOES UNDER

Suppose we repeat the story of Heartbreak Hotel for Fledgling Electronics. Everything is the same, except for the underlying real assets – not real estate, but a high-tech going concern, a growth company whose most valuable assets are technology, investment opportunities, and its employees' human capital.

Fledgling is of course more likely to get into trouble for a given degree of financial leverage than a hotel is, but the point here is to contrast what happens *if* a default occurs.

First, you would have a much more difficult time cashing in Fledgling's assets by just selling them off. Many of its assets are intangibles which have value only as part of a going concern.

Could the value of Fledgling, as a going concern, be preserved through default and reorganization? That would require a complete insulation of Fledgling's operating and investment plans from the bankruptcy process. Unfortunately, this is costly and probably infeasible.

Default creates a variety of operating and investment problems. The odds of defections by key employees are higher than if the firm had started out with less debt and had never gotten into financial trouble. Aggressive investment in new products and technology will be more difficult; each class of creditors will have to be convinced that it is in their interest for the firm to raise more money and put the money into risky assets.[6] Special guarantees may have to be given to customers who doubt whether the firm will be around to service its products. Finally, the time that management spends solving these and other problems has its own opportunity cost.

I have taken the extreme cases of the hotel and the electronics firm to make a crucial distinction: some asset values can pass through bankruptcy and reorganization largely unscathed. Other asset values are likely to be considerably diminished. The losses are greatest for the intangible assets that are linked to the health of the firm as a going concern, for example, technology, growth opportunities, and human capital.

The moral is: think not only of the probability that borrowing will bring trouble. Think also of the value that may be lost if trouble comes.

THE COSTS OF AVOIDING BANKRUPTCY

Since "You can make a lot more money by smart investment decisions than by smart financing decisions," financing decisions ought to be arranged to support investment decisions. However, when default or bankruptcy threatens, things can get turned around; the financing side can gain the upper hand. Managers may pass up good investment opportunities in an attempt to conserve cash and keep the firm "alive."

Suppose your hotel, under threat of default, reduces customer services, defers painting guest rooms and cuts corners in the restaurant kitchens. Assume these were sensible outlays – that is, they would have been undertaken if the firm had no debt, other things equal. Then we can say that the threat of default reduces the value of your firm's *real assets*, because it thwarts expenditures that would increase that value.[7] Even if default is avoided, there is still a cost of financial distress, equal to the value lost because of foregone investments.

Fledgling Electronics is liable to the same underinvestment problem, but the value loss could be much greater. A year's delay in painting a room may not permanently undercut that hotel's competitive position, but falling a year behind in technology or product design could wipe out a substantial fraction of Fledgling Electronics' value.

People say "You have to spend money to make money." The threat of default often leads managers *not* to spend as much as they should. The loss in value from good investments passed by is a cost of financial distress even if the firm finally regains its financial health. The extent of loss depends on how valuable the foregone investments are, and on how costly it would be for the firm to catch up. The loss is likely to be greatest for firms whose market value rests primarily on technology, human capital and growth opportunities – another reason why Fledgling Electronics should have a more conservative debt policy than a firm holding tangible assets such as real estate.

WHY SHOULD A FIRM EVER PASS UP GOOD INVESTMENTS?

Some financial economists find it hard to believe that a firm – even firms in financial distress – would ever pass up a positive net present value (NPV) investment. It's clearly in the *joint* interests of all debt and equity security-holders to raise the money to take such investments. There must be some hidden cost.

The costs do exist. They are fundamentally costs of producing and transmitting information. Because information is costly, it is difficult for creditors – or any outside investor – to know what the firm's true risks and prospects are. It becomes difficult for creditors to know when managers are "doing the right thing" for the firm, and when they are acting in their own narrower interests, or in the interests of stockholders. Debt contracts become costly to write and cumbersome for the firm.[8] It becomes costly for creditors to monitor the firm's performance. Finally, it becomes costly to renegotiate the firm's financing.

Consider the following questions with these information costs in mind.[9]

Q: Why don't stockholders and creditors of a firm in financial distress get together and *jointly* advance the funds necessary to undertake all positive-NPV investments?

A: Sometimes they do.[10] However, it's costly for outside investors to find out what the positive-NPV investments really are. (They may suspect managers of trying to raise money to keep the firm alive even if its prospects are not all that great.)

It is also costly and time-consuming to negotiate an agreement in which each class of security-holder makes its share of the sacrifices necessary to allow the firm to take the right investments. Such an agreement may end up being almost as costly and time-consuming as a complete reorganization of the firm's capital structure.

Despite these costs, creditors will make considerable sacrifices for firms they consider worth keeping afloat as going concerns. Think of Chrysler and International Harvester.[11]

However, it's costly to negotiate these sacrifices, sometimes so costly that the sacrifice is not made and good investments are passed by. With either outcome the *overall* value of the firm (i.e., its joint value to all creditors and stockholders) is diminished. This value loss could be avoided by not borrowing so much in the first place.

Q: If joint action by creditors and stockholders is costly, why doesn't the firm just issue stock to finance its positive-NPV investments? For that matter, why doesn't it eliminate the whole problem by issuing stock to pay off the debt?

A: Let's take the second question first. If the firm is in serious financial trouble, its debt is no longer a safe security. The debt's market value has fallen substantially below its par or face value. If the firm issues stock and repays the *face* value of debt, stockholders are buying back the debt for considerably more than it is worth. In other words, paying off the creditors at par is always a negative-NPV investment for stockholders of a firm in financial distress.[12]

Suppose equity is issued not to pay off creditors, but to finance additional *real* investment by the firm. The problem here is that stockholders will have to share the extra value created by these investments with the creditors. Every time the value of the firm increases by one dollar, creditors are better off. Shareholders do not capture the full reward their additional investment creates. When the firm is sound and the debt is safe anyway, the proportion of the extra value captured by creditors is small. However, when the firm is in trouble, the proportion can be substantial. Thus it is often not in the stockholder's interest for firms in financial distress to raise and invest new equity capital, except through a *negotiated* reorganization of the firm's financing – and that, as I have argued before, is costly and time-consuming.

BACK TO THE UNDERINVESTMENT PROBLEM

All this boils down to a few simple points: First, a firm that falls into financial distress may pass up good investment opportunities, or it (and its security holders) may have to renegotiate its financing in order to avoid passing up the good opportunities. Both possibilities are costly.

Second, firms can reduce the probability of these costs by not borrowing so much in the first place.

Third, *if* the firm lands in financial trouble, the magnitude of loss from underinvestment depends on how good its investment opportunities are. Who cares if a firm passes up investment opportunities if the opportunities are worth no more than they cost?

This gives one more reason for Fledgling Electronics, or any firm whose value depends on growth opportunities or intangible assets, to borrow less than a hotel chain. The "underinvestment problem" may explain the low debt ratios in the pharmaceutical industry, where value depends on continued success in research and development, and in consumer-products companies, where sustained, massive investment in advertising is necessary to maintain product recognition and market share. We can also understand why highly profitable growth companies, such as Hewlett-Packard, Digital Equipment Corporation and IBM, tend to use mostly equity financing. Recent empirical research by Michael Long and Ileen Malitz, and by Scott Williamson, confirms that firms whose assets are weighted towards intangible assets and growth opportunities borrow significantly less, on average, than firms holding mostly tangible assets-on-place.[13]

CONCLUSION

Let me try to sum up this article's main ideas. The first, most fundamental one is Modigliani and Miller's "no magic in leverage" proposition. The firm markets its *real* assets and *operating* income to investors by issuing a package of financial assets. However, if capital markets are doing their job, one package is as good as another. In particular, there is no presumption that borrowing is a good thing, even if debt is kept to "moderate" levels.

However, there does seem to be some tax advantage to borrowing for firms which make full use of interest tax shields. On the other hand, costs of financial trouble threaten firms that borrow too much. The financial manager should consider not just the probability of trouble, but also the value lost from trouble if it does occur. This value loss is greatest for firms with valuable intangible assets and growth opportunities.

Thus the choice of capital structure, when discussed with the broad brush required by this short article, boils down to taxes, risk and asset type. For example, a safe, consistently profitable company, with few intangible assets or growth opportunities, ought to find a relatively high debt ratio attractive. A risky growth company ought to avoid debt financing, especially if it has other ways of shielding its income from taxes.

I will cheerfully admit that this three-item checklist of taxes, risk and asset type does not tell the financial manager how much debt to issue. For example, a firm with average risk, lots of unsheltered taxable income, *but* few tangible assets, could use this article's qualitative arguments to support either a high or low debt ratio. Such a firm would probably decide that any middle-of-the-road debt ratio is OK, and base its financing choices on more down-to-earth considerations, such as issue costs, opportunities for subsidized financing, and so on.

Nevertheless, the checklist does tell the financial manager what's important and what isn't. It gives him or her a *framework* for thinking about optimal capital structure. As always, the financing *decision* finally rests on the manager's shoulders.

NOTES

1. The Fourth Law will appear in the second edition of R. A. Brealey and S. C. Myers, *Principles of Corporate Finance*, New York: McGraw-Hill Book Co.
2. See David Pyle, "Is Deep Discount Debt Financing a Bargain?," *Chase Financial Quarterly*, Vol. I, Issue 1, 1981.
3. "Debt and Taxes," *Journal of Finance*, May 1977.
4. *Principles of Corporate Finance*, New York, McGraw-Hill Book Co., p. 385.
5. Direct bankruptcy costs would virtually disappear if someone could design a "no fault" system of bankruptcy, in which the assets of the defaulting firm could be transmitted to the creditors by executing a few standard documents. But it is difficult to imagine this working for large firms, which typically have many classes of creditors with conflicting interests. No fault bankruptcy would also undercut another purpose of the law, which is to protect the firm as a going concern for time enough to give reorganization, instead of liquidation, a fair try.
6. The funds would probably be raised by giving a new class of creditors a prior claim on the firm's assets.
7. That is, expenditures with positive *net* present value.
8. Clifford Smith and Jerrold Warner give an excellent description of how debt contracts are written and why they are written as they are. See "On Financial Contracting: An Analysis of Bond Covenants," *Journal of Financial Economics*, June 1979.
9. I discuss these questions more carefully and extensively in "The Determinants of Corporate Borrowing," *Journal of Financial Economics*, November 1977.
10. For example, lenders often allow troubled firms to break covenants and defer debt service. When this is done, stockholders, and often employees, are expected to make sacrifices too: for example, no dividends to stockholders and no bonuses to managers.
11. They may still be forced to decide to let International Harvester sink.
12. Of course, shareholders can always try to buy the debt back at *market* value. Getting creditors to accept this offer is another matter, except as part of a negotiated reorganization.
13. Both studies hold risk constant. See M. Long and I. Malitz, "Investment Patterns and Financial Leverage." National Bureau of Economic Research, January 1983, and S. Williamson, "The Moral Hazard Theory of Corporate Capital Structure: Empirical Tests." Unpublished Ph.D. Dissertation, MIT, November, 1981.

'The Search for Optimal Capital Structure', by S. C. Myers, reproduced from *The Revolution in Corporate Finance*, 2nd Edition, edited by J. M. Stern and D. H. Chew.

CASE STUDY 3

Brand Owners and Capital Structure

Corporate Finance

If the merger of brand-laden corporates Guinness, the brewing and distilling group, and Grand Metropolitan, the food and drinks concern, teaches a lesson, it is that the branded consumer goods industry is facing ever-increasing levels of pressure to generate value for shareholders.

Much of this pressure stems from competition in the maturing markets of western Europe and North America. Retailers are bigger and far more powerful than they used to be. They are putting pressure on the branded goods companies to sell their products more cheaply. The pressure in the retail market is enhanced by the increasing presence of private labels, where the lower expenditure on marketing and packaging keeps costs down. In addition, sales potential is reduced as companies face slower population and economic growth. As companies seek to continue generating shareholder value, therefore, we are seeing two major trends.

First, the industry is consolidating, as the $40 billion merger of Guinness and GrandMet clearly shows. Second, companies are expanding into emerging markets, looking for opportunities to develop their brand franchises and expand their brand portfolios in markets that have been growing more quickly. Despite turmoil in Asia, plans for expansion into Latin America and central and eastern Europe still make sense in the long term.

In this environment the issue of creating value becomes increasingly important. And, judging by performance of corporates in this sector during the 1990s, those companies that have embraced value-based management have been the most successful in standing up to this pressure.

US enterprises in particular have taken value-based management on board since the early 1990s, with companies such as Campbell Soup and General Mills setting up programmes that incentivize the management to add value. But most companies in the UK and Europe are only now starting to examine value-based management ideas.

The graphs in Figure 1 vindicate this strategy. Over the period from 1980 to 1997 branded consumer goods groups in the US and the UK managed to outperform other industries. In the past five years, however, it is notable that, while US companies have surged ahead, UK companies have fallen back. And Interbrand's list of the top 10 brands in the world reveals that seven are from the US.

Value-based management begins with the process of identifying the drivers that a company believes lead to creating shareholder value. A variety of systems can be used to this end and one of the favourites is economic value added – EVA. However, in the case of branded consumer goods groups it is essential when looking at the capital base to capitalize the value

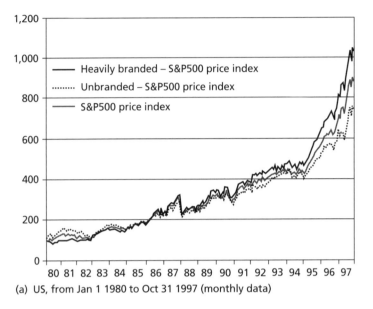

(a) US, from Jan 1 1980 to Oct 31 1997 (monthly data)

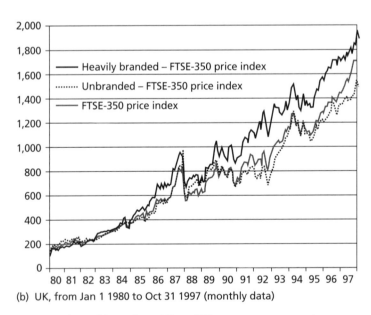

(b) UK, from Jan 1 1980 to Oct 31 1997 (monthly data)

Figure 1 Value of branding, US vs. UK (*Source*: Datastream)

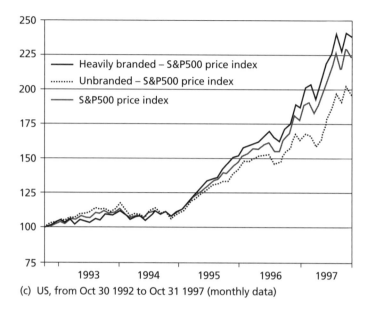

(c) US, from Oct 30 1992 to Oct 31 1997 (monthly data)

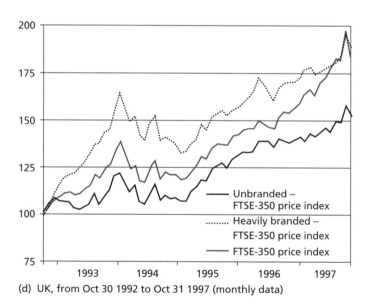

(d) UK, from Oct 30 1992 to Oct 31 1997 (monthly data)

Figure 1   *continued*

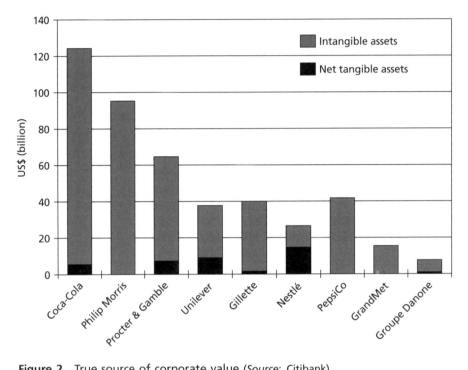

Figure 2 True source of corporate value (*Source*: Citibank)

of the brands – something that many equity analysts fail to do in their EVA analysis, probably because this information is hard to come by. Yet brands are vital assets to consider because, as Figure 2 shows, the feature that sets branded consumer groups apart from others is that the vast majority of their value derives from their intangible assets – mainly the brands themselves. In the majority of cases brand value is not expressed on the balance sheet. Coca-Cola perhaps represents the most extreme example of this valuation problem; it has a market capitalization of $163 billion yet has only $6.6 billion of net tangible assets.

Value-based management might sound like just another management consultant's empty buzz phrase, but the truth is that too few companies are maximizing the potential value of their brand names. In addition to analyzing the value of investment in increased capacity, companies should be assessing the return on their marketing spend, as branded goods companies spend between two and five, and sometimes as high as eight, times as much on marketing as they do on capital expenditure.

By creating a strategy that maximizes brand value, companies can improve performance in mature markets as well as in emerging markets. Says Patrick Hearne, vice-president and branded consumer goods specialist at Citibank: "Branded consumer goods groups should be at the forefront of managing intangibles for value."

BUILDING THE OPTIMAL CAPITAL STRUCTURE

Increasing pressure and competition mean that improving financial sophistication in brand management is now a necessity rather than a luxury. The philosophy of value-based management can be applied to devise the right capital structure for a branded consumer goods company.

Companies in this sector are huge generators of cash; the more successful the brands, the more cash they generate. But what have they been doing with this cash? Not much. A glance at the balance sheets of 1996 annual reports reveals that companies such as Nestlé, Unilever and Procter & Gamble all had cash mountains of more than $2.5 billion – and they are far from being the only examples. Companies in this sector should be putting this excess cash to work for them.

One capital structure philosophy implies that debt funds stable cashflows and equity funds variable cashflows. It is fair to say, then, that successful and mature branded consumer groups such as Unilever and Nestlé, which are able to generate a large stable cashflow, are in the right position to be able to reduce their cost of capital by gearing up their debt/equity ratio.

The priority for these cash-heavy companies should be to look for opportunities to reduce the mountain. Buying back shares is the most straightforward solution. Share buy-backs are no longer viewed by shareholders as the strategy of a management that can think of nothing better to do with its money. For some European companies buy-backs have been a problem because tax structures have made them economically unviable. But with its own recent Sfr1 billion buy-back, Swiss Re has demonstrated that the technique is now possible in the Swiss market

The argument against reducing the cash mountain has been that at least some of this money was needed as a form of emergency back-up, or as a facility to use in case an acquisition opportunity appeared. The answer is to take on more debt. If an opportunistic acquisition appears, the company has a safe cashflow against which it can raise debt. A company waiting for the right type of target to become available can, for example, set up a stand-by revolving credit facility.

Again, most branded consumer companies have been against the notion of taking on too much debt. If they change their capital structure radically they might put their credit rating at risk. The more cash-generative companies in the branded consumer goods sector do indeed have credit ratings in the upper region of the investment-grade range.

Nestlé, for example, has a triple-A credit rating from Standard & Poor's, which it has held to be sacred – and with good reason. A triple-A rating carries a great deal of kudos in the international capital markets and enables the company to raise debt at extremely attractive prices. Other companies with high credit ratings include UK/Dutch household goods maker Unilever (triple-A) and US breakfast cereal concern Kelloggs.

But the question must be asked whether maintaining a high investment-grade rating is the optimal strategy. Industry fundamentals suggest that

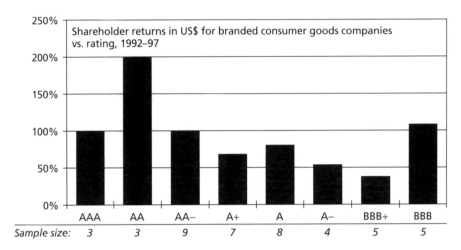

Figure 3 Rating impact (*Source*: Citibank)

companies should be more highly geared, and that their credit ratings are too high.

Says Citibank's Hearne: "In the longer term, companies in the branded consumer goods sector should be aiming to be in the mid to lower investment-grade area."

Figure 3 shows that companies with a double-A or triple-A rating are performing well compared with branded goods companies with lower ratings. This is due to the strength of their brands, from which the high cash generation has led to relatively low levels of debt. However, they could perform better by taking on more debt and lowering the cost of capital. Companies should take a leap of faith and lever off their balance sheet and borrow to fund investment in consolidation, expansion and share buy-backs.

In the past, companies looked for a strong credit rating because it allowed them to keep the cost of debt down. But, following the rules of value-based management, they should be keeping the overall cost of capital down – which is achieved by more debt and less equity funding. Indeed, companies like Nestlé and Unilever are now starting to realize that they are not benefiting from having such a high rating and are reviewing their ratings policy.

They should also bear in mind that branded consumer goods companies have a big advantage in the international capital markets over other sectors – name recognition. Retail investors particularly are attracted to a name when they are familiar with the product it makes. As a result, top names can access the Eurobond market more easily and at better pricing than companies with the same credit rating from other industries. Gillette is a good example; although it is rated double-A, the market lets it borrow as if it were a triple-A borrower.

Furthermore, since the share price is a more effective way of measuring the value of a branded goods company than book equity, it follows that the

---

Linking operational and financial exposures

According to traditional capital structure theory, long-term assets are best funded with long-term debt and short-term assets with short-term debt. The benefit of this guideline is that it allows management to lock in liquidity for the economic life of an asset and to simplify capital budgeting decisions by locking in the cost of financing for new investment.

The established approach, however, does not consider the dynamics of the cashflows generated by the asset. Because the term debt market has been a fixed-rate market this financing approach provides an economic match only if the cashflows generated by the asset can be viewed as fixed.

While a company's core assets have long economic lives, the cashflows generated by these assets are likely to be influenced by the economy. The core asset portfolio could therefore have the properties of a long-term variable-rate investment.

Funding variable core assets with fixed-rate debt creates a mismatch in cashflow that causes extra volatility in earnings.

Certain branded consumer businesses exhibit a positive link between interest rates and either unit sales and/or profit margins. This suggests that, because of the variability of the revenues and cashflows, the company would have a relatively short asset duration. (By duration we mean sensitivity to interest rates, not to the maturity of the liability, so the firm could have long-term debt but have the rate reset more often.) The implication is that such a firm should have a relatively short liability duration.

By hedging away some of the risk, earnings volatility would decline. Over time the reduction in volatility would reduce the firm's cost of capital and increase EVA and shareholder value.

---

best way of evaluating the capital structure is by working out a debt ratio based on market capitalization rather than straight debt/equity book value. This brings the value of the intangible assets into the equation and allows companies to determine the right level of leverage.

"This is important in building intangible value and giving value to shareholders," says Joel Schweitzer, vice president, global derivatives at Citibank. "If you are managing for shareholder value, investors will measure your performance by the share price, not the accounts."

Project Finance: Making the Right Financial Connections for Melbourne

M. Carapiet

The Melbourne City Link Project has involved the design, construction, financing, operation and maintenance of two major sections of toll road as well as an electronic tolling and traffic management system. The Southern Link and Western Link together represent about 22 kilometres of new and upgraded roadway.

Environmental studies undertaken by the Victoria state government indicated that the conditions on the existing road network would continue to deteriorate. It was estimated that by 2001 the volume of traffic on most major intersections within the transport corridors that are to be serviced by the Melbourne City Link would exceed 1.6 times their respective design capacities. If no action was taken, Melbourne would have two peak periods a day each lasting about two and a half hours by 2011.

The concession deed contains a number of state government objectives for the project including:

- ensuring that it is an integrated part of Melbourne's road system;
- generally facilitating the movement of traffic around the central activities district, rather than through it;
- improving access to the central activities district, to new state government initiatives such as the Southbank shopping and business area, Melbourne's Casino, the Exhibition Centre, the proposed new Docklands property development and to major sporting and entertainment venues, including the Melbourne Cricket Ground, the Arts Centre and Olympic Park;
- enhancing access for freight movements for manufacturing industry and primary producers to the Port of Melbourne, rail facilities, including the Melbourne Freight Terminal and the South Dynon Container Terminal, the wholesale markets and Melbourne Airport; and
- improving the environment around the Yarra River, the Royal Botanic Gardens, the Kings Domain and Moonee Ponds Creek.

The size of the Melbourne City Link Project was unprecedented for an Australian toll road financing. Further, the overall requirements of the state government with respect to risk allocation and design and technical requirements added to the complexity of the transaction.

When the two Melbourne City Link tenderers were shortlisted, virtually every major infrastructure debt and equity financier sought to be aligned with one of them, ensuring that the market constraints for both debt and equity were stretched to the limit. The Transurban Consortium appointed Macquarie Corporate Finance as financial adviser in July 1994.

Macquarie believed that a safe but unimaginative financing package was unlikely to win; equally, a structure that would create doubts as to its deliverability would have no better prospects. Macquarie's objective, therefore, was to strike the right financing balance and help the sponsors select the best team of debt and equity financiers.

The Transurban Consortium won the tender and the Melbourne City Link prospectus, issued in late February 1996, closed heavily oversubscribed with about 7,000 investors. The project raised A$510 million (US$400 million) of equity from public and institutional investors with support from the sponsors, including Macquarie Corporate Finance. The balance of the project financing consisted of a debt package of A$1.288 billion in a core project debt facility, supported by a A$350 million CPI (consumer price index-linked) bond facility, a A$1.249 billion infrastructure loan facility and a A$51 million subordinated loan.

OVERVIEW OF THE PROJECT

In July 1992, the Victoria government sought expressions of interest to design, build, own, operate and maintain the proposed Melbourne City Link. The Transurban Consortium, sponsored by Australian construction company Transfield Holdings and Japanese construction company Obayashi Corporation, lodged a submission and was one of two consortia shortlisted as a result of the expression of interest process.

The project was temporarily suspended following a change in state government and then relaunched on July 1 1994. On May 29 1995, after a nine-month competitive bid process, the Melbourne City Link Authority selected the Transurban Consortium as the preferred tenderer. Following a further five-month negotiation period, Transurban City Link Limited and Transurban City Link Unit Trust (jointly Transurban) executed a concession deed with the Melbourne City Link Authority and the state government and financial close was achieved on March 4 1996.

The concession deed grants Transurban the right to construct and operate the link and to impose tolls for a period of about 34 years after completion of construction. At the expiration of this concession period, Transurban's rights in respect of the link are surrendered to the State of Victoria for no consideration. Consequently, the project is an investment with a finite life-span and no anticipated residual value for investors. As such, distributions received by investors during the concession period comprise both distributions of profit and the return of capital.

The 22km link includes the 3.4km Burnley Tunnel and the 1.6km Domain Tunnel, both of which run under Melbourne's Royal Botanic Gardens and Yarra River, an elevated roadway between the Flemington Road interchange and the West Gate Freeway and a 30m high bridge near Melbourne's port.

Table 1 Refinements made as the deal progressed

Instrument	Initial bid	Revised bid	Financial close
Project debt	✓	✓	Increased size
CPI bonds	✓	Reduced terms	Increased size
Sponsor equity	✓	✓	Change in timing
Sub-contractor equity	✓	✓	✗
Underwritten equity	✓	✓	✓
Direct equity	✓	✓	✓
Develop Australia bonds	✓	Revised structure and increased size	Increased size and revised terms
Floating-rate notes	✓	✓	✗
Subordinated debt	✓	✓	Non-sponsor provided

The Western Link is scheduled to open by April 1999 and the Southern Link by December 1999. The most outstanding feature of the toll road is that it will be fully electronically tolled when completed in 1999.

There will be six toll zones strategically located throughout the Link and tolls for passenger vehicles will vary between 80¢ and A$1.00 per zone, with the tolls for light commercial vehicles and heavy commercial vehicles being 1.6 and 1.8 times the passenger car toll. Average weekday volumes are estimated to exceed 660,000 screenline crossings in 2001, increasing to more than 730,000 in 2011, with all vehicles being electronically tolled.

EVOLUTION OF THE FINANCE PLAN

The project's initial finance plan was subject to constant refinements throughout the course of the deal, as shown in Table 1. Although the earlier financing of the M2 Motorway in Sydney was a valuable starting point, the financing plan for the Melbourne project contained significant enhancements to the debt and equity structures previously implemented.

The A$1.78 billion (US$1.4 billion) ultimately required to complete construction and financing of the link has been funded by raising about A$510 million of equity and A$1.27 billion of net debt. The equity raising included a retail offer, an excluded institutional offer, and subscriptions by the project sponsors and other institutional and corporate supporters. The equity issue was completed in late February 1996 and the equity parcels were publicly listed in mid-March 1996.

RATIONALE FOR THE STRUCTURE

The driving forces that shaped the form of the investment structure included:

■ a requirement by equity investors for liquidity of their investment;

■ the strong preference expressed by institutional investors for receiving their equity returns in the form of pre-tax distributions;

- a need for equity to be subscribed upfront; and
- a need for equity distributions to be made during the construction phase.

The requirement for liquidity arose by virtue of the fact that, under the terms of their respective trust deeds, many of the institutional investors were permitted to invest only in listed or other liquid investments. This requirement alone meant that some form of listed investment structure would be required.

With the exception of the sponsors, institutional equity investors wished to subscribe funds up-front. They were reluctant to enter into long-term commitments to subscribe equity at some future time without receiving a return on the funds reserved for this eventual investment.

The preference to receive returns in the form of pre-tax distributions was expressed by various investors because the performance of many of the potential investors is judged on their gross pre-tax returns. Hence, even though optimizing after-tax returns was important, maximizing pre-tax returns was crucial in determining the corporate structure of this project. Thus, if the investment structure was to satisfy this requirement, a partnership or trust structure had to be put in place. A unit trust structure was chosen, as it is one that many investors are familiar with and, unlike a partnership, it can be listed on the Australian Stock Exchange. This provided the benefit of offering investors pre-tax distributions as well as liquidity for their investment.

The desire to receive early cashflow during the 45-month construction period resulted in the project effectively raising more capital than was required, as part of the capital raised is being repaid to investors in the form of tax-exempt infrastructure bond coupons during the construction period. The regular income stream during construction has served to provide a floor under the price of the listed securities, which have traded at a generous premium to the initial subscription price.

It was determined that the proposed distributions during the construction phase would be best achieved via a debt instrument, as the lack of accounting income effectively precluded any form of equity distribution (other than a return of capital). However, the Division 16L concessions in the Australian Income Tax Assessment Act contemplate infrastructure borrowings being made only through a company, and so a normal listed unit trust would not enable the dual benefits of the Division 16L concessions to be used and pre-tax trust distributions to be made. Therefore, the dual company/trust structure was developed whereby the company would be the infrastructure bond issuer and the trust would be the primary vehicle from which equity distributions would be made.

Another consideration that led to the separate company and trust vehicles was the requirement that the trust should not fall within the "trading trust" provisions of the Income Tax Act (Divisions 6B and 6C). Essentially, if Divisions 6B and 6C were to apply, the trust would be treated as a company for taxation purposes, thus removing the ability to distribute pre-tax income. To

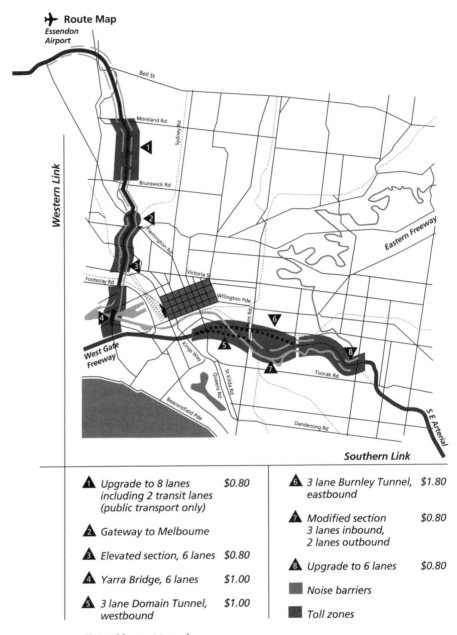

Figure 1   Melbourne's City Link Project

ensure that the trust does not fall within the trading trust provisions, the trust cannot participate in the operation of the tollway. Thus, the trust's role in the project is limited to the design and construction of certain sections of toll road that are leased to the company and the raising of project debt. The trust's income takes the form of rentals under the sublease to the company and interest on any loans provided to the company by the trust.

SOURCES OF DEBT AND EQUITY

The manner in which the structure and the funding sources are arranged is shown in Figure 2.

The debt raised for the project was a combination of long-term bank debt in two tranches with a term of 17 and 19 years respectively, a A$350 million CPI bond facility with a 27-year term, and a A$51 million subordinated debt facility with a six-year term. In addition, a nine-year infrastructure borrowing facility (now known as Develop Australia Bonds) of about A$1,250 million will be used, this facility being secured by cash deposits. This infrastructure borrowing facility was certified by the Development Allowance Authority (now known as Invest Australia), so that it qualifies for concessional taxation treatment under the Australian Tax Act.

A total of A$510 million in equity funding was sought for the project. Of this amount, the sponsors, Transfield and Obayashi, provided A$100 million. The remainder was raised from institutional and corporate investors and the public.

Because of the lengthy bidding process, Transurban was forced to rely primarily on its institutional investors. As the tendering process progressed, these investors were required to reconfirm their commitment to the project several times before the actual date for contribution of their funds. This provided the financial certainty that was required by the Victoria government and was a critical factor in the success of Transurban's bid. It was the first time that equity commitments from such a diverse range of investors were kept current for more than 15 months.

A retail share issue was deemed to be highly advantageous from both the government's and Transurban's viewpoint. Such an issue ensured a greater spread of investors to enhance liquidity and guarantee compliance with the Australian Stock Exchange listing rules. It also provided likely users of the link with the opportunity to invest directly in an asset that they will use regularly, and allowed for the promotion of the road to future users.

The state government expressed a strong preference for a retail issue in order that the public should have the opportunity to invest in this landmark infrastructure project. Accordingly, A$63.5 million was raised by way of a public offer. Having regard to the strong levels of retail demand and the imperative to achieve financial close, the public offer was closed three days after the issue of the prospectus, with the offer being heavily oversubscribed.

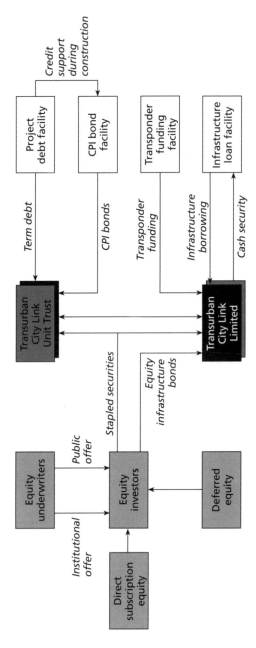

Figure 2 Funding structure

Table 2 Sources of equity

Public issue	Pursuant to a prospectus, the public was invited to apply for parcels of securities worth $63.5 million.
Institutional issue	Pursuant to a separate offering memorandum, institutional investors were invited to apply for parcels of securities worth $206.5 million. This was an excluded offer as defined in subsection 66(2) of the Corporations Law.
Direct subscription issue	Transfield Infrastructure Investments Pty Limited and a select group of institutional and corporate investors executed agreements to subsbcribe for parcels of securities worth A$185 million.

Table 3 Composition of each A$500 parcel in the initial equity

Quantity	Security	Issue price (A$)
499	Equity infrastructure bonds issued by the company at a price of A$1.00 each	499.00
1	Share in the company issued at 1 cent	0.01
1	Unit in the trust issued at 99 cents	0.99
	Total issue price	500.00

The initial equity was raised in three separate issues and accounts for $455 million of the total equity requirement of $510 million. The three separate issues are explained in Table 2.

Obayashi and Transroute (a major French toll road operator) each executed agreements by which they will subscribe for A$50 million and A$5 million of equity respectively. This deferred equity was committed at financial closing but is not scheduled to be paid up until 45 months after financial closing (the expected construction completion date). The obligations of Obayashi and Transroute to subscribe such deferred equity are supported by irrevocable letters of credit.

EQUITY INVESTMENT STRUCTURE

The initial equity was subscribed for in the form of A$500 parcels. The composition of each parcel during the construction period is shown in Table 3.

The single share and single unit in each parcel serve to establish investors' ownership and voting rights in the company and the trust. All 501 separate securities will be "stapled" together and cannot be traded separately.

During the construction phase, distributions will be paid to investors by way of quarterly interest coupons on the equity infrastructure bonds, which will be tax-exempt. These coupons are forecast to be A$50.00 per parcel per annum and, although the distribution is not guaranteed, the cost to the company of paying them has been factored into the financing plan.

Forty-five months after financial close, the 499 equity infrastructure bonds within each parcel are scheduled to be redeemed from an additional $454 million drawdown under the infrastructure borrowing facility. The redemption proceeds from each bond will be automatically subscribed (on behalf of investors) for stapled securities that comprise one share in the company and one unit in the trust.

For capital gains tax purposes, investors' cost base of each new stapled security is expected to equal the original issue price of the equity infrastructure bond plus any premium on redemption of the bond.

After redemption of the equity infrastructure bonds and the automatic subscription for stapled securities, each parcel will contain 500 shares and 500 units, each share being stapled to a unit. At this time, a parcel may be divided into individual stapled securities (each comprising one share and one unit). However, the stapling between each share and each unit cannot be undone.

Once the link is opened to traffic, returns to investors will depend on its operational performance (principally the volume of traffic using the toll road). Distributions during the operations phase will be primarily by way of pre-tax distributions from the trust. These are expected to contain tax-exempt and tax-deferred components arising from accumulated losses generated during the construction phase and depreciation allowances available to the company and the trust. To the extent that the company derives taxable income it is proposed to distribute that income to investors in their capacity as shareholders.

The parcels of securities were listed on the Australian Stock Exchange on Friday, March 15, 1996 and were trading at about an 80% premium to the issue price by the end of the year.

'Making the Right Financial Connections for Melbourne', by M. Carapiet, reprinted from *Corporate Finance*, Dec. Copyright 1996 *Corporate Finance*.

Dividend Cut: The Case of FPL

D. Soter and P. Evanson

On May 9, 1994, FPL Group, the parent company of Florida Power & Light Company, announced a 32% reduction in its quarterly dividend payout, from 62 cents per share to 42 cents. This was the first-ever dividend cut by a healthy utility. A number of utilities had reduced their dividends in the past, but only after cash flow problems – often associated with nuclear plants – had given them no other choice.

In its announcement, FPL stressed that it had studied the situation carefully and that, given the prospect of increased competition in the electric utility industry, the company's high dividend payout ratio (which had averaged 90% in the past four years) was no longer in its stockholders' best interests. The new policy resulted in a dividend payout of about 60% of the prior year's earnings. Management also announced that, starting in 1995, the dividend payout would be reviewed in February instead of May to reinforce the linkage between dividends and annual earnings. In so doing, the company wanted to minimize unintended "signaling effects" from any future changes in the dividend.

At the same time it announced this change in dividend policy, FPL Group's board authorized the repurchase of up to 10 million shares of common stock over the next three years; and FPL's management indicated that 4 million shares would be repurchased over the next 12 months, depending on market conditions. (In fact, the company repurchased 4 million shares in the last eight months of 1994 and 1.9 million shares in 1995, at a total cost of $193 million.) In adopting this strategy, the company noted that changes in the U.S. tax code since 1990 had made capital gains more attractive than dividends to shareholders. Whereas dividends are taxed at ordinary income rates, gains from stock sales are taxed at lower capital gains rates. Furthermore, capital gains are taxed only when realized, thus providing each shareholder the opportunity to defer that tax.

Besides providing a more tax-efficient means of distributing excess capital to its stockholders, FPL's substitution of stock repurchases for dividends was also designed to increase the company's financial flexibility in preparation for a new era of deregulation and heightened competition among utilities. Although much of the cash savings from the dividend cut would be returned to investors in the form of stock repurchases, the rest would be used to retire debt at Florida Power & Light and so reduce the company's leverage ratio. This deleveraging and strengthening of FPL's financial condition were intended both to prepare the company for an increase in business risk and to provide the financial resources to take advantage of future growth opportunities.

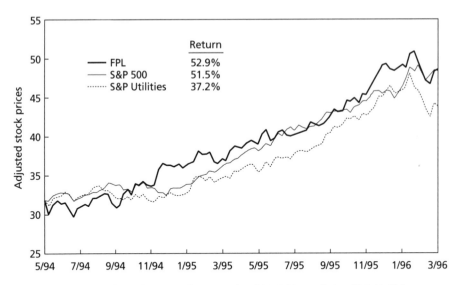

Figure 1 Adjusted stock prices for FPL, the S&P 500, and the S&P Utilities (5/6/94–3/29/96)

The stock market's initial reaction to FPL's announcement was negative. On the day of the announcement, the company's stock price fell from $31.88 to $27.50, a drop of nearly 14%. (Given that FPL's average stock price during the prior month was about $33.75, and that the stock under-performed the S&P Utilities Index by about 4% during that month, a better estimate of the market's negative response is probably about 18–20%.) But, as analysts digested the news and considered the reasons for the reduction, they concluded that the action was not a signal of financial distress but rather a strategic decision that would improve the company's long-term financial flexibility and prospects for growth. This view spread throughout the financial community, and FPL's stock began to recover.

On May 31, less than a month after the announcement, FPL's stock closed at $32.17 (adjusted for the quarterly dividend of 42 cents), or about 30 cents higher than the pre-announcement price. By the middle of June, at least 15 major brokerage houses had placed FPL's common stock on their "buy" lists. On May 9, 1995 – exactly one year after the announcement of the cut – FPL's stock price closed at $37.75, giving stockholders a one-year post-announcement return (including dividends) of 23.8%,[1] more than double the 11.2% of the S&P 500 Index and well above the 14.2% of the S&P Utilities Index over the same period. On April 1, 1996, FPL's stock was trading at $45.25 (or $48.73 adjusted for dividends), providing stockholders with a two-year post-announcement return of 52.9% – again, well above the 37.2% return of the S&P Utilities Index over the same period. (For a graphic illustration of FPL's stock return relative to the S&P Utilities Index, see Figure 1.)

Management's decision, however, was not an easy one. FPL had achieved the longest record of continuous annual dividend increases of any electric utility – 47 years – and the third longest of any company traded on the New York Stock Exchange. Moreover, dividend cuts are almost invariably followed by sharp reductions in stock price. Anticipating that the market's initial reaction would be negative, management undertook a major investor relations campaign to explain the company's change in dividend policy as a critical part of its overall business and financial strategy. That campaign took the form of a series of "road shows" comparable to those used in launching IPOs. The comparison seems apt because, in an important sense, FPL was becoming a *new* company – or at least it was a company in the process of transforming itself to confront a new competitive business environment.

FPL was not alone, however, either in reconsidering its dividend policy, or in making a partial substitution of stock repurchases for dividends. With companies in many industries facing greater competition, boards of directors are increasingly deciding that stock buybacks are a more effective means than dividends of committing management to distribute excess cash to stockholders. In the past three years, the dividend payout ratio of the S&P 500 has fallen from a 70-year historical average of about 55% to under 40%.[2] Stock market "bears" continue to point to a market dividend yield that has fallen from an historical average of about 4% to below 2.4%. What such analysis typically fails to recognize is the growing extent to which stock repurchases are being used to supplement dividends as a method of paying out excess cash. Between 1991 and 1995, total corporate dividends increased from $82.6 billion to an estimated $98.7 billion, an average annual growth rate of about 4%. Over the same period, the total amount of stock repurchased by U.S. companies grew from $21.3 billion to $55.3 billion, an average annual growth rate of over 30%.[3] In 1995 alone, over 800 U.S. companies announced plans to repurchase a total of $98 billion of stock – a 42% increase over the prior year.

Other utilities, as well as companies in other rapidly changing industries, are wrestling with the dividend issue. Neither financial economists nor Wall Street operators have a magic formula for establishing the optimal payout policy. Indeed, many academics are still engaged in a 35-year-old debate as to whether dividend policy matters at all. The FPL case can be seen as contributing to the dividend debate in the following sense: It suggests that while there may not be a single dividend payout ratio that maximizes a company's value, the wrong policy may end up reducing value. More important, it makes clear that the right dividend policy for an individual company depends primarily on the business environment in which the firm operates – and that changes in the business environment are likely to dictate changes in financial policy. As the FPL story also shows, making the right dividend decision is not a trivial undertaking.

NOTES

1. Measured from the $31.88 stock price prior to the announcement. If we measure the return instead from the prior month's average of $33.75, the return would have been about 17%, still above the S&P return of 14.2%.
2. See Jean Helwege, David Laster, and Kevin Cole, "Stock Market Valuation Indicators: Is This Time Different?" *Financial Analysts Journal* 52, May–June 1996, 56–64.
3. Ibid.

Section 4

Adding Value Through Risk Management

9

The Use of Risk Analysis Techniques in Capital Investment Appraisal

S. S. M. Ho and R. H. Pike

INTRODUCTION

The term 'risk' is often used to describe, characterize and rank new capital projects. Previous capital budgeting surveys indicate that actual practices of firms in handling risk have lagged well behind the theoretically prescribed probabilistic risk analysis (PRA) approach, despite the fact that there is a continuing trend towards greater formalization and sophistication of risk handling. Furthermore, the existing and somewhat aged information on risk handling practices, mostly collected and reported as a part of broader-based surveys, inevitably provides only a limited view of risk analysis practices and its related problems. The purpose of this article is to report findings from a survey of large UK firms on a wide range of issues related to the use of risk analysis, particularly the perceived barriers to, and benefits from, such use.

INVESTMENT APPRAISAL CRITERIA AND RISK HANDLING APPROACHES

In order to put the risk analysis issues in context, this section briefly reviews the three most commonly used financial appraisal techniques and the two major risk handling approaches in capital budgeting analysis.

Financial Appraisal Techniques

Net Present Value

In most cases a project will require an immediate initial outlay and this will result in a series of future cash flows. The net present value (NPV) of a project is the sum of all future cash flows discounted at the required rate of return *minus* the present value of the cost of the investment. A positive NPV implies that the project yields more than the cost of capital and a negative one that it yields less. Other things being equal, all projects showing a positive NPV should be accepted.

Internal Rate of Return

An alternative approach to NPV is to calculate an investment's internal rate of return (IRR), sometimes called the yield. The IRR is the rate of return which equates the anticipated net cash flows with the initial outlay. A project is acceptable if its yield or IRR is greater than the required rate of return on the project. In the vast majority of cases the IRR method of appraising capital projects gives exactly the same accept/reject decision as NPV, although there can be differences when comparing mutually exclusive projects, in which case NPV is generally preferred.

Payback Period

The payback period is the length of time required to repay the initial investment. The payback period is mainly used to test a manager's gut reaction to a project. It gives the manager a 'feel' as to the length of time cash is at risk. Payback period alone is usually inadequate to make a decision because it involves the subjective establishment of an acceptable payback period. It is often criticized as an appraisal method because it takes no account of big payoffs beyond the payback point. The payback period is very popular with managers, and when applied intelligently, combines well with the NPV method.

Risk Handling Approaches

Project risk usually denotes that the decision maker is uncertain as to the precise outcomes of a decision which involves the possibility of undesirable consequences or loss. Unlike 'pure' or 'non-speculative' risk usually discussed in the field of safety management (where there is usually no element of speculation or potential gain, i.e. the potential outcomes are loss or no loss), managers with entrepreneurial talent take certain 'strategic' or 'speculative' risks (where there are possibilities of gains as well as losses) in expectation of high returns. Unless otherwise specified, the term 'risk' in this chapter refers mainly to 'strategic risks'.

The integrative operational model for handling strategic risk developed by Ho (1990) suggests that all investment decisions in practice should go through a series of steps in a logical sequence. This requires first risk identification, then risk management and reduction, and lastly, risk evaluation – their subsequent incorporation in the final project decision process. After the measurement of risk at both project and portfolio level, a decision maker needs to judge whether some or all of the inherent pure risks can/should be avoided, reduced, tolerated or accepted. If the firm cannot tolerate some of the risks it would probably have to identify some methods to protect against unfavourable outcomes. If the project is still perceived as too risky (for example, in terms of maximum possible loss), it would be more likely to get rejected. Otherwise, the decision maker then has to make a risk-return tradeoff decision and decide to what extent the residual risks (largely probabilistic) can be accepted or compensated with a higher return. Finally, the manager must make an overall judgement about the project(s), and ultimately an accept/reject decision.

Except for some pure risk reduction methods such as diversification, acquiring insurance and vertical integration, approaches for handling strategic risk can generally be divided into two broad categories.

Simple Risk Adjustment (SRA)

Risk is handled by putting a more stringent requirement on financial evaluation (e.g. shortening required payback period or making more conservative cash flow estimates in the NPV or IRR model) or compensated with an intuitively determined risk premium (e.g. raising discount rate or required rate of return). This requires the analyst or decision maker to make a single best estimate of future cash flow variables, and provides a simple solution as to whether the project is or is not worth more than its cost. The major limitations of the two popular rule-of-thumb SRA methods to guard against risk can be summarized as below.

Reducing required payback period
It implies (amongst other things) that risk is time related and shortening the required payback period for a project to be accepted reduces the risk. The disadvantages of payback are several. First, as mentioned earlier, focusing on near future cash flows, it ignores earnings of an investment entirely after the investment was recovered and thus does not measure the true return of an investment. Second, it fails to consider the time pattern over which funds were recovered. Third, it overemphasizes liquidity as a goal of the capital investment programme. To resolve these problems, the discounted payback period method and the use of probabilities of meeting required payback period have been suggested.

Increasing discount rate intuitively
Clearly, the greater the risk, the higher will be the risk premium and discount rate in order to compensate for the added risk. There are, however, notable difficulties in applying this method. First, if risk does not increase constantly over time, using a single risk-adjusted discount rate is inappropriate. Second, setting the risk-adjusted discount rate arbitrarily without first conducting formal risk analysis or using a refined method such as the capital asset pricing model (CAPM) can cause other problems. Setting the

discount rates too high may lead to missed opportunities for profit and growth. An understating of these rates may result in unprofitable investment and a fall in market value.

Overall, most SRA methods usually do not explicitly assess the risk involved and risk adjustment is sometimes made without real understanding of the inherent risk. Combining risk estimation, risk preference and risk adjustment may ignore and hide information which could be valuable in investment decisions. Also, it is possible that several SRA methods will be applied to the NPV calculation which could make the final outcomes difficult to interpret and 'ultra-conservative'. Despite their apparent ease of use, SRA methods could lead decision makers to accept decisions against their original intentions if the assumptions were not clearly understood. Nevertheless, even though not using these primarily as tools and while some firms show greater acceptance of the more sophisticated techniques, the SRA approach still offers useful supplementary tools and should not be dismissed.

Probabilistic Risk Analysis (PRA)

More commonly known as 'risk analysis' in the literature, this approach advocates formal measurement of investment risk before any risk adjustment is made, and the analysis itself does not incorporate the decision maker's risk preference. The approach usually involves estimating the uncertainty surrounding forecasts and then deriving probability distributions and other derived statistics for performance criteria (such as NPV and IRR). The added information gives managers better insight into the risk situation so that they can make a more effective risk/return tradeoff decision. Commonly prescribed PRA techniques include those described below.

Sensitivity analysis (SA)
This aims to identify the uncertainty factors which have a significant impact on a project's return. This technique usually involves a series of 'what-if' questions by giving a percentage change to each key assumption one at a time. It is viewed as a first step to screen those factors to be specified in probabilities in more sophisticated methods.

Probability analysis (PA)
This includes all probability-based analytical methods (decision trees, $E-V$ rule, etc.). It provides answers to questions such as what is the probability of making a given NPV or IRR? One simple example is to assign probability distributions of future period-by-period cash flows and produce a probability distribution of NPV/IRR.

Hertz-type risk simulation (RS)
This models a situation where a number of key variables which impinge on a project could vary simultaneously. A computer is usually employed to

generate a series of possible returns for various combinations of values for these factors, and obtain a probability distribution achieved for the project's NPV/IRR.

More recently, the refined risk analysis approach incorporates both the risk simulation and some of the new CAPM concepts together in order to take account of the shareholders' preference. The CAPM measures the sensitivity of the investment's return to the changes in the return on market portfolio and it assumes only the undiversifiable risk requires a premium. As such the higher an investment's beta, the higher is its required discount rate.

It is suggested in the literature that the risk analysis approach has a valuable role to play in the process of corporate strategic planning through its input into such areas as: forecasting, firm risk positioning, environmental scanning, and managerial communication. Risk analysis enables the decision makers to examine, discuss, and eventually understand why one course of action might be more desirable than another. If applied properly, risk analysis techniques should foster managerial judgement rather than replace it in the decision-making process.

LITERATURE REVIEW ON IMPLEMENTATION ISSUES

Proponents of the PRA or 'risk analysis' approach argue that the increased quantitative information on the risks inherent in a project and the increased understanding of the precise nature of those risks lead to better decision outcomes and, ultimately, enhanced corporate performance. However, considerable disagreement exists in the business community as to the 'bottom-line' impact of using risk analysis. Many managers refuse to use risk analysis because there is little evidence that such use could improve corporate profitability. The limited empirical research investigating the impact of capital budgeting sophistication on firms' performance has been mixed and inconclusive (Schall, Sundem and Geijsbeek, 1978; Pike, 1984; Haka, Gordon and Pinches, 1984). Ho and Pike (1989, 1991 and 1992), using an interrupted time-series experimental design, also found no evidence that the adoption of probabilistic risk analysis led to a significant change in relative capital expenditure and profitability within firms.

Another major reason for the lack of widespread acceptance of risk analysis is that it is marred by some inherent and implementation problems still to be resolved. For instance, Vandell and Stonich (1973) argue that the use of sophisticated evaluation techniques is based on erroneous assumptions that risk can and should be measured. In addition, these techniques tend to add rigidities and 'bureaucratic rituals' to the capital budgeting process that:

- increase the resources necessary to process an attractive idea;

- reduce the output of worthwhile investment ideas; and

■ decrease the ability of management to review the real merits of an
   investment proposal.

They argue that most managers are suspicious of return calculations even
when accompanied by measures of dispersion. In the first place, managers
often disagree on what the distribution of probabilities should be, and second, there is a high probability of misuse of the information.

One of the most significant and extensive studies of the implementation
of risk analysis in business was carried out by Carter (1972) who focused
on the experience of four American oil companies in using risk analysis
with varying degrees of success. Carter found several persistent problems
in risk analysis and his findings reveal that management's basic attitude
towards risk analysis, the understanding of the approach, and the support
and participation of all levels of management in the implementation process
play an important part in its use and acceptance. Operational commitment,
as opposed to staff curiosity, is the key to success.

In a survey of financial modelling users in the United Kingdom, McGregor (1983) found only about 10% of FCS-using firms surveyed used the
risk analysis module in investment decisions. The major problems in building risk analysis models were the lack of sufficient data, the difficulties in
obtaining probability estimates and understanding probability concepts, correlation assumptions between variables and across time, and the understanding of the output information.

Despite these studies, many standard prescriptions for implementing
management science techniques and other planned organizational changes
have been developed in the past two decades, which should help to alleviate
some of those problems mentioned above. Others indicate the importance
of top management support, manager participation and training, and the fit
of the technique into the company's existing capital budgeting procedures
as well as the managers' decision process. Cooper and Chapman (1987)
further stress that successful risk analysis requires a flexible and easy-to-
understand model, supported by sophisticated interactive decision support
systems, a wide range of relevant expertise, and the experience and leadership to design and integrate models.

The many practical methods proposed for eliciting decision makers'
subjective probabilities necessary for risk analysis together with the increasing use of those user-friendly microcomputer modelling packages may well
mean that some of the implementation problems mentioned above are far
less applicable today. The risk analysis approach should, therefore, have
experienced an increase in both recognition and use in recent years.

Of interest in this article is whether many of these implementation issues
still concern UK managers, given the many technical and managerial developments in the 1980s. We also examine these managers' attitudes towards
risk analysis, whether they use risk analysis for certain types of projects
only, the difficulties and problems encountered, and the perceived impact
and overall satisfaction of using risk analysis.

Table 9.1   Industrial breakdown of responding firms

1st digit SIC code	Industry	Sample number	%
1	Energy and oil	11	7.5
2	Mining and manufacture of metals, mineral and chemical products	25	17.1
3	Engineering and vehicles	41	28.1
4	Consumer and other manufacturing	33	22.6
5	Construction	9	6.2
6	Distribution and trade	15	10.3
7, 8	Public and business services	12	8.2
Total		146	100.0

Table 9.2   Use of risk analysis techniques (total number of responses: 142 firms)

	Extent of use (%)					
Approach and technique	Never 1	Rare 2	Little 3	Some 4	Often 5	Very often 6
1. Sensitivity analysis	15.2	11.0	10.3	23.4	17.9	22.1
2. Probability analysis	49.0	10.5	10.5	13.3	9.8	7.0
3. Risk simulation	78.0	8.5	5.0	5.7	2.8	0.0
4. Capital asset pricing model (Beta analysis)	73.6	10.0	1.4	9.3	3.6	2.1

RISK ANALYSIS AND USER EXPERIENCES

For the current study, primary data were derived mainly through large-scale postal questionnaires and supplemented by interviews with 10 selected organizations. The pilot-tested questionnaires were distributed to named finance directors in the largest 350 companies in *The Times 1000* (1987), defined by sales turnover. After three mailings the whole process resulted in responses from 154 companies, 146 usable for this study (an actual response rate of 42.5%). Follow-up telephone and on-site interviews with selected respondents were carried out to seek further clarification on certain issues and obtain a more detailed picture of certain aspects of risk handling in the capital budgeting process. The industrial distribution of the sample firms presented in Table 9.1 suggests that the respondents were representative of the original sample.

Table 9.2 shows, on a six-point frequency scale (ranging from 'never' through 'sometimes' to 'very often'), the extent to which responding firms use each of the risk analysis techniques: sensitivity analysis, probability analysis, Hertz-type risk simulation, and CAPM. These techniques are not mutually exclusive and many firms make use of a combination of methods. Respondents were also requested to list any other project risk analysis methods they employed. These included scenario modelling, earning per share (EPS) impact analysis, breakeven analysis, profitability index analysis, and several enhanced versions of sensitivity analysis.

Among the various analysis techniques listed, sensitivity analysis was found to be the most commonly used technique, with 85% using it – the majority on a regular basis. In its most basic form, sensitivity analysis requires little subjective probability estimating, and is therefore found by managers to be reliable and easy to use, particularly when supported by a computerized spreadsheet package. Such analysis entails varying input variables, one at a time, over their entire range to determine their relative effects on a project's predicted return. It provides decision makers with answers to a whole range of 'what-if' questions, and assists managers to screen and isolate the key variables requiring further evaluation.

Over one-half of the respondents (57%) use subjective probability estimates for key variables, with 30% of respondents using it regularly. Interviews with executives show that some use is made of decision trees for structuring the important factors in sequential decision problems, and analysing mutually exclusive options; but only occasionally are subjective probabilities assigned to the 'trees' for statistical analysis.

Other more advanced techniques, although highly developed in theory, are not in widespread use in the capital budgeting process. Table 9.2 clearly shows that Hertz-type risk simulation and CAPM are rarely used. In practice, as the interviews showed, the type of 'simulation' used by some firms is not necessarily the Hertz-type as described in existing literature (Hertz and Thomas, 1983). These firms simply develop financial models consisting of all the key variables, with a subsequent 'simulation' of the performance measures, subject to changes in a few key assumptions. Such an approach does not necessitate the assignment of probability distributions for the key variables, as proposed in the Hertz approach. Probabilistic simulation and the CAPM technique are not new but their practical use is still in its infancy. In most firms visited, the production of a risk-return profile is still not a standard procedure in the evaluation of capital investment proposals. While many variations of risk analysis models are employed, one consistent requirement is that of flexibility in pursuing alternative analyses.

As a result of differences in project types approval levels (headquarters vs. divisions) and approval criteria, many companies are making use of multiple risk analysis methods. Over half of the sample firms use two or more formal techniques. The most popular combinations are sensitivity analysis and probability analysis (used by 20%), followed by all four techniques (used by 12%) and sensitivity analysis-probability analysis-risk simulation (used by 6%). The majority of companies using simulation also employ probability and sensitivity analysis in the decision-making process. For example, two firms visited for in-depth study used sensitivity analysis to identify key variables and subsequently used probability analysis of cash flows to find the best alternative. A simulation could then be conducted to build a risk profile and classify the project risk.

Table 9.3 Risk reduction and control (total number of responses: 143)

Risk reduction method	Percentage of total respondents
1. Maintain tighter control of project implementation	86.4
2. Diversify the risk (e.g. joint venture)	53.0
3. Modify policies and staffing of the company	40.9
4. Subcontract critical parts of project	31.0
5. Operate a contingency fund in the event of need	23.5
6. Secure market via vertical integration	15.9
7. Acquire commercial insurance coverage	8.3

Respondents were also further asked to identify the three primary methods that they use to reduce risk during both project implementation and operation, given a choice of seven risk reduction methods commonly described in the literature. Table 9.3 shows that the three most popular risk reduction methods are 'maintaining tighter project control' (86%), 'diversifying the risk' (53%), and 'modifying policies and staffing within the company' (41%). Other risk reduction methods mentioned include conducting market research, phased approval/development, guaranteed supply agreement with customers, taskforce approach, obtaining 'expert' advice prior to implementation, and minimizing 'upfront' commitment.

To ensure that the respondents' perceptions are based on real experience, only organizations which used or planned to use probability analysis and/ or risk simulation were included in the study of implementation problems below. In other words, 'PRA' or 'risk analysis' users in this study refer to those who formally and systematically determine the probabilistic distributions and its derived statistics of a project's performance.

CHANGE IN ROLE OF RISK ANALYSIS

Prior surveys suggest that the use of risk analysis is growing, even if at a slow rate. To confirm this trend before examining other implementation issues, respondents were asked if the importance of risk analysis in their firms had changed over the last five years. They were then asked to estimate the changes over the next five years. The percentages of responses to the question are summarized in Table 9.4. A total of 41% of respondents stated that over the past five years risk analysis had become more important – less than 2% perceiving it to be less important over the same period. For the next five years, over half of the sample firms expect risk analysis to become more important, while no firm predicts it to become less important.

Interview discussions revealed that the greatest change is in the increased use of microcomputers for risk measurement. The interest of firms in greater use of risk analysis has been apparent, with additional emphasis on the use of probability concepts. If the observed trend continues, formal risk

Table 9.4 Changes in the role of risk analysis

	More important (%)	No change (%)	Less important (%)
1. Over the last five years risk analysis has been	41.4	57.1	1.4
2. Over the next five years risk analysis will become	54.0	46.0	0.0

Table 9.5 Reasons for using risk simulation techniques

Reason	Percentage of total ($N = 39$)
1. Size of projects	73.7
2. Complexity of projects	73.7
3. New product development	47.4
4. New market	36.8
5. Payback period of project	26.3
6. Sponsor of projects	5.3

analysis may become as standard a technique for larger projects as discounted cash flow methods are today.

CHARACTERISTICS OF PROJECTS USING RISK ANALYSIS

Sample firms claiming use of risk analysis techniques were asked whether they use the techniques for certain types of projects only, and if so, what are the specific reasons for their use. Among the 39 risk simulation users who replied, 35 reported that they use simulation for certain project decisions, while 4 use it for all investment decisions (see Table 9.5).

Analysis of these results suggests that the size of a project and its complexity of implementation are the most important factors in the choice of risk analysis technique. This indicates that the application of risk analysis is not primarily correlated with the type of project (i.e. replacement, obligatory, strategic, etc.) but rather the use is very much dependent on management's perception of risk within the specific project. Payback period and track record of the project sponsor appear to be of relatively little importance in the choice of techniques. Among the 'other reasons' mentioned were: high uncertainty of cash flow estimate, 'territory', past experience of similar projects, and required rate of return.

Clearly, while the risk analysis approach is widely advocated and can be applied on a 'blanket-basis', the study findings suggest that usage is very much situation dependent. The main criteria adopted being that of size and complexity.

Table 9.6 Primary users of risk analysis

User level	Number of respondents	Percentage of total
Departmental managers	42	40.8
Budgeting/planning staff	34	33.0
Top executives/board	21	20.4
EDP/OR staff	1	1.0
Others	5	4.8
	103	100.0

PRIMARY USERS OF RISK ANALYSIS

This section aims to identify the personnel who actually use the risk analysis the most and to determine whether they are specialists or functional managers. Table 9.6 shows that the departmental/divisional managers involved in the project decision process use risk analysis most widely (41% of the total responses), followed by budgeting/corporate planning staff (33%) and top executives (20%). Only 1% of firms have electronic data processing/operations research (EDP/OR) staff as the primary users of risk analysis. Discussions with executives revealed that modelling for risk analysis is usually carried out by a project team under the general guidance of a steering committee composed of representatives from various interest groups. In many cases, there is a combination of financial analysts, accountants, and EDP personnel, who together build the model.

These results are indeed encouraging; they indicate that in over one-half of the companies using risk analysis, line managers rather than the EDP/OR specialists, are using the models. The use of risk analysis by top management was also impressive. There is much evidence in the literature that senior manager-user participation is important in the success of any computer systems development and its implementation.

ATTITUDES TOWARDS RISK ANALYSIS

One of the factors affecting the likelihood that managers will accept and beneficially employ risk analysis, is their underlying attitudes towards risk analysis. Such attitudes may well depend on their personal risk attitude and experiences of past investment decision outcomes. The survey examined such attitudes using a measurement of five items which pertain to the respondents' general attitudes towards several aspects of risk analysis. Respondents were asked to indicate how much they agreed or disagreed with each item ('1' = strongly agree, '6' = strongly disagree).

The average responses for each item and the overall attitudes are presented in Table 9.7. The respondents generally expressed a slightly favourable attitude regarding risk analysis (overall mean = 4.2). Focusing on

Table 9.7 Attitudes towards formal risk analysis (total number of responses 141 firms)

	Strongly disagree			Strongly agree			
	1	2	3	4	5	6	
Attitude statement			%				Mean
1. Capital budgeting involves uncertainty	0.0	2.8	5.0	16.3	27.0	48.9	5.14
2. I am personally in favour of formal risk analysis	0.7	4.3	15.8	28.8	30.2	20.1	4.47
3. Managers prefer to make a range of estimates rather than a single-point estimate for an uncertainty factor	2.1	10.6	16.3	29.8	29.1	12.1	4.09
4. Project uncertainty requires formal risk analysis	0.7	9.9	29.1	27.1	25.5	7.1	3.89
5. Project uncertainty can be measured quantitatively	3.5	14.9	29.8	32.6	12.8	1.4	3.36
Overall mean				4.179;	SD = 0.712		

responses with scores of '5' or '6', it was found that while almost 76% of respondents agreed that capital budgeting involves uncertainty, only about 14% agreed that project uncertainty can be measured quantitatively and only 33% that project uncertainty requires formal risk analysis. Despite the lack of enthusiasm for risk measurement, over 40% of respondents agreed that managers prefer to make a range of estimates rather than a single-point estimate for an uncertainty factor.

The implication from both the survey and interview findings is that, for risk analysis to be effective, first, management should acknowledge that they are making a decision that involves uncertainty, and more importantly, should recognize that uncertainty requires some formal analysis. Second, management's understanding of the approach may greatly affect these attitudes. While it may not be necessary to have formal training programmes, at least managerial interaction and involvement during all phases of the risk analysis process appear to be important to ensure understanding and acceptance. Interview findings revealed that user acceptance can be enhanced when managers realize that the information provided conforms to their decision process and can be helpful to them in their decision responsibilities. Future studies may investigate the influence of other personal factors, such as age, personality, experience, and risk-taking attitude on a decision maker's attitude towards formal risk analysis.

It is important to recognize that these attitudes are not static and may change as social, technological, organizational and investment conditions change. As business competition becomes more intense, environmental changes become more difficult to forecast, and managers become more conversant with information technology, they may demand more risk analysis information. Some evidence of this has emerged from this study, particularly among those young business-school-trained managers who are directly involved in capital investment decisions.

DIFFICULTIES AND PROBLEMS IN USE OF RISK ANALYSIS

A number of barriers or problem areas were identified in the literature as well as in the preliminary stages of this study which would block the effective use of risk analysis in companies. These barriers occur both in the organization itself and in its management.

Respondents were asked the extent to which they have experienced each of the problems listed in Table 9.8 in the implementation and use of risk analysis in their companies. Again, a six-point scale ranging from 'not at all' to 'very much' was used. In general, seven out of the eleven problems listed can be considered as common, as at least half of the respondents rated these seven problems as 'some', 'much' or 'very much'. These are:

- Managers' understanding of techniques (69%)
- Obtaining input estimates (62%)
- Time involvements (60.8%)

Table 9.8 Barriers to implementation and use of risk analysis (total number of responses: 137 firms)

	Not at all 1	Rare 2	Little 3	Some 4	Much 5	Very much 6	Mean
			%				Mean
Inherent problem encountered							
1. Obtaining input estimates	5.2	11.9	20.7	31.3	23.0	8.1	3.79
2. Time involvement	3.7	14.1	21.5	32.6	23.0	5.2	3.73
3. Understanding output of analysis	3.6	16.8	24.1	25.5	22.6	7.3	3.69
4. Tradeoff between risk and return	6.2	13.8	23.8	33.8	22.3	0.0	3.52
5. Managers cannot agree on estimates/judgement	5.2	22.2	29.6	31.9	10.4	0.7	3.22
6. Cost-justification of techniques	15.8	17.3	19.5	30.8	15.8	10.8	3.16
Implementation problem encountered							
7. Managers' understanding of techniques	2.2	14.6	13.9	35.0	23.4	10.9	3.96
8. Human/organizational resistance	3.7	16.2	23.5	35.3	14.7	6.6	3.61
9. Finding suitable methods	9.6	18.4	24.3	27.2	16.9	3.7	3.35
10. Lack of top management support	11.2	19.4	21.6	24.6	17.9	5.2	3.34
11. Lack of computing resources and assistance	25.6	23.3	25.6	17.3	5.3	3.0	2.62

■ Cost-justification of techniques (57%)

■ Human/organizational resistance (56%)

■ Tradeoff between risk and return (56%)

■ Understanding output of analysis (55%)

For the purpose of analysis, these problems can be divided into two types: inherent and implementation problems. Among the inherent problems, Table 9.8 indicates that the respondents perceived the problem of obtaining input estimates to be the most important. Over 31% of respondents reported they have had 'much' or 'very much' experience of this problem in their companies. For new strategic-type projects, project estimates are usually based on subjective judgement made by managers. Discussion with executives revealed that 3-point estimates are most popular, although 5-point estimates and normal distribution estimates are also used occasionally. Particular difficulties mentioned by the managers are the quantification of qualitative factors, measuring interrelationships between variables, personal biases, and over-conservatism, etc.

Effective probabilistic risk analysis requires substantial amounts of internal as well as external data. Sample firms in this survey were also asked to indicate how often the various types of desired information for risk analysis and investment decisions was obtained from their formal information systems. The results indicate that the project-specific data, such as estimates of cash flow, cost of capital, and economic life were seen to be quite adequate by the respondents. The vast majority of these data are collected either by updating previous forecasts or from internal historical record files. However, information on macroeconomics, competitors' behaviour and post-audit review was found to be far less adequate than other project-specific data. External future-information in many firms had to be collected through other unstructured, inconsistent and less reliable channels. It is believed that without a supportive information system, managers would find it very difficult to carry out any sophisticated or meaning risk analysis.

Interpreting and use of output information is another major problem; about 30% of respondents seeing it as 'much' or 'very much' a problem. Other comments regarding output include too much data to read, improper interpretation of output, and understanding limitations of the approach. As far as time and cost are concerned, some executives expressed that the costs are insignificant in terms of computer usage and other tangible costs. A more significant cost is incurred in assigning estimates in the form of personal judgement to be used in the analysis.

Regarding the implementation problems, Table 9.8 indicates the firms are most concerned with managers' knowledge of risk analysis, and least restricted by the problem of a lack of computing resources. Managers with little quantitative background would find the concepts of probability distribution, expected value and variance, difficult to use. Although many executives appreciate the potential of risk analysis, they have to become more familiar with the technique before it can become a part of their capital budgeting system. It seems that knowledge of risk analysis has not reached many intended practising managers through the proper channels.

About 21% found 'managerial resistance' and 'lack of top management support' 'much' or 'very much' of a problem. Resistance problems are possibly due to a lack of communication between managers and the OR/ budgeting specialists who implement risk analysis, in addition to the lack of manager-user involvement in the implementation process. Top management (including board directors) also play a vital role in risk analysis – they are the final authority for acceptance or rejection of new evaluation methods and investment proposals.

While the findings indicate that few companies suffer from lack of computing resources, many companies still only use deterministic models and very limited 'built-in' decision support functions of the financial modelling package (such as computing a project's NPV/IRR and conducting 'what-if' analyses). The study found that the probabilistic risk simulation module is used less frequently than most of the other functions, and indeed in over half of the companies is never used. Over 40% of user firms do not have access to external on-line databases, and only about 15% of respondents frequently use a database management system.

Summarizing these responses, while firms experience a number of barriers to the introduction and use of risk analysis, two main difficulties emerge: obtaining input estimates and understanding of the technique. This indicates only moderate progress in overcoming those persistent problems which have been recognized in the literature over the last two decades. However, these two problems seem increasingly solvable given the continuous improvement in information technology and our understanding of cognitive psychology. It should also be noted that the problems discussed above should be balanced by the benefits experienced, and other favourable responses by respondents, described in the next section.

PERCEIVED IMPACTS AND USER SATISFACTION OF RISK ANALYSIS

Probabilistic risk analysis can offer numerous benefits to managers and to the firm as a whole. For example, Hertz and Thomas (1983) advocate that the use of risk analysis provides a systematic and logical approach to investment decision making, helps communication within the organization, allows managerial judgement to be presented in a meaningful way, and ultimately improves firm performance. However, criticisms of risk analysis, such as rendering proposals more difficult to accept, reducing managers' enthusiasm to generate investment ideas, and thus leading to lower capital expenditure, also found in the literature (e.g. Vandell and Stonich, 1973). To examine such an important issue, nine specific items covering both tangible and intangible types of impacts were used in the questionnaire. It expands

Table 9.9 Perceived impacts of risk analysis (total number of responses 114 firms)

Formal risk analysis	Strongly disagree				Strongly agree		Mean
	1	2	3	4	5	6	
	(%)						
Positive impacts							
1. Providing a useful insight into the project	0.7	2.8	10.6	29.1	38.3	18.4	4.57
2. Improves quality of investment decisions	0.7	0.7	12.4	35.0	38.0	13.1	4.48
3. Increases confidence in investment decisions	0.0	2.1	13.6	34.3	39.3	10.7	4.30
4. Improves efficiency of investment decisions	0.7	3.6	23.2	38.4	23.2	10.9	4.12
5. Enhances communication among managers	2.9	16.5	33.1	29.5	14.4	3.6	3.47
6. Improves ultimate project performance	5.8	17.5	29.2	30.7	11.7	5.1	3.40
Negative impacts							
7. Makes it more difficult to accept proposals	6.6	28.7	30.1	25.7	8.8	0.0	3.01
8. Reduces managers' enthusiasm to generate/sponsor projects	8.0	32.1	28.5	20.4	9.5	1.5	2.96
9. Leads to lower capital expenditure	9.8	30.1	29.3	20.3	9.8	0.8	2.93

the concepts of risk analysis effectiveness to include 'process impacts' in addition to the commonly used 'outcome impacts'.

Table 9.9 reveals that the majority of respondents are reasonably happy with their use of risk analysis. The only two statements for which there was no reasonably clear consensus of concern were whether the use of risk analysis would improve:

1. communication among the managers involved; and
2. ultimate project performance.

In general, however, more managers agreed rather than disagreed with statements of a positive or favourable impact nature. With statements of a negative or unfavourable nature, more managers indicated disagreement than agreement. The majority of respondents agreed that risk analysis is particularly useful for providing an insight into the project decision (mean = 4.57), improving quality of investment decisions, and increasing confidence in investment decisions.

Overall, the survey findings show that the perceived impact of risk analysis on the investment decision process has been substantial, but its impact

Table 9.10 Satisfaction with using risk analysis

% distribution								
1 I	2 I	3 I	4 I	5 I	6 I	Mean	Median	SD
0.0	8.1	25.3	47.5	18.2	1.0	3.79	4	0.872

Note: 1 = not satisfied; 6 = very satisfied.

on the decision outcomes is less conclusive. Most respondents tend to agree that formal risk analysis has offered useful information to the decision maker in making his/her decision. In addition, even though the decision makers find risk analysis more difficult to use, it appears that the new information give rise to greater confidence in the final decision.

In order to assess the overall effectiveness of risk analysis, users were further asked to rate their overall satisfaction with the risk analysis techniques. Table 9.10 shows the summarized responses from managers. The majority of users are moderately pleased with their use of formal risk analysis (66.7% rated risk analysis in the top half of the scale). Users typically rated risk analysis better than '3' (fairly satisfied) giving the approach an acceptable 3.79 average satisfaction rating. However, the results also show that many users are still ambivalent to risk analysis and there is much room for further improvement of the application.

The findings in this study suggest that, while various problems of risk analysis do exist, they do not negate the usefulness of risk analysis for many companies. In many decision situations, the qualitative benefits of using risk analysis were perceived to be substantial. This, in fact, supports Carter's (1972) observation that 'perhaps the greater benefits of risk analysis come from the preparation of the model, not from the results' (p. 78).

DISCUSSIONS AND CONCLUSIONS

This article has examined managers' preferences for handling risk within capital budgeting contexts, based on the authors' survey conducted in 146 larger-sized UK organizations. The main finding is that firms prefer relatively simple risk adjustment and sensitivity analysis. While risk analysis is more commonly employed on larger, more complex projects, there is still a sizeable gap between normative theory and observed practice. The major limitations most frequently found for the application of risk analysis are:

■ obtaining input estimates; and

■ managers' inadequate understanding of the risk analysis approach.

However, the findings revealed that most managers view risk in capital investment decisions as important, and over half of the respondents expressed favourable attitudes regarding formal risk analysis. The major problem is that they simply do not possess the required knowledge to apply formal approaches, or are unable to find an approach which is systematic, easy to apply and cost effective.

Several lessons can also be drawn from the study. First, risk analysis should formalize managers' judgement about project uncertainty in a more precise way and also allow them to modify their judgement in the light of new information or 'second thoughts'. Second, regarding the problem of collecting probability estimates, further development and refinement of practical methods for eliciting the subjective probabilities necessary for risk analysis are required. With some prior discussion and training, we believe that such assessment can generally be obtained. As executives become more comfortable in dealing with outputs from these models, managers should be less concerned with the apparent over-emphasis on exactness and more concerned with the underlying assumptions. Misuse of risk analysis information can also be minimized as knowledge of the techniques increase.

More recently, the increasing widespread use of microcomputers in financial modelling packages has added to the potential, ease of use and efficiency of risk analysis in capital budgeting. Data are more readily available and can be analysed with more flexible statistical techniques and models in an interactive, end-user computing environment. This makes it easier to understand and use risk analysis in a more cost-effective manner, and with less dependence on traditional OR specialists. Gordon and Pinches (1984) argue that a computer-based decision support system (DSS) environment provides the kind of conditions within which theoretically preferred risk analysis methods can become more effective.

The many implementation problems discussed earlier in this chapter, while being more procedural in nature, certainly require attention. For instance, more studies into the motivation for selecting particular types of risk models and information will be valuable. Other related research, which the authors believe to be worthy of further investigation, includes the extent to which:

■ the methods of forecasting; and

■ the presentation/manipulability of the models affect risk analysis effectiveness.

Overall, the study provides a timely review of risk analysis practice in capital budgeting in the United Kingdom, and the perceived barriers and benefits. Some possible suggestions to bridge the gap between theory and practice were discussed. These findings may help executives to re-evaluate and improve their own risk handling practice in the light of the revealed practices and problems of others. They also provide important research insights into several important aspects of risk management.

REFERENCES

Carter, E. E. (1972). What are the risks in risk analysis? *Harvard Business Review*, July–August, 72–82.

Cooper, D. and Chapman, C. (1987). *Risk Analysis for Large Projects: Model, Methods and Cases*, John Wiley & Sons.

Gordon, L. A. and Pinches, G. E. (1984). *Improving Capital Budgeting: A Decision Support System Approach*, Addison-Wesley, Reading, Mass.

Haka, S. F., Gordon, L. A. and Pinches, G. E. (1984). Sophisticated capital budgeting selection techniques and firm performance, *The Accounting Review*, October, 651–69.

Hertz, D. B. and Thomas H. (1983). *Risk Analysis and its Applications*, John Wiley and Sons, NY.

Ho, S. S. M. (1990). An integrative operational framework for strategic risk analysis, in K. Borcherding, O. I. Larichv and D. M. Messick (eds), *Contemporary Issues in Decision Making*, Elsevier–North Holland, pp. 305–14.

Ho, S. S. M. and Pike, R. H. (1989). The impact of adopting risk analysis in capital budgeting on firm performance: a time-analysis analysis in *Proceedings of the International Symposium on Risk Management and Corporate Finance*, European Institute for Advanced Studies in Management, Brussels, Belgium.

Ho, S. S. M. and Pike, R. H. (1991). Information systems and decision supports for capital budgeting decisions, Working Paper, Faculty of Business Administration, The Chinese University of Hong Kong, 1991.

Ho, S. S. M. and Pike, R. H. (1992). Adoption of probabilistic risk analysis in capital budgeting and corporate investment, *Journal of Business Finance and Accounting*, **19**(3), 387–401.

McGregor, J. M. (1983). What users think about computer models, *Long Range Planning*, **16**(5), 45–57.

Pike, R. H. (1984). Sophisticated capital budgeting systems and their corporate performance, *Managerial and Decision Economics*, **5**(21), 91–7.

Schall, D. L., Sundem, G. L. and Geijsbeek, W. R. (1978). Survey and analysis of capital budgeting methods, *Journal of Finance*, **XXXIII**(1) March, 281–6.

Vandell, R. F. and Stonich, R. D. (1973). Capital budgeting: theory or results? *Financial Executive*, August, 46–56.

10

Operating Exposure

D. R. Lessard and J. B. Lightstone

Treasurers are familiar with the impact of changes in exchange rates on the dollar value of assets and liabilities denominated in foreign currencies. The impact of changes in exchange rates on *operating profit* expressed in home currency, which we will call *operating exposure*, is often more important to the company but much less understood. Interest in the effects of exchange rates on operating profit has been increased by the growing awareness of global competition, as well as by the ongoing debate over the accounting treatment of exchange gains and losses.

Operating exposure is often the major cause of variability in operating profit from year to year and an understanding of operating exposure is a necessary input into many decisions of the company. In the long term, operating exposure should be considered in setting strategy and world-wide product planning. In the short term, an understanding of operating exposure will often improve operating decisions. At a business unit level, the quality of a business and the effectiveness of its managers should be evaluated after taking into account exchange rate effects on reported performance which are outside management control.

The increased importance of operating exposure has developed in several ways. Exchange rates are volatile in the current world of managed floating rates. Also, markets are becoming increasingly global. For example, the US no longer has a dominant world market share in key industries but shares markets more equally with Europe and Japan. As a result of these changes, we expect exchange rate effects to impact the operating profits of companies in globally competitive industries, whether or not they export their products. In fact, the effect of changes in exchange rates on operating profit is often important for companies with no foreign operations or exports but which face significant foreign competition in their domestic market.

This article outlines the concept of operating exposure and the appropriate business and financial responses to manage this exposure and has three parts:

1. Exchange rate environment.

2. Understanding operating exposure.

3. Measuring operating exposure.

EXCHANGE RATE ENVIRONMENT

To understand the impact of exchange rates on operating profit, we need to understand both the long- and short-term behaviour of exchange rates.

The exchange rate environment is characterised by a long-term tendency for changes in the nominal US dollar/foreign currency exchange rate to be approximately equal to the difference between the rates of inflation in the price of traded goods in the US and the foreign country.[1] If the inflation rate in the US is 4 per cent greater than the German inflation rate during the year, the Deutschmark will tend to strengthen approximately 4 per cent against the dollar. This long-term relationship between exchange rates and price levels – usually called purchasing power parity (PPP) – implies that changes in competitiveness between countries, which would otherwise arise because of unequal rates of inflation, tend to be offset by corresponding changes in the exchange rate between the two countries. However, in the short-term of six months to several years, exchange rates are extremely volatile and have a major impact on the relative competitiveness of companies selling into the same market but sourcing from different countries.

This change in relative competitiveness in the short term is the result of changes in the nominal exchange rate which are not offset by the difference in inflation rates in the two countries. If the Deutschmark strengthens 4 per cent against the US dollar and the German inflation rate is 1 per cent, a US exporter into a German market served primarily by German producers would see his dollar price increase by 5 per cent. However, if the inflation rate in the US is 4 per cent, which is 3 per cent higher than the inflation rate in Germany, the operating margin of the US producer will only increase by one percentage point. This example (and other examples developed later in more detail) show that the change in relative competitiveness does not depend on changes in the *nominal* exchange rate – the number of Deutschmarks we obtain for each US dollar – but on changes in the *real* exchange rate, which are changes in the nominal exchange rate from which are subtracted the difference in inflation rates in the two countries.[2] In the case of our US exporter into Germany, the change in the nominal exchange rate is 4 per cent but the change in the real exchange rate (which flows through to operating profit) is only 1 per cent.

Changes in real exchange rates reflect deviations from purchasing power parity, so that the cumulative change in the real exchange rate tends to be smaller than that of the nominal exchange rate over a long period of time. In the short term of six months to several years, both nominal and real exchange rates are volatile, with implications for the profitability of the company. This volatility of real exchange rates in the time-frame of six months to several years gives rise to an exaggerated variability in operating margin.

	Accounting exposure	Operational exposure
Financial items considered	Contractual (debt, payables, receivables)	Non-contractual (revenue, cost, profit)
Inputs to measure exposure	Company's accounting statements	Company's competitive position
Exchange rate which impacts profit	Nominal	Real

Figure 10.1 Currency exposure

UNDERSTANDING OPERATING EXPOSURE

The traditional analysis of currency exposure (Figure 10.1) emphasises contractual items on the company's balance sheet, such as debt, payables and receivables, which are denominated in a foreign currency and whose US dollar value is affected by changes in the nominal exchange rate. The company may enter into forward contracts to cover this contractual exposure. A traditional analysis recognises two types of impacts on the profits of the company, which arise from translation of outstanding contractual items as of year-end and transactions involving contractual items closed out during the year. The information required to define this contractual or accounting exposure is obtained from the accounting statements of the company. Under the US accounts standard FASB 52, physical assets also enter into the calculation of translation gains and losses. However, in general these translation gains or losses will bear little or no relationship to the operating exposure of the company.

In economic terms, these contractual items are properly identified as exposed to changes in exchange rates. Our problem lies in the fact that, in many cases, this contractual exposure captures only a small part of the total impact of exchange rates on the company, which should properly include the effect of changes in real exchange rates on non-contractual items, such as revenues, costs and operating profit. If a company covers its contractual exposure, it may be increasing its total exposure because of the operating exposure component of total exposure which has not been separately identified. The operating exposure and contractual exposure of the company may have different origins, so that in many cases the two exposures will indeed have opposite significance.

Both contractual exposure and operating exposure must be taken into account by the company, so that the two approaches are complementary and not mutually exclusive. Unfortunately, the difference in emphasis in considering each type of exposure tends to introduce a sense of defensiveness in practitioners who have historically only managed contractual exposure. A balanced perspective is not helped by the fact that the effects of changes in nominal exchange rates are separately identified in the income statement

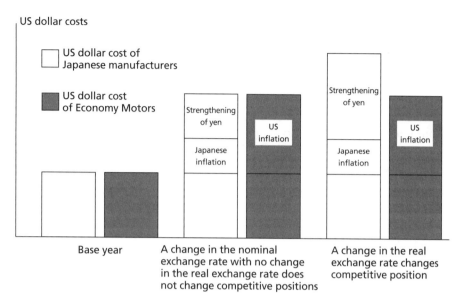

Figure 10.2 The competitive position of Economy Motors

but the effects of changes in real exchange rates on revenues and costs are not similarly recognised.

The effects of changes in exchange rates on operating profits can be separated into margin effects and volume effects. We shall illustrate each kind of effect by a series of examples based on composites of companies studied.

Example 1

Economy Motors is a US manufacturer of small cars, that purchases inputs in the US and sells exclusively in the domestic market and has no foreign debt. From a traditional point of view, Economy Motors has no exposure to changes in exchange rates: in fact, however, the operating profit of Economy Motors is exposed to changes in the real yen/US dollar exchange rate.

Economy Motors competes in the US small car market with Japanese manufacturers which are the market leaders. The Japanese companies take into account their yen costs in setting a dollar price in the US. The competitive position of Economy Motors is shown in Figure 10.2. In some base year when the yen and the dollar are at parity, the dollar costs of Economy Motors are assumed to be equal to the dollar equivalent costs of its Japanese competitors and Economy Motors enjoys a normal operating profit margin.[3] In some later year, if the yen strengthens in line with PPP, to offset a higher inflation rate in the US than in Japan, there is no change in the competitive position of Economy Motors. The increase in the dollar equivalent costs of the Japanese companies from Japanese inflation plus the effect of the yen appreciation is equal to the increase in the costs of Economy Motors from US inflation. In this case, the nominal exchange rate has changed with no change in the real exchange rate and there is no change in the competitive position of Economy Motors. However, if the yen strengthens relative to the dollar by a greater amount than required by PPP, the dollar equivalent costs of the Japanese companies will be greater than the costs of Economy Motors and there will be a strengthening in the competitive position of Economy Motors relative to its Japanese competition.

This example illustrates several characteristics of operating exposure:

- Operating exposure bears no necessary relationship to accounting or contractual exposure.

- Operating exposure is determined by the structure of the markets in which the company and its competitors source inputs and sell products. The measurement of operating exposure must accordingly take into account the nature of the company and its competition. The measurement of accounting exposure has traditionally looked to the company alone.

- Operating exposure is not necessarily associated with the country in which goods are sold or inputs sourced. Economy Motors, for example, is a US manufacturer selling in the US market and has a significant yen exposure.

- Operating exposure is not necessarily associated with the currency in which prices are quoted.

- Operating profit varies with changes in the real exchange rate. The nominal exchange rate may change without any change in the real exchange rates and with no effect on operating profit. Conversely, the nominal exchange rate may remain constant while the real exchange rate is changing and impacting operating profit.

The importance of the details of market structure in determining operating exposure is easily seen in Examples 2 and 3.

Example 2

Specialty Chemicals (Canada) Limited is the Canadian subsidiary of a US company which distributes chemicals produced in the US by its parent. As a distribution subsidiary with few fixed assets, it has little debt. It quotes prices in Canadian dollars. When the Canadian dollar weakens relative to the US dollar, there is a decline in the US dollar value of its Canadian dollar receivables and, from an accounting viewpoint, Specialty Chemicals is exposed because of these receivables.

When we look beyond the accounting treatment, we recognise that when the Canadian dollar weakens, the cost of Specialty Chemicals will increase in Canadian dollars. This raises a number of questions:

- Does Specialty Chemicals have a Canadian dollar operating exposure?
- Should Specialty Chemicals construct a Canadian manufacturing plant to match revenues and costs?
- Should the company issue Canadian dollar debt, so that if the Canadian dollar weakens, there will be a reduced US dollar value of its repayments?

We cannot answer these questions by looking at Specialty Chemicals alone; we have to examine the structure of the marketplace in which it sells its products. We find that Specialty Chemicals and all its competitors import products from the US, with no significant production in Canada. Any increase in Canadian dollar costs will be felt equally by all companies, without any change in their relative competitive position, and will be reflected very quickly in an increased price. The responsiveness in price offsets the cost responsiveness so that there is no operating exposure except in the very short term. Issuing Canadian dollar debt or building a plant in Canada will introduce a new operating exposure where there was no operating exposure previously.

Operating exposure often differs substantially among companies which at first glance appear similar but where the companies sell into markets which have a different structure. For example, Home Products (Canada) Limited, like the previous case, is also a Canadian subsidiary of a US company which purchases product from its US parent. However, the competitors of Home Products (Canada) Limited have manufacturing facilities in Canada and have the major share of the Canadian market. If the Canadian dollar weakens in real terms, the Canadian dollar costs of Home Products will increase without any associated increase in price. There is a cost responsiveness without any offsetting price responsiveness, so that Home Products has a Canadian dollar/US dollar operating exposure.

Changes in the real Canadian dollar/US dollar exchange rate will affect a Canadian exporter into the US with a small share of the American market in opposite ways to Home Products. When the Canadian dollar weakens in real terms, there will be a decline in the profits of Home Products but an increase in the profits of the Canadian exporter.

Home Products can reduce this exposure by building a plant in Canada or entering into a financial hedge which offsets the effect of the change in the real exchange rate. Alternatively, if Home Products increases its share of the Canadian market to become the market leader, it may be able to raise prices to offset some or all of the increased Canadian dollar costs caused by a weakening Canadian dollar and thereby reduce its operating exposure.

Figure 10.3 illustrates the effect of various combinations of cost responsiveness and price responsiveness on the magnitude of the resulting operating exposure.

Example 3

The same analysis can be applied to the more realistic but also more complex case of companies that compete globally rather than in specific

Price responsiveness \ Cost responsiveness	Low	Moderate	High
Low	SMALL		LARGE Home Products
Moderate		SMALL	
High	LARGE Economy Motors		SMALL Specialty Chemicals

Figure 10.3 Operating exposure matrix

national markets. Consider the case of International Instrumentation, a US company that sells precision measurement instruments throughout the world and is the market leader in its industry. Its prices are approximately uniform across countries, as product requirements do not vary from country to country and transhipment costs are small relative to the value of the product.

Demand is insensitive to price, as its products represent a small fraction of the total costs of its customers. Nevertheless, prices and margins are not allowed to be so high that other firms possessing the relevant technologies would be encouraged to enter the market. International Instrumentation will set its prices with a view toward its costs and the costs of actual and potential competitors. If most of its potential competitors are also based in the US, its prices in dollars will be relatively independent of exchange rates. If International Instrumentation is attempting to discourage potential competitors which are located in other countries, it will set lower dollar prices in periods of relative dollar strength.

Example 4

Contrast the above example with Earthworm Tractors, a US-based manufacturer of heavy construction equipment. Its prices vary somewhat across countries because of variations in product specifications and substantial shipping costs, but it nevertheless faces substantial global competition. However, in contrast to International Instrumentation, it faces two major competitors: West Germany and Japan. The cost positions of the three firms are such that exchange rate changes shift cost and price leadership and, as a result, basic world prices, whether measured in US dollars, yen, or Deutschmarks, respond to exchange rate changes.

These examples illustrate some further characteristics of operating exposure:

- Operating exposure is introduced by differences between competitors in sourcing or technology or country of manufacture.

- Companies which are market leaders will tend to have a reduced operating exposure.

- Operating exposure is specific to a particular business. A company is likely to have a variety of operating exposures among its subsidiaries doing business in any given country and the operating exposures of these business units must be evaluated separately. This is in contrast to a standard accounting treatment which aggregates the exposure of the various businesses in a company.

- It will generally be possible to identify two companies which have opposite operating exposures with respect to the same real exchange rate.

So far we have focused on the impact of changes in the real exchange rate on operating margin. In some cases, changes in real exchange rates will have their most important impact on volume.

Example 5

United Kingdom Airways is a UK-based charter airline which sells airline transportation and package tours to the US. When sterling weakens relative to the US dollar in real terms, there were fewer UK travellers to the US. As travel cost is only about 30 per cent of the total cost of a vacation, there is little that a seller of travel services can do to offset the increasing cost of a trip to the US.

Laker Airways had a similar operating exposure. Laker was a UK-based company whose marketing seems to have been primarily directed to UK travellers. With a marketing strategy which was more evenly balanced between travel originating in the US and the UK, changes in the real exchange rate would have had relatively little effect on the demand for total air travel between the two countries. Fewer British tourists would visit the US when the US is relatively expensive from a British perspective but this would be offset by more US travellers to Britain. Laker transported an increasing number of British tourists until 1980. This was to a large extent the result of a sterling strengthening beyond its parity with the dollar, with the implication that eventually sterling would again weaken to regain parity. However, in 1980, Laker financed new aircraft purchases in US dollars, in effect doubling its exposure to the subsequent weakness in the pound.

In summary, several factors contribute to the nature and severity of the company's competitive exposure. These include the degree of cross-border market integration, the extent of global competition, the extent to which the cost structure of the industry is variable versus fixed, and the extent to

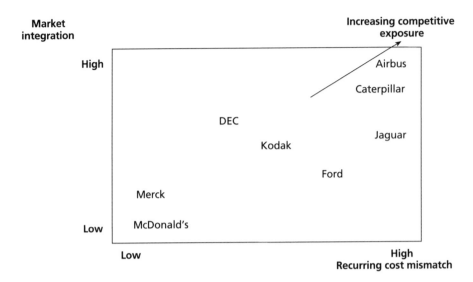

Figure 10.4 Determinants of competitive exposure

which the industry is characterised by lead competitors with differing costs. Figure 10.4 illustrates the competitive exposure of various companies combining the degree of currency mismatch in costs and the relative importance of variable versus fixed costs.

Turning to actual examples, Airbus is a company with an extreme competitive exposure. It sells its product in international markets in direct competition with Boeing and McDonnell Douglas, although almost all its costs are in European currencies. The market is almost completely integrated and the variable cost component of aircraft manufacturing is substantial. Caterpillar is another company that has a similar high degree of competitive exposure, because the market for its products is highly integrated and it faces in most of those markets a key competitor, Komatsu, which has a very different cost structure.

At the other extreme lie some pharmaceutical companies such as Merck. Here, market integration across national boundaries is low as national regulation serves as an effective barrier to transhipment. Also, the variable cost component of producing products is low, and substantial advertising and distribution costs are incurred in the country of sale. Another company with relatively low competitive exposure is McDonald's, which receives franchise fees as a percentage of sales from its operations in various countries. These fees are effectively denominated in local currency as relatively few people cross the Atlantic to arbitrage the 'Big Mac' and there is little cross-border integration of markets and most variable costs are incurred in the country of sale.

Jaguar is an example of a company with a moderately high competitive exposure, as it has a variable cost mismatch as great as that of Airbus or Caterpillar, but a somewhat lesser degree of market integration between

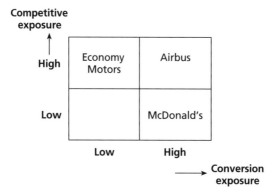

Figure 10.5 Components of operational exposure

Europe and the US because of the greater differentiation of its product and its ability to control distribution channels. Nevertheless, even though Jaguar is a unique product, its pricing in the US cannot differ substantially from the pricing of other luxury cars. Companies such as Kodak and DEC also fit into this middle category.

Companies such as Merck and McDonald's, which have low levels of competitive exposure, nevertheless have substantial operating exposure to exchange rate changes because of the conversion effect. Their US dollar profitability from foreign operations will change in time with real exchange rates. Figure 10.5 shows companies with various combinations of competitive and conversion exposures.

MEASURING OPERATING EXPOSURE

Contractual or accounting exposure is readily identified with any desired degree of precision from accounting statements. However, operating exposure cannot be directly estimated from accounting records, and will not have the precision of an estimate of contractual exposure. On the other hand, the operating exposure of a company may be far greater than its contractual exposure.

We have been able to estimate operating exposure in two ways, a bottom-up estimate, which relies on a detailed understanding of the competitive position of the various businesses of the company and a top-down estimate, which is derived from an analysis of the historical profitability of the company.

Bottom-up Estimates

A bottom-up measurement of operating exposure requires an understanding of:

- the structure of the markets in which the company and its competitors source inputs and sell their products; and

- the degree of flexibility of the company and its competitors in changing markets, product mix, sourcing and technology.

We have been successful in obtaining this information in a structured dialogue with operating management. Most managers have the information to answer these questions but lack the analytical framework to use this information, and usually the treasury group will have the responsibility of coordinating the process of measuring operating exposure. For many companies this represents a closer involvement of the treasury group with operations and an enlarged treasury responsibility. This involvement of the treasury function in operating considerations reflects the fact that the impact of exchange rates on the profitability of the company is in some sense a financial effect, to a large extent outside the business control of the company, and yet it corresponds to a very important aspect of the external competitive environment.

This exposure audit with operating management will typically include the following types of questions:

- Who are actual and potential major competitors in various markets?

- Who are low cost producers?

- Who are price leaders?

- What has happened in the past to profit margins when real exchange rates have become overvalued and undervalued?

- What is the flexibility of the company to shift production to countries with undervalued currencies?

These questions are usually well received by operating management, because an understanding of the operating exposure of a company can be used directly to improve operating decisions and it is critical to measure management performance after taking into account exchange rate effects. In Example 1, Economy Motors is likely to be more successful in increasing market share during a period of weakness in the dollar, when its Japanese competitors are seeing decreasing yen equivalent prices, if management has previously anticipated this set of circumstances in contingency planning. There is also less conflict in the management of operating exposure between the welfare of a partly owned foreign subsidiary and its parent whereas these conflicts are often present in the management of contractual exposure.

Top-down Estimates

The bottom-up process of dialogue with operating management is likely to be time-consuming and costly. We have also developed top-down analytical techniques to estimate operating exposure at the company level or at the level of individual business units. This analysis can be performed quickly.

We have found that it is an effective method of communicating the operating exposure of the company to senior management, in particular when the exposure of the company arises from import competition in the domestic market.

The top-down estimate is derived from an analytical comparison of the historical profitability of the company with the changes in profitability expected on the basis of changes in real exchange rates assuming that the competitive position of the company is constant during the period of the comparison and that the company has not undergone major structural changes at the level of aggregation under review.

The effect of changes in real exchange rates on the profitability of the company will be determined by the volatility in exchange rates and the fraction of revenues exposed. The top-down analysis identifies both the principal exchange rates to which the company is exposed and the fraction of revenues exposed.

If the exporter has some market power in the overseas marketplace, the exposure will be limited to some fraction of his total revenue and there will be less volatility in mark-up and operating profit. Similarly, the exposure of Economy Motors (Example 1) is limited to some fraction of its revenues which corresponds to the power of Japanese importers in the US marketplace. However, in general, the volatility in earnings may be a cause of financial distress to the company. In an environment where there is not a good understanding of the exchange rate cause of this volatility, management decisions will often not take advantage of the underlying business opportunity.

The top-down estimates of operating exposure have identified many companies where a large part of the variability in the profits of the company results from exposure to real exchange rate effects, in some cases with only a small fraction of the revenues exposed. In the absence of an analytical framework to demonstrate these operating exposure effects, there is a tendency for them not to be fully recognised by management, whose culture in many cases will want to attribute the success of the company to the performance of its operating management.

NOTES

1. The exact relation is that $\dot{S}_{12} = (\dot{P}_1 - \dot{P}_2)/(1 + \dot{P}_2)$. where $\dot{S}_{12}$ is the fractional change in the spot exchange rate (currency 1/currency 2) and $\dot{P}_1$ and $\dot{P}_2$ are the annual inflation rates in country 1 and country 2.
2. More exactly, the fractional change in the real exchange rate is $\dot{S}_{12} - [(\dot{P}_1 - \dot{P}_2) /(1 + \dot{P}_2)]$.
3. The argument can be extended to the case when the US dollar costs of Economy Motors in the base year bear their normal relationship (but are not necessarily equal) to the US dollar equivalent costs of its Japanese competitors.

'Operating Exposure', by D. R. Lessard and J. B. Lightstone, reproduced with permission from *Management of Currency Risk*, edited by B. Antl. Copyright 1989 Euromoney Books, tel 0171 779 8542, fax 0171 779 8541, e-mail embks@dial,pipex.com.

11

Modules for Standardizing
the Process

A. Steyn and A. Boessenkool

Every corporate treasurer appreciates the difficulty of trying to convey unfamiliar concepts about instrument pricing and portfolio management to decision-makers more at ease with engineering or economic thinking. This is because treasury risk management draws from the knowledge base of a variety of disciplines – economics, mathematics, statistics and computer science. Treasury risk management is technically complex, but the board nevertheless needs to take an active interest in the subject, given its strategic significance for the business[1].

The treasurer therefore has to find a way to communicate the necessary information to the board. This can be achieved by adopting a process approach to treasury risk management. This not only enhances the understanding of the entire corporate treasury function, it also creates the opportunity for part or piecemeal implementation rather than an all-or-nothing scheme. In this process approach, it is important that strict design criteria, visualization, pre-determined flexibility and a focus on intuitive risk/return set-off are meticulously observed.

Corporate treasury risk management can be divided into four distinct modules, enabling treasury managers to choose the level of complexity that they believe they can expose their corporate board to, and to provide a path for progression as its understanding develops.

It should be recognized that the maturity of different corporations in market risk management varies. Rather than suggesting sophisticated management techniques that might alienate a board regularly confronted with negative publicity about spectacular business failures caused by mismanagement of treasury risks, a logical, positive, educational and modularized developmental approach would be more constructive in achieving the objective of managing market risk. In this article simple quantitative techniques are used to illustrate that treasury risk management concepts can be translated into practically usable information for decision-making.

The process approach will be discussed in separate modules that can be adopted sequentially as each module is mastered and implemented; the process may be terminated after any module. Adoption of the modules will depend on the skills, technology and other resources available at a particular

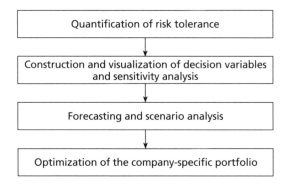

Figure 11.1 Progression of the market risk management process*
  (*Source*: Nampak Management Services)
* The process may be implemented module-by-module.

corporate treasury. The process stages as embodied in the distinct modules can be correlated almost directly with the stages of development of risk analysis as defined by Vlahos[2] – naïve decision-making, educated guesses (sensitivity analysis), calculated risk-taking (scenario analysis) and quantitative decision analysis (see Figure 11.1).

MODULE 1 – QUANTIFYING RISK TOLERANCE

The risk tolerance of a corporation must be clearly defined in qualitative and quantitative format at board level. This step is important for a number of reasons, notably that board members are not treasury risk management specialists but general management practitioners with an intuitive grasp of risk/return set-offs. There is no excuse, however, for accommodating the common belief that the most prudent approach to market risk is not to involve the corporation in treasury risk management at all.

The board needs to be made aware that, as a consequence of financial market risks, the corporation has exposures with regard to its future earnings. Also, treasury can do its own cause much good by stating that it intends to manage existing risks to make the company more competitive in the commercial marketplace, as opposed to creating new risks of its own.

To conduct market risk management requires certain resources, among which risk capital is the most important, and these resources must be determined scientifically and the allocation agreed formally with the board. No treasurer can make this decision on his own and neither would an ad hoc allocation of risk capital on a case-by-case basis be practically workable.

The first step in quantifying risk appetite (Figure 11.2) is to identify the types of risk that the company is exposed to. These will typically be liquidity risk (the inability to meet commitments as they come due or having to

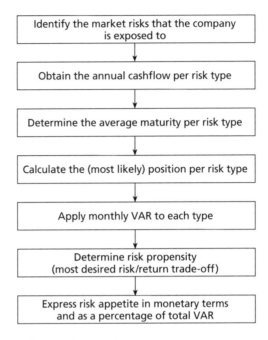

Figure 11.2 Quantifying risk appetite (*Source*: Nampak Management Services)

pay excessively to obtain the required cash at short notice); interest rate risk (earnings negatively affected by an adverse move in market interest rates); foreign exchange risk (earnings or asset values negatively affected by a movement in exchange rates detrimental to the home currency); and commodity price risk (earnings negatively affected by a rise in the cost of manufacturing raw materials).

Next, extract from accounting records the value of annual cashflow related to each of the risks identified. Then determine the average maturity of positions resulting from these cashflows – a more demanding task, especially in a corporation where focus on market risk management has been inadequate. In the crudest of circumstances, an 80/20 rule may need to be applied where the objective should be to identify those elements in each of the exposure groups where the major cashflows occur and researching the most likely life-span of such resulting exposures (for example, "We mostly finance our requirements using three-month debt instruments", or "We normally buy raw materials sourced in US dollars on fixed six-month price agreements").

The risk types are analyzed separately, mainly because of differing volatilities and hence costs of hedging in the different markets – they have different risk/return characteristics. Separate analysis allows risk capital to be allocated accordingly to manage risk in different markets. Dividing the annual cashflow of a particular risk type by the likely maturity will deliver the likely position in that risk type at any moment.

Knowing what the likely position in each of the risk types is and what the major constituents of those positions are (for example, three-month banker's acceptances in interest rate risk or LME aluminium in commodity price risk) enables you to apply value at risk (VAR) methodology. Because of the customary reporting frequency, monthly VAR will mostly be applied in the corporate environment.

Depending on how familiar the corporate treasurer is with mathematical statistics, he or she can either calculate the measures of location and distribution of major constituents of the portfolio on the basis of sufficient month-end data or use public-domain data such as JP Morgan's RiskMetrics[3]. Covariance matrices will also need to be drawn up to view the market exposures in portfolio context.

The value that is at risk whether the exposures are managed or not may now be defined quantitatively within a chosen predetermined confidence interval. A 90% confidence interval is used in our examples because that is widely seen as being prudent without being extreme and because it allows comparison with the RiskMetrics database, which uses the same interval. The results of the exercise to identify and quantify the company's market risk exposures are summarized in Table 11.1. This table is self-explanatory, but for a detailed discussion the reader is referred to other research by the authors[4].

Given the proven value at risk, it must now be established what monetary value (that is, risk capital) the board is prepared to allocate to management of the stated risks. The treasurer should convert this figure, which will probably be determined subjectively, into a percentage of the known VAR to arrive at a risk appetite for the corporation regarding each type of risk (for example, 50% currency mismatches may be incurred, 30% commodity hedging mismatches may be incurred, and so on).

Before this recommendation will be accepted, the treasurer will need to calculate the maximum hedging cost that could be saved per year by managing the risks within the suggested risk appetite limits. This will appeal to the average corporate board member's intuitive grasp for risk/return trade-off. It may also lead to a reassessment of the capital that the board is prepared to allocate to managing financial market risk. The result of this step will be a set of policy limits based on risk capital allocated as determined by comparing VAR against the maximum possible saving in hedging cost (Table 11.2).

Quantifying the board's risk appetite is important because the result will determine whether the treasury should be established as a cost centre or a profit centre (or a service centre with elements of both) – with all the implications for resource requirements such as capital, staffing and systems and for risk management policy and procedures. Moreover, the VAR limits determined in this exercise per risk type, per instrument, per country, per counterpart and so on dictate the wide policy parameters that will be used as constraints in a mathematical programming model under which an optimal portfolio is to be tailored for the corporation. To ensure the confidence of

Table 11.1 Quantitative description of unmanaged monthly VAR

	Historical 1-month volatility	Average exposure at any time	Monthly VAR (90% confidence interval)	Total monthly VAR per risk category*	Cost of 100% hedge per year	Total cost in home currency*	Ratio of monthly VAR (1:) to cost
Interest rate risk				**R583,234**		**R10,950,000**	**18.77**
Rand call loans	5.26%	R200,000,000	R216,975		R2,000,000		
Rand 3-month loans	3.40%	R400,000,000	R280,500		R4,000,000		
US dollar 3-month loans	2.10%	$110,000,000	$19,058		$1,100,000		
Foreign exchange risk				**R14,396,400**		**R102,600,000**	**7.13**
US dollar	1.42%	$100,000,000	$1,420,000		R45,000,000		
Sterling	1.39%	£80,000,000	£1,112,000		R57,600,000		
Commodity price risk				**R18,227,250**		**R22,050,000**	**1.21**
Aluminium	5.92%	$20,000,000	$1,184,000		$1,400,000		
Paper pulp	5.10%	$35,000,000	$1,785,000		$2,450,000		
HDPE	7.21%	$15,000,000	$1,081,500		$1,050,000		
				Total: R33,206,884		**Total: R135,600,000**	**4.08**

US dollar/rand spot: 4.5
Sterling/rand spot: 7.2
* Monthly VAR figures converted to the home currency (South African rand) at spot rates in order to prevent double counting.
Source: Nampak Management Services

Table 11.2 Board policy decision on the allocation of risk capital

Risk category	Total exposure (home currency)	Total monthly VAR	Risk capital allocated	Minimum per cent hedge	Maximum unhedged exposure	Cost of full hedging	Maximum hedging cost recovery
Interest rate risk	R1,095,000,000	R583,234	R583,234	0%	R1,095,000,000	R10,950,000	R10,950,000
Foreign exchange risk	R1,026,000,000	R14,396,400	R5,468,638	62.0%	R389,737,880	R102,600,000	R38,973,788
Commodity price risk	R315,000,000	R18,227,250	R1,175,012	93.6%	R20,306,340	R22,050,000	R1,421,444
		Total: **R7,226,883**					Total: **R51,345,232**

Note: Capital allocated to result in identical risk/return characteristics for all categories of risk. Other considerations, such as the quantum of risk management costs that can be recovered, may (within reason) be applied in practice.
Source: Nampak Management Services

the board in treasury risk management, the actual results must be continuously monitored against the anticipated VAR limits to prevent disproportionate deviations from the expected.

MODULE 2 – CONSTRUCTION AND VISUALIZATION OF DECISION VARIABLES

At this point, risk managers might feel that, with market risk sufficiently defined, they may now launch into forecasting and scenario analysis as the basis for formulating market strategies. An essential link in the process, however, still needs to be forged. For the sake of comparability, the risk of individual components of the portfolio of risk types must be described in a standardized way. By defining risk at the level of individual instruments the concept becomes easier to visualize and to communicate by graphic means to non-specialists.

At the most basic level, a financial market portfolio consists of a collection of cashflow events, each of which may be described by a limited set of quantitative variables, such as its quantity (nominal value), time of occurrence and variability (that is, uncertainty of eventual outcome). This commonality offers a good opportunity for generalization on the level of individual instruments – that is, they may be seen as a collection of related cashflows. The ability to represent each instrument as a geometric vector in space enables risk behaviour to be illustrated graphically; and, as a set of related vectors, the portfolio can be represented graphically to show the relative risk behaviour of a set of instruments.

In describing the variables of an individual instrument, the first derivative of the series (the change of value from period to period) is of particular concern in risk management. For this purpose measures of location and of dispersion must be defined. Some commentators prefer to use the mean of a historic distribution as a measure of location, assuming a normal distribution of historic changes in value.

As for finding a measure of dispersion, a number of specialists have concluded that implied volatility performs no better than historic volatility as an estimator of future volatility. It has therefore been argued that standard deviation can be used to estimate future volatility as long as it is remembered that historical data is not necessarily serially uncorrelated. This approach, however, applies only in specific circumstances – for example, to a large portfolio (20 to 30 elements) of highly tradable securities, provided it is not rich in options. This seems an unacceptable limitation, given that we are trying to standardize the risk management process.

We propose a simpler approach to describing individual instruments, based on a deterministic approach free of the constraints of having to assume normality in the limit. Our method may be easier to apply and yet captures the essence of the risk. Basically, the mode rather than the mean of historic changes in value may be used as a measure of location. The mode is that value in a data set that is most frequently observed as opposed to the mean or average, which may indeed never coincide with the value of any one actual observation in the data set.

The choice of the mode is also important in terms of the generation of forecasts, in that forecasters will typically project the value that they expect most likely to occur (the mode), rather than forecasting the average of the distribution. The mode of a data set is independent of the actual distribution of the population and, moreover, its value is not influenced by outliers to the extent that the mean of a sample is.

Also, in practice, decisions are based on the value of financial instruments at a given time at an actually observed market price/rate rather than on the value of some historic average. With this approach, event risk is more visible to the treasurer and is therefore provided for more specifically in terms of sensitivity analysis – as discussed later in this module. Mode is also recognized as a much more robust measure of location[5].

In determining a measure of dispersion, a sufficient sample of historic data of the correct frequency (that is, matching the forecasting or reporting horizon) might be used to create a histogram of change in value from one period to the next. This is a direct way of graphic visualization of the characteristics of the distribution of a variable and therefore aids understanding of the risk behaviour of a financial instrument.

The quality of the forecast of the future distribution may then be improved (that is, the histogram smoothed) by using a resampling technique such as Bootstrapping or Monte Carlo simulation[6]. The required confidence interval can be calculated as the symmetric area of desired proportion (that is, probability), a concept illustrated in Figure 11.3.

To explain this approach in simple terms, a numeric example will be used. Let us assume that the spot US dollar/rand exchange rate is one of the exposures in a portfolio of market risks. Given that we are interested in describing the characteristics of the monthly variability of this portfolio constituent, the data series we start off with is the month-end exchange rate over the past 60 months (Figure 11.4). However, for the purposes of managing financial market risk, what we are really interested in is the month-on-month percentage change in the value of the series (Figure 11.5).

The data in this chart can, however, be grouped in percentage change bins to construct a histogram (Figure 11.6). This histogram may be smoothed by using a resampling technique, but for the purposes of ease of illustration we will use the histogram as is. Through its data points we then fit a least-squares polynomial that gives the best fit. We employ this technique because of its simplicity in allowing us to describe accurately the distribution function as a single formula that may be used to analyze the risk behaviour of the data series. The equation of this polynomial is:

$$y = 3.61799 + 0.430734x - 0.297542x^2 - 0.0788773x^3 - 0.00498662x^4$$

The area under the curve represents the probability of a particular percentage change being observed as the actual outcome at a given point in

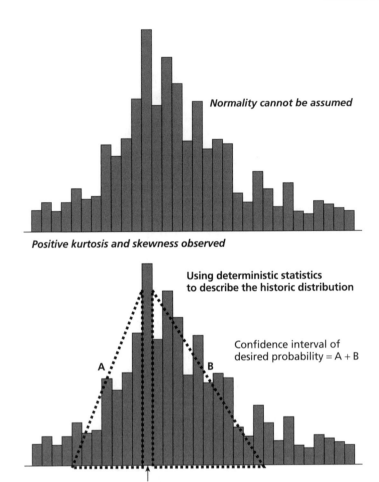

Figure 11.3 Typical distribution of historical price changes of a financial instrument (*Source*: Nampak Management Services)

time. The total area under the curve between the limits of −8.5% and 2.5% represents all the possible outcomes – that is, a 100% probability. To calculate the area, it is necessary to determine the integral of the polynomial. The function describing this integral is as follows:

$$\int(y) = 3.61799x + 0.215367x^2 - 0.00991807x^3 - 0.019793x^4 - 0.000997324x^5$$

This function is plotted in Figure 11.7. It is clearly a monotone-increasing function, which confirms that it describes the cumulative probability of the distribution of the series. The range of the function between −8.5% and 2.5% is 20.9413. The offset of the function at −8.5% is −12.9676 – that is, the required shift upwards for the curve to cross the x-axis at −8.5%. Therefore,

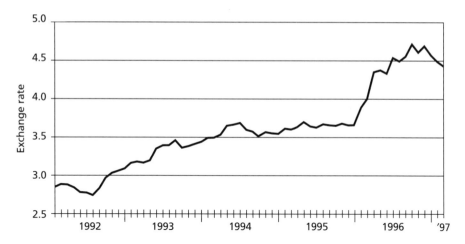

Figure 11.4 Historic month-end US$/R exchange rate (*Source*: Nampak Management Services)

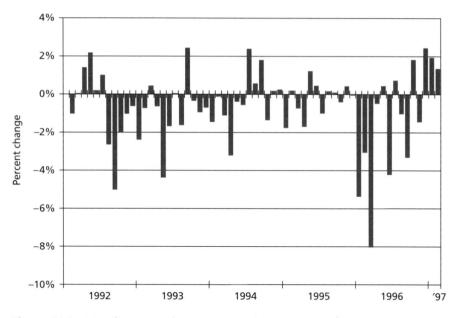

Figure 11.5 Month-on-month percentage change in R/US$ value (*Source*: Nampak Management Services)

the value of any percentile of the probability distribution can now be calculated where:

$$\int(y) - \text{Percentile}_i \text{ (Range)} - \text{Offset} = 0 \qquad 11.1$$

Solving for x in equation 11.1 at the fifth and 95th percentile allows one to describe the dispersion of a 90% confidence interval. This confidence

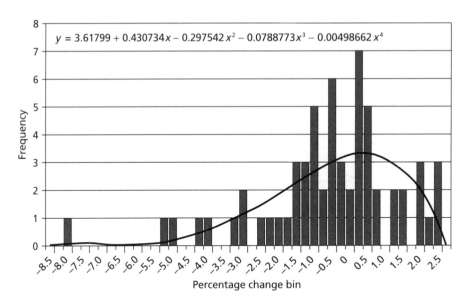

Figure 11.6 Distribution of historic m/o/m change in US$/R rate (*Source*: Nampak Management Services)

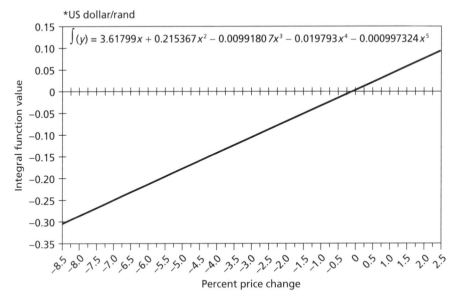

Figure 11.7 Function of integral of m/o/m price change distribution*
(*Source*: Nampak Management Services)

interval will have a lower boundary of −7.514% and an upper boundary of 1.988%.

The next step in describing the characteristics of the probability distribution in this way – the measure of location – still needs to be taken.

Computationally it can be determined that the mode of the distribution (0.18%) falls on the 61.23th percentile. As a matter of interest, the median of the distribution is on -0.731% and the average on -0.7%. It is therefore clear that these other (mean and median) measures of location have been affected more by the left-handed skewness (value -1.099242) of the historic distribution than the mode has.

The process can be used as a standard way to define the characteristics of the historic distribution of any market series – which is good progress towards our goal of standardization of market risk management. The historic distribution of the data series has now been described completely, and this description can be used to visualize risk and to qualify forecasts – as will be demonstrated.

Having described how to determine the location (nominal value) and dispersion (uncertainty) of a set of cashflows, the last step to a complete description of the variables of any instrument is to accommodate the time of occurrence of individual cashflows in a standardized manner. This can be achieved by describing the present value at time $t = 0$ of a financial instrument as the sum of a Maclaurin series[7] of discrete cashflow events (C_m) related to the mode expectation of the price/rate of the instrument at a point in future and applying discount rates (r_m) on a market forward curve. This function would take the form

$$\sum_{t=0}^{m} f \frac{(t)(0)}{t!} C^t = C_0 + C_1\left(\frac{1}{1 + (r_1 \times n/365)}\right) + C_2\left(\frac{1}{1 + (r_2 \times n/365)}\right)^2$$
$$+ \ldots + C_m\left(\frac{1}{1 + (r_m \times n/365)}\right)^m$$

where n = number of days from the previous cashflow, and the number of days per year depends on the currency of the instrument.

of which the well-known compound interest formula is a special case that uses a single fixed interest rate instead of rates on a forward curve.

Armed with this information about the distribution and current value of individual instruments, we can proceed to describe these instruments as geometric vectors, using an adaptation of the methodology suggested by Zerolis[8]. This is done to visualize the interrelationships between financial instruments in the context of a portfolio. This methodology exploits the fact that if, say, three currencies are put at the vertices of a triangle with the length of each side being scaled equivalent to the volatility of that currency cross, then the correlation between the price changes of any two of these currencies as measured in the third is described as the cosine of the angle at the opposite end. Figure 11.8 depicts this concept for US dollars, sterling and the rand.

For the purposes of the deterministic description of price/rate change distributions discussed earlier, different triangles should be constructed for upside (profit) risk and downside (loss) risk. This methodology would

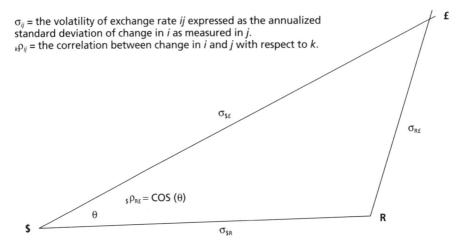

σ_{ij} = the volatility of exchange rate ij expressed as the annualized standard deviation of change in i as measured in j.
$_k\rho_{ij}$ = the correlation between change in i and j with respect to k.

Figure 11.8 Visualization of risk and return in portfolio context (*Source*: Nampak Management Services)

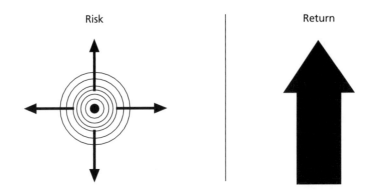

Risk   Return

Risk increases in all directions, return in only one

Figure 11.9 Geometric visualization of risk and return (*Source*: Nampak Management Services)

typically be applied to express the return or cost of various other instruments in terms of the base currency for that risk type.

The idea can be expanded for a portfolio of securities, since the return of a portfolio is a linear function of the returns on its constituent elements. The magnitude of volatility is not changed by the direction of the constituent vectors, and neither are the cross-relationships. The object may therefore always be orientated so that the return of any element is directed as a linear function of one of the primary directions – say, the Z-axis given the ease of visual inspection permitted in identifying positive and negative returns in this arrangement (Figure 11.9). With this orientation, the magnitude of returns can be directly compared, whereas the risk associated with that return can be visualized as the distance of the vector from the origin.

The visualization of risk and return (or cost, depending on the objective of the portfolio) has now been achieved at the same time as the standardization of the description of the variables of individual instruments and portfolios of instruments, and risk is expressed in a format that can be brought directly in line with VAR and the policy limits defined in module 1.

The next step would be to apply sensitivity or shock analysis and what-ifs to the portfolio in the interests of investigating the effect of event risk (market crashes and similar abnormal occurrences) on the value of instruments and the portfolio as a whole. Given that the suggested method of visualization takes covariance into consideration, skewing the 90% confidence interval value of any element to provide for the effect of a subjectively perceived chaotic event will bring the effect on the relative return of other elements of the portfolio into consideration. In this sense the methodology will provide a robust way to illustrate the real dangers in the portfolio and a methodology for evaluating alternative hedge strategies.

This concludes the second module – at which point an exit is again offered for the treasury that is still developing. A practical ability to manage portfolio structuring and event risk and to implement transaction-based hedging is nevertheless provided. Decision variables have now been stated in a standardized format that simplifies their use in a mathematical optimization model for the more advanced treasury. Before we describe that action in the last module, we need to first discuss the next step in the refinement of the risk management process: that of going beyond catastrophe management to controlled scenario analysis, which makes the taking of calculated risks possible.

MODULE 3 – FORECASTING AND SCENARIO ANALYSIS

In addition to the crude approach of worst-case anticipation, the corporate treasury should also consider the effect of a number of more likely scenarios on the performance of the portfolio of exposures that it manages. These scenarios would be designed to show the possible outcomes of the future prices/rates of elements in the portfolio under more normal circumstances, rather than the extreme effect of event risk considered in the previous module.

The objective of the process is to forecast the value of the mode of the distribution of selected key instruments at selected points in the future. This exercise will, of course, be undertaken in an effort to anticipate market movements and, as a consequence, to save on hedging costs.

Casual observation would lead one to believe that forecasters normally forecast mode (the most likely outcome) rather than the average outcome of market prices/rates. In line with the standardized method of describing the variables of elements of the portfolio, we are interested in the change in the value of the mode of the distribution of the element – that is, the return of the element from time t_0 to a series of selected points t_m in future. On the basis of the reasoning discussed earlier, historic volatility will continue to be applied in a discrete distribution to describe future volatility, with that volatility distinguished as favourable and unfavourable. Certainly, a number of forecasting techniques may be considered, but, given the unique stability of the chosen measure of location – the mode – we believe this method to be particularly suitable. We will now discuss that proposal in detail.

Because of the relative stability of the mode of the month-on-month price change (return) of any market series, a good fit may be achieved by fitting a polynomial curve through the series of historic percentage (price or rate) changes over time using a least-squares-fit approach. Again, this method is used to describe the historic price movement of financial market variables in a way that allows easy but accurate graphical analysis.

As a refinement of the technique, the first derivative (that is, the function differentiated once) of this series can then be calculated to determine the turning points and inflection points of this curve, and the market cycle divided into four parts as a consequence of this calculation (first up, second up, first down and second down). Sectional correlations between the historic values for key series and secondary series must then be calculated to make provision for the possible change in relative behaviour in different segments of the market cycle. Forecasting techniques ranging from statistical methods to econometric models to Delphi may then be employed to forecast the mode value of the selected key series at pre-determined intervals in the future. These forecasts should be displayed visually.

Next, the forecast values in at least three scenarios should then be calculated for the key series – a worst (fifth or 95th percentile, depending on the direction of an unfavourable price move), expected (mode) and best (again fifth or 95th percentile value). The calculated correlations (applicable to the particular phase, if so refined) should then be applied to the other elements in the portfolio to forecast their relative mode values. The calculated returns relative to key elements can now be input into the standardized method of describing and visualizing decision variables as discussed in module 2, and the VAR visualized again with a view to identifying opportunities and threats and planning risk management activity accordingly.

This process is illustrated by making use of a numerical example, again involving the US dollar/rand exchange rate. Figure 11.10 illustrates the result of fitting the first polynomial curve to the month-on-month percentage change in US dollar/rand, which is for this purpose regarded as a key series. For the sake of simplicity, we then calculate the correlation between the price change series for US dollar/rand and sterling/rand (a secondary series) without executing the refinement. This correlation is found to be 93.5% with a *beta* of 0.76.

We proceed to forecasting the percentage change value for the US dollar/ rand series for three months using any forecasting method. These values

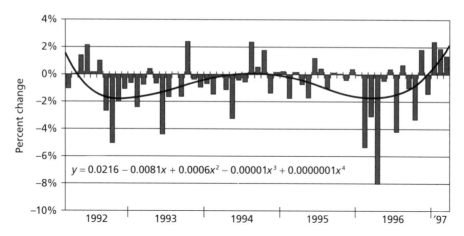

Figure 11.10 Polynomial function fitted to the series of m/o/m percentage change in value of R/US$ (*Source*: Nampak Managment Services)

Table 11.3 Forecasting the future distribution of a dependent series

	Month 1	Month 2	Month 3
US dollar/rand forecast mode	1.50%	1.75%	2.00%
Sterling/rand mode by correlation	1.14%	1.33%	1.52%
Sterling/rand worst case (5th percentile)	−6.16%	−5.97%	−5.78%
Sterling/rand best case (95th percentile)	3.17%	3.36%	3.55%

Independent series (key series): month-on-month price-change in US$/R
Dependent series (secondary series): month-on-month price-change in £/R
Source: Nampak Management Services

may, for argument's sake, be as summarized in Table 11.3, to which the calculated *beta* is then applied to the sterling/rand series in order to calculate the mode values for that series. Finally, the fifth and 95th percentile volatility calculated for the sterling/rand price-change series (*not shown*) will then be applied to the calculated mode of that series to determine respectively the worst- and best-case price-change percentage values.

At this stage calculated risk-taking becomes possible. However, the risk management process must remain subject to quality control – forecasts are bound to be wrong to a greater or lesser extent. Continued control and rebalancing of the portfolio will be required to the extent that contingency planning based on the forecast scenarios may not provide the required resistance to adverse moves or enable favourable movements in market rates to be exploited. For this purpose, control charts such as those routinely used in the manufacturing process[9] (Figure 11.11) can be used successfully to monitor continuously the suitability of a forecast scenario and its consequences for portfolio performance.

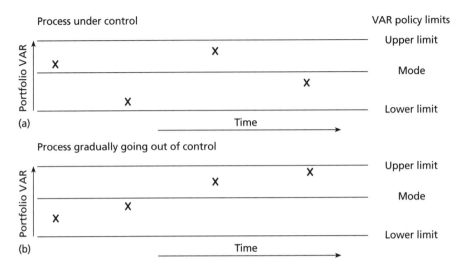

Figure 11.11 Use of control charts to monitor market risk continuously against VAR limits (*Source*: Nampak Management Services)

An added benefit of this control measure is that the change in portfolio performance may be brought in relation to VAR limits and the decision made visible and simple as to whether the process is in control or gradually getting out of control.

For all the virtues of the process thus far, the sophisticated treasurer is bound to ask whether the strict design criteria applied so far and the standardization of the description of the variables of the portfolio elements offer benefits beyond that gained from visualization and calculated risk-taking. Indeed, the ultimate usefulness of this approach lies in the ability to construct a mathematically optimal portfolio for each individual corporation to provide a precise match for the risk appetite and market views formulated by the decision-makers of that business. However, treasurers not comfortable with the mathematics of optimization may well choose to remain with the tools provided up to this point only.

MODULE 4 – OPTIMIZING THE TAILORED PORTFOLIO

At this stage, risk-tolerance limits have been determined based on VAR and expressed both as maximum percentage mismatches allowed and as maximum monetary loss per risk type that may be incurred. The decision variables have also been described as vectors in standardized format. By adding further constraints, the treasurer should be able to employ linear programming to arrive at what will, in terms of market expectations and operational limitations, be the optimal portfolio in the executable area that can be constructed for the company.

Because the price behaviours of financial market instruments have now been described as linear vectors, with a complex set of interrelationships, linear programming is chosen as the simplest and most efficient way of compiling these instruments into a customized portfolio. The following should be added to obtain a comprehensive set of constraints: minimum and maximum (percentage or value) exposures to classes of instruments, countries and counterparts (credit risk) as static constraints; and maximum and minimum exposure to given maturities, currencies and commodities as dynamic constraints determined on the basis of market expectations. Pre-determined hedges decided on as a result of visual inspection (to prevent catastrophe) in the second module should also be included. Having completed the set, linear programming that can minimize with respect to cost or maximize with respect to return can now be set up in standard format, as shown below:

Maximize with $$z = c_1x_1 + c_1x_2 + ... + c_nx_n$$

$$a_{11}x_1 + a_{12}x_2 + ... a_{1n}x_n = b_1$$
$$\vdots$$
$$a_{m1}x_1 + ... + a_{mn}x_n = b_m$$

and

$$x_1 \geq 0, ..., x_n \geq 0$$

The result of this optimization will be an unambiguous shopping list that can be executed by dealing staff in a controlled manner. The benefits of this final step in the process can clearly be seen in the ability to consider a multitude of different factors in a scientific way. The methodology does not prescribe a best portfolio that every corporation should strive to attain (efficiency frontier), but a unique optimal portfolio for the specific corporation, given its objective and the limitations of its own risk appetite and market views.

CONCLUSION

Managing market risk is a repetitive process that needs to be executed on a regular basis and subjected to continuous quality control. In any circumstances the process will remain computationally intensive. This requirement can be alleviated by the availability of data in the public domain, such as the JP Morgan RiskMetrics database, credit ratings and electronic market information that can be imported directly into an executable version of the process.

To automate the process as much as possible, these data sources should be linked to the corporation's risk management system – indeed, it is in this context that the process approach comes into its own. The process can clearly be automated using the suggested methodology, but, more than that, it is very visually driven and expresses all risks in a known quantity (the monetary value in home currency). These characteristics will make the process highly accessible to the board of an average corporate.

Finally, the modular design deserves special mention. Its purpose is to enforce a certain discipline in the risk management process and, beyond that, to ensure that the risk management approach adopted by each treasury is compatible with the intended function of that operation and the grasp of the treasury staff of the intricacies of the techniques applied.

Objections to the standardization of market risk management in recent research history tend to centre on the limiting assumptions made (such as normality in price change distribution) that compromise the general applicability of a particular approach. This attempt at standardizing market risk management suffers from none of these artificial constraints and as such may be applied to any individual instrument or portfolio of instruments with equal validity.

NOTES

1. M Van der Nat, "Treasury Policies in the Supervisory Board", Global Treasury Handbook, *Treasury Management International*, March 1997.
2. K Vlahos, "Taking the risk out of uncertainty", *Mastering Management (Business Day)*, vol 5, 1996.
3. TM Guldiman, "RiskMetrics – Technical Document", Morgan Guaranty Trust Company, New York, 1994.
4. A Steyn & AL Boessenkool, "VAR in the Corporate Environment", *Treasury Management International*, April 1997.
5. J Neter, W Wasserman *et al*, "Applied Statistics", Allyn & Bacon Inc, Boston, 1982.
6. D Bunn, "Applied Decision Analysis", McGraw-Hill, 1984.
7. RL Finney & GB Thomas, "Calculus", Addison-Wesley Publishing, Reading, Massachusetts, 1990.
8. J Zerolis, "Triangulating Risk", *Risk*, vol 9, no. 12, December 1996.
9. AC Laufer "Production and Operations Management", South-Western Publishing Co, Cincinnati, 1984.

'Modules for Standardizing the Process', by A. Steyn and A. Boessenkool, reproduced with their permission.

12

How Financial Engineering Can Advance Corporate Strategy

P. Tufano

Leaders of successful businesses build long-term relationships with customers, suppliers, employees, and shareholders. They make farsighted investments to support and develop their core competencies. They act quickly to ensure that short-term obstacles do not disrupt their long-term strategies. In conceiving and implementing corporate strategies, managers have always drawn on the skills of many specialists, from marketers to production experts. Now a small but growing number of senior managers have found that practitioners of a new technical specialty – financial engineering – can help them achieve their companies' strategic objectives. They have found that, like other technological breakthroughs such as cheap computing power, financial engineering has the potential not only to reduce the cost of existing activities but also to make possible the development of new products, services, and markets.

The notion that financial engineering – the use of derivatives to manage risk and create customized financial instruments – can advance a company's strategic goals might contradict the impression one gets from recent stories in the press. In many of these tales, traders within the finance staff use derivatives to speculate on the steepness of the yield curve or on movements of exchange rates. It appears that these bets have not been driven by the company's business strategy and that senior managers have been unaware of choices made deep within their finance organizations. When misguided wagers backfire, companies lose millions and executives lose their jobs. Managers who seek to avoid disasters certainly must pay careful attention to these cautionary tales. Nevertheless, these accounts could easily give the impression that financial engineering is not used, and indeed should not be used, by nonfinancial companies to advance core business goals. That impression would be wrong.

It is well to recognize the pitfalls of new technologies, but failure to appreciate their true competitive value can be shortsighted and ultimately hazardous. Forward-looking managers need to keep abreast of their rivals' successful uses of promising breakthroughs like financial engineering. Unfortunately, those are the stories that remain untold. Were they to be told, managers would learn of leading organizations that have used financial engineering to solve classic and vexing business problems. These are not narrow finance problems that involve shaving a few basis points off financing costs or shedding transaction exposures arising from sales abroad. Rather, they are broad strategic problems – in marketing, production, human resources, investor relations, and strategic restructuring – for which advanced financial techniques have offered new solutions. This article presents five case studies that illustrate innovative applications of financial engineering and offers managers guidance for determining when such techniques are appropriate.

The cases highlight five corporations – three headquartered in the United States, one in France, and one in Mexico – that produce and market gas, electricity, chemicals, cement, or oil. Although the companies faced different management challenges, their goals were clear and their opportunities well defined. Traditional approaches toward achieving their objectives, however, seemed inadequate – either the costs or the risks appeared to be too high. The outline of a new, nontraditional solution was not hard to discern. But the innovative approach required that the companies commit themselves to bearing risks that their customers, employees, or counterparties sought to shed. Without a means of structuring, valuing, and mitigating those risks, the strategic initiatives that management pursued seemed doomed to failure. In the end, the innovative approach was made possible by the concepts, tools, and markets of financial engineers.

The cases demonstrate that close collaboration between general managers and financial engineers can help create a competitive edge in a variety of ways: by differentiating products through enhanced price and delivery options, by increasing production capacity with flexible alternatives to capital investment, by changing the risk characteristics of holding stock, or by keeping strategic mergers on track through the creation of win-win situations. The underlying aim of the cases is to follow the eye of the financial engineer who thinks like a strategist (or the strategist who thinks like a financial engineer). That means "following the risk" through the process of identifying the sources of risk, evaluating the strategic advantage of bearing risk, creating financial instruments to transfer risk, and using financial markets to value and shed risk.

CONTROLLING VOLATILITY: ENRON CAPITAL & TRADE RESOURCES

Producers and distributors of regulated commodity products, such as natural gas or electricity, have not generally been known for their sophisticated marketing programs. Before deregulation, there was little need or incentive to differentiate their products. But price decontrols, open distribution systems, and market economics have changed all that. How, then, can a commodity producer succeed in a competitive environment? Elementary strategy suggests that the company must either be the lowest-cost provider or distinguish its product from the competition. And yet it would seem almost senseless for a company to establish a brand name for a product like methane, which can be fully described as one molecule of carbon attached to four molecules of hydrogen.

This was the challenge confronting Enron Capital & Trade Resources (ECT), a subsidiary of Enron Corporation of Houston, Texas – a diversified natural gas company that explores for and produces gas, operates pipelines, and builds and operates power plants around the world. ECT's recent success in the natural gas business can be attributed in part to its ability to create a line of product and service options by using financial engineering. As Jeffrey K. Skilling, chairman and CEO of ECT, puts it, "Selling natural gas is getting to be a real business, like selling washing machines. We're taking the simplest commodity there is, a methane molecule, and we're packaging and delivering it under a brand name, the way General Electric does."

ECT's managers had learned from a decade of instability in the natural gas market that their product was about more than carbon and hydrogen and that users of natural gas cared very much about such characteristics as reliable delivery and predictable prices. From 1938 to 1978, the price of natural gas had been under regulatory control, and buyers and sellers had known that prices would be fairly predictable. In the early 1970s, price controls together with the oil embargo in the Middle East led to severe gas shortages and precipitated the industry's deregulation from the wellhead to the end user. A series of legal rulings and market developments abrogated the standard industry contracts, which presold fixed quantities of gas at fixed prices. By 1990, more than three-fourths of all gas sales were at spot prices. Natural gas prices were more volatile than oil prices and, on occasion, four times as volatile as the Standard & Poor's 500 index.

In the late 1980s, ECT's managers sensed a market opportunity. Their vision was to create a "gas bank" that would serve as an intermediary between buyers and sellers, allowing both to shed their unwanted risks. Focusing on buyers, ECT's marketers reasoned that bundling methane molecules, reliable delivery, and predictable prices into a single package would define a clear product line and communicate the company's unique skills. Further, by giving the package a distinctive name, they could perform the seemingly impossible trick of creating a brand name for methane.

Accordingly, ECT developed a family of products called EnFolio Gas Resource Agreements – gas-supply contracts that could be customized according to the quantity, time period, price index, and settlement terms specified. One local gas utility could buy EnFolio GasBank and be assured of a fixed volume at a fixed price. Another might prefer EnFolio Index, which offered a fixed volume at a price tied to a natural gas index. A third might choose EnFolio GasCap, which delivered a fixed volume at a price tied to a natural gas index and capped at a previously determined level. Given the range of variables, each product could be sold under a nearly infinite set of specific conditions. ECT's marketing strategy, which stressed the company's ability to help gas consumers avoid unpredictable prices, included an amusing advertising campaign that featured a large black dot called Spot, representing the spot price of gas. In one ad, Spot was in a hospital bed. An erratic chart tracked its vital signs, and the caption read, "See Spot. See Spot having problems long-term."

ECT's crucial insight was that the extraordinary volatility of natural gas prices and the fluctuations in supply offered the company the opportunity to distinguish its product and to profit by managing the risks of uncertainty experienced by gas producers and consumers. Buyers and sellers would, in effect, pass their risk on to ECT. But ECT realized that it would have to manage the gas bank's long-term contracts carefully to avoid falling into the trap that had plagued the savings and loan industry, in which fixed-rate, long-term mortgages were funded by short-term interest rates paid to depositors. That mismatch of assets and liabilities had nearly bankrupted an entire industry when interest rates rose. ECT's risk managers have clear instructions to develop a hedging strategy that minimizes net gas exposures, and the company has invested millions of dollars in hardware, software, and hundreds of highly trained personnel to eliminate mismatches and ensure that fluctuations in gas prices do not jeopardize the company's existence.

Understanding customers' needs and developing a supporting marketing strategy did not require any knowledge of financial engineering. But creating the contracts and ensuring that the company did not expose itself to excessive risks were classic exercises in financial engineering. ECT's success – measured by both market share and profits – illustrates how financial engineers, working with marketers and strategists, can differentiate a commodity product without taking on undue risk.

ADDING CAPACITY WITH VIRTUAL BRICKS AND MORTAR: TVA

Senior managers facing projections of increased demand have to confront difficult decisions about whether to make or buy production capacity to meet that demand. The problem can be particularly vexing when building new capacity entails large-scale capital financing that may limit precious flexibility in a rapidly changing market. Costly production assets with projected useful lives of several decades could be rendered obsolete almost overnight. For the managers of Tennessee Valley Authority, the problem was even more acute because government policy limited their ability to finance new projects, and their industry was in a period of unprecedented upheaval. How could TVA meet its customers' needs without exposing itself either to market uncertainties or to large investments?

Founded in 1933, TVA was set up by Congress to manage the waters of the Tennessee River to produce electricity for the southeastern United States. At first, TVA built hydroelectric dams, and in later years, coal-fired-steam and nuclear power plants. Throughout its history, TVA met the increased demand for power by turning to its engineers, who transformed bricks, mortar, turbines, and reactors into energy. By mid-1994, TVA's demand forecasts indicated that for all but its lowest projections, it would have to continue to add capacity; for its highest projections, additional peak capacity would be required as soon as 1997.

But building new capacity is not inexpensive. One estimate puts the cost of TVA's nuclear power program over its 28-year history at $25 billion. In mid-1994, the capital expenditures necessary for TVA to meet its forecasted demand by the year 2000 were projected to be about $1.7 billion per year for the next six years. Numbers like these were putting pressure on TVA's capital budget.

Two other factors complicated TVA's ability to meet increasing demand. First, by setting TVA's debt ceiling at $30 billion, Congress limited the company's ability to finance new projects. In 1994, TVA's debt already stood at $26 billion, and its own board had set an internal cap approximately 10% below that imposed by Congress. Second, the deregulation of the electric power industry had begun, and the electricity market was in a state of flux. In the new market for power, electricity could be bought and sold for spot or future delivery. In the United Kingdom, brokers of power already could trade primitive futures contracts. In the western United States, the Western Systems Power Pool operated as a power exchange for its members. And the New York Mercantile Exchange was actively discussing the specifications of an exchange-traded futures contract on electric power. By the end of 1994, 80 entities had applied to the Federal Energy Regulatory Commission to become over-the-counter brokers or marketers of power in what was thought to be the beginning of one of the nation's biggest emerging markets.

The evolving markets for power clearly offered TVA a way to meet increasing demand by buying power rather than making it with bricks and mortar. Buying long-term fixed-price and fixed-quantity contracts might require a smaller up-front capital investment than would building new generating plants. But that strategy wouldn't necessarily solve the problem of uncertain demand – the question of when and how much to buy. TVA could vary the amount of energy its power plants produced in a matter of minutes; and because electricity is not easily stored, that flexibility was a critical aspect of the business. Given the volatility of prices in the emerging power markets, flexibility was becoming even more important. Thus for *buying* power to be an adequate substitute for *making* power, it would have to give TVA the same flexibility that the company's power plants could. It looked as though long-term contracts that locked in fixed amounts at fixed prices would not fit the bill.

In early 1994, members of the Customer Planning Group at TVA, all engineers by training, began to discuss a new idea. Why couldn't TVA purchase call options on power that would give it the right, but not the obligation, to buy power from other utilities? By purchasing call options on electricity, TVA could buy additional power as needed. The call options could create a virtual power plant for TVA that acted like the real options that the company had in its bricks-and-mortar plants. Just as TVA could decide the level at which to operate a particular generating source – sometimes on a daily basis, based on market demand and prices – so it could choose whether to exercise its options to buy power. If the company's low energy forecasts were borne out, it might choose to buy less additional power, but if the demand for energy was strong, it could exercise all its options. Similarly, it could choose whether to exercise its options on the basis of prevailing energy prices.

A number of questions remained: How could TVA ensure that its power counterparties would perform both technically and financially on their contracts? How should the option contracts be structured? How would TVA evaluate and price the various contracts? Through the spring and summer of 1994, the TVA team hammered out the mechanism for soliciting market prices from potential sellers of options. In July 1994, it issued a request for proposals for option purchase agreements (OPAs), formally seeking quotations on electricity options. By December 1994, it had received 138 separate bids totaling nearly 22,000 megawatts of power. During the winter and spring of 1995, the team evaluated the proposals, created a shortlist, and began to negotiate with potential counterparties.

The insight that TVA needed flexibility in acquiring new capacity did not require any financial engineering skills, but the implementation of the option purchase plan did. Concepts borrowed from the financial markets will help TVA value its OPAs, compare them with the traditional alternative (building plants), and manage the risk of an options portfolio. The financial engineers who structure, value, and manage these portfolios of option contracts may someday prove to be as valuable to a utility's future as the engineers who design hydroelectric, coal, and nuclear power plants. Perhaps as important, the information that electric power markets will provide to both producers and consumers will allow managers to make better investment decisions, even about traditional bricks-and-mortar projects.

REDUCING STOCKHOLDERS' RISKS: RHÔNE-POULENC AND CEMEX

When investors shy away from a stock, it is probably because they think that the risks of investment are too high relative to the likely return. The managers whose stocks are avoided, however, may believe that such judgments are unwarranted or ill informed. They may want to educate investors and communicate confidence in their company's stock, especially when the potential investors are their own employees. Many managers and scholars agree that workers tend to be most productive when their financial interests are aligned with those of the company's shareholders. One way to achieve this community of interests and to motivate workers is to tie compensation to stock price performance through executive stock ownership or employee stock ownership plans. Although companies can, of course, give stock to employees, they obviously would prefer that employees purchase shares. But they may find it difficult to persuade them to buy, especially when the prevailing business culture has made workers risk averse and there is no tradition of employee stock ownership in any form.

That was the problem confronting officials of the French government and managers of Rhône-Poulenc, the leading French life sciences and chemical company. Rhône-Poulenc had been nationalized in 1982, but more than a decade later a new regime sought to return the organization to private ownership, and a massive equity offering was planned to sell shares to global investors. Government officials and Rhône-Poulenc managers, deeming that broad participation by employees was critical to the private entity's long-term success, were excited by the prospect of employees having a direct interest in the value of its stock. When, in early 1993, an initial block of Rhône-Poulenc shares was sold in a partial privatization, both the government and the company took measures to encourage employees to buy shares. The state granted employees a 10% discount off the market price of the shares, and Rhône-Poulenc sweetened the deal by giving them an extra 15% discount in addition to the right to pay for the stock over 12 months. Despite those incentives, the employees' response was disappointing: Only 20% chose to participate, and only three-fourths of the employee allotment was sold.

As full privatization approached in late 1993, managers of Rhône-Poulenc and their counterparts at the French Treasury considered even more aggressive traditional incentives, such as further discounts, free shares, and interest-free loans. These sweeteners, however, had two problems: First, they might prove very costly both to the government and to Rhône-Poulenc. Second, the Treasury and the managers suspected that even these measures would be insufficient because they failed to address the employees' fundamental fear of holding stock – the fear of losing their entire investment. The managers and the government worried that employees, whose economic well-being was already largely dependent on Rhône-Poulenc, would not take on a greater stake in the company; they needed a solution that would reduce or eliminate the risks of stock ownership for employees *and* avoid prohibitive costs or risks to themselves. How could they meet both those goals?

This was another classic opportunity for financial engineering, and the company's financial advisers at Bankers Trust offered the following solution: Why not provide employees with a guaranteed minimum return on their investments, which could be paid for by forgoing a part of their interest in the stock if it appreciated? In simple terms, employees could be offered a stock investment in Rhône-Poulenc that gave them voting rights and guaranteed a minimum return of 25% over four and a half years plus two-thirds of the appreciation of the stock over its initial level. If the company performed poorly, employees would not suffer any loss, and if it did well, they would gain, although not as much as they would have had they held regular shares. Thus the agreement would address the employees' fear of losing their money, as was amply demonstrated by their overwhelming acceptance of the plan. The proposed guaranteed shares, described in information sessions and on videotapes, turned out to be a successful portion of Rhône-Poulenc's oversubscribed offering.

But what about the costs to Rhône-Poulenc and the French government? Neither wanted to bear the risk of the guarantees if share prices fell. Here, too, they turned to their financial intermediaries, who assumed responsibility for managing the risk of the employee portfolio in financial markets. The financial engineers who structured the deal and managed the portfolio profited from the transaction while attracting praise and new business with their novel proposal. More important, by using the tools of risk management, they supported a well-conceived human resources policy that was an integral part of the company's strategy. And, thanks to financial engineering, Rhône-Poulenc's innovative approach had a net cost that was no higher than it would have been had the company used any of the traditional sweeteners. Management's insight that guaranteeing a minimum return on employee stock ownership would alleviate workers' concerns did not require any special knowledge of finance. Nor did the rank and file have to understand that they were financing the purchase of a put option by selling calls. But the skills of financial engineers were essential to ensure that Rhône-Poulenc kept the promises it made to employees.

Rhône-Poulenc's need to communicate confidence in its stock highlights a common management concern. Virtually every manager at one time or another believes that his or her stock is undervalued. If a company is using its stock to acquire other companies or if executive compensation is based on stock-price appreciation, undervaluation may be especially troublesome. Consider the case of Cemex, the largest cement producer in the Americas and the second-largest industrial company in Mexico. In 1992, when Cemex announced its strategic acquisition of two Spanish cement manufacturers, its stock fell dramatically in response. The market undervaluation was both extreme and crippling. What could Cemex do to communicate its confidence to investors?

The managers' first line of defense, meeting with investors and analysts, apparently failed, and the second "normal" solution, a stock buyback, was complicated by Mexican law. Cemex's financial advisers at J. P. Morgan then suggested an alternative that would comply with Mexican law while achieving the same purpose as a buyback: Instead of *buying* its stock, Cemex could *sell* investors an option (the right but not the obligation) to sell their stock back at any time over the next year for a fixed price. In the financial engineers' terminology, Cemex could issue a put on its own stock. In effect, it would commit to buy back its shares, guaranteeing a minimum price to any investor who bought the put. Whereas companies sometimes quietly sell (or write) puts in conjunction with their stock-buyback programs, J. P. Morgan was recommending a well-publicized sale of puts to communicate Cemex's conviction that its share price was too low.

Cemex had publicly committed to bearing a large portion of its investors' risks, but there was one remaining problem: If the company's share price plummeted, Cemex would not have the resources to honor its guarantees. The company's advisers at J. P. Morgan, however, were willing to issue and back the securities, called equity buyback obligation rights (EBORs), themselves. The proposal was a classic example of financial engineering: The specialists could price the EBORs and manage their risks in the financial markets.

Cemex's puts were a close cousin of the guarantees that Rhône-Poulenc offered its employees and apparently were just as effective. Between the time of the board meeting at which the EBORs were discussed and the actual offering, the company's stock recovered nearly half of its earlier decline. It is impossible to tell whether the response was caused by the public signal sent by Cemex, the trust implied by J. P. Morgan's issuance of the securities, or unrelated movements in the stock's price. Regardless of the cause, financial engineering (in this case, the sale of puts) offered a viable alternative to communicating confidence in stock through press releases and straight buybacks.

BRIDGING THE GAP BETWEEN BUYER AND SELLER: MW PETROLEUM CORPORATION

For the thousands of mergers and acquisitions consummated in a given year, there are probably thousands more that never get completed. Although some of those deals fail because of big differences in the perceptions of buyer and seller, others fail even though the gaps between the two parties are quite small. Given the right technical resources, skilled negotiators often can find ways to close the gaps, removing impediments to the fulfillment of their company's strategic plans.

In early 1991, a proposed transaction that would help both Amoco Corporation and Apache Corporation achieve their strategic goals looked as if it might bust. Amoco, an integrated petroleum and chemical corporation with sales of more than $28 billion, had emerged from a long-term, multi-year strategic assessment of its business with the conclusion that, given the company's cost structure, it should dispose of marginal oil and gas properties. So it created a new organization, MW Petroleum Corporation, as a freestanding exploration and development entity with working interests in 9,500 wells in more than 300 producing fields. Among Amoco's options was the ability to sell MW Petroleum as a midsize independent petroleum company. Amoco and its financial adviser, Morgan Stanley Group, then marketed MW Petroleum to potential international and domestic buyers. Among them, Apache Corporation, an independent oil and gas company with revenues of $270 million, showed the most serious interest. Apache was an aggressive acquirer of oil and gas properties whose strategy was to acquire properties that majors like Amoco believed were marginal and then use its expertise and low-cost operations to achieve substantially higher profits. According to Apache's chairman and CEO, Raymond Plank, the strategy "is a bit like a pig following a cow through the cornfield. The scraps are pretty good for someone with our particular mission." The MW Petroleum deal was an attractive set of scraps.

The sale of MW Petroleum to Apache looked like a strategic win-win for both companies – if they could find an acceptable price. In the spring of 1991, however, the oil and gas markets had just passed through a tumultuous period. Iraq's invasion of Kuwait had not only pushed oil prices to historic highs but also increased uncertainty about their direction. In this environment, Amoco was bullish and Apache bearish about future oil prices. So although Amoco and Apache agreed on most of the technical characteristics of MW Petroleum, their differences over oil prices set a roadblock to the deal. More important, Apache's bankers, who would fund the acquisition, were very conservative about future oil prices and based their proposed loan on worst-case scenarios. With the gap between buyer and seller equaling perhaps 10% of the transaction value, the deal appeared to be dead. Strategic goals are fine, but only if they can be accomplished at a reasonable price.

That might have been the end of the story – another set of discussions derailed by a failure to agree, with neither party willing to take the risk of a compromise. In this case, however, the disagreement was about future commodity prices, not about the inherent characteristics of the business being bought and sold. Although both parties were committed to their forecasts, they eventually realized they could find common ground by sharing the risk of future oil price movements while at the same time addressing the concerns of the bankers financing the deal. The solution hinged on a remarkably simple piece of financial engineering.

Amoco, which was more optimistic about oil and gas prices, could write Apache a capped price-support guarantee. Under the guarantee, if oil prices fell below a designated "price support" level in the fist two years after the sale, Amoco would make compensating payments to Apache. With this support in hand, Apache would see short-term revenues and profits bolstered were oil and gas prices to soften. In turn, its lenders would be assured of sufficient cash flow to make the required debt service. In return for the guarantee, Apache would pay Amoco if oil or gas prices exceeded a designated "price sharing" level over the next five to eight years. Although Apache would end up paying more for MW Petroleum if oil or gas prices rose, the corresponding rise in revenues would provide the means to make the payments. By forgoing some of the upside, Apache could insure itself against the downside. The agreement was a win-win solution because each party would get the price it had forecast if that forecast was right – so both parties felt that they got the better deal.

By the same token, either company might regret having structured the transaction as it did. Nevertheless, by using a simple piece of financial engineering, both could accomplish their strategic goals in an environment of great uncertainty about future commodity prices. They found a way of sharing risks that made the chief executives and boards of both companies comfortable with the transaction. It did not take financial engineering skills to recognize that the risks of this deal could be shared. Nor did the buyer and seller have to understand that they had created a *collar* – a combination of a call option and a put option. Financial engineers, however, could value the collar by using actual data and financial models. Moreover, their pricing exercise was not merely theoretical. After the deal was closed, both sides were approached to sell off their positions and thus had the choice of monetizing the options and closing their risk exposures.

APPLYING FINANCIAL ENGINEERING

All the case studies presented here show how financial engineering can offer solutions to intractable problems. Although the cases differ in many respects, managers in each one recognized the need, for the sake of their own strategic goals, to help others bear risks. Financial engineers were then able to structure, value, and manage the transfer of those risks. Further similarities among the cases raise a number of questions that managers should consider when deciding whether it is appropriate to apply financial engineering techniques.

Is your ability to commit to bearing additional risk critical to your strategic success?
The use of financial engineering in these five cases contrasts with traditional forms of risk management, in which financial managers, seemingly divorced from the rest of the organization, inherit a set of exposures and manage their risk. Business leaders in these five cases knowingly took on risks to satisfy their customers, employees, stockholders, or negotiation counterparties. They did not seek to take on risk for risk's sake but, rather, risk for strategy's sake. The anticipated value of their transactions would come primarily from the strategic gains made possible by them. Although ECT, for example, sold fixed-price gas contracts, its primary goal was not to gain when gas prices rose or fell but rather to profit over the long term by differentiating its product. Similarly, Rhône-Poulenc's primary purpose was not to profit from movements in its stock value but to benefit from the increased personal investment and productivity of its employees.

Is there an existing or potential market for the kinds of risks you need to bear?
Financial engineers are experts in transforming the risk-and-return characteristics of investments, and they are assisted by deep markets with low transaction costs. The more closely they can correlate the risk they seek to modify to a traded market with established contract forms, the more likely they are to find a feasible solution. Some risks, such as a potential rise or fall in a broad stock index, are very common, and claims on these risks are actively traded in public and private markets. Other risks are more idiosyncratic. But even a risk as personal as the potential property loss due to an auto accident can be mitigated – not in a market but through the risk sharing of property insurance. Financial engineering has proved to be most useful in protecting against potential failures caused by or related to movements

in financial or commodity markets – in the present cases, the stock markets for Rhône-Poulenc and Cemex, and the commodity markets for the others.

Financial markets offer the opportunity to exchange risks at reasonably low transaction costs. Managers and academics should recognize that an efficient market, being essentially a zero-sum game, makes it difficult if not impossible to profit by taking on fairly priced risks. And they should be skeptical about whether companies should assume those risks. But again, it should be remembered that the five companies used financial engineering, in large measure, to shed the risks they took on. To the extent that they accepted risk, the "profits" they sought were not in the financial markets but rather in the product "market" for reliable gas, the labor "market" for committed French employees, or the acquisition and divestiture "market" for marginal oil properties. In an important sense, the companies were arbitraging risks between efficient financial markets and less efficient non-financial markets.

What is remarkable about these companies is their willingness to pursue financial engineering even though the relevant markets they faced were not very deep or well developed. None of them could find a pre-made derivative contract at an exchange that would answer their needs. Yet the importance of their problems and the lack of traditional business solutions motivated them to construct tailor-made solutions. While these tailored solutions may have been expensive, they were less expensive and more effective than the alternatives.

Can you structure a contract that transfers the risk at a reasonable price without forcing you to incur unacceptable risks?
Financial engineering, of course, is not free, and transactions that transfer risk characteristically require cash payments or entail other contingent risks owing to the nature of the transactions. Managers who use financial engineering must understand those costs or new risks.

Managers obviously need to consider the cash costs of selling risks. For example, the owner of a stock portfolio might pay cash for a put option that gives him or her the right to sell the portfolio for a fixed price at some future time, thereby setting a floor value on the stock-and-option package. Cemex's EBORs and TVA's proposed purchase of call options both involve such up-front cash payments. Furthermore, when companies use financial engineering to obtain flexibility, they should understand and allow for the additional cash costs they may incur if they later change their plans.

Often, the price of shedding risk is taking on another risk or giving up some of the upside potential of a future transaction or rate movement. That is how Apache, Rhône-Poulenc's employees, and the purchasers of EnFolio GasBank products protected themselves against adverse movements in the price of oil, stock, or gas. In these forms of risk barter, the terms of trade were explicit and understood by all parties, but the allegations surrounding some recent cases of leveraged swaps underscore the need to make such understandings very clear.

In addition to these explicit costs or risks, managers using financial engineering should be mindful of other contingencies that are harder to quantify. As in other corporate transactions, there is some degree of credit risk because financially engineered solutions generally involve fallible counterparties. Financial engineers have devised various ways to mitigate credit risk, from collateralization agreements to AAA-rated derivative subsidiaries. Nevetheless, when you buy a commodity contract from a financial institution, you often are trading price risk for counterparty risk. A closely related problem arises from performance risk, or the risk that the counterparty in a commodity market will not be able to produce or deliver the product as specified in the contract. Clearly, if TVA's proposed option contracts are to work as planned, its counterparties must be able to deliver power.

Another contingency is basis risk, which you encounter when you cannot find a market that trades precisely the kind of risk you want to shed, and you have to use a close substitute that behaves similarly. ECT, Apache, and Amoco wrote contracts tied to specific grades of gas or oil, delivered at particular locations; users of these types of contracts may have to contend with differences between their individual exposure and the benchmarks in the industry. Other contracts might entail liquidity risks. For example, if a company uses short-term contracts to hedge long-term risks, the consequence may be sudden and unexpected cash-flow requirements. If so, a strategy intended to protect company value may turn out to be worse than no strategy at all. Perhaps the most troublesome risks that parties bear arise from legal, tax, and regulatory uncertainties. Courts, commissions, legislatures, and politicians may suddenly change the rules or simply abrogate existing contracts. As a result, it is not uncommon for "legal engineers" to work alongside financial engineers to ensure the reliability of their agreements.

MAKING THE DECISION ON RISK AND RETURN

When a business decision is about to be made, it is always useful to repeat the mantra "risk and return." The two concepts are simple, but the cases presented here emphasize that a full understanding of how they are related often requires the collaboration of financial engineers and general strategists. Financial engineers can help to measure and moderate risks by answering such questions as, Based on the current market, what's a fair price for shedding oil-price risk? How much upside must I surrender to buy downside protection on a stock price? But ultimately, the most significant returns on transactions can be understood and valued only by the general manager, who must answer such questions as, What is it worth for the company to have its employees own stock? Will divesting a large part of our business allow us to make significant gains elsewhere? Each party has some of the relevant risk-and-return information. Working alone, neither the financial engineer nor the general manager has enough information to make a prudent decision. Working together, they may. What is most interesting about these five cases is not their technical virtuosity; on the contrary, the financial engineering employed was quite simple. Rather, the cases are exciting because they demonstrate that collaboration between financial engineers and general strategists can produce concepts and insights capable of meeting complex challenges.

The potential for this kind of collaboration will vary from company to company and from situation to situation. But the cases presented here should suggest that the possibilities are broader than might at first be imagined. Equity derivatives that address employees' concerns or signal confidence in a company's stock can be applied widely, as long as the company has traded common stock. The use of derivatives in an acquisition can be beneficial if the contract is structured around the subsequent accounting or stock market performance of the unit being sold. The use of futures markets and indices in commodity settings can also be applied much more broadly – for example, there are new real estate indices, as well as new derivative contracts on the indices. By using these contracts, a real estate brokerage could differentiate its services from those of its rivals by protecting a home seller or buyer against marketwide moves in prices between the time of listing and the time of sale or purchase.

Surely not all experiments in financial engineering will be successful. Some returns may be smaller than anticipated, some risks larger than expected. New technologies like computing or financial engineering usually produce winners and losers. In the case of computing, we remember the survivors – companies made richer by capitalizing on low-cost technology. Yet if we think back a decade or two, we also will remember companies whose experiments failed. Similarly, there are companies whose experiments with financial technology have been uninspiring. The debacles reported in the headlines represent our generation's technological washouts. What they seem to have in common is a degree of myopia on the part of senior management. We often learn that the specifications, design, execution, and oversight of these programs were all performed by the same technicians, without strategic direction and review. Facing a new specialty, senior managers sometimes throw their hands up and abdicate responsibility. The results are not surprising: An advanced financial program designed without reference to the business and its strategy, like a computer system built without input from end users, runs the risk of missing the mark.

The companies studied here adopted financial solutions as integral parts of their core business processes. The financial engineering used in these cases was remarkably simple, but it was able to solve complex managerial problems. Furthermore, these experiments with financial wizardry promise to accomplish the objectives that management established: capturing market share and profit with minimal risk, developing new production capacity, persuading employees and shareholders to buy stock, and bringing an important acquisition to completion. Although such success stories produce blander headlines than do dramatic tales of derivatives disasters, they should be more suggestive and inspiring to forward-thinking leaders.

13

New Ways with Derivatives

S. Brady

Those seeking innovation in the derivatives market will find it in three main varieties: the introduction of a new instrument; new uses for established products; and the penetration of a new user base by an established product.

NEW PRODUCTS

Of the first class, the most interesting is the credit derivative. The basic credit derivative is the credit default swap. It is a bilateral financial contract in which one counterparty (the protection buyer) pays a periodic fee, typically expressed in fixed basis points on the notional amount, in return for a floating payment contingent on the default of one or more third-party reference credits. This floating payment is designed to mirror the loss incurred by creditors of the reference credit in the event of its default. It is usually calculated as the fall in price of a reference security below par at some pre-designated point in time after the reference credit has defaulted.

Elaborates Rob Reoch, vice-president of credit derivatives at JP Morgan: "Counterparties typically wait from one week to three months after default in order to give the price of the reference security time to settle at a new level. Since most securities become due and payable in the event of default, most plain vanilla securities will trade at the price that reflects the market's estimation of recovery following a default, irrespective of maturity or coupon."

This type of cash-settled transaction is commonest, but transactions in which there is physical delivery of the reference security at par are also structured.

One of the clearest applications for the default swap is the synthetic reallocation of credit risk between the loan and bond portfolios of banks. Providers of the swaps envisage a liquid market in which financial institutions will use credit swaps to free up lines filled up by loan transactions and bond and derivatives portfolios.

By paying another financial institution to take over the default risk on a loan or bond, or on a swap or option exposure to a single counterparty, commercial and investment banks can manage their credit limits quickly and confidentially, without having to enter complex assignment negotiations.

This will enable banks, for the first time, to hedge the most pernicious risks they face: concentration risk, correlation risk and the conflict between external regulatory and internal economic capital adequacy requirements.

So, in a simple example, a bank wishing to free up its credit lines to Italy at five years might enter into a five-year default swap with an Italian government bond as the reference security. The bank would pay a premium – say, 20bp a year – to the counterparty. The counterparty makes a payment in exchange only if Italy defaults on its debts, in which case the payment might be par less the final price of the security multiplied by the notional principal amount of the swap.

In the simplest example the hedging bank holds the same value of the underlying bond as the notional swap principal. So if Italy defaults and the reference bond falls to 85%, the bank collects the 85% from the market and the remaining 15% from the swap counterparty.

However well tailored the credit swap may seem for the bank market, it has a number of significant uses for non-financial corporations. Many companies are heavily exposed to a small number of key customers. Take an engineering company all of whose heavy drilling equipment in the next three years will be sold to a particular customer. This is not unusual in some areas of mining, where highly specialized equipment can take years to build and where two or three companies dominate a particular field and are therefore the main customers. If the customer goes bust, the manufacturer is left out of pocket holding machinery that no-one else will buy. If the risk to its survival is serious enough the supplier can now buy a credit swap on a notional principal that gives it either the value of the machinery or some breakeven amount.

Then there is project finance. An equity sponsor to a large project may be happy with the operational and project risk but not with the sovereign risk on the guarantees. He may have protected himself against 70% of this risk via an export credit agency-backed facility. However, he wants protection against the remaining 30%. He could enter into a credit default swap with a notional principal equal to the amount covered by the sovereign guarantee, with the same maturity, such that, if the sovereign defaulted, he would receive the cash.

Says one banker: "The corporate sponsor might say: 'Well, we know LNG [liquefied natural gas] and are happy with the project risk, but we are not happy about Indonesia.' They will pay us so that if Indonesia defaults, then we pay up."

A more complex version of a project financing hedge is where a company involved in a project or other enterprise is due a predictable payment stream. The company may want to ensure that this payment stream continues in the event of default. Credit swaps can be structured in such a way that the company pays a premium in exchange for which, on default of a swap counterparty, the present value of that payment stream is payable to the company.

More generally, large exporters, particularly in the heavy plant sector, are taking advantage of the new-found ability to buy tailored protection against country risk that is either not available or too expensive to obtain from traditional political risk insurers.

Says a spokesman at CIBC Financial Products: "We have just completed a transaction for a European manufacturer of heavy goods who has bought credit protection against its exposure to certain emerging markets. This transaction is very rare right now, but such deals will become much more popular."

Another important potential use of credit derivatives for larger corporations is to mitigate the large credit exposures they have to the banking sector under swap contracts. Ford, for example, had derivatives with a notional principal of $66 billion outstanding in 1994, many of which were interest rate swaps. Any deterioration in the credit quality of the bank counterparties to these swaps implies a change in the mark-to-market value of the swap (though few corporations take the precaution of marking to market) and also an increase in the risk that the bank will not be able to maintain any payments due under the swap.

One way round this problem – which has become particularly acute in the Japanese bank sector, especially in combination with dollar/yen currency swaps – is the swap guarantee. This is a credit swap whose notional principal is directly linked to the mark-to-market value of a reference swap. The swap guarantee pays out if the reference swap defaults.

Example 1   A match for toll earnings

Italian toll road operator Autostrade has long been known for leading the way in international finance, having issued the first Eurobond in 1963. More recently it took advantage of JP Morgan's derivatives expertise to launch an inflation-indexed private placement.

The L100 billion ($64.1 million) seven-year deal sold at the end of last year pays a coupon tied to the real earnings of the company. The toll tariffs it charges are adjusted by a calculation based on the percentage change in the cost of living minus productivity savings. The bond's interest payments are thus better aligned with the company's earnings than a normal floating-rate note.

Using derivatives, JP Morgan created two assets, stripping the credit component out of the real rate asset. The deal was about nine months in the making and the bank is coy about the details, but other companies should be interested in following Autostrade's lead: utilities whose price increases are linked to inflation are the obvious example.

Studies have also shown that the consumer price index is far less volatile than Libor or swap rates. The US Treasury is the latest sovereign debt issuer to be convinced of the benefits.

REAL OPTIONS

Another new product – at least, new in the sense that it has only recently attracted anything other than academic interest – is the real option.

Explains Simon Hotchin, deputy general manager at Tokai Bank in London: "Real options are real in the sense that the option exists within physical assets, as opposed to paper-based assets. They are options in the sense that the resulting payoff profile is non-linear."

In other words, a real option gives its owner a choice: to exercise or not to exercise. However, the option is embedded in a business operation. It is the option that a mining company has to extract or not to extract the metals or minerals it sells. It is the option a power utility has to switch between fuel sources. It is the option an oil refiner has to produce different distillates from its crude input.

Described in this way, most companies are long real options as a result of their physical operations, their purchase and sale contracts, their lease agreements and other financing contracts. So what should companies do with them?

The simple answer is to sell a financial equivalent and capitalize the option. This may hedge an underlying operation or financing and it can generate capital better deployed in other ways. A one-product natural resource business like oil is simplest. Assume that a particular well may be worth operating only if the price of oil rises above a breakeven of $20 a barrel and that oil is equally likely to rise to $22 or fall to $18. The company that owns the well has several choices: pump oil only when the oil price rises above $20, in which case it gains if the price rises but does not lose if it falls – its average oil price received is therefore $21; pump regardless and be as likely to lose money as to make a profit – its average price received is $20; sell forward to lock in the average price of $20 and make neither profit nor loss.

In this example, the company that uses its option not to exercise does best and the value of its option is $1 per barrel. To capitalize this option the company would sell a call on oil at $20 per barrel to generate $1 of premium per option. If oil rose above $20, the company would receive $20 from the holder of the calls and keep its $1 in premium – the same position as under the real option situation.

What has the company got from this transaction? A guaranteed average cashflow in exchange for the possibility of doing better or worse than average. This is likely to appeal more to smaller, higher-cost producers whose access to financing may be improved by capitalizing their options.

Real examples are more complex. Most firms make investment and operational decisions of this type using discounted cashflow analysis. Real options analysis can be used not simply to identify optionality that can be replicated in the financial options markets, but to provide a different approach to decision-making.

Explains Hotchin: "The key to applying a real options approach to evaluate an asset is to frame the problem so that its cashflows can be modelled through time, and then to isolate the sources of optionality that give rise to potential non-linearities in these cashflows. Accurately depicting the contingent nature of the pay-off through exploiting the source of embedded flexibility is key to understanding and, more importantly, monetizing this potential hidden value.

"Even when no flexibility is embedded in the asset, a real options approach can still be a useful tool to place alongside a DCF technique, since it may provide a different asset valuation, and it avoids having to make difficult decisions on considerations such as the appropriate risk-weighted discount rate to apply to future asset cashflows."

In general, the real options approach, when applied to a more complex realworld example such as a project financing, reveals a complex series of option positions. While it may or may not be possible to sell these for a profit in the financial options markets, these positions can be used to provide a basis for the valuation of assets, leases or production contracts that is significantly different from DCF or traditional accounting valuations.

Example 2   A barrel of puts

A Latin American oil company wanted to raise funds by securitizing the payment stream due to it under a long-term contract to deliver oil. However, if the oil price fell too far, the number of barrels of oil pledged to the deal would generate insufficient revenue to service the bond. To guard against this, the oil company purchased a string of puts on oil from Credit Suisse Financial Products, thus guaranteeing the revenue stream.

The total size of the transaction was $400 million, and the transaction extended out to seven years.

Investors viewed the credit risk on the bond as that of the buyer of oil. The bank had a better rating than the oil company, and the cost of the puts was outweighed by the lower cost of funds that resulted from the better rating.

HYBRID DERIVATIVES

Taking the idea of real options to its natural conclusion, companies are realizing that one of the drawbacks of traditional hedging programmes is their tendency to manage only one variable in isolation. At its most extreme, this meant that companies focused on one type of risk – usually interest rate or foreign exchange – to the exclusion of others.

"The craziest examples were in the oil sector," says one provider of derivative products. "You had oil companies spending vast amounts of time looking at interest rate risk management when movements in interest rates were hundreds of times less important than the risk of a fall in the price of oil."

One way around this problem is to manage all risks simultaneously. However, unless this is done within a framework that analyzes the correlations between the different underlying risks being hedged, this approach will almost certainly lead to overhedging. For example, interest rates and commodity prices have a correlation of close to zero: commodity prices and interest rates are as likely to move in opposite directions as in the same direction. This means that a derivative instrument that requires the same directional move in both interest rates and commodities is cheaper than two derivative instruments that separately require the same directional move.

This has significant implications in the commodity and natural resource sectors, because when commodity prices rise, companies have more free cashflow with which to service debt. So, for example, an oil producer could buy an oil-linked interest rate cap: this is a standard interest cap except that, if oil hits a certain price, the cap is knocked out. The buyer sets the level of the knock-out so that interest rate protection disappears only when profits can cope with the increase in interest rates. This type of cap will vary in price depending on the level of the knock-out and the correlation between interest rates and the commodity price. However, it will never cost more than a simple cap.

A similar hedge can be constructed so that the hedger's interest rate costs drop if the price of the commodity he produces falls below a certain point. An oil producer might enter into a semi-fixed swap structured so that he pays a fixed rate of 5% if the price of oil remains above $18 a barrel, but if oil falls below a floor of $16 then the company's interest rate falls by 75bp.

Most recently, the disciplines of the insurance industry have been combined with financial engineering to produce almost bizarre hybrids. Example 3 shows how the trigger for the knock-in or knock-out of a financial derivative – in this case a foreign exchange rate hedge – can be a non-financial, actuarially calculated event such as the launch of a satellite. Interest rate hedges have been linked to earthquakes and other catastrophes, usually in the form of options embedded in fixed-income instruments.

Example 3   AIG launches combined risk option

AIG Combined Risks, the investment banking subsidiary of the US insurance group, has developed a family of event-contingent financial hedges. Although rivals view the group as too much of a niche player, the deals it has done put it high in derivatives innovation.

One client, a satellite launch company, was faced with a contingent risk: it would have a dollar/yen exposure only if a satellite launch failed and the satellite had to be rebuilt and relaunched – several of the major components required for a rebuild are manufactured by companies in Japan.

This exposure could be hedged by selling dollars forward to receive yen, but if the launch succeeds the launcher is left with a dollar/yen exposure on the forward. The company could also try using a call option to buy yen, but with only a relatively small chance of the launch failing the premium makes the deal look expensive.

AIG Combined Risks provided the company with a combined risk option. In this case the instrument is a call option on the price of yen, but the price reflects the probability of it being needed. It is much cheaper than a conventional optional on yen and provides a cost-effective solution to match the client's event-driven financial exposure.

OPERATIONAL RISK MANAGEMENT

This blurring of the distinction between commercial insurance and financial derivatives has resulted in the new science of operational risk management. A number of large industrial corporations, notably UK oil company BP, analyzed the premiums they were paying for insurance and found that they were much greater than the amount they had claimed for. BP found that during the 1980s it had claimed $250 million but paid $1.2 billion in premiums. It decided to buy insurance only for losses of less than £10 million – where claims administration from insurers is routine – and buy none against larger losses.

This type of analysis, relying as it does on a thorough examination of the risks inherent in the operational processes that would be involved in a catastrophic equipment failure, has been developed by financial institutions as the third leg of their risk management discipline after credit and market risks. Bankers Trust is at the forefront of these developments and has created a system that analyzes the operational risks faced by banks (technology risks, staff risks, relationship and client risks and risks associated with physical assets), values them and allocates capital to cover them.

Comments Doug Hoffman, managing director responsible for Bankers Trust's operational risk management capital allocation system: "By taking the best from the disciplines of financial risk management and insurance-related actuarial sciences and applying the combination to the problem of catastrophe insurance, companies can begin to derive quantitative answers to the question of how to finance and hedge operational risk."

This bank-driven analysis is important because it can be applied both to existing corporate organizations and to new investment decisions. Also, as multinational corporations create larger, more complex cross-border treasury, payment and cash management systems, they begin to create risk profiles in the non-operational side of their business that are closer to those faced by banks than to traditional corporate risks.

For example, Procter & Gamble, the US consumer products group, has its parent treasury centre in Cincinnati, regional centres in Brussels and Dublin and a complex cash management, inter-company lending and foreign exchange netting and pooling system involving two specialized entities that are effectively banks.

According to Lionel Smith, P&G's European regional treasurer for the past three years, one of the main motivations behind the setting up of the system was to reduce the number of banks with which the company deals by "doing things ourselves which we are as good at as the banks – such as lending ourselves our own money".

However, the new system means that local operating businesses rely on the central pooling system to make up shortfalls in their working capital and to manage their foreign exchange risks – to take just two activities. Any technological failures could expose the company to unexpected forex losses; it could incur unplanned overdraft expenses. These operational risks themselves must be managed.

Example 4   A level of confidence

Société Générale's derivatives team has gained a reputation for success in the more tailored end of the market. At the beginning of this year the bank had a German client that wanted to borrow a certain amount of Deutschmarks on a fixed-rate, long-term basis. At that time the yield curve was quite steep and volatility fairly high. Entering into a plain vanilla swap was not attractive because of the shape of the curve.

The bank designed a specific swap in which the customer pays a fixed rate well under the normal fixed-rate swap as long as Libor stays under a limit, which was then 3% above prevailing six-month Libor. If Libor goes above the predetermined limit the swap is de-activated for the remainder of the period concerned.

According to Vincent Lauwick at SocGen in Paris, this product is among the best strategies for borrowers who expect a rise in interest rates but do not believe the rise will go beyond a certain level.

NEW USES

Because the pace of new product innovation is inevitably slowing, derivatives providers are eager to find new applications for existing products. One area in which they have been successful, and where corporations seem keen for innovation to continue is equity derivatives.

The highest-profile use of equity derivatives by non-financial corporations has been in acquisitions and acquisition financing. The recent sale of 12.5% of UK power utility National Grid to Crescent Holdings, part of Olayan Group, an Athens holding company, was structured as a derivatives trade with brokers James Capel.

Derivatives have played a prominent part in acquisition attempts by diversified UK group Trafalgar House and its former parent Hong Kong Land. However, according to one equity derivatives expert, "these deals are few and far between. The bread-and-butter corporate transactions are the employee share options scheme trades and those involving strategic cross-shareholdings."

Example 5   Safer cross-border bids

One of the interesting ways in which foreign exchange options can be used to tailor innovative risk management solutions to specific one-off needs for corporates is in mergers and acquisitions, where compound options can provide the transaction profile-matching that simpler instruments cannot.

The use of compound options in M&A is similar to that for companies submitting a bid on any project or contract payable in a foreign currency.

Consider an Italian corporate that wants to buy a German rival and is funding the Deutschmark purchase out of its lira reserves. The deal, like most of this type, is not certain to go through but the acquiring company has some idea of the likelihood of completion. It will know in three months' time whether its bid has been successful, and if it is, the company knows that payment is due after a further three months.

The simplest measure the company could take is to buy Deutschmarks six months forward, but this would expose it to transaction risk. If the Deutschmark rate were to depreciate against the lira over the next three months, the foreign exchange position would generate a loss.

This loss should be offset by the falling cost of the target company in lira terms, but if the acquisition were not to proceed for, say, regulatory reasons, the offset would disappear and the Italian company would be sitting on a loss-making hedge with no offsetting position. The same would be true for any option strategy where options had been sold to finance the purchased cover.

Forwards are clearly not the best way to hedge a contingent exposure. Purchased options are better, because the most that can be lost on the hedge is the premium spent on it.

An even better way to hedge the exposure might be with compound options, which are options that give their holder the right to buy a particular option in the future for a pre-agreed price.

The Italian company in the example could buy an option to buy itself protection in three months' time when it knows whether the acquisition is proceeding. It could even buy an option on a collar (guaranteeing it a minimum exchange rate in return for the company giving away some of its potential upside) without incurring the type of potential liability it could face if it did not have the right to walk away from the hedge.

The more a company pays upfront for a compound the less it needs to pay to exercise if the acquisition proceeds. If the Italian company were reasonably certain of success it would want to pay more upfront and less when the time comes to exercise its right to be hedged. If the chances of success were lower it might be prudent to pay less upfront so that walking away from the hedge if the bid failed would involve lower costs.

The upfront premium could thus be thought of as part of the fixed costs of acquisition, like legal fees.

Example 6   Lonrho stake sold via risk reversal

Dieter Bock's transformation of hotels-to-mining conglomerate Lonrho continues to make the headlines, but less well known is how equity derivatives were used to sell his Lonrho stake to South African mining group Anglo American.

Bock held an 18.5% stake in the company when he announced his intention to separate Lonrho's mining and non-mining assets in an historic demerger. Former chief executive Tiny Rowland had a put option to sell Bock a further 5.9% stake, on which Bock had a call option to buy the same shares.

Rowland decided to exercise his put for £91 million (£137.5 million). Anglo American wanted to buy these shares as a means of gaining exposure to Lonrho's mining assets. However, regulatory and foreign exchange issues made a straight share purchase difficult to execute because Anglo needed to buy shares from a local exchange in local currency.

SBC Warburg bought the 5.9% stake for £91 million and bought a risk-reversal from Anglo, purchasing a put option from Anglo and selling it a call option. The bank listed the shares on the local South African exchange, where it sold them to Anglo in rand, by exercising its put at option maturity. The bank hedged its own rand/sterling exposure.

Anglo has subsequently acquired an option to buy Bock's 18.5% stake.

NEW USERS

But perhaps the most long-lasting innovations in risk management are those that introduce a new set of users to derivatives-based risk management. One institution that has, by necessity, been successful in this area is a relative newcomer to the non-Canadian markets – CIBC Financial Products. Started in the aftermath of the original Procter & Gamble lawsuit, CIBC benefited from the back-to-basics reaction of the corporate marketplace. In the mass of reorganizations that followed the corporate disasters CIBC was also able to build up its 300-man operation with high-profile hires, concentrating on people with five years' or more experience and an established client base.

The bank has pursued the policy of client education with a unique strategy. A travelling school of risk management has taken its seminars to cities around the US and Europe, encouraging companies to re-examine derivatives and to focus on fundamentals rather than more transient market opportunities.

"Previously, corporates focused increasingly on market-driven transactions that had seemed more appropriate to investment organizations," says David Visher, head of corporate marketing at CIBC Financial Products. "Now we see companies coming back to a much more fundamental approach to hedging their underlying business exposures."

In the US, where the bank has been a leading lender to the media, oil and gas and financial institution sectors, CIBC has identified a number of sectors it believes will provide a new and lasting source of demand for risk management services. One is utilities. A mixture of lack of competitive pressures and a regulatory environment that has forced companies to pass on hedging gains to clients but take hedging losses onto the profit and loss has kept these firms out of the derivatives market. Amendments to the regulations and increased competition have changed the operating environment and utilities are now poised to enter the market for the first time.

14

Rethinking Risk Management

R. M. Stultz

This article explores an apparent conflict between the theory and current practice of corporate risk management. Academic theory suggests that some companies facing large exposures to interest rates, exchange rates, or commodity prices can increase their market values by using derivative securities to reduce their exposures. The primary emphasis of the theory is on the role of derivatives in reducing the variability of corporate cash flows and, in so doing, reducing various costs associated with financial distress.

The actual corporate use of derivatives, however, does not seem to correspond closely to the theory. For one thing, large companies make far greater use of derivatives than small firms, even though small firms have more volatile cash flows, more restricted access to capital, and thus presumably more reason to buy protection against financial trouble. Perhaps more puzzling, however, is that many companies appear to be using risk management to pursue goals other than reducing variance.

Does this mean that the prevailing academic theory of risk management is wrong, and that "variance-minimization" is not a useful goal for companies using derivatives? Or, is the current corporate practice of risk management misguided and in urgent need of reform? In this article, I answer "no" to both questions while at the same time suggesting there may be room for improvement in the theory as well as the practice of risk management.

The article begins by reviewing some evidence that has accumulated about the current practice of corporate risk management. Part of this evidence takes the form of recent "anecdotes," or cases, involving large derivatives losses. Most of the evidence, however, consists of corporate responses to surveys. What the stories suggest, and the surveys seem to confirm, is the popularity of a practice known as "selective" as opposed to "full-cover" hedging. That is, while few companies regularly use derivatives to take a "naked" speculative position on FX rates or commodity prices, most corporate derivatives users appear to allow their views of future interest rates, exchange rates, and commodity prices to influence their hedge ratios.

Such a practice seems inconsistent with modern risk management theory, or at least the theory that has been presented thus far. But there is a plausible defense of selective hedging – one that would justify the practice without violating the efficient markets tenet at the center of modern financial theory. In this article, I attempt to explain more of the corporate behavior we observe by pushing the theory of risk management beyond the variance-minimization model that prevails in most academic circles. Some companies, I argue below, may have a comparative advantage in bearing certain financial risks (while other companies mistakenly think and act as if they do). I accordingly propose a somewhat different goal for corporate risk management – namely, the *elimination of costly lower-tail outcomes* – that is designed to reduce the expected costs of financial trouble while preserving a company's ability to exploit any comparative advantage in risk-bearing it may have. (In the jargon of finance specialists, the fundamental aim of corporate risk management can be viewed as the purchase of "well-out-of-the-money put options" that eliminate the downside while preserving as much of the upside as can be justified by the principle of comparative advantage.)

Such a modified theory of risk management implies that some companies should hedge all financial risks, other firms should worry about only certain kinds of risks, and still others should not worry about risks at all. But, as I also argue below, when making decisions whether or not to hedge, management should keep in mind that risk management can be used to change both a company's capital structure and its ownership structure. By reducing the probability of financial trouble, risk management has the potential both to increase debt capacity and to facilitate larger equity stakes for management.

RISK MANAGEMENT IN PRACTICE

In one of their series of papers on Metallgesellschaft, Chris Culp and Merton Miller make an observation that may seem startling to students of modern finance: "We need hardly remind readers that most value-maximizing firms do not hedge."[1]

Culp and Miller refer to survey evidence – in particular, to a Wharton-Chase study that sent questionnaires to 1,999 companies inquiring about their risk management practices.[2] Of the 530 firms that responded to the survey, only about a third answered "yes" when asked if they ever used futures, forwards, options, or swaps. One clear finding that emerges from this survey is that large companies make greater use of derivatives than smaller firms. Whereas 65% of companies with a market value greater than $250 million reported using derivatives, only 13% of the firms with market values of $50 million or less claimed to use them.

What are the derivatives used to accomplish? The only uses reported by more than half of the corporate users are to hedge contractual commitments and to hedge anticipated transactions expected to take place within 12 months. About two thirds of the companies responded that they never use derivatives to reduce funding costs (or earn "treasury profits") by arbitraging the markets or by taking a view. Roughly the same proportion of firms also said they never use derivatives to hedge their balance sheets, their foreign dividends, or their economic or competitive exposures.

The Wharton-Chase study was updated in 1995, and its results were published in 1996 as the Wharton-CIBC Wood Gundy study. The results of the 1995 survey confirm those of its predecessor, but with one striking new finding: Over a third of all derivative users said they sometimes "actively take positions" that reflect their market views of interest rate and exchange rates.

This finding was anticipated in a survey of Fortune 500 companies conducted by Walter Dolde in 1992, and published in this journal in the following year.[3] Of the 244 companies that responded to Dolde's survey, 85% reported having used swaps, forwards, futures, or options. As in the Wharton surveys, larger companies reported greater use of derivatives than smaller firms. And, as Dolde notes, such a finding confirms the experience of risk management practitioners that the corporate use of derivatives requires a considerable upfront investment in personnel, training, and computer hardware and software – an investment that could discourage small firms.

But, as we observed earlier, there are also reasons why the demand for risk management products should actually be greater for small firms than for large – notably the greater probability of default caused by unhedged exposures and the greater concentration of equity ownership in smaller companies. And Dolde's survey provides an interesting piece of evidence in support of this argument. When companies were asked to estimate what percentages of their exposures they chose to hedge, many respondents said that it depended on whether they had a view of future market movements. *Almost 90% of the derivatives users in Dolde's survey said they sometimes took a view.* And, when the companies employed such views in their hedging decisions, the smaller companies reported hedging significantly greater percentages of their FX and interest rate exposures than the larger companies.

Put another way, the larger companies were more inclined to "self-insure" their FX or interest rate risks. For example, if they expected FX rates to move in a way that would increase firm value, they might hedge only 10% to 20% (or maybe none) of their currency exposure. But if they expected rates to move in a way that would reduce value, they might hedge 100% of the exposure.

Like the Wharton surveys, the Dolde survey also found that the focus of risk management was mostly on transaction exposures and near-term exposures. Nevertheless, Dolde also reported "a distinct evolutionary pattern" in which many firms "progress from targeting individual transactions to more systematic measures of ongoing competitive exposures."[4]

The bottom line from the surveys, then, is that corporations do not systematically hedge their exposures, the extent to which they hedge depends on their views of future price movements, the focus of hedging is primarily on near-term transactions, and the use of derivatives is greater for large firms than small firms. Many of the widely-reported derivative problems of recent years are fully consistent with this survey evidence, and closer inspection of such cases provides additional insight into common risk management practices. We briefly recount two cases in which companies lost large amounts of money as a result of risk management programs.

Metallgesellschaft

Although the case of Metallgesellschaft continues to be surrounded by controversy, there is general agreement about the facts of the case. By the end of 1993, MGRM, the U.S. oil marketing subsidiary of Metallgesellschaft, contracted to sell 154 million barrels of oil through fixed-price contracts ranging over a period of ten years. These fixed-price contracts created a huge exposure to oil price increases that MGRM decided to hedge. However, it did not do so in a straightforward way. Rather than hedging its future outflows with offsetting positions of matching maturities, MGRM chose to take "stacked" positions in short-term contracts, both futures and swaps, and then roll the entire "stack" forward as the contracts expired.

MGRM's choice of short-term contracts can be explained in part by the lack of longer-term hedging vehicles. For example, liquid markets for oil futures do not go out much beyond 12 months. But it also appears that MGRM took a far larger position in oil futures than would have been consistent with a variance-minimizing strategy. For example, one study estimated that the minimum-variance hedge position for MGRM would have required the forward purchase of only 86 million barrels of oil, or about 55% of the 154 million barrels in short-maturity contracts that MGRM actually entered into.[5]

Does this mean that MRGM really took a position that was long some 58 million barrels of oil? Not necessarily. As Culp and Miller demonstrate, had MGRM adhered to its professed strategy and been able to obtain funding for whatever futures losses it incurred over the entire 10-year period, its position would have been largely hedged.[6]

But even if MGRM's net exposure to oil prices was effectively hedged over the long haul, it is also clear that MGRM's traders had not designed their hedge with the aim of minimizing the variance of their net position in oil during the life of the contracts. The traders presumably took the position they did because they thought they could benefit from their specialized information about supply and demand – and, more specifically, from a persistent feature of oil futures known as "backwardation," or the long-run tendency of spot prices to be higher than futures prices. So, although MGRM was effectively hedged against changes in spot oil prices, it nevertheless had what amounted to a long position in "the basis." Most of this long position in the basis represented a bet that the convenience yields on crude oil – that is, the premiums of near-term futures over long-dated futures – would remain positive as they had over most of the past decade.

When spot prices fell dramatically in 1993, MGRM lost on its futures positions and gained on its cash positions – that is, on the present value of its delivery contracts. But because the futures positions were marked to market while the delivery contracts were not, MGRM's financial statements showed large losses. Compounding this problem of large "paper losses," the backwardation of oil prices also disappeared, thus adding real losses to the paper ones. And, in response to the reports of mounting losses, MG's management chose to liquidate the hedge. This action, as Culp and Miller point out, had the unfortunate consequence of "turning paper losses into realized losses" and "leaving MGRM exposed to rising prices on its remaining fixed-price contracts."[7]

Daimler-Benz

In 1995, Daimler-Benz reported first-half losses of DM1.56 billion, the largest in the company's 109-year history. In its public statements, management attributed the losses to exchange rate losses due to the weakening dollar. One subsidiary of Daimler-Benz, Daimler-Benz Aerospace, had an order book of DM20 billion, of which 80% was fixed in dollars. Because the dollar fell by 14% during this period, Daimler-Benz had to take a provision for losses of DM1.2 billion to cover futures losses.

Why did Daimler-Benz fail to hedge its expected dollar receivables? The company said that it chose not to hedge because the forecasts it received were too disperse, ranging as they did from DM1.2 to DM1.7 per dollar. Analysts, however, attributed Daimler-Benz's decision to remain unhedged to its view that the dollar would stay above DM1.55.[8]

These two brief case studies reinforce the conclusion drawn from the survey evidence. In both of these cases, management's view of future price movements was an important determinant of how (or whether) risk was managed. Risk management did not mean minimizing risk by putting on a minimum-variance hedge. Rather, it meant choosing to bear certain risks based on a number of different considerations, including the belief that a particular position would allow the firm to earn abnormal returns.

Is such a practice consistent with the modern theory of risk management? To answer that question, we first need to review the theory.

THE PERSPECTIVE OF MODERN FINANCE

The two pillars of modern finance theory are the concepts of efficient markets and diversification. Stated as briefly as possible, market efficiency means that markets don't leave money on the table. Information that is freely accessible is incorporated in prices with sufficient speed and accuracy that one cannot profit by trading on it.

Despite the spread of the doctrine of efficient markets, the world remains full of corporate executives who are convinced of their own ability to predict future interest rates, exchange rates, and commodity prices. As evidence of the strength and breadth of this conviction, many companies during the late '80s and early '90s set up their corporate treasuries as "profit centers" in their own right – a practice that, if the survey evidence can be trusted, has been largely abandoned in recent years by most industrial firms. And the practice has been abandoned with good reason: Behind most large derivative losses – in cases ranging from Orange County and Baring Brothers to

Procter & Gamble and BancOne – there appear to have been more or less conscious decisions to bear significant exposures to market risks with the hope of earning abnormal returns.

The lesson of market efficiency for corporate risk managers is that the attempt to earn higher returns in most financial markets generally means bearing large (and unfamiliar) risks. In highly liquid markets such as those for interest rate and FX futures – and in the case of heavily traded commodities like oil and gold as well – industrial companies are unlikely to have a comparative advantage in bearing these risks. And so, for most industrial corporations, setting up the corporate treasury to trade derivatives for profit is a value-destroying proposition. (As I will also argue later, however, market efficiency does not rule out the possibility that management's information may be better than the market's in special cases.)

But if the concept of market efficiency should discourage corporations from *creating* corporate exposures to financial market risks, the companion concept of diversification should also discourage some companies from *hedging* financial exposures incurred through their normal business operations. To explain why, however, requires a brief digression on the corporate cost of capital.

Finance theory says that the stock market, in setting the values of companies, effectively assigns minimum required rates of return on capital that vary directly with the companies' levels of risk. In general, the greater a company's risk, the higher the rate of return it must earn to produce superior returns for its shareholders. But a company's required rate of return, also known as its cost of capital, is said to depend only on its non-diversifiable (or "systematic") risk, not on its total risk. In slightly different words, a company's cost of capital depends on the strength of the firm's tendency to move with the broad market (in statistical terms, its "covariance") rather than its overall volatility (or "variance").

In general, most of a company's interest rate, currency, and commodity price exposures will not increase the risk of a well-diversified portfolio. Thus, most corporate financial exposures represent "non-systematic" or "diversifiable" risks that shareholders can eliminate by holding diversified portfolios. And because shareholders have such an inexpensive risk-management tool at their disposal, companies that reduce their earnings volatility by managing their financial risks will not be rewarded by investors with lower required rates of return (or, alternatively, with higher P/E ratios for given levels of cash flow or earnings). As one example, investors with portfolios that include stocks of oil companies are not likely to place higher multiples on the earnings of petrochemical firms just because the latter smooth their earnings by hedging against oil price increases.

For this reason, having the corporation devote resources to reducing FX or commodity price risks makes sense only if the cash flow variability arising from such risks has the potential to impose "real" costs on the corporation. The academic finance literature has identified three major costs associated with higher variability:

1. higher expected bankruptcy costs (and, more generally, costs of financial distress);

2. higher expected payments to corporate "stakeholders" (including higher rates of return required by owners of closely-held firms); and

3. higher expected tax payments.

The potential gains from risk management come from its ability to reduce each of these three costs – and I review each in turn below.[9]

Risk Management Can Reduce Bankruptcy Costs

Although well-diversified shareholders may not be concerned about the cash flow variability caused by swings in FX rates or commodity prices, they will become concerned if such variability materially raises the probability of financial distress. In the extreme case, a company with significant amounts of debt could experience a sharp downturn in operating cash flow – caused in part by an unhedged exposure – and be forced to file for bankruptcy.

What are the costs of bankruptcy? Most obvious are the payments to lawyers and court costs. But, in addition to these "direct" costs of administration and reorganization, there are some potentially larger "indirect" costs. Companies that wind up in Chapter 11 face considerable interference from the bankruptcy court with their investment and operating decisions. And such interference has the potential to cause significant reductions in the ongoing operating value of the firm.

If a company's shareholders view bankruptcy as a real possibility – and to the extent the process of reorganization itself is expected to reduce the firm's operating value – the expected present value of these costs will be reflected in a company's *current* market value. A risk management program that costlessly eliminates the risk of bankruptcy effectively reduces these costs to zero and, in so doing, increases the value of the firm.

The effects of risk management on bankruptcy costs and firm value are illustrated in Figure 14.1. In the case shown in the figure, hedging is assumed to reduce the variability of cash flow and firm value to the degree that default is no longer possible. By eliminating the possibility of bankruptcy, risk management increases the value of the firm's equity by an amount roughly equal to Bc (bankruptcy costs) multiplied by the probability of bankruptcy if the firm remains unhedged (pBU). For example, let's assume the market value of the firm's equity is $100 million, bankruptcy costs are expected to run $25 million (or 25% of current firm value), and the probability of bankruptcy in the absence of hedging is 10%. In this case, risk management can be seen as increasing the current value of the firm's equity by $2.5 million (10% × $25 million), or 2.5%. (Keep in mind that this is the contribution of risk management to firm value *when the company is healthy*; in the event that cash flow and value should decline sharply from

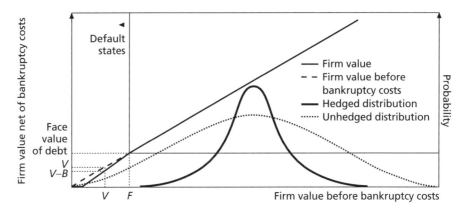

Figure 14.1 Debt, equity, and firm value with bankruptcy costs

current levels, the value added by risk management increases in absolute dollars, and even more on a percentage-of-value basis.)

This argument extends to distress costs in general. For instance, as a company becomes weaker financially, it becomes more difficult for it to raise funds. At some point, the cost of outside funding – if available at all – may become so great that management chooses to pass up profitable investments. This "underinvestment problem" experienced by companies when facing the prospect of default (or, in some cases, just a downturn in earnings[10]) represents an important cost of financial distress. And, to the extent that risk management succeeds in reducing the perceived *probability* of financial distress and the costs associated with underinvestment, it will increase the current market value of the firm.

Risk Management Can Reduce Payments to "Stakeholders" (and Required Returns to Owners of Closely Held Firms)[11]

Although the shareholders of large public companies can often manage most financial risks more efficiently than the companies themselves, the case may be different for the owners – or owner-managers – of private or closely held companies. Because such owners tend to have a large proportion of their wealth tied up in the firm, their required rates of return are likely to reflect all important sources of risk, those that can be "diversified away" by outside investors as well as those that cannot. In such circumstances, hedging financial exposures can be thought of as adding value by reducing the owners' risks and hence their required rates of return on investment.

And it's not just the owners of closely held companies that value the protection from risk management. In public companies with dispersed ownership, non-investor groups such as managers, employees, customers, and suppliers with a large stake in the success of the firm typically cannot diversify away large financial exposures. If there is a chance that their "firm-specific" investments could be lost because of financial distress, they are likely to require added compensation for the greater risk. Employees will demand higher wages (or reduce their loyalty or perhaps their work effort) at a company where the probability of layoff is greater. Managers with alternative opportunities will demand higher salaries (or maybe an equity stake in the company) to run firms where the risks of insolvency and financial embarrassment are significant. Suppliers will be more reluctant to enter into long-term contracts, and trade creditors will charge more and be less flexible, with companies whose prospects are more uncertain. And customers concerned about the company's ability to fulfil warranty obligations or service their products in the future may be reluctant to buy those products.

To the extent risk management can protect the investments of each of these corporate stakeholders, the company can improve the terms on which it contracts with them and so increase firm value. And, as I discuss later in more detail, hedging can also facilitate larger equity stakes for managers of public companies by limiting "uncontrollables" and thus the "scope" of their bets.

Risk Management Can Reduce Taxes

The potential tax benefits of risk management derive from the interaction of risk management's ability to reduce the volatility of reported income and the progressivity (or, more precisely, the "convexity") of most of the world's tax codes. In the U.S., as in most countries, a company's effective tax rate rises along with increases in pre-tax income. Increasing marginal tax rates, limits on the use of tax-loss carry forwards, and the alternative minimum tax all work together to impose higher effective rates of taxation on higher levels of reported income and to provide lower percentage tax rebates for ever larger losses.

Because of the convexity of the tax code, there are benefits to "managing" taxable income so that as much of it as possible falls within an optimal range – that is, neither too high nor too low. By reducing fluctuations in taxable income, risk management can lead to lower tax payments by ensuring that, over a complete business cycle, the largest possible proportion of corporate income falls within this optimal range of tax rates.

RISK MANAGEMENT AND COMPARATIVE ADVANTAGE IN RISK-TAKING

Up to this point, we have seen that companies should not expect to make money consistently by taking financial positions based on information that is publicly available. But what about information that is not publicly available? After all, many companies in the course of their normal operating activities acquire specialized information about certain financial markets. Could not such information give them a comparative advantage over their shareholders in taking some types of risks?

Let's look at a hypothetical example. Consider company X that produces consumer durables using large amounts of copper as a major input. In the process of ensuring that it has the appropriate amount of copper on hand, it gathers useful information about the copper market. It knows its own demand for copper, of course, but it also learns a lot about the supply. In such a case, the firm will almost certainly allow that specialized information to play some role in its risk management strategy.

For example, let's assume that company X's management has determined that, when it has no view about future copper prices, it will hedge 50% of the next year's expected copper purchases to protect itself against the possibility of financial distress. But, now let's say that the firm's purchasing agents persuade top management that the price of copper is far more likely to rise than fall in the coming year. In this case, the firm's risk manager might choose to take a long position in copper futures that would hedge as much as 100% of its anticipated purchases for the year instead of the customary 50%. Conversely, if management becomes convinced that copper prices are likely to drop sharply (with almost no possibility of a major increase), it might choose to hedge as little as 20% of its exposure.[12]

Should the management of company X refrain from exploiting its specialized knowledge in this fashion, and instead adhere to its 50% hedging target? Or should it, in certain circumstances, allow its market view to influence its hedge ratio?

Although there are clearly risks to selective hedging of this kind – in particular, the risk that the firm's information may not in fact be better than the market's – it seems quite plausible that companies could have such informational advantages. Companies that repurchase their own shares based on the belief that their current value fails to reflect the firm's prospects seem to be vindicated more often than not. And though it's true that management may be able to predict the firm's future earnings with more confidence than the price of one of its major inputs, the information companies acquire about certain financial markets may still prove a reasonably reliable source of gain in risk management decisions.

The Importance of Understanding Comparative Advantage

What this example fails to suggest, however, is that the same operating activity in one company may not necessarily provide a comparative advantage in risk-bearing for another firm. As suggested above, the major risk associated with "selective" hedging is that the firm's information may not in fact be better than the market's. For this reason, it is important for management to understand the source of its comparative advantages.

To illustrate this point, take the case of a foreign currency trading operation in a large commercial bank. A foreign currency trading room can make a lot of money from taking positions provided, of course, exchange rates move in the anticipated direction. But, in an efficient market, as we have seen, banks can reliably make money from position-taking of this sort only if they have access to information before most other firms. In the case of FX, this is likely to happen only if the bank's trading operation is very large – large enough so that its deal flow is likely to reflect general shifts in demand for foreign currencies.

Most FX dealers, however, have no comparative advantage in gathering information about changes in the value of foreign currencies. For such firms, management of currency risk means ensuring that their exposures are short-lived. The most reliable way to minimize exposures for most currency traders is to enlarge their customer base. With a sufficient number of large, highly active customers, a trading operation has the following advantage: If one of its traders agrees to buy yen from one customer, the firm can resell them quickly to another customer and pocket the bid-ask spread.

In an article entitled "An Analysis of Trading Profits: How Trading Rooms Really Make Money," Alberic Braas and Charles Bralver present evidence suggesting that most FX trading profits come from market-making, not position-taking.[13] Moreover, as the authors of this article point out, a trading operation that does not understand its comparative advantage in trading currencies is likely not only to fail to generate consistent profit, but to endanger its existing comparative advantage. If the source of the profits of the trading room is really the customer base of the bank, and not the predictive power of its traders, then the bank must invest in maintaining and building its customer base. A trading room that mistakenly believes that the source of its profits is position-taking will take large positions that, on average, will neither make money nor lose money. More troubling, though, is that the resulting variability of its trading income is likely to unsettle its customers and weaken its customer base. Making matters worse, it may choose a compensation system for its traders that rewards profitable position-taking instead of valuable coordination of trading and sales activities. A top management that fails to understand its comparative advantage may waste its time looking for star traders while neglecting the development of marketing strategies and services.

How can management determine when it should take risks and when it should not? The best approach is to implement a *risk-taking audit*. This would involve a comprehensive review of the risks to which the company is exposed, both through its financial instruments and liability structure as well as its normal operations. Such an audit should attempt to answer questions like the following: Which of its major risks has the firm proved capable of "self-insuring" over a complete business cycle? If the firm chooses to hedge "selectively," or leaves exposures completely unhedged, what is the source of the firm's comparative advantage in taking these positions? Which

risk management activities have consistently added value without introducing another source of volatility?

Once a firm has decided that it has a comparative advantage in taking
certain financial risks, it must then determine the role of risk management
in exploiting this advantage. As I argue below, risk management may para-
doxically enable the firm to take *more* of these risks than it would in the
absence of risk management. To illustrate this point, let's return to our example
of company X and assume it has valuable information about the copper
market that enables it to earn consistently superior profits trading copper.
Even in this situation, such trading profits are by no means a sure thing; there
is always the possibility that the firm will experience signific-ant losses.
Purchasing far-out-of-the-money calls on copper in such a case could actually serve to increase the firm's ability to take speculative positions in copper. But, as I argue in the next section, a company's ability to withstand
large trading losses without endangering its operating activities depends not
only on its risk management policy, but also on its capital structure and
general financial health.

THE LINK BETWEEN RISK MANAGEMENT, RISK-TAKING, AND CAPITAL STRUCTURE

In discussing earlier the benefits of risk management, I suggested that companies should manage risk in a way that makes financial distress highly unlikely
and, in so doing, preserves the financing flexibility necessary to carry out
their investment strategies. Given this primary objective for risk management,
one would not expect companies with little or no debt financing – and, hence,
a low probability of financial trouble – to benefit from hedging.

In this sense, risk management can be viewed as a direct substitute for
equity capital. That is, the more the firm hedges its financial exposures, the
less equity it requires to support its business. Or, to put it another way, the
use of risk management to reduce exposures effectively increases a company's debt capacity.

Moreover, to the extent one views risk management as a substitute for
equity capital – or, alternatively, as a technique that allows management to
substitute debt for equity – then it pays companies to practice risk management only to the extent that equity capital is more expensive than debt. As
this formulation of the issue suggests, a company's decisions to hedge financial risks – or to bear part of such risks through selective hedging – should
be made jointly with the corporate capital structure decision.

To illustrate this interdependence between risk management and capital
structure, consider the three kinds of companies pictured in Figure 14.2. At
the right-hand side of the figure is company AAA, so named because it has
little debt and a very high debt rating. The probability of default is essentially zero; and thus the left or lower tail of AAA's distribution of potential
outcomes never reaches the range where low value begins to impose financial

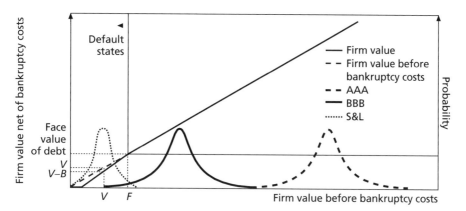

Figure 14.2 Optimal hedging for firms AAA, BBB, S&L

distress costs on the firm. Based on the theory of risk management just presented, there is no reason for this company to hedge its financial exposures; the company's shareholders can do the same job more cost-effectively. And, should investment opportunities arise, AAA will likely be able to raise funds on an economic basis, even if its cash flows should decline temporarily.

Should such a company take bets on financial markets? The answer could be yes, provided management has specialized information that would give it a comparative advantage in a certain market. In AAA's case, a bet that turns out badly will not affect the company's ability to carry out its strategic plan.

But now let's consider the company in the middle of the picture, call it BBB. Like the company shown in Figure 14.1 earlier, this firm has a lower credit rating, and there is a significant probability that the firm could face distress. What should BBB do? As shown earlier in Figure 14.1, this firm should probably eliminate the probability of encountering financial distress through risk management. In this case, even if management feels that there are occasional opportunities to profit from market inefficiencies, hedging exposures is likely to be the best policy. In company BBB's case, the cost of having a bet turn sour can be substantial, since this would almost certainly imply default. Consequently, one would not expect the management of such a firm to let its views affect the hedge ratio.

Finally, let's consider a firm that is in distress – and let's call it "S&L." What should it do? Reducing risk once the firm is in distress is not in the interest of shareholders. If the firm stays in distress and eventually defaults, shareholders will end up with near-worthless shares. In these circumstances, a management intent on maximizing shareholder value will not only accept bets that present themselves, but will *seek out* new ones. Such managers will take bets even if they believe markets are efficient because introducing new sources of volatility raises the probability of the "upper-tail" outcomes that are capable of rescuing the firm from financial distress.

Back to the capital structure decision. As we saw in the case of company AAA, firms that have a lot of equity capital can make bets without worrying about whether doing so will bring about financial distress. One would therefore not expect these firms to hedge aggressively, particularly if risk management is costly and shareholders are better off without it.

The major issue that such companies must address, however, is whether they have too much capital – or, too much equity capital. In other words, although risk management may not be useful to them *given their current leverage ratios*, they might be better off using risk management and increasing leverage. Debt financing, of course, has a tax advantage over equity financing. But, in addition to its ability to reduce corporate taxes, increasing leverage also has the potential to strengthen management incentives to improve efficiency and add value. For one thing, the substitution of debt for equity leads managers to pay out excess capital – an action that could be a major source of value added in industries with overcapacity and few promising investment opportunities. Perhaps even more important, however, is that the substitution of debt for equity also allows for greater concentration of equity ownership, including a significant ownership stake for managers.

In sum, the question of what is the right corporate risk management decision for a company begs the question of not only its optimal capital structure, but optimal *ownership* structure as well. As suggested above, hedging could help some companies to increase shareholder value by enabling them to raise leverage – say, by buying back their shares – and increase management's percentage ownership. For other companies, however, leaving exposures unhedged or hedging "selectively" while maintaining more equity may turn out to be the value-maximizing strategy.

CORPORATE RISK-TAKING AND MANAGEMENT INCENTIVES

Management incentives may have a lot to do with why some firms take bets and others do not. As suggested, some companies that leave exposures unhedged or take bets on financial markets may have a comparative advantage in so doing; and, for those companies, such risk-taking may be a value-increasing strategy. Other companies, however, may choose to take financial risks without having a comparative advantage, particularly if such risk-taking somehow serves the interests of those managers who choose to expose their firms to the risks.

We have little convincing empirical evidence on the extent of risk-taking by companies, whether public or private. But there is one notable exception – a study by Peter Tufano of the hedging behavior of 48 publicly traded North American gold mining companies that was published in the September 1996 issue of the *Journal of Finance*.[14] The gold mining industry is ideal for studying hedging behavior in the sense that gold mining companies tend to be single-industry firms with one very large price exposure and a wide range of hedging vehicles, from forward sales, to exchange-traded gold futures and options, to gold swaps and bullion loans.

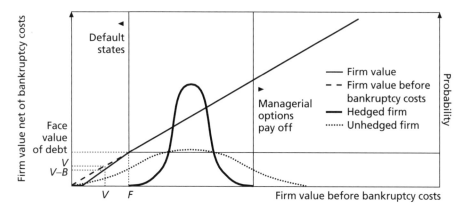

Figure 14.3 Impact of options in managerial compensation contracts

The purpose of Tufano's study was to examine the ability of various corporate risk management theories to explain any significant pattern of differences in the percentage of their gold price exposures that the companies choose to hedge. Somewhat surprisingly, there was considerable variation in the hedging behavior of these 48 firms. One company, Homestake Mining, chose not only to hedge none of its exposure, but to publicize its policy while condemning what it called "gold price management." At the other extreme were companies like American Barrick that hedged as much as 85% of their anticipated production over the next three years. And whereas about one in six of these firms chose to hedge none of its exposure and sold *all* of its output at spot prices, another one in six firms hedged 40% or more of its gold price exposure.

The bottom line of Tufano's study was that the only important systematic determinant of the 48 corporate hedging decisions was managerial ownership of shares and, more generally, the nature of the managerial compensation contract. In general, the greater management's direct percentage share ownership, the larger the percentage of its gold price exposure a firm hedged. By contrast, little hedging took place in gold mining firms where management owns a small stake. Moreover, managerial compensation contracts that emphasize options or option-like features were also associated with significantly less hedging.

The propensity of managers with lots of stock options but little equity ownership to leave their gold price exposures unhedged is also easy to understand. As shown in Figure 14.3, the one-sided payoff from stock options effectively rewards management for taking bets and so increasing volatility. In this example, the reduction in volatility from hedging makes management's options worthless (that is, the example assumes these are well out-of-the-money options). But if the firm does not hedge, there is some probability that a large increase in gold prices will cause the options to pay off.

What if we make the more realistic assumption that the options are *at the money* instead of far out of the money? In this case, options would still have the power to influence hedging behavior because management gains more from increases in firm value than it loses from reductions in firm value. As we saw in the case of the S&L presented earlier, this "asymmetric" payoff structure of options increases management's willingness to take bets.[15]

But if these differences in hedging behavior reflect differences in managerial incentives, what do they tell us about the effect of risk management on shareholder value? Tufano implies that neither of the two polar risk management strategies – hedging none of their gold exposure vs. hedging 40% or more – seems designed to increase shareholder value while both appear to serve managers' interests. But can we therefore conclude from this study that neither of these approaches benefits shareholders?

Let's start with the case of the companies that, like Homestake Mining, choose to hedge none of their gold price exposure. As we saw earlier, companies for which financial distress is unlikely have no good reason to hedge (assuming they see no value in changing their current capital structure.) At the same time, in a market as heavily traded as gold, management is also not likely to possess a comparative advantage in predicting gold prices. And, lacking either a motive for hedging or superior information about future gold prices, management has no reason to alter the company's natural exposure to gold prices. In further defense of such a policy, one could also argue that such a gold price exposure will have diversification benefits for investors seeking protection against inflation and political risks.

On the other hand, because stock options have considerably more upside than downside risk, such incentive packages could result in a misalignment of managers' and shareholders' interests. That is, stock options could be giving managers a one-sided preference for risk-taking that is not fully shared by the companies' stockholders; and, if so, a better policy would be to balance managers' upside potential by giving them a share of the downside risk.

But what about the opposite decision to hedge a significant portion of gold price exposures? Was that likely to have increased shareholder value? As Tufano's study suggests, the managers of the hedging firms tend to hold larger equity stakes. And, as we saw earlier, if such managers have a large fraction of their wealth tied up in their firms, they will demand higher levels of compensation to work in firms with such price exposures. *Given that the firm has chosen to concentrate equity ownership*, hedging may well be a value-adding strategy. That is, if significant equity ownership for managers is expected to add value by strengthening incentives to improve operating performance, the role of hedging is to make these incentives even stronger by removing the "noise" introduced by a major performance variable – the gold price – that is beyond management's control. For this reason, the combination of concentrated ownership, the less "noisy" performance measure produced by hedging, and the possibility of higher financial leverage[16] has the potential to add significant value. As this reasoning suggests, risk management can be used to facilitate an organizational structure that resembles that of an LBO![17]

To put the same thought another way, it is the risk management policy that allows companies with large financial exposures to have significant managerial stock ownership. For, without the hedging policy, a major price exposure would cause the scope of management's bet to be too diffuse, and "uncontrollables" would dilute the desired incentive benefits of more concentrated ownership.

Although Tufano's study is finally incapable of answering the question, "Did risk management add value for shareholders?," the study nevertheless has an important message for corporate policy. It says that, to the extent that risk-taking within the corporation is decentralized, it is important to understand the incentives of those who make the decisions to take or lay off risks.

Organizations have lots of people doing a good job, and so simply doing a good job may not be enough to get promoted. And, if one views corporate promotions as the outcome of "tournaments" (as does one strand of the academic literature), there are tremendous incentives to stand out. One way to stand out is by volunteering to take big risks. In most areas of a corporation, it is generally impossible to take risks where the payoffs are large enough to be noticeable if things go well. But the treasury area may still be an exception. When organized as a profit center, the corporate treasury was certainly a place where an enterprising executive could take such risks and succeed. To the extent such possibilities for risk-taking still exist within some corporate treasuries, top management must be very careful in establishing the appropriate incentives for their risk managers.

CONCLUSION

This article presents a theory of risk management that attempts to go beyond the 'variance-minimization' model that dominates most academic discussions of corporate risk management. I argue that the primary goal of risk management is to eliminate the probability of costly lower-tail outcomes – those that would cause financial distress or make a company unable to carry out its investment strategy. (In this sense, risk management can be viewed as the purchase of well-out-of-the-money put options designed to limit downside risk.) Moreover, by eliminating downside risk and reducing the expected costs of financial trouble, risk management can also help move companies toward their optimal capital and ownership structure. For, besides increasing corporate debt capacity, the reduction of downside risk could also encourage larger equity stakes for managers by shielding their investments from "uncontrollables."

This article also departs from standard finance theory in suggesting that some companies may have a comparative advantage in bearing certain financial market risks – an advantage that derives from information it acquires through its normal business activities. Although such specialized information may occasionally lead some companies to take speculative positions in commodities or currencies, it is more likely to encourage selective hedging, a practice in which the risk manager's view of future price movements influences the percentage of the exposure that is hedged. This kind of hedging, while certainly containing potential for abuse, may also represent a value-adding form of risk-taking for many companies.

NOTES

1. Christopher Culp and Merton Miller, "Hedging in the Theory of Corporate Finance: A Reply to Our Critics," *Journal of Applied Corporate Finance* 8 (Spring 1995), p. 122. For the central idea of this article, I am indebted to Culp and Miller's discussion of Holbrook Working's "carrying-charge" theory of commodity hedging. It is essentially Workings' notion – and Culp and Miller's elaboration of it – that I attempt in this article to generalize into a broader theory of risk management based on comparative advantage in risk-bearing.
2. The Wharton School and The Chase Manhattan Bank, N. A., Survey of Derivative Usage Among U.S. Non-Financial Firms (February 1994).
3. Walter Dolde, "The Trajectory of Corporate Financial Risk Management", *Journal of Applied Corporate Finance* 6 (Fall 1993), 33–41.
4. Dolde, p. 39.
5. Mello, A., and J. E. Parsons, "Maturity Structure of a Hedge Matters: Lessons from the Metallgesellschaft Debacle," *Journal of Applied Corporate Finance* Vol. 8 No. 1 (Spring 1995), 106–120.
6. More precisely, Culp and Miller's analysis shows that, ignoring any complications arising from basis risk and the daily mark-to-market requirement for futures, over the 10-year period each rolled-over futures contract would have eventually corresponded to an equivalent quantity of oil delivered to customers.
7. Culp and Miller, Vol. 7 No. 4 (Winter 1995), p. 63.
8. See *Risk Magazine*, October 1995, p. 11.
9. For a discussion of the benefits of corporate hedging, see Clifford Smith and René Stulz, "The Determinants of Firms' Hedging Policies," *Journal of Financial and Quantitative Analysis* 20 (1985), pp. 391–405.
10. This argument is made by Kenneth Froot, David Scharfstein, and Jeremy Stein in "Risk Management: Coordinating Corporate Investment and Financing Policies," *Journal of Finance* 48, (1993), 1629–1658.
11. The discussion in this section and the next draws heavily on Smith and Stulz (1985), cited in footnote 9.
12. For a good example of this kind of selective hedging policy, see the comments by John Van Roden, Chief Financial Officer of Lukens, Inc. in the "Bank of America Rroundtable on Corporate Risk Management," *Journal of Applied Corporate Finance*, Vol. 8 No. 3 (Fall 1995). As a stainless steel producer, one of the company's principal inputs is nickel; and Lukens' policy is to allow its view of nickel prices to influence how much of its nickel exposure it hedges. By contrast, although it may have views of interest rates or FX exposures, such views play no role in hedging those exposures.

13. See Alberic Braas and Charles Bralver, "How Do Trading Rooms Really Make Money?," *Journal of Applied Corporate Finance*, Vol. 2 No. 4 (Winter 1990).

14. Peter Tufano, "Who Manages Risk? An Empirical Examination of the Risk Management Practices of the Gold Mining Industry," *Journal of Finance* (September, 1996).

15. Additional empirical support for the importance of the relation between the option component of managerial compensation contracts and corporate risk-taking was provided in a recent study of S&Ls that changed their organizational form from mutual ownership to stock ownership. The study finds that those "converted" S&Ls where management has options choose to increase their one-year gaps and, hence, their exposure to interest rates. The study also shows that the greater the percentage of their interest rate exposure an S&L hedges, the larger the credit risk it takes on. The authors of the study interpret this finding to argue, as I do here, that risk management allows firms to increase their exposures to some risks by reducing other risks and thus limiting total firm risk. See C. M. Schrandt and H. Unal, "Coordinated Risk Management: On and Off-balance Sheet Hedging and Thrift Conversion," 1996, unpublished working paper, The Wharton School, University of Pennsylvania, Philadelphia, PA.

16. Although Tufano's study does not find that firms that hedge have systematically higher leverage ratios, it does find that companies that hedge less have higher cash balances.

17. For a discussion of the role of hedging in creating an LBO-like structure, see my study, "Managerial Discretion and Optimal Financing Policies," *Journal of Financial Economics* (1990), pp. 3–26.

CASE STUDY 6

Ring of Confidence

G. Cooper

Global brands, global investment, global growth is the theme of Colgate-Palmolive's annual report. A quick review of the company's business outside its US base shows these claims to be fully justified. Few companies in the world can match the consumer product group's geographical spread of activities. Its annual sales of $8.4 billion come from 194 countries and it has production facilities in 87. Its leading brands, such as Palmolive soap, Colgate toothpaste and Ajax cleaning products, are all sold in well over 100 countries and have the lion's share of the market in most of them.

The potentially daunting foreign exchange risks arising from this spread of business find a natural partial hedge in Colgate's wide manufacturing base and its strong market position. But the company is also a firm believer in the benefits of hedging with derivatives, assistant treasurer Hans Pohls-chroeder told delegates at the Risk 95 Congress held in June in Newport, Rhode Island.

Two cardinal rules govern the firm's approach to derivatives, he said: the treasury is not a profit centre, and risk reduction is the overriding aim of its currency and interest rate management effort.

Other key features of its risk management policy are the involvement of senior management in decisions regarding derivatives. Treasury staff propose ideas within a hedging framework defined by management but approval from senior managers is required for major transactions. "I sometimes make presentations personally to the chairman (on major hedging positions)," said Pohlschroeder.

The corporate risk management committee meets every three months and lays down detailed written policies. In such a large company, it is important that these should be written down, he added, so that they can be effectively and promptly transmitted to the many subsidiaries around the world.

Other strengths of the company's derivatives policy, he said, are the close involvement of accounting, tax and legal specialists in all transactions, the use of state-of-the-art software systems, rigorous accounting and documentation of all deals, regular marking to market, stress testing of positions and credit limits on counterparties.

Colgate itself has an A+ rating from Standard & Poor's for its long-term debt and requires its bank counterparties to have at least this rating. It now deals with 21 banks and has separate exposure limits for each.

To simplify its interest rate risk management, the company has a policy of not borrowing in countries where rates are very high. It has no debt in Latin America at present, even though this region accounts for 23% of total sales. Colgate boasts of being a pioneer in emerging markets since the

1920s and has entered 22 new markets since 1989. In both Latin America and Asia/Africa it achieved double-digit sales growth (in dollar terms) last year and together these regions account for 42% of total sales.

In Mexico, for example, almost all the products sold there are made there, greatly reducing the impact of fluctuations in the dollar/peso exchange rate. The company claims to have more than 90% of the Mexican toothpaste market (against 52% for the whole world). Between 1989 and 1994, dollar sales in Latin America have risen at a compound annual rate of 16%.

Another cornerstone of Colgate's financing policy is to maintain a healthy credit rating. "We want to be a strong A not a double A or a triple A," said Pohlschroeder. This gives the company a reasonably low cost of capital which feeds through into earnings and helps it compete with its rivals.

Peer review is an important element of the firm's approach to hedging and it regularly monitors the risk management techniques of 20 major competitors. "The board is very interested in what [the company's] peers are doing," said Pohlschroeder.

This is not to say that it copies what its rivals do. Procter & Gamble, for example, is a direct competitor in many markets but the aggressive treasury operations which eventually resulted in the notorious 1994 loss of $175 million on highly leveraged swaps would be anathema to the Colgate treasury team.

As well as maintaining a continuous dialogue with senior management to establish its objectives and risk tolerance, the risk management committee continuously monitors and measures the various risks to which the company is exposed.

Regarding its interest rate risk, the firm has a clear target that floating-rate debt should represent 30–35% of the total in each capital market in which Colgate has debt. This is the optimum mix for obtaining the lowest cost of capital consistent with an acceptable level of risk, Pohlschroeder said (see Figure 1). Similarly, it tries to ensure that short-term borrowings account for around a third of total debt.

Interest rate swaps are the main instruments used to achieve this debt mix but caps are also used. At the end of December 1994, the notional amount of swaps outstanding was $222 million.

Only unleveraged swaps are allowed, Pohlschroeder stressed, and any derivatives used must be related to an underlying exposure. As examples, he cited the company's 1989 $1 billion sale of health care company Kendall, which eliminated the company's short-term debt and pushed floating-rate debt down to 8% of the total. Interest rate swaps covering some $300 million were used to restore the desired fixed/floating mix. In 1993, the company launched a share buy-back programme which resulted in floating-rate debt rising to 44% of the total. Again, swaps were quickly arranged to restore the desired 2:1 ratio of fixed to floating-rate debt. The instruments used were a 30-year swap to fix a rate of 6.6% on an underlying $100 million and a 10-year swap at a fixed rate of 5.7% on an underlying $75 million. Both hedges have made money as 30-year and 10-year rates have both risen.

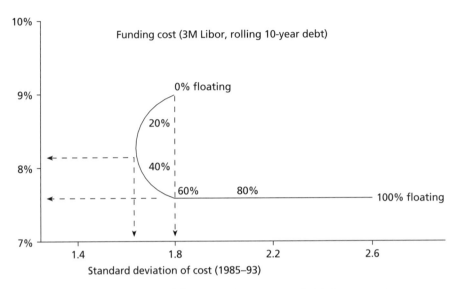

Figure 1 How floating rate debt can reduce cost and risk (*Source*: Colgate-Palmolive)

But, in these cases and all others, Pohlschroeder insisted, derivative hedges were the appropriate course of action whether or not they resulted in a gain or loss. Once a hedge position is taken, it will not be lifted just to take a view on the market, he said.

The same rule applies to foreign exchange risk. Colgate uses forward forex contracts principally to hedge foreign currency exposures associated with its investments in its extensive foreign operations and inter-company loans. The aim is to minimise the impact of foreign exchange rate movements on the company's financial position. Most such contracts have maturities of less than three years. At year-end 1994, the company held $390.7 million of outstanding forex contracts in which foreign currencies were purchased and just $6.9 million in which foreign currencies were sold.

Around 20% of all forex contracts were to hedge net investments in foreign subsidiaries, 60% hedged inter-company loans, 10% were related to third party commitments and the remaining 10% were anticipatory hedges related to other transactions.

While the vast majority of Colgate's forex hedging is achieved with currency forwards, Pohlschroeder said plain vanilla options are sometimes used for contingent exposures. Option writing to obtain premium income is rare. Currency hedging never covers 100% of exposures; the precise amount hedged varies according to the strength of the dollar and the duration of the exposure.

To facilitate control of the company's various financial hedges, a sophisticated software package is essential, Pohlschroeder said. It helps provide an audit trail of transactions, simplifies accounting procedures and helps avoid human errors. It also facilitates marking to market and sensitivity studies and raises alarms when limits on various risks are reached.

Colgate also subjects its derivatives positions to stress tests. This involves identifying the critical underlying variables, analysing abnormal market and price movements including worst-case scenarios, calculating the positions' sensitivities to each risk source and presenting the conclusions for management review.

Section 5

Measuring Performance

15

Using Earnings and Free Cash Flow to Evaluate Corporate Performance

R. G. Sloan

There is general agreement that a company's value should be established with reference to the net present value of the cash distributions it is expected to generate. There is considerable disagreement, however, concerning practical applications of the valuation process. Security analysts, managers, and the business press focus heavily on accounting earnings in evaluating firm performance. Investors appear to share the focus on earnings, given the well-documented stock price responses to earnings announcements and earnings forecasts issued by analysts and managers. In marked contrast, modern finance texts typically advocate a focus on "free cash flow" and caution against the use of earnings. These texts acknowledge and puzzle over the popularity of earnings, and then go on to illustrate the pitfalls associated with using earnings. Accountants, for their part, remain adamant that earnings and not cash flows summarize firm performance. Indeed, financial statements are expressly prohibited from reporting cash flow per share on the grounds that this would falsely imply that cash flow is an alternative to earnings per share as a measure of firm performance.

Faced with such disagreement, students of finance often become confused about the role of earnings and free cash flow in performance evaluation. What is captured by earnings that is not captured by free cash flow? How should earnings and free cash flow be used in security valuation? Do analysts, investors and managers place too much emphasis on earnings performance? If so, does this cause equity securities to be incorrectly priced? In this article, I provide some answers to these questions.

WHAT DO ACCOUNTING EARNINGS MEASURE?

A company's accounting earnings are not unrelated to its free cash flow. In large part, earnings are the result of taking the cash flows generated by a firm's operating and investing activities, and accruing or deferring certain cash flows to earlier or later periods. These accruals and deferrals are designed to facilitate performance evaluation, rather than to obfuscate the analysis of free cash flow. Specifically, earnings for a particular period are the result of an attempt to measure the free cash flow generated by sales transactions taking place during that period, *regardless* of the timing of the underlying cash receipts and disbursements.

Two principles guide the earnings measurement process. The first is the *realization principle*, which states that revenue should be recognized when a good or service is provided, rather than upon the receipt of cash. The cash proceeds expected from a sale are recognized in earnings in the period the sale is made, rather than the period in which the cash is collected. As long as the amount of cash to be collected from a sale is known with reasonable certainty, a company's ability to generate cash receipts is limited only by its ability to generate sales. Therefore, the cash receipts expected to be generated by sales made during the period provide a better measure of periodic performance than the cash that happened to be collected during the period.

The second principle guiding the earnings measurement process is the *matching principle*. This principle states that the cash disbursements associated with the production and sale of a product should be recognized in earnings in the period that sale is made, rather than in the period that the cash happens to be disbursed. As long as it is known with reasonable certainty that the cash disbursements associated with producing a product will result in the sale of the product, a company's ability to generate free cash flow depends primarily on the difference between the sales price and the cash disbursements associated with producing the sale (that is, the profit margin). Because the cash disbursements associated with producing a saleable product often occur in prior or future periods, cash disbursements incurred during a period provide a poor measure of the costs associated with producing products that are sold during that period.

Together, the realization and matching principles attempt to measure the free cash flow attributable to sales generated during the period, regardless of the timing of the underlying cash receipts and disbursements. By measuring the net free cash flow pertaining to sales made during a period, accountants aim to provide a better measure of periodic performance than simply measuring the net free cash flow generated during the period.

While accountants produce earnings in an attempt to provide a superior measure of firm performance, earnings suffer from three limitations. First, the periodic earnings number makes no attempt to measure the expected effects of events occurring in the current period on the free cash flow to be derived from sales expected to take place in subsequent periods. For example, expectations of future sales growth from product innovations or expectations of reductions in production costs from technological innovations are not reflected in current earnings.

While there is little doubt that such innovations will lead to revised expectations about future free cash flow and future earnings, the accountant makes no attempt to measure them in current earnings. Earnings represent an attempt to measure the periodic performance of a company, *given* the conditions present during the period, including sales volume, input and output prices and production technology. The task of predicting how these conditions will change in the future and the expected effects of any changes on future free cash flow is left to managers, security analysts, and investors.

The second limitation of earnings is that the realization and matching principles cannot always be easily and objectively applied. In cases of extreme subjectivity, accountants tend to move back toward a cash-based performance measurement system. For example, if the amount of cash to be collected from a sale is highly uncertain, then revenue is not recognized until cash is collected. Also, if costs cannot be matched to a saleable product, then they are expensed in the period in which they are incurred. Such is typically the case with selling, administrative, and research and development costs. In less extreme cases, generally accepted accounting principles specify accounting methods that can be objectively applied, but introduce some arbitrariness into the matching of costs and revenues. Examples include the use of the FIFO and LIFO cost flow assumptions for inventory, the amortization of acquisition premiums, and the use of straight line and accelerated methods of depreciating property, plant, and equipment.

The third limitation of earnings is that the application of the realization and matching principles often requires accountants and managers to incorporate subjective estimates into earnings. Whether by mistake or design, these subjective estimates may be incorrect. For example, if bad debts are underestimated, the amount of cash to be collected from sales made during the current period will be overestimated. Costs can also be misstated if, for example, the productive life of a piece of machinery is incorrectly estimated or inventory becomes obsolete. The subsequent correction of past misstatements leads to a "catch up" adjustment in the earnings of subsequent periods.

The recent wave of corporate restructuring charges, in which the costs of entire idled plants are charged against the earnings of a single period, are symptomatic of this problem. In the eyes of many earnings critics, this third limitation is most severe, because it allows managers to manipulate earnings to meet their own objectives. The considerable discretion afforded to managers by the realization and matching principles is often argued to seriously diminish earnings' ability to measure firm performance.

Given the above limitations, it seems reasonable to ask whether in fact earnings are a superior measure of firm performance relative to free cash flow. A detailed analysis of this question, by Patricia Dechow of the Wharton School, came to the conclusion that earnings are indeed a better summary measure of corporate performance.[1] The intuition behind her findings is illustrated in Figure 15.1, which contains plots of future free cash flow for portfolios of companies formed on the basis of their current earnings and current free cash flow.

Free cash flow is defined as the sum of net cash flow relating to operating activities and net cash flow relating to investing activities, as reported by Compustat. To provide a simple but crude control for the size of the investment base, each performance measure is scaled by total assets.[2] All companies were then ranked using the respective performance measures, and

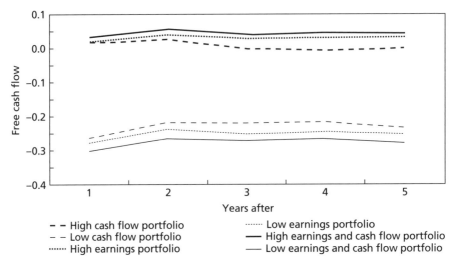

Figure 15.1 Plots of subsequent annual average free cash flow for portfolios of firms*

* Porfolios of firms formed on (i) current free cash flow; (ii) current earnings; and (iii) a weighted average of current earnings and current free cash flow. Each portfolio consists of firms in either the highest or lowest 10% of firms when ranked according to that portfolio's performance measure.

portfolios are constructed consisting of the top and bottom 10% of firms as ranked by each performance measure.

The performance measures are evaluated by their ability to predict *future* free cash flow. The greater the spread in future average free cash flows between the top and bottom 10% of firms, the better the measure is judged to be at summarizing firm performance.

As shown in Figure 15.1, the high current earnings portfolio has systematically higher future free cash flow than the high current free cash flow portfolio, and the low current earnings portfolio has systematically lower future free cash flow than the low current cash flow portfolio. (We will return to the third measure that combines earnings and free cash flow later in the article.) This finding demonstrates that current earnings is a better leading indicator of future free cash flow, and forms the basis for the study's conclusion that current earnings provide a better summary measure of corporate performance than current free cash flow.

HOW DO EARNINGS AND CASH FLOWS RELATE TO CORPORATE VALUATION?

From the above discussion, it should be clear that neither current earnings nor current free cash flow alone is sufficient for valuation. Neither measure incorporates how changes in future business conditions are expected to affect future free cash flow. Nevertheless, firm value can be readily expressed in terms of future free cash flow or future earnings, because future cash distributions are paid out of future free cash flow or future earnings.

Consider the following two popular versions of the dividend discounting model:

$$P_0 = \sum_{t=1}^{\infty} \frac{CFO_t - CFI_t}{(1+r)^t} = \sum_{t=1}^{\infty} \frac{Earn_t \times Payout_t}{(1+r)^t}$$

where

P_0 = value of security at the end of period 0
r = cost of capital
CFO_t = cash from operating activities for period t
CFI_t = cash used for investing activities for period t
$Earn_t$ = accounting earnings for period t
$Payout_t$ = the dividend payout ratio for period t

Both of the valuation models simply equate firm value with the present value of future dividends.[3] The models differ in that they define dividends in terms of different variables. The first model is the classic textbook valuation model, in which dividends represent the excess of operating cash flows over investing cash flows. The second model corresponds to models frequently used in practice, in which dividends are inferred by applying a dividend payout ratio to reported earnings.

The two valuation models are equivalent from a theoretical standpoint, since both models require forecasts of future dividends, and neither model restricts the information that can be used to forecast future dividends. But, from a practical standpoint, the earnings-based model can be argued to offer an advantage over the cash-based model.

Specifically, the earnings-based model implicitly fosters a two-stage valuation *heuristic*. In the first stage, future earnings is forecast, focusing attention on the fundamental value drivers: future cash receipts from sales and the margin earned on the sales. The realization and matching principles that guide the computation of earnings encourage such a focus. In the second stage, the task of establishing the exact timing of the cash distributions is addressed. By implying that the second stage is of secondary importance in the valuation process, I am not suggesting that the timing of cash distributions is irrelevant. What I am suggesting is that, in most practical situations, forecasting future sales and the margins they will generate is usually considered more important than forecasting the exact timing of future investment expenditures. For example, forecasting whether investments in working capital will be made at the end of one year or the beginning of the next may have a significant impact on the cash flow forecasts of each year, but will typically have relatively little impact on firm value.[4]

In contrast to the earnings-based model, the model requiring the direct forecasting of future operating and investing cash flows focuses attention on the exact timing of future cash inflows and outflows. In particular, one must consider timing issues associated with the collection of cash receipts and investments in working capital. While these timing issues can have a material impact on the cash flows of particular periods, their net effect on the cash flows of adjacent periods is usually fixed, reducing their importance in the valuation process. In short, for the same reason that earnings provide a superior summary measure of current performance, they also provide a useful heuristic for generating forecasts of future performance.

IS CURRENT FREE CASH FLOW USEFUL IN PERFORMANCE EVALUATION?

Having established that earnings provide an effective summary measure of current performance, and a useful heuristic for generating forecasts of future performance, it is perhaps not surprising that investors, managers, and security analysts focus heavily on earnings. However, the fact that earnings happens to be a good summary measure of performance does not imply that other sources of information should be ignored. For example, the fact that current earnings are better than current free cash flow at forecasting future free cash flow does not imply that information in current free cash flow is not *incrementally* useful in forecasting future free cash flow.

This incremental importance of free cash flow is illustrated in Figure 15.1. Besides including current free cash flow and current earnings performance, Figure 15.1 also includes a third performance measure that combines information in both current free cash flow and current earnings. The "high earnings and cash flow portfolio" consists of the top 10% of companies when ranked on a weighted average of earnings and cash flow performance. Conversely, the "low earnings and cash flow portfolio" consists of the bottom 10% of firms when ranked on a weighted average of cash flow and earnings performance. The relative weights placed on earnings and free cash flow are determined through the statistical analysis of historical data. Note that this is a simple and crude way of extracting some of the additional information in current free cash flow. In practical applications, the additional information would be extracted through a more sophisticated analysis of the components of earnings and free cash flow.[5]

Figure 15.1 illustrates that the performance measure combining information in both current earnings and current cash flow proves better than either of the individual current earnings or current cash flow measures in predicting future free cash flow. Specifically, companies with high combined current earnings and current free cash flow have the highest future free cash flow, while firms with low combined current earnings and current free cash flow have the lowest future free cash flow. Note also that since we have used a crude technique to extract the additional information in free cash flow, Figure 15.1 represents a lower bound on the incremental information about firm performance that can be gleaned from current free cash flow.

The intuition behind the superiority of the combined performance measure is straightforward. Earlier in this article, we recognized that the application of the realization and matching principles requires accountants to make subjective accruals and deferrals of future and past cash flows. The more of these subjective accruals and deferrals there are in current earnings, the poorer is its ability to predict future cash flow. By weighting both earnings and cash flows, the combined performance measure places relatively less weight on the accruals and deferrals.

This is not to say that the accruals and deferrals are not useful as predictors of future free cash flow. It simply says that both earnings and free cash flow tend to be less reliable predictors of future free cash flow when earnings contain large net accruals or deferrals. Thus, a performance measure that weights both free cash flow and the accruals/deferrals, but places a relatively higher weight on free cash flow, is superior to a performance measure that either ignores the accruals/deferrals (that is, current free cash flow) or weights cash flows and accruals/deferrals equally (that is, current earnings).

Some Examples

To make these ideas more concrete, it is useful to consider some common types of situations that cause earnings to contain a significant number of accruals or deferrals:[6]

Condition 1: Earnings are high relative to cash flows.
Symptoms: The firm is accruing a significant amount of expected future cash receipts as current revenues and/or deferring a significant amount of current cash disbursements as future expenses.
Possible Causes:

1. The firm is growing and therefore increasing its capital investments. Expanding levels of sales and production require additional investments in receivables, inventory, property, plant, equipment, etc.

2. The firm is using accounting methods that tend to increase reported income. For example, using the FIFO cost flow assumption for inventory in times of rising input prices and growing inventories or using straight-line depreciation on a growing asset base.

3. The firm is using accounting estimates that tend to increase reported income. For example, underestimating the provision for bad debts on future collectibles or overestimating the remaining useful life of its asset base.

Condition 2: Free cash flow is high relative to earnings.
Symptoms: The firm is collecting a significant amount of cash receipts that were generated by prior period sales and/or expensing a significant amount of cash disbursements that were deferred in prior periods.
Possible Causes:

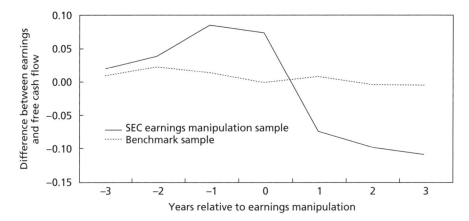

Figure 15.2 The difference between earnings and free cash flow*
* for a sample of 66 firms subject to enforcement actions by the SEC for manipulating earnings and for a sample of benchmark firms matched by size, industry, and fiscal year (Year 0 is the year in which the SEC alleges that earnings were overstated).

1. The firm is contracting and therefore reducing its capital investments. Declining levels of sales and production lead to reduced investments in receivables, inventory, property, plant, equipment, etc.

2. The firm is using accounting methods that tend to reduce reported income. For example, using the FIFO cost flow assumption for inventory in times of falling input prices and growing inventories or using straight-line depreciation on a contracting asset base.

3. The firm is using accounting estimates that tend to decrease reported income. For example, overestimating the provision for bad debts on future collectibles or underestimating the remaining useful life of its asset base.

It is difficult to generalize about the relative importance of the different causes described above for the superiority of the combined performance measure illustrated in Figure 15.1. Nevertheless, there is evidence that suggests that corporate choices of accounting methods and estimates play a significant role. In a recent study on which I collaborated with Patricia Dechow and Amy Sweeney (of the Harvard Business School), we examined the performance of companies that were subjected to enforcement actions by the SEC for allegedly overstating earnings.[7]

Some results from this research are summarized in Figure 15.2. The figure plots the average *difference* between earnings and free cash flow for the seven years centered on the year of the alleged earnings manipulation. The figure includes both a plot for the sample of firms investigated by the SEC and for a benchmark sample of firms matched on industry, size and fiscal year. The difference between earnings and free cash flow is large and positive for the SEC sample in the year of the alleged earnings manipulations. This suggests that managerial manipulation of earnings may be an important source of differences between earnings and free cash flow.

Figure 15.2 also illustrates that in the years following the alleged earnings manipulations, the situation reverses sharply and cash flows become significantly larger than earnings. There are two lessons to learn from this. First, it demonstrates that attempts to increase earnings today through the choice of accounting methods and estimates will lead to relatively lower earnings in the future. The accounting system requires that past misstatements of earnings be reflected in the earnings of subsequent periods. From the perspective of a manager attempting to increase perceptions of firm value, earnings manipulation is, at best, a shortsighted solution.

Second, the earnings reversal in the SEC sample illustrates exactly why information in free cash flow is incrementally useful. Had we relied on earnings to forecast future free cash flow, our forecasts of future free cash flow in the manipulation year would have been overly optimistic. This excessive optimism would have been corrected in the subsequent years with the dramatic earnings reversals. However, had we used information in *both earnings and free cash flow*, our forecasts of future free cash flow in the manipulation year would have been tempered by the relatively low free cash flows for that year. In sum, the large difference between earnings and free cash flow in the manipulation year tends to be a leading indicator that earnings performance is going to be relatively poor in subsequent years.

Empirical evidence is not restricted to companies attempting to maximize the difference between reported earnings and free cash flow. Some firms choose to use conservative accounting techniques relative to their industry counterparts, resulting in free cash flow that is high relative to earnings. An interesting case in point is Harnischfeger Industries, which is examined in detail by Krishna Palepu of the Harvard Business School. Harnischfeger traditionally had a policy of using conservative accounting techniques relative to its industry counterparts. In 1984, it reversed this policy, resulting in a substantial increase in its earnings. Interestingly, management's stated motive for the changes was that investors did not understand the earnings effects of Harnischfeger's more conservative accounting policies.

Another similar and well-publicized case was General Motors Corporation. Prior to 1987, GM had a long-standing tradition of using conservative accounting relative to its industry counterparts. During 1987, in the face of declining profits and market share, GM adopted what it referred to as "more realistic assumptions," resulting in a timely boost to its earnings.

In sum, companies can report cash flows that are high relative to earnings either because:

- they are currently using conservative accounting or,
- they have used aggressive accounting in the past, the effects of which are being reversed in current earnings.

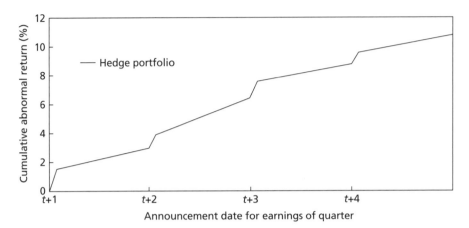

Figure 15.3 Cumulative abnormal returns for a hedge portfolio taking a long
position in the stock of firms with low earnings and high free cash flow and
a corresponding short position in the stock of firms with high earnings and
low free cash flow*

* Holding periods are formed by splitting the period netween adjacent earnings
announcement dates into a three-day announcement window (day –2 to day 0) and a
non-announcement window. While actual non-announcement windows vary in length,
the mean value of 60 trading days is used to illustrate the differential price responses
occurring in the two windows.

DO INVESTORS PLACE TOO MUCH EMPHASIS ON EARNINGS?

The results illustrated in Figures 15.1 and 15.2 clearly indicate that the evaluation of corporate performance requires the consideration of information
in both earnings and free cash flow. Nevertheless, the tremendous focus
of managers, analysts, and the business press on earnings raises the question of whether investors fully exploit information in free cash flow. At a general level, it is well documented that security prices respond to information
other than earnings. For example, the announcement of management changes,
new projects, corporate restructurings, and a host of other events are known
to lead to stock price revisions. The specific question of whether investors
supplement analysis of earnings performance with analysis of free cash flow
is the topic of one of my own recent studies,[8] and the results are rather
surprising. Efficient market theory predicts that stock prices should act as
if investors correctly use information in both current earnings and current
free cash flow in predicting future performance. However, my research indicates that stock prices react as if investors use earnings, but largely ignore
the incremental information in free cash flow.

The intuition underlying the findings of this study is illustrated in Figure
15.3. This figure plots the returns to a trading strategy that is designed to
exploit investors' overemphasis on earnings performance. The trading strategy takes a long position in companies with low current earnings but high

current cash flows and a short position in firms with high current earnings but low current cash flows. If stock prices act as if investors efficiently incorporate the information in current free cash flow, then the hedge portfolio should yield an average return of zero. However, if stock prices act as if investors overemphasize information in current earnings relative to information in current free cash flow, then the strategy should yield a positive return. This is because firms with low current earnings *and* high current free cash flow have higher future free cash flow than firms that simply have low current earnings. If investors base their expectations of future free cash flow on current earnings alone, then they will underestimate the future cash flow to the low earnings/high free cash flow portfolio. The subsequent realization of higher than expected future free cash flow will lead to higher than expected future earnings, causing an upward revision in investors' assessments of firm value. The converse reasoning applies to the high earnings/ low free cash flow portfolio, causing a subsequent downward revision in investors' assessments of firm value. Hence the hedge portfolio should yield positive returns if investors overemphasize earnings relative to free cash flow.

The results in Figure 15.3 are consistent with investors placing too much emphasis on earnings relative to free cash flow. Not only is the hedge portfolio return positive, but much of the positive return is concentrated around subsequent earnings announcements. Investors do not appear to learn about the information in current cash flows until this information is released through subsequent earnings announcements.

The size of the return to the strategy is also surprising. The results in Figure 15.3 are computed by implementing the strategy each year from 1963 to 1993 using all stocks trading on the New York Stock Exchange and the American Stock Exchange. The average annual hedge portfolio return over this period is about 11%.

Given the large body of existing evidence and opinion in support of the efficient market hypothesis, these results should be interpreted with caution. It is difficult to understand how these investment opportunities went unexploited, and even harder to believe that they will persist into the future. Nevertheless, I am not aware of a satisfactory alternative explanation for these results.

IMPLICATIONS

This article summarizes recent research that comes to the following conclusions:

- current earnings provide a better summary measure of performance than current free cash flow;

- earnings provide a useful heuristic for generating forecasts of future performance for use in valuation;

- the evaluation of corporate performance should go beyond the use of simple summary measures such as current earnings;

- current free cash flow provides information about corporate performance that is not contained in current earnings; and

- stock prices behave as if investors place too much emphasis on current earnings in generating forecasts of future free cash flow.

This last result should be interpreted with caution, because it contradicts existing evidence and academic opinion in support of the efficient markets hypothesis. Nevertheless, taken at face value, this result also has some interesting implications. The efficient markets hypothesis has traditionally led academics to the conclusion that it doesn't "pay" to manipulate earnings. However, the results reported in Figure 15.3 clearly raise the possibility that management may be able to influence stock prices through the manipulation of earnings. In fact, some recent research suggests that managers have raised their stock prices just before equity offerings through the use of earnings manipulation.[9]

A second implication of investors' overemphasis on earnings is that the accounting rules mandated by standard setting bodies, such as the FASB, may influence stock prices. Corporate managers have long been concerned that accounting rules forcing them to report lower earnings make it more difficult for them to access capital markets. If investors place too much emphasis on reported earnings, then managers' concerns may be justified. Pushing this implication to its extreme, the decisions of accounting standard-setters become critical, because they influence reported earnings and hence the allocation of capital.

The above implications are far-reaching, but have yet to be substantiated by a strong body of empirical evidence. In the meantime, it would be wise for investors and managers alike to be alert to the limitations of earnings and other common summary measures of firm performance.

NOTES

1. P. Dechow, "Accounting Earnings and Cash Flows as Measures of Firm Performance: The Role of Accounting Accruals," *The Journal of Accounting and Economics* (1994).
2. Construction of a measure of firm performance requires consideration of (1) future free cash flow, (2) the size of the investment base, and (3) the cost of capital. In this article, I restrict my focus to the ability of current earnings and current free cash flow to predict future free cash flow. Note that because I compare earnings and free cash flow using the exact same sample of firms, the size of the investment base and the cost of capital are held constant. The reason I scale by total assets is to avoid giving too much weight to large firms in my results.
3. For simplicity, I assume an all-equity capital structure and use the term "dividends" to refer to the net cash distributions made to all equity holders.

4. Of course, in cases where capital expenditures are relatively large and irregular, the timing of future cash flows can also be an important value driver (for example, a utility with a small number of facilities).

5. For example, Stern Stewart & Co. has identified some 120 performance measurement issues that require the adjustment of accounting earnings to eliminate distortions in measuring economic performance in the computation of its EVA measure.

6. For brevity, the examples that follow focus on revenue accruals and expense deferrals. The underlying logic also applies to revenue deferral (for example, collection of advance payments) and expense accrual (e.g., expensing of expected future employee retirement benefits).

7. See P. Dechow, R. Sloan, and A. Sweeney, "Causes and Consequences of Earnings Manipulation: An Analysis of Firms Subject to Enforcement Actions by the SEC," *Contemporary Accounting Research* (1996).

8. See Richard Sloan, "Do Stock Prices Reflect Information in Accruals and Cash Flows About Future Earnings?," *Accounting Review* (1996).

9. I am referring to research in progress by S. Rangan at Northwestern University.

The Case of UK Convertible Securities: Creative Compliance in Financial Reporting

A. K. Shah

In many countries, accounting regulation is based on a system of detailed rules prescribed in standards and the law. However, rule-based systems can rarely be water-tight. There may be gaps in the rules, and places where the rules are vague or even incomplete. Of equal, if not greater significance is the fact that regulatees may develop schemes which fulfil the letter of the rules, but undermine their spirit. Regulators may find themselves constantly lagging behind the avoidance activities of the regulatees (McBarnet, 1988). In such circumstances, effective regulation breaks down. Hopwood (1990, p. 80) observed that:

> Corporate financial accounting and the subsequent audit function are subject to a... lack of operational specificity, enabling a certain fluidity to enter into the corporate accounting domain. Discretion and choice are thereby made import-ant elements of the accounting function, providing a zone of strategic choice for management and a basis for a negotiated rather than purely procedural audit function.

In the United Kingdom, extensive evidence of the existence of such "creat-ive accounting" emerged upon the publication of *Accounting for Growth* by Smith (1992). This raised a public outcry and the share prices of some of the companies named by Smith declined at the time of publication.

In their study on the effectiveness of legal regulation of accounting prac-tice, McBarnet and Whelan (1991) explain this process of "creative com-pliance" as (p. 848).

> ... the active response of those subject to the law, not just in political lobby-ing over legislation but in *post hoc* manipulation of the law to turn it – no matter what the intentions of the legislators or enforcers – to the service of their own interests and to avoid unwanted control.

The aim of this study is to examine further this process of creative com-pliance in accounting. By focusing in detail on one particular scheme which was popular in the United Kingdom in the late 1980s, the paper traces the "dialectic of creativity" – from avoidance to rules to avoidance again. Par-ticular attention is placed on the development of the scheme and the manner in which the process of obtaining effective compliance is managed and articu-lated. Despite the significant evidence on the practice of creative account-ing, there is no study in the literature which traces the process by which such schemes are developed and avoid breaching accounting regulations. Tracing this process is the principal aim of this article. The findings expose the active involvement of those whose very job it is to be familiar with the rules – lawyers and accountants. This evidence appears to support McBarnet and Whelan's (1991, p. 873) central thesis that effective legal control, particularly of those with the resources to resist, may not be attainable.

During the period 1987–90, convertible securities attracted a lot of attention from financial engineers (Shah, 1993). At the time, there were no specific accounting standards or laws which defined the accounting treatment of convertibles. Thus no rules stated whether or not convertibles should be classified as equity from the outset, nor was there any statement on how the coupon interest should be treated in the profit and loss account. It was this gap in the rules which provided a range of creative accounting opportunities (Pope and Puxty, 1991). Smith (1992, Chap. 13) devotes a chapter to one such instrument – the premium put convertible bond. This study examines the process of creative compliance through the issuance of convertible securities.

A DIALECTIC OF CREATIVITY

A conventional convertible security is a combination of a bond and an option to convert the bond into shares of the underlying company at a future date. For accounting purposes, the common treatment in the U.K. and North America at the time (McInnes *et al.*, 1991) was to treat the bond as debt and the coupon as an expense until it is converted, whereupon the debt transforms into equity. During 1987–90, there was considerable innovation in the U.K. convertible market such that several variants from the conventional convertible were developed (Pope and Puxty, 1991). The first such instrument was the premium put convertible bond (issued by Burton Group in January 1987), where the interest rate was set lower than the coupon for conventional convertibles in the first five years. However, to compensate for the low interest return, investors were promised a much larger increase in the share price. If the increase failed to materialize, investors had the option to redeem their bond and collect the back-interest for the previous five years (hereafter called supplemental interest). Hence, the central accounting issue here is whether or not the supplemental interest should be accrued in the annual accounts of the issuer during the first five years.

In March 1988, a variant of the premium put convertible bond was invented – the offshore premium put convertible preference shares (first issued by United Biscuits). Here, the unique additional feature was that as the securities were preference shares, they escaped debt classification in the early years, hence improving the gearing position considerably. In addition, the equity classification helped issuers to create a significant reserve which could subsequently be used to write off the goodwill that arose from the acquisition which the security was financing. The offshore issuance structure helped ensure that the preference dividends did not attract advance corporation tax and could be offset against profits in a manner similar to interest on debt securities (Hughes and Lubbock, 1989). Thus the instrument was

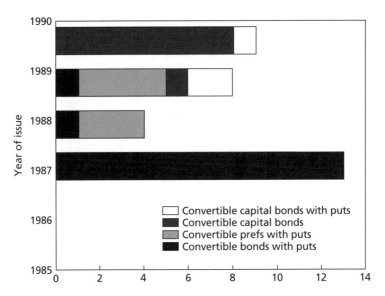

Figure 1 Number of new issues

designed to take advantage of gaps in both the accounting and the tax rules. As one senior investment banker explained when interviewed: "It was a wonderful instrument designed to meet a particular need."

In April 1989, the Inland Revenue hardened its attitude on such structures by rewriting the double tax agreement with the Netherlands Antilles where the finance subsidiaries were sheltered and as a result, the preference share dividends could no longer be offset for tax purposes (Morgan, 1990). This change in tax regulations led to the development and issuance of yet another variant of the convertible security – the Convertible Capital Bond (CCB). This instrument was designed to benefit from the tax and accounting advantages of the offshore convertible preference shares and get around the change in attitude towards the Netherlands Antilles – it was now issued through a specially created Jersey subsidiary.

Figure 1 demonstrates the rise and fall of the different variants of the convertible securities during the period 1987–90 – from the premium put convertible bond, to the offshore convertible preference share and finally the convertible capital bond. The move from premium put convertible bonds to offshore convertible preference shares retained the accounting benefits of the premium put structure and built on these by structuring the instrument in such a way as to allow equity classification. The change from offshore convertible preference shares to convertible capital bonds was driven by a change in tax regulations. It is worth noting that each time a new variant was developed it immediately phased out the previous instrument. Companies issued the most beneficial instrument prevailing at the time.

In all, thirty-two large publicly quoted companies issued the above convertibles and raised $3,584 million of new finance. Of these, some firms made more than one issue of the security. Most of the issuers were well-known quoted companies such as British Airways (£320m), Saatchi and Saatchi (£177m) and Blue Circle (£90m). The average size of each issue was £112m. Almost all of these companies had a number of creative accounting practices according to the analysis presented in Smith (1992, Chap. 16), the now infamous "blob index" – which lists the names, types and range of creative accounting practices adopted by large listed U.K. companies. The issuers came from a range of industrial groups, although companies in food retailing and stores were amongst the most common issuers.

During the period 1987–90 there were no specific accounting standards in the United Kingdom which dealt with the treatment of convertibles. Under Statement of Accounting Practice 2 (Accounting Standards Committee, 1971), which outlines some of the fundamental accounting concepts, the accruals and prudence concepts would suggest amortization of the supplemental interest from the date of issue. This interpretation was formalized in January 1988, when the Institute of Chartered Accountants in England and Wales issued a technical release (TR677) (ICAEW, 1988) which recommended the accrual of supplemental interest for premium put convertibles. This document did not have the force of an accounting standard as it was issued by a professional body and not the Accounting Standards Committee. However, its contents act as an indicator of best practice where no alternative pronouncements exist. However, there was no rule or pronouncement relating to the debt or equity classification of convertibles, and the latter securities (offshore convertible preference shares and convertible capital bonds) were designed specifically to exploit this gap in the accounting rules (Dow, 1990; Pope and Puxty, 1991). Debt classification would project an image of high gearing and hence greater risk for investors and lenders. Issuers were keen to obtain equity classification as this would reduce the perceived gearing ratio and provide significant benefits for the write-off of acquisition goodwill. Through creating "new reserves" issuers were able to avoid amortizing goodwill against reported profits which would have otherwise led to reduced earnings per share.

Thus, not only were the initial designs geared toward accounting and tax avoidance, but when there was a change in the rules, the market was quick to respond and retain the previous advantages despite the new rules. There was a dialectic of creativity. The principal factor driving the innovations was the creativity of the professionals and the attitude of the Inland Revenue. Standard accounting rules did not change during this period so they were not a problem[1], although the "discovery" of the "offshore" preference shares (which could be classified as equity) helped significantly in portraying a strong financing position (i.e. lower indebtedness). Changes in tax rules meant a redrafting of the terms of the convertibles to retain the original tax advantages. It has been suspected that regulators are always behind in the "game" of creative compliance, and this may mean that effective rule-based regulation is unachievable in practice (McBarnet and Whelan, 1991). In the case of convertibles, the regulatees appear to be always ahead in the "game" of creative compliance.

NOTES

1. There was a technical release issued by a professional body relating to the accounting treatment of the supplemental interest. However, this did not have the force of a standard.

REFERENCES

Dow, R., 'Convertible Capital Bonds: The New Financing Solution', *Practical Law for Companies* (August 1990) pp. 7–14.

Hopwood, A., 'Ambiguity, Knowledge and Territorial Claims: Some Observations on the Doctrine of Substance over Form: A Review Essay', *British Accounting Review* (March 1990) pp. 79–87.

Hughes, N. and Lubbock, E., 'Euroconvertible Preference Shares', *The Treasurer* (April 1989) pp. 43–45.

McBarnet, D., 'Law, Policy and Legal Avoidance: Can Law Effectively Implement Egalitarian Policies', *Journal of Law and Society* (Spring 1988) pp. 113–121.

McBarnet, D. and Whelan, C., 'The Elusive Spirit of the Law: Formalism and the Struggle for Legal Control', *The Modern Law Review* (November 1991) pp. 848–873.

McInnes, W., Draper, P. and Marshall, A., 'Accounting for Convertible Loan Stock: A Decomposition Approach', *Accounting and Business Research* (Summer 1991) pp. 253–263.

Morgan, B., 'Convertible Capital Bonds: Equity or Debt', *The Treasurer* (December 1990) pp. 12–16.

Pope, P. F. and Puxty, A. G., 'What is Equity? New Financial Instruments in the Interstices between the Law, Accounting and Economics', *The Modern Law Review* (November 1991) pp. 889–911.

Shah, A., 'Accounting Policy Choice: The Case of Financial Instruments', Unpublished doctoral dissertation, London School of Economics (April 1993).

Smith, T., *Accounting for Growth: Stripping the Camouflage from Company Accounts* (London: Century Business Publications, 1992).

CASE STUDY 8

Queens Moat Houses P.L.C.

The following text is extracted from the Notes to the Accounts for the year to 31 December 1992 of Queens Moat Houses P.L.C.

PRIOR YEAR ADJUSTMENTS AND RECLASSIFICATIONS

Following an investigation into the affairs of the group, including a review of the group's accounting policies and the treatment of certain transactions in prior years, the current directors have concluded that the accounts for 1992 and future years would be unlikely to give a true and fair view of the group's results and financial position if such policies and treatments continued to be adopted. Accordingly, certain changes have been made which, in the opinion of the the current directors, ensure that the accounts are prepared in accordance with best practice and give a fairer presentation of the groups's results and financial position. In order to ensure comparability, the 1991 accounts have been restated to reflect these changes. In addition, certain profit and loss account and balance sheet items have been reclassified. Further details of the prior year adjustments and reclassifications are set out below together with a summary of their effects on the accounts as at 31 December 1991 and for the year then ended.

Prior Year Adjustments

(a) Licence Fees

Previously, licence fees receivable from hotel operations not directly managed by the group were included in income in full at the commencement of the period of the licence and the turnover and net operating costs of such operations were included in group turnover and net operating costs. These policies have been changed and licence fees are now recognised on a straight line basis over the period of the licence. Furthermore, in view of the fact that the group's only contractual entitlement in respect of such operations is the receipt of a licence fee, the turnover and net operating costs of these operations are no longer recognised in the group's profit and loss account.

(b) Hotel Sale and Leaseback Transactions

Previously, sale and leaseback transactions which the group entered into with respect to certain UK hotel properties were accounted for as sales and operating leases, with the sales proceeds and profit on sale included in group turnover and operating profit respectively. In view of the nature of the leases, the current directors consider that they should, more appropriately, be accounted for as finance leases. Accordingly, this treatment has been changed and sale and leaseback transactions of this type are now accounted for as finance leases and the sales proceeds and profit on sale are no longer recognised in the accounts. The accounts have been restated accordingly.

(c) Office Properties Held under Finance Leases

As at 31 December 1991, the group held certain office properties under finance leases in connection with which there were outstanding liabilities amounting to £12.1 million. The properties were included in stocks as properties held for development at their cost of £12.1 million and the outstanding liabilities of £12.1 million were netted off in arriving at the total amount disclosed for stocks. The current directors consider that the nature of these properties was such that it was inappropriate to include them in stocks and that they should have been included in tangible fixed assets at their market value, which has subsequently been determined by the group's independent property advisers at £6.5 million and that the outstanding finance lease obligations of £12.1 million should have been included in creditors and not netted against stocks. The accounts have been restated for these and certain other related adjustments.

(d) Depreciation and Repairs and Maintenance Expenditure

Previously, certain tangible fixed assets comprising fixtures, fittings, plant and equipment were revalued annually and not depreciated. In addition, certain expenditure in respect of hotel repairs and maintenance was capitalised in tangible fixed assets. These policies have been changed, and all fixtures, fittings, plant and equipment, other than certain integral fixed plant, are now depreciated on a straight line basis over periods of four to fifteen years and expenditure in respect of hotel repairs and maintenance is now charged to the profit and loss account when incurred.

(e) Acquisition of Globana

During 1991, the company acquired the remaining 51% interest in the Globana (France) group of companies ("Globana"). As part of the overall transaction the company received a fee of £10.3 million in respect of the cancellation of the management contract under which it previously managed the hotels owned or leased by Globana. This fee was included in the group's turnover in 1991. The current directors consider that the fee was part of a series of transactions which resulted in the acquisition of the remaining 51% of Globana and, accordingly, that it should have been treated as a reduction in the purchase price and not as income to the group. The accounts have been restated accordingly.

(f) Rationalisation Costs

Previously, rationalisation costs incurred in connection with the acquisition of new hotels, comprising principally wages, replacements, stationery and advertising for a period of six months following acquisition, were capitalised as part of the cost of acquisition. This policy has been changed and all such costs are now charged to the profit and loss account when incurred.

(g) Loan Finance Costs

Previously, certain loan finance costs incurred in connection with the acquisition, construction or redevelopment of hotel properties were capitalised in fixed assets. This policy has been changed and all such loan finance costs are now charged to the profit and loss account when incurred.

(h) Deferred Revenue Expenditure

Previously, expenditure incurred in the creation and marketing of new projects was deferred and charged to the profit and loss account over a five year period, commencing when income was first derived. This policy has been changed and all such expenditure is now charged to the profit and loss account when incurred.

(i) Acquisition of the Ashford Group

Shares issued by the company as consideration for the acquisition of Ashford Group Holdings Limited ("Ashford Group") in September 1989 were recorded in both the company's accounts and the group accounts at their nominal value and no share premium or merger reserve was created. As a result, in the consolidated accounts the consideration was not recorded at its fair value, the effect of which was to reduce the amount of goodwill arising on the acquisition. Adjustments have now been made to record the consideration at its fair value by creating additional share premium in both the company's accounts and the consolidated accounts and to increase the amount of goodwill written off to the consolidated profit and loss account. Furthermore, no accrual was made as at 31 December 1991 for deferred consideration payable in respect of the acquisition of the Ashford Group. Such deferred consideration was dependent on the profits of the companies of the Ashford Group for the year then ended, and the current directors consider that an accrual should have been made. The accounts have been restated accordingly.

(j) Profit on Disposals of Fixed Assets

Previously, profits and losses arising on the disposal of fixed assets carried at valuation were included in the profit and loss account based on the difference between the sales proceeds and depreciated historical cost. In accordance with the requirements of FRS 3 this policy has been changed and such profits and losses are now included based on the difference between the sales proceeds and net carrying amount, whether at valuation or at depreciated historical cost.

(k) Exchange Rates

Previously, the results of overseas subsidiary undertakings were translated into pounds sterling at the rates ruling at the balance sheet date. This policy has changed and such results are now translated at the average rates of exchange for the year.

(l) Sale and Repurchase of Land

During 1991, the group disposed of an interest in land which was subsequently repurchased under an option entered into at the time of the sale contract. The current directors consider that the nature of the agreement was such that a realised profit should not have been recognised and that, rather, the sale proceeds should have been treated as a short term loan. The accounts have been restated accordingly.

(m) Bonuses Capitalised

During 1991, a bonus paid to an executive director of the company was capitalised as part of the cost of the company's investment in a subsidiary undertaking which was acquired from the director in March 1988. In view of the nature of the bonus arrangements, this treatment has been changed and all such bonuses are now charged to the profit and loss account.

(n) Other Changes

Certain other changes have been made in order that the accounts are prepared on a more prudent basis. These include: the accrual of holiday pay, the reversal of an adjustment to goodwill written off in prior years which was released to profit and loss account in 1991 and the deferral of part of the profit recognised on a sale and leaseback transaction where the sale was at above market value.

Reclassifications

(a) Stocks

Certain stocks held by hotels as at 31 December 1991, which were previously included in tangible fixed assets or debtors, have been reclassified to stocks.

(b) Non-hotel Properties

Certain non-hotel properties, including the group's head office, which were included in stocks as properties held for development as at 31 December 1991, have been reclassified to tangible fixed assets.

(c) Telephone Revenue

Previously, both revenue and expenditure arising from the use of telephones by guests in the group's United Kingdom hotels were included in net operating costs. This has been changed and the revenues arising in this regard are now included in turnover and the related expenditure remains in net operating costs.

(d) Deferred Tax Write Back

During 1991, £1.7 million was credited to operating costs, being the write back of certain deferred tax provisions no longer required. This amount has now been reclassified to taxation in the profit and loss account.

(e) Finance Lease Creditors

Finance lease creditors amounting to £30.5 million, which were included in other creditors as at 31 December 1991, have been reclassified to bank and other borrowings as obligations under finance leases.

Company Balance Sheet

Certain of the above prior year adjustments and reclassifications, principally those relating to the acquisition of Globana, the acquisition of the Ashford Group and bonuses capitalised, also affect the accounts of the company. In addition, certain loan finance costs and deferred revenue expenditure were previously capitalised into the cost of the company's investment in subsidiary undertakings. Adjustments have been made to restate the accounts of the company for the year ended 31 December 1991 on a basis consistent with the revised accounting policies and treatments adopted by the group in the 1992 accounts. Furthermore, as at 31 December 1991, the balance sheet of the company included cash at bank and in hand amounting to £36.8 million which the current directors consider should have been included in the accounts of certain subsidiary undertakings; accordingly, adjustments have now been made to include such amounts in group balances.

A summary of the effects of the above prior year adjustments and reclassifications on consolidated net assets and on the consolidated profit and loss on ordinary activities before taxation for the year ended 31 December 1991 is set out in Table 1.

Table 1

		Net assets (£m)	Profit/(loss) on ordinary activities before taxation (£m)
As previously reported		1,297.9	90.4
(a)	Licence fees	(48.6)	(13.5)
(b)	Hotel sale and leaseback transactions	(33.3)	(9.8)
(c)	Office properties held under finance leases	(7.9)	(8.5)
(d)	Depreciation and repairs and maintenance expenditure	(2.5)	(50.9)
(e)	Acquisition of Globana	–	(10.3)
(f)	Rationalisation costs	3.0	(5.9)
(g)	Loan finance costs	(0.5)	(14.6)
(h)	Deferred revenue expenditure	(5.2)	(1.4)
(i)	Acquisition of the Ashford Group	(5.0)	–
(j)	Profit on disposals of fixed assets	–	(24.2)
(k)	Exchange rates	–	1.5
(l)	Sale and repurchase of land	(0.2)	(0.3)
(m)	Bonuses capitalised	(1.2)	(1.2)
(n)	Other changes	(3.9)	(7.6)
		(105.3)	(146.7)
As restated		1,192.6	(56.3)

16

Making Accounting More International
Why, How, and How Far Will It Go?

R. Ball

There is a strong and growing movement to make accounting practices more uniform across national borders – to "internationalize" or "harmonize" the rules of accounting. It could transform the practice of accounting in many countries. It could require managers in corporations to quickly become familiar with a new set of rules. And because of the complex interaction between accounting rules and the ways in which business is conducted, it could have substantial effects on corporate affairs.

Commonly-asked questions include:

- Why does it make sense to make accounting rules more global?
- Why is it happening now?
- How is the globalization of accounting being accomplished?
- Why were there national differences in the first place?
- Will individual countries still put their own national stamp on their accounting rules, or will there be essentially uniform international rules?
- Is it desirable to eliminate national accounting differences?
- How far should the U.S. go in supporting international accounting standards, and what should be my corporation's position?

Before attempting to provide answers to these questions, it may be worth a short digression on why we have accounting rules in the first place and why accounting is important.

Stated as briefly as possible, we have accounting rules so there can be general agreement about how important commercial transactions are to be implemented. For example, in order to write and enforce loan agreements that restrict a borrower's ratio of debt to total assets, one requires rules – acceptable to both borrowers and lenders – for counting debts and counting assets. As another example, public corporations raise large amounts of capital in public markets; and, to allow their shareholders and creditors to monitor their performance, such companies must have rules – acceptable to both managers and shareholders – that govern the amount and type of information to be publicly disclosed to investors. To compensate managers on the basis of profits, companies require rules – acceptable to both managers and shareholders (and compensation committees) – for counting profits. The common thread in these examples is that accounting information is used in a variety of corporate transactions, and acceptable rules of accounting must be arrived at to allow them to proceed.

In sum, generally-accepted accounting rules are an integral part of how corporations transact. Change the accounting rules and you change how corporations behave.

THE ECONOMIC AND POLITICAL PRESSURE TO INTERNATIONALIZE

Accounting rules are set and administered by standard-setting bodies that tend to develop in one of two basic ways. One is to grow out of the accounting profession and remain part of the private sector, as have the U.S. Financial Accounting Standards Board (FASB) and the U.K.'s Accounting Standards Board. The alternative is for such accounting bodies to originate in and remain part of government, of which the French Conseil National de la Comptabilité is the classic example. But, regardless of whether the standard-setting body is part of the private or the public sector, accounting rules everywhere are shaped ultimately by two forces: market economics and politics.[1]

The main determinant of accounting rules is market demand. In many market settings, financial statements are used in transacting with corporations, so corporations incur the cost of preparing them. The other determinant of accounting rules is politics – and politicians, by virtue of their control over regulators, find ways to interfere with almost everything. The relative importance of market and political influences varies across countries, across time, and with the accounting issue involved.

Not surprisingly, the pressure for more uniform international accounting rules therefore comes from two directions: increased globalization of the markets in which accounting reports are used, and increased internationalization of the political processes that regulate those markets. I discuss each in turn.

Market Demand for Accounting

Accounting information is used in a wide variety of market transactions. Stock market investors use accounting information in their buying and selling decisions, and thus in setting stock prices. In short-term debt markets, lenders use accounting information in loan decisions. For example, banks analyze accounting reports when assessing the creditworthiness of potential clients, or when evaluating loans they have already made to clients. In long-term corporate debt markets, accounting information is also used both for credit assessment and subsequent evaluation decisions, though typically in more complex ways than in the case of short-term lenders. For example, contracts for unsecured long-term borrowing by public companies usually include covenants under which the company agrees to limit the proportion of its assets financed with debt, or to maintain a minimum level of working capital (current assets minus current liabilities), or not to pay out the contributed capital as dividends.

Accounting reports also are used in evaluating and compensating managers based on their company's reported performance. It is difficult to conceive of investors contributing enormous amounts of risk capital to corporations run by professional managers without an independent score-keeper. And, besides outside investors and creditors, there are other potential "consumers" of corporate accounting information. A company's suppliers, its employees, its managers, and even its customers have an interest in receiving information about its financial position. This is true whether they are individuals or companies. Indeed, the demand for accounting information arises from all parties who could potentially transact with the corporation, including those who might buy its shares, write analysts' reports about it, lend to it, work for it, or even buy its products (especially when the products come with long-lived commitments or warranties).

And because the range of actual and potential parties transacting in markets with publicly traded corporations is so large, virtually all democracies – particularly common-law countries – have a tradition of "public disclosure," of providing free accounting (and other) information to all. The enormous variety of market uses creates the primary demand for accounting information, and the market is thus the primary influence on the rules accountants use to report that information.

Political Regulation of Accounting

The second effect on accounting is politics. In most countries, the political process has a large say when it comes to writing the accounting rules, though the mechanisms for doing so differ substantially. Under the U.S. Securities Acts, an agency of the U.S. Government (the Securities and Exchange Commission) has legal oversight over U.S. accounting rules. And even though it delegates this function to a private-sector body (the Financial Accounting Standards Board), it flexes its regulatory muscle whenever it disapproves of what is being done. For example, the SEC put a lot of pressure on the FASB to "mark to market" (that is, record on balance sheets at market value rather than historical cost) a wider range of corporate investments in financial securities, including derivative products.

Recently, the FASB bowed to political pressure and abandoned its proposed new rule on accounting for stock options granted to executives by their corporations. The proposed rule would have booked the value of the granted options as a component of executive compensation expense, which would in turn have reduced granting corporations' reported earnings. Concerted lobbying by prominent executives caused Congress to pressure the FASB and the SEC to abandon the proposal. Although the executives allegedly feared adverse investor reaction to lower reported earnings, cynics thought they feared disclosing their total compensation. Ironically, one of the leading lobbyers of Congress was Bill Gates, founder of Microsoft and erstwhile defender of unregulated markets. Executives of Silicone Valley firms, including Microsoft, have unusually large stock option schemes.

The politics of accounting differ across countries. The SEC normally attempts to maintain at least the appearance of protecting small investors from losses, whereas Japanese rule-making, for example, has been dominated by the interests of companies and institutional lenders and investors. In Japan, the Ministry of Finance codifies accounting rules under the guidance of the Business Accounting Deliberation Council, with the Japanese Institute of Certified Public Accountants fulfilling an essentially interpretative role. In spite of the differences in political machinery, accounting rules everywhere are influenced in some way by politics.

Politics also influences how managers exercise any choice among accounting methods they are allowed by the rules (for example, in choosing among various depreciation methods). This is especially important in politically-sensitive areas such as defence contracting, utilities (with large numbers of geographically-concentrated voters), and corporations with large organized-labor payrolls. These corporations are more likely to choose conservative accounting methods that make them look less profitable and so avoid attracting political attention.[2]

Another way that the political process affects accounting is through tax accounting rules. In some countries (including France, Germany, Japan, and most of South America), tax laws have a large direct effect on accounting rules because the same or similar rules are used to calculate both a company's taxable income and the income it reports in its public financial statements. For example, German corporations routinely take charges against taxable income that are essentially extra depreciation charges; and because the German tax rules and the Commercial Code require this practice to be mirrored in the published accounts, German companies routinely report highly conservative income statements and balance sheets.

Tax rules have less effect in the U.S., where there are substantial differences between tax and reported ("book") income. But even in countries that do not equate reported accounting income and taxable income, there are subtle interactions between tax rules and accounting rules because the firm's transactions-recording system is used to prepare both. So, while accounting rules are shaped primarily by the various needs of users, they also are affected by politics.

WHY NOW?

Because accounting rules are shaped ultimately by economics and politics, it should come as no surprise that the push for international accounting rules is being driven by two related developments. First and foremost is the progressive globalization of the markets in which accounting reports are used. A secondary, but nevertheless important, factor is increased internationalization of the political influences on accounting – particularly, the growth of efforts among nations to coordinate their regulation of capital markets.

The recent acceleration in the globalization of markets and political processes is no doubt due to many things. Without question, however, the largest single driving force is the drastic reduction in recent times of the costs of producing, communicating, accessing, processing and interpreting information. It is becoming clear that the most important invention since the wheel is not atomic power, but the electronic computer.[3] Enormous (and related) breakthroughs have been made in satellite and fiber-optic information transmission, communications software, software for database management and processing, organizational decentralization, management education, and all aspects of information handling. Invention after invention has cut almost every component of information costs at an astonishing pace. When accumulated over decades, the effect has been truly revolutionary.

Cross-border transacting has mushroomed as a consequence. International communications and transactions that today are routine for low-level operational employees were, until very recently, the province of a managerial elite. Low-cost access to an abundance of international information has reshaped many markets. To an unprecedented degree, managers, employees, suppliers, investors, and customers now live and work in a "global village." When such people use accounting information in international transactions – say, in lending to a foreign corporation, investing in its shares, deciding to work for it, or buying its products – they create a demand for the internationalization of accounting. That is, they create a demand for accounting standards that transcend national boundaries. Cross-border trading requires cross-border trading institutions.

Politics is becoming more international as well. Voters and politicians are better informed about the actions of foreign politicians and their consequences. For example, the U.S. press now closely follows the politics of German monetary policies, French interest rate policies, European Union farm subsidies, and Japanese auto and rice imports. In this fashion, public opinion in one country becomes a political issue in others.

Information costs continue to fall apace, so the trend to internationalize commerce and politics, and thus accounting, continues almost unabated. Below, I outline the way in which accounting rules are becoming more global, including the operation of the International Accounting Standards Committee (IASC). But first it is necessary to describe the base from which this process is working – that is, the way in which accounting rules differ across countries, and why.

NATURE AND CAUSES OF NATIONAL DIFFERENCES IN ACCOUNTING RULES

Why are there national accounting differences in the first place? Here again, the reason is that accounting is an integral part of each country's own economic and political institutions. As one might expect, there are enormous differences among countries in how markets and politics are conducted. Nevertheless, it is useful to think of countries as falling into three distinct accounting groups: Anglo-American, Continental European, and South American.[4]

Anglo-American

This is the largest group, comprising over 30 countries. Its accounting institutions were developed in England and Scotland. They were exported to most former British Colonies (including the U.S.) and to countries that were early in building multinational corporations (notably, the Netherlands). The group includes Canada, Hong Kong, India, Indonesia, Israel, Kenya, Mexico, Nigeria, Philippines, Singapore, South Africa, and Zimbabwe.

Because these tend to be "common-law" countries, case law and precedent have a greater impact on accounting than does codified law. "Common law" is so-called because it arises organically from the commonly-accepted practices of the marketplace. When a practice becomes commonplace, the courts "read it in" to subsequent commercial agreements, and this practice becomes a rule.

Common law allows parties to a transaction who share no close ties to reach an agreement with the assurance that an independent body (the courts) will interpret it against a rich background of common practices. If a contract does not unambiguously provide for a particular eventuality, then common practice fills in such "gaps." Close ties between parties are thus not needed when entering complex, long-term transactions, which can be described as "arm's-length." In part because this style of legal system supports transacting by parties without close ties, common-law countries tend to have active public capital markets that attract widespread individual investment from the public at large.

Not surprisingly, accounting rules in the Anglo-American group have been determined largely in the private sector and have been oriented toward disclosure across an arm's-length market to interested parties. These parties are presumed by the courts (and by agencies such as the SEC) to rely entirely on publicly-disclosed information because they have no close ties to the corporation. Chief among them are investors – shareholders, creditors, bankers, and long-term lenders of debt capital – many of whose only communication with the corporation is through public disclosure.

Continental European

This group comprises a variety of countries in which the legal system and the accounting rules are codified by government ministries. Close interplay between government and major players is necessary because codified law, lacking the organic origin and evolutionary mechanisms of common law, relies upon the government ministries possessing an acute knowledge of contemporary commercial affairs. For the system to work, the major players must be few in number, so corporate capital is largely supplied by banks and other institutional investors. And because the players must be in close contact with one another, the governing boards of public corporations have representation from banks (Deutsche Bank alone sits on over 100 German boards), labor unions, and perhaps major suppliers or customers. Transactions in such countries tend to be based more on private information and less on public information than in common-law countries.

Most of continental Europe falls into this group (including Belgium, Denmark, France, Germany, Italy, Norway, Spain, and Sweden), as do several small former colonies. Japan also belongs to this group owing to its incorporation of the German commercial code and the French accounting code during the Meiji Era (1868–1910). In this group of countries, the comparatively close interplay between markets and governments in most aspects of business also extends to the setting of accounting rules. The accounting and tax rules in these countries are remarkably similar and, in many cases, even identical.

In Japan and much of continental Europe, then, public disclosure plays a comparatively modest role in shaping accounting rules due to the dominating role of private communication with banks and other groups with close links to the companies and to government. One consequence of the reduced emphasis on public disclosure is fewer public corporations. In 1993, for example, Germany had 425 corporations with publicly-listed shares, whereas Britain – a much smaller European economy operating under a different tradition – had 1,950.

South American

In most South American countries, the dominating influences are the legal and administrative systems inherited from Spanish (and Portuguese) colonization, and the highly political environment that results from such systems. The most notable differences between South American and Continental European accounting, which can both be characterized as government-administered systems, come from the special problems and requirements imposed by the persistently high inflation experienced by these countries. Inflation requires extensive modification of accounting rules. For example, countries like Brazil and Argentina have been forced to implement accounting rules to provide constant-dollar financial statements, with inflationary gains and losses clearly and separately identified.

Institutional Diversity is the Norm

The institutional differences among these groups – especially, between the Anglo-American and the other two groups – are significant and fundamental.

While such differences are being eroded by modern communication costs, they seem resilient. And within the three individual categories cited above, there are further differences. To European accountants, it would seem strange to place Germany, France, and Italy in the same box. Stereotypes notwithstanding, the German accounting code is written in general terms and allows considerable discretion, whereas the French code is more rigid.

Further, some countries do not fit within any category very well. For example, accounting in Finland evolved to meet the needs of its once-dominant forest-products industry. In this industry, companies create value largely by planting, managing, and growing forests. But because the Anglo-American accounting model does not record profits until decades later when the forest is cut and then sold, Finland developed its own accounting model to meet its special requirements. Nevertheless, as it has opened its economy to foreign investment, Finland has embraced the IASC's international rules (described below).

Switzerland, which has almost made a business out of secrecy, has minimum financial disclosure rules. To be sure, all large multinational Swiss corporations disclose well in excess of these requirements because they transact with international lenders, investors, customers, suppliers, labor unions and managers; but other Swiss firms are under no requirement to do so. As in many continental European accounting systems, Swiss accounting allows companies to have particularly large "hidden reserves" arising from undisclosed or undervalued assets.

What we learn from international comparisons of accounting systems, then, is that there is no one "true" way of doing accounting. Rather, accounting rules evolve as an integral part of the markets and politics of each country, and these forces differ substantially among countries.

HOW INTERNATIONALIZATION IS BEING ACCOMPLISHED

The differences, however, are narrowing. In response to the breathtaking collapse in the cost of transacting internationally, institutional structures are changing rapidly. As part of this, accounting is internationalizing at a rapid pace. I now summarize the principal ways in which this is happening.

Corporate Solutions

Some companies have adopted their own solutions. One simple solution is preparing "convenience statements," which merely translate a firm's financial statements into a foreign language while still using home-country accounting rules. Some companies prepare "parallel" financial statements, under the rules of one or more foreign countries in which they do business. Perhaps, the most highly publicized example of such parallel reporting occurred when Daimler-Benz in 1993 became the first German corporation to list on the NYSE. To comply with SEC regulations, Daimler-Benz was required to issue statements prepared according to U.S. GAAP. German corporate executives in general viewed the corporation's compliance with U.S. rules, which meant disclosure of large U.S.-GAAP losses, as a breaking of ranks. German accounting rules, like those of many other European countries, allow profits to be under-reported during good years by burying "hidden reserves" in the accounts that can later be drawn down to cover losses in bad times. And, just as it was for many of its corporate compatriots, 1993 was a bad year for Daimler-Benz. Although the company had reported DM168 million profit under German rules, that profit became a first-half loss of DM949 million (then $590 million) under U.S. GAAP.[5]

Few other European firms have yet followed the lead of Daimler-Benz, nor are they likely to do so soon. Nevertheless, some are moving toward more globally acceptable accounting methods. For example, more than 20 large French, German, and Swiss corporations now prepare their consolidated group financial statements under International Accounting Standards Committee (IASC) rules – rules that, as explained below, are likely to accommodate many aspects of Anglo-American accounting practice. Companies have incentives to adopt these solutions because they make it easier for foreign investors, suppliers, customers, and governments to transact with them.

Accounting Firms Become Multinational

As accounting firms' clients engage in more international transactions (for example, opening an overseas plant, entering joint ventures with foreign corporations, buying or selling internationally, borrowing from a consortium of foreign banks, or listing one's shares for trading on the London, Tokyo or New York stock exchanges), the accounting firms that audit the transactions have incentives to become more international. Thus, there has been a spate of worldwide mergers of accounting firms, with each of the majors (the "Big Six" seeking a permanent office in most large cities of the world.

Competition Among Financial Markets

Financial markets increasingly are competing on a worldwide basis to attract listing by foreign corporations. This puts pressure on markets and regulators to accept financial statements prepared under foreign or IASC rules. The London and Hong Kong stock exchanges now accept financial statements prepared under IASC standards as satisfying their listing requirements. The World Federation of Stock Exchanges encourages its members to accept IASC statements. The International Organization of Securities Commissions (IOSCO), a worldwide coalition of regulatory bodies, is working with IASC in developing its standards and has representatives on the IASC

Consultative Group. IOSCO has announced that it will defer considering recognition of IASC standards until they are essentially completed, but it is expected to increase the pressure on countries' regulatory bodies to accept IASC standards.

There are costs and benefits for corporations in listing their stock on foreign exchanges. Benefits include widening the base for raising new debt and equity capital, increased liquidity, and better matching of the country profile of the firm's investors with that of its profit (that is, better hedging of its profits against the currency risk faced by investors). The costs include listing fees and costs of complying with foreign regulations, including (if required) the considerable costs of preparing foreign-rule accounts. As one example of the trend toward global listing, Philip Morris, the tobacco and consumer products company, is listed on 13 exchanges outside the U.S.

The SEC has been adamant that foreign firms listing in the U.S. must comply with U.S. rules, including filing U.S.-GAAP statements. Its view is reported to be that statements prepared under non-U.S. GAAP are misleading.[6] The SEC does allow foreign corporations to trade American Depository Receipts (ADRs), which mimic (but are not) foreign shares under U.S. law, without filing U.S.-GAAP financial statements. However, trading in ADRs is restricted to the over-the-counter market, which has little depth and liquidity. One effect of the SEC's position is that U.S. financial markets are getting less international business than otherwise. If New York decides to challenge London as the largest international financial market in the world, it may pressure the SEC to relax its hardline stance.

International Accounting Standards Committee (IASC)

The IASC is a London-based coalition of professional accounting bodies from over 80 countries.[7] Formed in 1973, it has adopted the delicate task of promulgating international accounting rules. Until recently, the influence of the IASC has been limited by its not yet having assembled a complete set of accounting rules, but it has accelerated its standard-setting program and plans to complete a comprehensive set of rules by 1999. By the end of 1994, IASC had published 29 accounting standards that address accounting for inventory, R & D, construction contracts, joint ventures, hyperinflation, and other issues.[8] Its meager $2 million 1994 budget was financed 42% by professional accounting bodies and 23% by corporate contributions (including 2% by U.S. corporations).

The influence of the IASC is growing quickly. Most national accounting professions have actively supported the IASC, though U.S. support has been lukewarm. Several countries (including Singapore, Malaysia and Hong Kong) have adopted IASC rules as their own after a small amount of requisite rewriting. The Chinese Ministry of Finance is creating that country's first set of accounting rules, starting with IASC standards and revising them to better suit Chinese institutions and politics. Moreover, most national bodies, when drafting their rules in relation to an emerging problem such as accounting for derivatives, now seek information on the consensus solution worldwide. In such cases, the IASC plays a coordinating role.

IOSCO

IOSCO – the international club of market regulators – has requested its members to recommend one IASC standard (on cash flow disclosures) for acceptance in their own countries. In the U.S., the SEC has agreed to that request, with the effect that U.S.-registered corporations can choose between the FASB and IASC rules. IOSCO has announced that it will defer endorsement of IASC standards until they are complete. Since work on the remaining 16 standards – on topics such as financial instruments and interim reporting – is scheduled for completion in mid-1999, we can expect a millenium-induced bout of international accounting fever.

European Union (EU)

The EU requires companies operating in its member countries to comply with various EU directives. Among other things, these specify EU-side accounting rules, disclosure practices, and requirements for practicing as an auditor. Like many aspects of European unionization, implementation of the important Fourth Directive remains controversial in many EU countries. For example, its Article 2 states: "The annual accounts shall give a true and fair view of the company's assets, liabilities, financial position and profit or loss." The "true and fair" requirement is of British common-law origin and under-lies the Anglo-American accounting model, and thus differs sharply from the Continental-European model of codifying exact accounting rules. It specifies a criterion for rules to satisfy, and requires judgment to be exercised by an independent accountant in deciding whether the accounts are "true and fair," but it does not codify those rules. Since EU and national laws operate jointly, one effect of Article 2 has thus been to insert a common-law concept of "true and fair" into the codified legal systems of some EU countries.

Other International Accounting Institutions

As might be expected, a wide variety of groups is involved. To take one example, the International Federation of Accountants (IFAC) is a worldwide coalition of accounting bodies that operates in parallel to IASC by issuing non-binding standards for independent auditing of accounts. In addition to the IFAC, other participating groups include the International Chamber of Commerce, the International Association of Financial Executives Institutes, the International Banking Association, the International Bar Association,

O.E.C.D., and the United Nations Division on Transnational Corporations and Investment.

Finally, it is important not to overlook Eastern Europe and China. As these countries convert from planned to market economies, accounting firms are discovering an enormous opportunity to contribute to and profit from their development of accounting institutions "from the ground up." Accounting in the former Soviet Union has been described as a conspiracy between accountant and plant manager to prove that the plant met its output quota. Against this background, the creation of a truly independent accounting profession in Eastern Europe is no easy task. Whatever the outcome, much of it will be imported from other countries.

From this short survey, we can see that internationalization of accounting is proceeding apace, but along complex and somewhat uncertain paths.

THE ECONOMIC AND POLITICAL LIMITS TO INTERNATIONALIZATION

There are limits to how far internationalization can go. While the concept of a "global village" is a partial reality, most of us transact most of the time in a "local village." We will use our own locally-adapted business practices and political processes for the foreseeable future. One reason is that economic and political institutions change slowly; history, as they say, is destiny. The other reason is that the clear majority of commercial and political activity remains *intra*national, so the primary driving force behind the majority of actual accounting practices remains domestic in nature. It does not make sense to adopt a single set of accounting rules when the contexts in which accounting information is used vary substantively across countries. Equivalently, it would only make sense to have fully integrated accounting rules if the world had fully integrated markets and politics. It would take a truly remarkable transformation of the capital-market institutions for most European countries to embrace Anglo-American accounting rules.

Perhaps the greatest barrier to worldwide adoption of IASC rules is that they are perceived as being "too American." A German group of accountants recently complained that the international accounting standards being developed by the IASC "are largely based on Anglo-Saxon principles of accounting, which give priority to the matching of revenues and expenses, as compared to the continental European principle of conservatism."[9] By contrast, the French accounting profession is currently pressing hard for IASC standards to be adopted in place of their present system of centrally-codified rules (which originated in the Napoleonic Code). But even this proposal is being resisted by the French bureaucracy, due to its legendary conservatism and also to French managers' objections to detailed disclosures under IASC rules.

Domestic commercial and political factors are highly unlikely to go away. Until capital markets become *fully* integrated, with similar methods of raising capital and controlling managers, it will probably be rational to maintain different accounting practices across countries. Perhaps this is what the Europeans have in mind when they describe their move toward accounting rules that are more uniform as a process of "harmonization" as opposed to "integration."

GLOBAL ACCOUNTING RULES WOULD BE TOO RIGID AND TOO POLITICAL

Nor is complete internationalization of accounting rules a good idea. A single, centrally-planned, worldwide set of accounting rules would be Marx's dream. Its governing body would be a United Nations of the participating countries' professional accounting associations, regulatory bodies, stock exchanges, corporate lobby groups, labor unions, banks, stock exchanges and financial analysts' associations, among others. Such a body would also likely invite participation by organizations such as the World Bank, the IMF, OECD, worldwide and regional political and trade groups, and the U.N. itself.[10] Politics would become the driving force behind accounting rules. There would be excessive gridlock. The bureaucracy administering the rules would have neither the incentive nor the institutional capacity to respond to – much less encourage or participate in – productive innovations in business practice.

Two factors are worth keeping in mind. First, the fundamental source of the United States' great wealth and its role in the world – and also the driving power behind its great corporations – is its open, innovative institutional structure. By both historical and current world standards, the inventive energy of its free markets is comparatively unrestrained by political interference. In general, wealthy societies exhibit a long history of experimentation with institutional practices, a process whereby less efficient practices are discarded if they cannot compete with more efficient innovations.[11] Wealth is not guaranteed by possessing natural resources or by access to advanced technologies, as even a casual glance at nations like Russia and Argentina will show. Switzerland, Japan, Hong Kong, and Singapore are poorly endowed with natural resources, but are wealthy in comparison with their better-endowed neighbors. In poorer societies, institutional evolution is comparatively more suppressed by the political sphere, and institutional practices are less efficient.[12] The conclusion: nurture the free evolution of business institutions in general.

Second, because accounting rules are an integral part of the evolving institutional structure, they cannot simply be laid down once and for all time. They require continual maintenance. A case in point is the emergence of long-term non-cancellable leases as a widespread financing method in the early 1970s. Under the old accounting rules, which naturally had not anticipated the innovation of financial leases, these transactions were not recorded on balance sheets, even if the lessor had full recourse to the lessee/

borrower's assets. The protection afforded lenders by balance-sheet debt-ratio covenants suddenly was rendered less effective because a prevalent form of full-recourse long-term financing was not recorded as debt.

In 1976, to restore the usefulness of their balance sheets, U.S. accountants implemented new rules to capitalize leases that, according to several objective criteria, are financing transactions. The new rules book the present value of qualifying lease payments as a leased asset, and a lease liability of the same amount, even though no such asset and no liability to pay such an amount exists in law. Thereafter, corporations and lenders to corporations were able to write debt-ratio covenants that better reflected the economic substance of corporate financing transactions rather than their narrow legal form. As a consequence, one could lend to a corporation with greater assurance that its leverage was effectively constrained by agreement. The new accounting rule thus increased the efficiency with which future debt contracts were written.[13]

This adaptation of the accounting rules, however, could not have been introduced a decade earlier, when discounted present value still was a largely academic concept. At that time, present values would not have been understood by most balance-sheet readers, and it would have been extremely difficult to convince a court that a strictly notional present value calculation should be counted among a corporation's liabilities. This episode reveals how accounting rules and corporate transactions (in this case, long-term debt covenants and long-term leasing) evolve together. It also illustrates that accounting rules, which can affect all firms' financial statements and all users of financial statements, must be based on generally-accepted commercial concepts (in this case, acceptance of the present value technique and the idea that certain leases are essentially financing agreements).[14]

More recently, accountants have sought to find rules to better reflect innovative corporate transactions in financial derivatives. Better accounting rules for derivatives would mean that investors and lenders could transact with greater assurance about the extent and nature of a corporation's risk exposure. And this in turn would reduce the "information costs" to corporations of using derivatives in even legitimate hedging transactions – costs that today are very large.

Accounting practices have evolved over millennia (many of the surviving Babylonian clay tablets are accounting records), as an integral part of the evolution of commerical practice. If the evolution of accounting rules is impeded, then innovation in business practice generally is impeded. The conclusion: nurture the free evolution of accounting rules.

Eliminating the untidy spectacle of different countries evolving different rules might appeal to some, but in my view it should not be an objective. This is *not* to say that the trend toward internationalizing accounting rules will not or should not continue: the increasing internationalization of markets and politics suggests the trend will and should continue. Corporations engaging in significant crossborder transacting can prepare supplemental reports under IASC rules, or simply provide foreign-language "convenience statements," at small cost, without their home countries completely abandoning their local standards. IASC standards can be adopted piecemeal by smaller countries, emerging countries, and countries in which transactions using accounting information are largely international, without placing worldwide accounting under the control of one planning body. Diversity among nations' accounting rules can be reduced voluntarily, as nations compete in increasingly-integrated world markets for financial and other transactions, without legis-lating its elimination.

I hasten to add that this conclusion is *not* based on any opinion that U.S. accounting standards (or those of any other country) are better than IASC (or any other) standards. It is based on an opinion about the best *process* for the evolution of accounting standards across the world.

CONCLUSION

We have not yet experienced the full impact of the massive reduction in information costs over recent decades. One important consequence of the "information revolution" is that further integration of both markets and pol-itics seems inevitable on a worldwide scale. Accountants are scrambling to provide financial communication that is more intelligible across national boundaries because countries differ remarkably in their accounting rules, in the philosophies underlying their entire accounting systems, and even in their attitudes to public disclosure generally. There is pressure to reduce diversity in accounting rules, and the International Accounting Standards Committee (IASC) rules are growing in volume, stature, and usage.

On the other hand, economic and political integration is far from com-plete, and it seems highly likely to remain so. While further international-ization will reduce some or much of the diversity in accounting rules and practices across nations, it will not eliminate it. Nor should it.

NOTES

1. For the pioneering research on the economics and politics of accounting, see Ross L. Watts and Jerold L. Zimmerman, *Positive Accounting Theory* (Engle-wood Cliffs, N.J.: Prentice-Hall, 1986).
2. Watts, Ross L. and Jerold Zimmerman, "Towards a Positive Theory of the Deter-mination of Accounting Standards," *Accounting Review* (Jan. 1978): 112–134.
3. *The New York Time* (8 January 1995) has estimated that in 20 years the cost of executing a given number of instructions per second fell below one-millionth of that of a 1975 I.B.M. mainframe. And anyone who programmed during the 1960s knows what a tremendous improvement a 1975 mainframe was.
4. Digests of accounting rules worldwide are provided in: F. D. S. Choi (ed). *Handbook of International Accounting* (New York: John Wiley & Sons Inc, 1991); and F. D. S Choi and G. G. Mueller, *International Accounting* (Engle-wood Cliffs. N.J.: Prentice-Hall, 1992). See also *Miller's European Account-ing Guide* (New York: Harcourt Brace & Company, 1995).

5. See *Wall Street Journal* 25 February 1994 and *The Economist* 25 September 1993.
6. *International Herald Tribune* 28 April 1992.
7. At the end of 1994, there were 81 members. Details are in the IASC *Annual Review* (IASC: 167 Fleet Street, London EC4A 2ES).
8. An excellent summary of IASC rules is provided by Price Waterhouse, *An Introduction to International Accounting Standards*, 1994.
9. Working Group on External Financial Reporting of the Schmalenbach-Gesellschaft-Deutsche Gesellschaft fur Betriebswirtschaft, "German Accounting Principles: An Institutionalized Framework," *Accounting Horizons*, Vol. 9 No. 3 (September 1995), pp. 92–99.
10. The UN's involvement began in 1986, with the formation of the Intergovernmental Working Group of Experts on International Standards of Accounting and Reporting (ISAR), a group within the United Nations Conference on Trade and Development (UNCTAD). The group now includes representatives from at least 32 countries.
11. The term "institutional practices" refers to all routine ways of transacting in the economy, ranging from the broad forms under which corporations and markets are organized, through the most intricate details of managerial, legal, financial and accounting techniques.
12. For a fine historical account of the effect on wealth (and also on health, education, enlightenment and liberty) of separating the political and economic spheres, see N. Rosenberg and L. E. Birdzell, Jr., *How the West Grew Rich: The Economic Transformation of the Industrial World* (Basic Books, New York, 1986). Their account includes a history of the joint stock corporation – the institutional giant of the twentieth century – and in my view is a "must read" for reflective managers.
13. *Ex post*, the new accounting rule (FAS 13) adversely affected corporations that were exposed to unrecorded lease obligations. Existing leases suddenly were put onto balance sheets as long-term debt, and thus existing debt-ratio covenants became more binding overnight. Imhoff and Thomas provide (in "Economic Consequences of Accounting Standards: The Lease Disclosure Change," *Journal of Accounting and Economics*, 10 (1988), pp. 277–310) an analysis of the *ex post* effects of FAS 13 on corporate financing practice. My focus is on the *ex ante* contracting efficiency of the accounting standard.
14. In the U.S., the notion that accounting rules ultimately must form a widely-accepted basis for contracting is reflected in the term "generally accepted accounting principles" (GAAP), used to describe U.S. rules. In many countries which inherited British accounting, the notion is reflected in requirements that accounts be "fair." Because fairness is a property of the relative treatment of all interested parties, it is a different way of expressing acceptance by all. Common law invokes notions such as common practice, caselaw precedent and the representative "prudent man," when deciding what is "fair."

'Making Accounting More International: Why, How and How Far It Will Go?', by R. Ball, reproduced with permission from *Journal of Applied Corporate Finance* 8(3). Copyright 1995 Stern Stewart Management Services.

CASE STUDY 9

International Accounting and Daimler-Benz

D. Hawkins

WHICH EARNINGS?

Investors in Daimler-Benz have the choice of three earnings numbers to use in their equity investment decisions – the company's reported German GAAP[1] income, analysts estimates of the DVFA income,[2] and the company's reported U.S. GAAP income. We suggest that investors at this time and most probably in the longer run should use the company's U.S. GAAP figure.

At the present time, investor interest in Daimler-Benz is focused on a number of major issues including how quickly the company can recover from its present difficulties. In our view, the best income figure for equity investors to use for valuation purposes at this time is the one that best:

■ Measures the depth of the company's difficulties and its actual rate of recovery from these difficulties.

In the long run, we believe that the best Daimler-Benz income measurement for equity investors is the one that best:

■ Reflects the economic realities of the company's financial condition and operations.

■ Measures the level of risk associated with the company's earnings.

■ Alerts investors to both positive and negative changes in the company's fortunes on a timely basis.

THREE DIFFERENT APPROACHES

In order to answer the question "Which earnings?", it is first necessary to understand the principal conceptual and application differences between German GAAP, the DVFA method, and U.S. GAAP.

German GAAP Income

Two principal characteristics of German GAAP earnings that make them unsuitable for equity valuation purposes are:

1. The overarching financial reporting requirement that the prudence concept be observed.
2. The tax code requirements that book accounting conform in many areas to the accounting methods elected for tax purposes.

The prudence concept requires that all anticipated risks and losses be recognized. It prohibits recognition of unrealized profits. This concept also requires an item-by-item approach to valuation.

The problem created for equity investors by the prudence concept is that it can lead to:

■ Gross understatements of income in good business years as companies build up provisions for future known and unknown losses through charges to income.

■ Gross overstatement of income in bad business years as losses are charged directly to existing provisions and reserves and old provisions are released to income.

These distortions coupled with poor disclosure of provisions and reserves and many other data important to equity investors can leave equity investors in the dark with respect to the company's actual financial and operating condition.

The German income tax regulations require corporations in many areas to use the same accounting for financial reporting as elected for tax purposes. This requirement further makes German GAAP earnings unsuitable for equity valuation purposes because:

■ The objective of the tax regulations is not necessarily to determine a measurement of income that reflects the economic reality of the reporting corporation.

■ The corporate bias in electing tax accounting principles, methods, and estimates typically is to minimize taxable income and defer tax payments.

Despite these equity valuation limitations of German GAAP earnings, which are well known to equity investors, some analysts who follow German equities believe that reported German GAAP earnings are the best comparative income measure to use between German and non-German corporations using Anglo-Saxon type accounting, such as U.K. and U.S. GAAP.

Table 1, which is a comparison of Daimler-Benz earnings on three different accounting bases, suggests that in the case of Daimler-Benz, this has not been a reasonable assumption over at least three and a half years because:

■ While close in some periods, Daimler-Benz's German GAAP earnings have been consistently higher than its U.S. GAAP earnings.

■ In two periods, 1990 and the first 6 months of 1993, Daimler-Benz's German GAAP earnings have been considerably higher than the company's U.S. GAAP earnings.

■ Daimler-Benz's German GAAP income is significantly less volatile than its U.S. GAAP income.

■ While Daimler-Benz's 1991–92 German and U.S. GAAP earnings are reasonably close, an examination of the many adjustments required to restate the company's earnings from a German to a U.S. GAAP basis suggests that this is purely a statistical coincidence (See Table 2).

Table 1 Daimler-Benz net income under alternative reporting models

	DM millions			
	1993 (6 months)	1992	1991	1990
Reported net income under German GAAP	168	1,451	1,942	1,795
Earnings according to DVFA	–	1,379	2,580	2,230
Net income in accordance with U.S. GAAP	(949)	1,350	1,886	884

Source: Various Daimler-Benz reports

Table 2 Reconciliation of Daimler-Benz's German GAAP income to U.S. GAAP

	DM millions			
	1993 (6 months)	1992	1991	1990
Net income as reported in the consolidated income statements under German GAAP	168	1,451	1,942	1,795
Less: Income and losses applicable to minority shareholders	(51)	(33)	(70)	(111)
Adjusted net income under German GAAP	117	1,418	1,872	1,684
Add: Changes in appropriated retained earnings provisions, reserves and valuation differences	(1,615)	774	64	738
	(1,498)	2,192	1,936	2,422
Other adjustments required to conform with U.S. GAAP:				
Long-term contracts	30	(57)	(32)	(14)
Goodwill and business acquisitions	(33)	(76)	(270)	(251)
Business dispositions	–	337	(490)	0
Pensions and other post-retirement benefits	(135)	96	(66)	(153)
Foreign currency translation	(7)	(94)	155	46
Financial instruments	(293)	(438)	86	35
Earnings of Deutsche Aerospace Airbus	–	–	636	(512)
Other	67	88	57	69
Deferred taxes	920	(646)	(126)	(758)
Net income in accordance with U.S. GAAP before cumulative effect of a change in accounting principle	(949)	1,402	1,886	884
Cumulative effect of change in accounting for postretirement benefits other than pensions as of January 1, 1992, net of tax of DM 33	–	(52)	–	–
Net income in accordance with U.S. GAAP	(949)	1,350	1,886	884
Earnings per share in accordance with U.S. GAAP	(20.37)	29.00[1]	40.52	18.99
Earnings per American Depository Share in accordance with U.S. GAAP[2]	(2.04)	2.90[1]	4.05	1.90

Notes: 1 Includes the negative effect of the change in accounting for postretirement benefits other than pensions of DM 12 per share (DM 0.11 per American Depository Share).
2 Earnings per American Depository Share are calculated on the basis of ten American Depository Shares for every Ordinary Share.
Source: Daimler-Benz Form 20-F, September 17, 1993

■ Daimler-Benz's 1992 German and U.S. GAAP figures are almost identical. Some might argue that this is more representative of what might be expected in the future, particularly since in contrast to 1990–91 Daimler-Benz's 1992 German GAAP income includes Deutsche Aerospace Airbus' operating results for the first time. This may be a reasonable position over the long haul, but at least in the short-term the significant gap between the German and U.S. GAAP 6 month 1993 income figures argue against this position.

DVFA Method

Two earnings figures are quoted for listed German companies – earnings measured by German GAAP and earnings estimated by the DVFA method. The DVFA earnings are generally considered to be useful to equity investors for making earnings comparisons between German companies.

The principal DVFA method adjustments to German GAAP earnings are:

■ Eliminate extraordinary items – which in German GAAP includes many more items than U.S. GAAP – from net income. A DVFA method objective is to determine what a company could have earned if the extraordinary items had not occurred.

■ Eliminate the effect of excessive provision and pension expense accounting entries that hide or boost income. In making this adjustment, the analysts often must rely on management for the information.

■ Eliminate depreciation expense due to special and accelerated tax valuations. Since a goal of DVFA is to put German firms on the same footing and all German firms use the same tax depreciation schedules, no depreciation adjustment is made for regular tax conforming book depreciation lives that might be shorter than the economic lives of the related assets.

■ Eliminate capitalized goodwill charges.

■ Eliminate any minority interest included in the consolidated income.

DVFA income is not a good proxy for U.S. GAAP measured earnings. While the DVFA method may reconcile some of the differences between German and U.S. GAAP, it is generally recognized that typically the DVFA method often leads to income figures for German companies that are substantially higher than both their comparable German and U.S. GAAP income. With the exception of 1992, Table 1 indicates that this was true in the case of Daimler-Benz in 1990–91. A comparison of the relatively few adjustments and their magnitude required to convert Daimler-Benz's 1991 German GAAP income to a DVFA basis[3] and the many adjustments needed to convert Daimler-Benz's German GAAP income to U.S. GAAP basis (see Table 2) suggest the closeness of the 1991 DVFA and U.S. GAAP income figures is a statistical coincidence unrelated to the two approaches to measuring income.

U.S. GAAP

The objective of U.S. GAAP is to measure income in a way that is useful to public investors. In the pursuit of this goal, U.S. GAAP has gone a long way to eliminate many of the alternative ways of accounting for similar transactions, freeing book accounting from tax accounting, making the accounting between companies comparable, and moving accounting for earnings closer to reflecting a firm's current economic reality. In particular, it has eliminated the use of the kind of "hidden" and "general" reserves permitted by German GAAP. While not perfect and not free of controversy, U.S. GAAP is generally regarded as serving public investors well in their security valuation decisions.

U.S. GAAP PREFERRED

Daimler-Benz's U.S. GAAP earnings most probably will be used by equity investors in their valuations of the company's equity because its U.S. GAAP earnings are:

- Along with its DVFA earnings, two of the three possible earnings figures the company could release that are designed to be responsive to public equity investor information needs.

- The company's only earnings figure that is comparable to the earnings data of the other New York Stock Exchange listed companies, which most probably will be the group of comparative companies referred to in determining Daimler-Benz's equity values. While designed for equity investors, the company's DVFA earnings figure with its bias to over-statement relative to U.S. GAAP will not be useful for this purpose.

- Reflective of the company's current difficulties. A comparison of the company's 1993 first six months German and U.S. GAAP earnings and the legitimate German GAAP use of provision accounting to turn a significant loss into small profit clearly demonstrates this point (See Table 2).

- A more reliable indicator of the company's rate of recovery from its current difficulties. Under U.S. GAAP management will have to earn its way out of its current problem. The German GAAP option of using past provisions to give the appearance of recovery is not available to it on such a large magnitude under U.S. GAAP.

- A better measure of the level of risk attached to the company's earnings. Earnings volatility is an important measure of equity risk. U.S. GAAP based earnings tend to reflect the volatility of earnings inherent in a company's business better than German GAAP, which tends to result in smoothed earnings.

It is sometimes argued that equity investors are better served by German GAAP than U.S. GAAP because German GAAP better reflects a company's sustainable earnings, which is better than any one year's earnings for equity valuation purposes. While this argument has some theoretical appeal, we do not find it convincing. To make fully informed buy, hold, and sell decisions, investors need to know on a timely basis when a company is in earnings trouble. The freedom German GAAP gives management to use hidden and general reserves to smooth earnings and cover up the full extent of earnings problems may deny investors this timely information. Failure to reflect the full extent of earnings problems in reported income on a timely basis also increases the probability that markets will not be fair by giving insiders a potential time and information advantage.

QUALITY OF EARNINGS

Determining the accounting quality of a company's earnings is an important part of equity valuation. The price-earnings multiples of companies with high quality earnings tend to be higher than those of companies whose earnings are judged to be of low accounting quality. This should not be surprising. High quality accounting practices tend to consistently result in understatement of income, give investors more confidence in the reporting company management, and produce earnings figures that are earned rather than created by accounting, transaction, and financial manipulations.

As equity investors move toward using Daimler-Benz's U.S. GAAP earnings, they will have to assess the accounting quality of the company's U.S. GAAP earnings. While it is premature given the company's limited operating period under U.S. GAAP to assess its U.S. GAAP earnings quality, the following observations can be made:

■ Adherence to the thrust of the prudence concept within a U.S. GAAP context should lead to conservative U.S. GAAP earnings reports. Whether Daimler-Benz will approach its U.S. GAAP accounting in this manner is difficult to forecast, but given the prudence concept's strong hold on the minds of German accountants and managers, there is a reasonably high probability that the company may adopt a conservative approach to the application of U.S. GAAP.

■ The U.S. GAAP accounting principles adopted by the company suggest its earnings will be of average accounting quality. The principles adopted are mostly prescribed by the FASB and are fairly typical of major U.S. corporations.

■ Accounting quality is often best revealed by the judgments management
   makes in selecting the assumptions necessary to apply accounting principles. The company's selection of pension and postretirement benefit
   assumptions are small, but important indicators of a management seeking to report above average accounting quality earnings.

A CAUTIONARY NOTE

As investors move toward viewing Daimler-Benz on a U.S. GAAP basis,
they must be careful that the company's U.S. GAAP data reflects the way
management views and manages the company, and are not simply a set of
accounting data prepared for U.S. investors disconnected from the way the
company is actually managed. Disconnected U.S. GAAP accounting could
be a poor indicator of future U.S. GAAP results. While there is no evidence
one way or the other at this time, investors should note that Daimler-Benz's
restatement from German to U.S. GAAP is done at the corporate level, the
company's operating units appear still to operate on a German GAAP basis,
and the company's principal corporate stockholders' report on a German
GAAP basis. It also should be noted that during the six-month period ended
June 30, 1993, the company did change under German GAAP a number of its
accounting practices to move them towards U.S. GAAP.[4] Only time will tell
whether this cautionary note turns out to be a problem for equity investors.

   Daimler-Benz's decision to report the company's earnings on a U.S. GAAP
basis made possible its listing on the New York Stock Exchange. This
broadened the stock's trading base and gives the company access to U.S.
capital markets which are the largest in the world. The U.S. GAAP decision
should also enhance the attractiveness of the company in other financial
markets where investor-oriented financial data is expected and demanded by
investors. It is hard to see how U.S. GAAP reporting is going to be anything
but a positive for Daimler-Benz's long-run success.

NOTES

1. Appendix A provides a detailed description of German GAAP. For a comparison
   of German GAAP with the accounting practices of other European Community
   countries, International Accounting Standards, and U.S. GAAP, see "Comparative European Community Accounting Standards: An Investor's Perspective",
   October 1992. For earlier similar coverage of non-U.S. accounting practices,
   see Accounting Bulletin No. 1, "Dealing With International Accounting Diversity: International Accounting Standards", May 1990; Accounting Bulletin
   No. 2, "Direct Transnational Financial Statement Analysis. Converting IAS to
   U.S. GAAP", September 1990; Accounting Bulletin No. 8, "Measuring and Analyzing Mexican Peso Profits", July 26, 1991; and Accounting Bulletin No. 15,

"International Accounting Standards Update", February 1993. All copyrighted by Merrill Lynch, Pierce, Fenner & Smith, Incorporated.

2. The DVFA method is a series of adjustments to the German GAAP income of companies made by German companies and/or financial analysts acting independently or through a joint negotiations process to facilitate the comparison of the earnings of German companies. The adjustments include elimination of such items as extraordinary items, minority interests, excess depreciation, excess provisions, and goodwill expense. DVFA stands for the initials in German of the German Association of Financial Analysts and Investment Advisors, the developer of the DVFA method.

3. The DVFA method adjustments to Daimler-Benz's German GAAP income in 1992 (1991) were: +DM 160 (+86) million for depreciation and amortization; −DM (+573) million for provision; −DM 33 (−70) million for minority interest income; and, −DM 111 (−171) million for other items. 1991 DVFA adjustments included a +DM 220 million extraordinary item.

4. The accounting policy changes involved accounting for certain accrued expenses, including accrued sales commissions, accrued internal expenses for such items as major repairs, restructuring and year end closing costs, accrued anniversary payments, accrued maintenance expenses, and accrued apprentice training costs. The net effect of these changes on ordinary business activities for this period was to release DM 1.8 million of provisions to the German GAAP income statement.

Appendix A Comparison of Daimler-Benz Consolidated Financial Reporting Policies and U.S. GAAP[a]

Item	Daimler-Benz	U.S. GAAP	Comments
Consolidation	Consolidates fully all material companies in which parent has effective control.	Consolidates all companies that parent has ownership in excess of 50% and effective control.	While seldom used, under German GAAP subsidiaries may be excluded from consolidated entity if inclusion would be detrimental to a true and fair presentation. Not permitted under U.S. GAAP.
Minority interest	Included in stockholders' equity and net income not adjusted for minority interest in net income of subsidiaries.	Excluded from stockholders' equity and excluded in net income measurement.	German GAAP is based on the entity view of consolidation. The consolidated statements present the company results from the total corporate point of view. U.S. GAAP is based on the parent company stockholder's interest in the net assets and net income of the consolidated entity. Therefore, minority interests are excluded in consolidated statements. DFVA adjustments eliminate minority interest income and losses from income.
Joint ventures	Certain joint venture companies are accounted for using the pro rata method of consolidation.	Equity method.	Pro rata consolidation increases consolidated assets and liabilities, but has no effect on stockholders' equity and net income
Significant 20–50% ownership investments	Equity method.	Similar.[b]	In both German and U.S. GAAP, equity method is used for non-consolidated invested companies where the investor holds at least 20% of the voting stock. Under German GAAP, 20–50% ownership investments valued at acquisition cost in the parent company statements.

a As of June 30, 1993.
b "Similar" should be interpreted to mean "similar in concept and thrust, but not necessarily in all of the details".

Appendix A (Cont'd)

Item	Daimler-Benz	U.S. GAAP	Comments
Investments less than 20% ownership	Cost method.	Similar.	
Hedges	Reserve established for unrealized losses related to financial instruments covering foreign currency risks. Unrealized gains not recognized until realized.	Hedge accounting permits deferral of unrealized gain and losses on hedges of known transactions. All other hedges marked to market and unrealized gains and losses recognized in income.	In general, German GAAP requires futures contracts to be valued at market with unrealized losses recognized and gains deferred. One major exception is unrealized gains on hedges related to foreign currency receivables. These gains can be deferred as offsets against the receivables.
Foreign currency receivables and payables	Recorded at historical exchange rates unless use of current exchange rates would result in an unrealized loss. Unrealized losses are recognized currently. Unrealized gains are not recorded until realized.	Record at current exchange rate. Recognize unrealized gains and losses in income.	
Translation of foreign currency balance sheets	Non-current assets translated at historical exchange rates. All other assets and liabilities are translated at period end exchange rates.	If the foreign entity operates primarily in its local currency, all assets and liabilities are translated at period end exchange rates. If the foreign entity operates primarily in a U.S. dollar environment, inventory and fixed assets are translated at historical exchange rates. All other assets and liabilities are translated at period end exchange rates.	German GAAP does not specify any particular translation methods. A variety of methods is used. The Daimler-Benz method is similar to the U.S. GAAP accounting for foreign subsidiaries that operate primarily in parent company currency environments, which is the U.S. dollar for U.S. parent companies.

Translation of foreign currency income statements	Expense and income items generally translated at average exchange rates. Depreciation, amortization, and profit and loss from disposal of non-current assets translated at historical currency rates. Net income is translated at period end currency rates. Translation gains and losses included in income.	Expense and income items translated at weighted average exchange rates of the period except in situations where the entity operates in a U.S. dollar environment. In this situation, cost of sales and depreciation are translated at historical exchange rates. Translation gains and losses are included in income, except when the foreign entity operates primarily in a U.S. dollar environment. In this situation, translation gains and losses are included in income.	German GAAP does not specify any particular translation method. A variety of methods is used. The Daimler-Benz method is similar to the U.S. GAAP method is similar to the U.S. GAAP accounting for subsidiaries that operate primarily in parent company currency environments, which is the U.S. dollar for U.S. parent companies.
Financial instruments (securities and financial assets)	Investment classified as current (securities) reported at lower of acquisition cost or market. A lower valuation can be used if permitted for tax purposes. Investments classified as long-term (financial assets) carried at cost.	Marketable securities held with the intent to hold to maturity recorded at cost. Trading securities are accounted for at market with unrealized gains and losses recognized in income. Securities held for sale recorded at market with unrealized gains and losses treated as a direct adjustment of stockholders' equity. This standard is effective in 1994.	The valuation of investments under German GAAP depends on their balance sheet classification as either current or non-current. U.S. GAAP valuation of securities depends on the holder's intent. German GAAP permits provisions for temporary impairment of financial asset values. DVFA adjustments add back precautionary temporary writedowns to income.
Hyperinflation economies	Accounts of foreign subsidiaries operating in hyper-inflation economies translated using period end currency rates.	Translate as if the entity operated in a U.S. dollar environment (see above).	German GAAP does not specify any particular translation method.
Revenue recognition	Recognized when title passes or services are rendered net of discounts, customer bonuses and rebates granted.	Similar.	

Appendix A (Cont'd)

Item	Daimler-Benz	U.S. GAAP	Comments
Long-term contracts	Revenue is recognized upon the attainment of milestones where practicable or on the completed contract method.	The presumption is that percentage-of-completion accounting will be used.	The completed contract method is used almost exclusively in Germany.
Finance receivables	Interest method.	Similar.	
Operating lease income	Recognized when earned.	Similar.	Lease accounting in Germany follows its treatment for tax purposes.
Property, plant and equipment	Historical cost. Property and plant generally are depreciated on a straight line basis. Accelerated depreciation used for equipment.	Historical cost. Straight line, declining balance, sum-of-the-years digits and unit of production used.	German GAAP permits same depreciation methods as U.S. GAAP. DVFA adjusts for underdepreciation resulting from excessive writedowns of depreciable assets.
Leased equipment	Cost. 5-year accelerated depreciation used.	Similar, but depreciation schedule not specified.	
Excess depreciation	Special tax deductible depreciation used for both book and tax purposes.	Not permitted.	DFVA adjustments eliminate special and accelerated tax depreciation.
Business combinations	Purchase method. Assets acquired prior to 1988 valued at historical cost. After 1987 acquired assets valued at fair value.	Pooling of interest method permitted only if very restrictive conditions met. All other business combinations accounted for as purchases with acquired assets and liabilities valued at fair value.	German GAAP permits pooling of interest accounting if at least 90% of shares acquired and cash consideration paid not exceed 10% of compensation. Pooling of interest avoids goodwill and the fair value of assets and liabilities being recorded. In the case of Daimler-Benz gains or losses on assets sold that were acquired through purchase transactions prior to 1988 will be measured using their historical costs, not their fair value.

Item	German GAAP	U.S. GAAP	Comment
Acquisition goodwill	Capitalized and amortized over 5–15 years.	Similar. Amortization period cannot exceed 40 years.	German GAAP also permits goodwill to be charged directly to reserves and thereby avoid goodwill charges to earnings. Not permitted by U.S. GAAP. If goodwill is capitalized and amortized, DVFA adds back the expense to earnings.
Restructuring goodwill	Charged directly to retained earnings.	Recognize income as part of restructuring charge.	
Strategic alliance goodwill	Portion related to expansion of the group amortized over useful life. Remainder charged directly to retained earnings.	No comparable concept.	
Business dispositions	Record at date of signed contract.	Record at exchange of consideration date.	
Intangible assets (other than goodwill)	Capitalize at cost if acquired for consideration. Amortized over useful life. Self-generated intangibles expensed as incurred.	Capitalized if acquired. Cost of internally developed identifiable intangibles with determinable lives may be capitalized and amortized over their useful lives.	German GAAP is comparable to the preferred U.S. accounting for intangibles.
Pension costs and similar obligations	Present value of future payments based on actuarial studies. Pension costs based on entry age method.	Present value of future payments based on actuarial studies. Pension costs based on projected unit credit method.	Pension obligations are rarely funded in Germany. In contrast to U.S. GAAP, German GAAP permits recognition of actuarial gains and losses currently rather than spread over a number of years. German companies often limit their pension expense to actual payments. DVFA deducts excess pension expense from income.

Appendix A (Cont'd)

Item	Daimler-Benz	U.S. GAAP	Comments
Inventory	FIFO. Includes direct labor and materials and applicable overheads including depreciation charges.	LIFO, FIFO, average cost, moving average and specific identification methods used. Cost includes manufacturing costs and certain storage, general and administrative costs.	German GAAP permits LIFO, FIFO, moving average and specific identification inventory methods. German GAAP also permits companies to value inventory at its direct cost only. DVFA adjustments restate direct costing based cost of goods sold to a fully manufactured cost basis relying typically on data provided by the company.
Income taxes	Liability method. Deferred taxes recognized only to the extent consolidated deferred tax liabilities exceed deferred tax assets. Deferred tax assets not recognized for operating loss carryforwards.	Liability method. All temporary differences between book and tax accounting included in measurement of deferred taxes. Deferred tax assets including the tax benefits of operating loss carryforwards recognized to the extent that it is better than 50/50 probability that they will be realized in the future.	
Advertising, sales promotion and other product expenses	Expense as incurred.	Similar.	
Research and development	Expense as incurred.	Similar, except computer software research and development costs must be capitalized under certain circumstances.	Research and development costs are normally not capitalized by German firms.
Warranty provisions	Recognized at time products are sold.	Similar.	
Interest cost	Expense as incurred.	Interest costs must be capitalized for assets that require a period of time to be prepared for their intended use. All other interest costs expensed as incurred.	Under German GAAP interest may be capitalized as part of an asset whose manufacture extends over a long period of time.

Accounts receivable	Non-interest bearing receivables at present value. Provision made for doubtful accounts.	Similar.	Only instance in German GAAP where imputation of interest permitted.
Provisions, reserves and valuation differences	Provisions made for uncertain liabilities, asset risks, and loss contingencies. Provisions for future losses on open production orders include all internal expenses, including indirect selling and administrative expenses. No recognition of contingent gains.	Contingent losses only recognized when information is available that indicates it is probable that an asset has been impaired or a liability incurred and the amount of the loss can be reasonably estimated. No recognition of contingency gains permitted.	The prudence concept requires German companies to not recognize contingent gains and to accrue estimates of all contingent losses that are likely to occur. The prudence concept also permits writedowns of assets even if the loss is temporary. The prudence concept does not exist in U.S. GAAP which has a significantly more restrictive view of when contingency losses can be recognized. DVFA attempts to adjust for excessive provisions, but has to rely on data provided by the company.
Release of provisions to income	Practiced.	Permitted if actual costs are less than the contingency provisions for those costs.	DVFA adjustments eliminate from income if material.
Extraordinary items	Unusual and infrequent transactions, including gains and losses on sale of subsidiaries and restructuring charges.	Events that are both unusual in nature and occur infrequently when considered in relation to the reporting company's operations.	German GAAP defines extraordinary income and expense as items that arise outside of ordinary business activities. U.S. GAAP's definition is considerably more restrictive. Consequently German companies tend to include more items in the extraordinary category. There is no comparable provision in German GAAP to the U.S. GAAP requirement to segregate in the income statement discontinued operations' profits and losses. DVFA adjustments add extraordinary items back to reported earnings in an attempt to measure what the company could have earned had the extraordinary item not occurred.

17

The Balanced Scorecard
Measures That Drive Performance

R. S. Kaplan and D. P. Norton

What you measure is what you get. Senior executives understand that their organization's measurement system strongly affects the behavior of managers and employees. Executives also understand that traditional financial accounting measures like return-on-investment and earnings-per-share can give misleading signals for continuous improvement and innovation–activities today's competitive environment demands. The traditional financial performance measures worked well for the industrial era, but they are out of step with the skills and competencies companies are trying to master today.

As managers and academic researchers have tried to remedy the inadequacies of current performance measurement systems, some have focused on making financial measures more relevant. Others have said, "Forget the financial measures. Improve operational measures like cycle time and defect rates; the financial results will follow." But managers should not have to choose between financial and operational measures. In observing and working with many companies, we have found that senior executives do not rely on one set of measures to the exclusion of the other. They realize that no single measure can provide a clear performance target or focus attention on the critical areas of the business. Managers want a balanced presentation of both financial and operational measures.

During a year-long research project with 12 companies at the leading edge of performance measurement, we devised a "balanced scorecard" – a set of measures that gives top managers a fast but comprehensive view of the business. The balanced scorecard includes financial measures that tell the results of actions already taken. And it complements the financial measures with operational measures on customer satisfaction, internal processes, and the organization's innovation and improvement activities – operational measures that are the drivers of future financial performance.

Think of the balanced scorecard as the dials and indicators in an airplane cockpit. For the complex task of navigating and flying an airplane, pilots need detailed information about many aspects of the flight. They need information on fuel, air speed, altitude, bearing, destination, and other indicators that summarize the current and predicted environment. Reliance on one instrument can be fatal. Similarly, the complexity of managing an organization

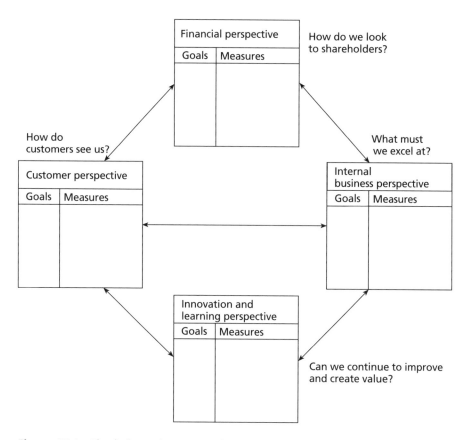

Figure 17.1 The balanced scorecard links performance measures

today requires that managers be able to view performance in several areas simultaneously.

The balanced scorecard allows managers to look at the business from four important perspectives as shown in Figure 17.1 and provides answers to four basic questions:

1. How do customers see us? (customer perspective)

2. What must we excel at? (internal perspective)

3. Can we continue to improve and create value? (innovation and learning perspective)

4. How do we look to shareholders? (financial perspective)

While giving senior managers information from four different perspectives, the balanced scorecard minimizes information overload by limiting the number of measures used. Companies rarely suffer from having too few measures. More commonly, they keep adding new measures whenever an employee or a consultant makes a worthwhile suggestion. One manager described the proliferation of new measures at his company as its "kill another tree program." The balanced scorecard forces managers to focus on the handful of measures that are most critical.

Second, the scorecard guards against suboptimization. By forcing senior managers to consider all the important operational measures together, the balanced scorecard lets them see whether improvement in one area may have been achieved at the expense of another. Even the best objective can be achieved badly. Companies can reduce time to market, for example, in two very different ways: by improving the management of new product introductions or by releasing only products that are incrementally different from existing products. Spending on setups can be cut either by reducing setup times or by increasing batch sizes. Similarly, production output and first-pass yields can rise, but the increases may be due to a shift in the product mix to more standard, easy-to-produce but lower-margin products.

We will illustrate how companies can create their own balanced scorecard with the experiences of one semiconductor company – let's call it Electronic Circuits Inc. ECI saw the scorecard as a way to clarify, simplify, and then operationalize the vision at the top of the organization. The ECI scorecard was designed to focus the attention of its top executives on a short list of critical indicators of current and future performance.

CUSTOMER PERSPECTIVE: HOW DO CUSTOMERS SEE US?

Many companies today have a corporate mission that focuses on the customer. "To be number one in delivering value to customers" is a typical mission statement. How a company is performing from its customers' perspective has become, therefore, a priority for top management. The balanced scorecard demands that managers translate their general mission statement on customer service into specific measures that reflect the factors that really matter to customers.

Customers' concerns tend to fall into four categories: time, quality, performance and service, and cost. Lead time measures the time required for the company to meet its customers' needs. For existing products, lead time can be measured from the time the company receives an order to the time it actually delivers the product or service to the customer. For new products, lead time represents the time to market, or how long it takes to bring a new product from the product definition stage to the start of shipments. Quality measures the defect level of incoming products as perceived and measured by the customer. Quality could also measure on-time delivery, the accuracy of the company's delivery forecasts. The combination of performance and service measures how the company's products or services contribute to creating value for its customers.

To put the balanced scorecard to work, companies should articulate goals for time, quality, and performance and service and then translate these goals into specific measures. Senior managers at ECI, for example, established general goals for customer performance: get standard products to market

Financial perspective	
Goals	Measures
Survive	Cash flow
Succeed	Quarterly sales growth and operating income by division
Prosper	Increased market share and ROE

Customer perspective	
Goals	Measures
New products	Percent of sales from new products
	Percent of sales from proprietary products
Responsive supply	On-time delivery (defined by customer)
Preferred supplier	Share of key accounts' purchases
	Ranking by key accounts
Customer partnership	Number of cooperative engineering efforts

Internal business perspective	
Goals	Measures
Technology capability	Manufacturing geometry vs. competition
Manufacturing excellence	Cycle time Unit cost Yield
Design productivity	Silicon efficiency Engineering efficiency
New product introduction	Actual introduction schedule vs. plan

Innovation and learning perspective	
Goals	Measures
Technology leadership	Time to develop next generation
Manufacturing learning	Process time to maturity
Product focus	Percent of products that equal 80% sales
Time to market	New product introduction vs. competition

Figure 17.2 ECI's balanced business scorecard

sooner, improve customers' time to market, become customers' supplier of choice through partnerships with them, and develop innovative products tailored to customer needs. The managers translated these general goals into four specific goals and identified an appropriate measure for each (see Figure 17.2).

To track the specific goal of providing a continuous stream of attractive solutions, ECI measured the percent of sales from new products and the percent of sales from proprietary products. That information was available internally. But certain other measures forced the company to get data from outside. To assess whether the company was achieving its goal of providing reliable, responsive supply, ECI turned to its customers. When it found that each customer defined "reliable, responsive supply" differently, ECI created a database of the factors as defined by each of its major customers. The shift to external measures of performance with customers led ECI to redefine "on time" so it matched customers' expectations. Some customers defined "on-time" as any shipment that arrived within five days of scheduled delivery; others used a nine-day window. ECI itself had been using a seven-day window, which meant that the company was not satisfying some of its customers and overachieving at others. ECI also asked its top ten customers to rank the company as a supplier overall.

Depending on customers' evaluations to define some of a company's performance measures forces that company to view its performance through customers' eyes. Some companies hire third parties to perform anonymous customer surveys, resulting in a customer-driven report card. The J. D. Powers quality survey, for example, has become the standard of performance for the automobile industry, while the Department of Transportation's measurement of ontime arrivals and lost baggage provides external standards for airlines. Benchmarking procedures are yet another technique companies use to compare their performance against competitors' best practice. Many companies have introduced "best of breed" comparison programs: the company looks to one industry to find, say, the best distribution system, to another industry for the lowest cost payroll process, and then forms a composite of those best practices to set objectives for its own performance.

In addition to measures of time, quality, and performance and service, companies must remain sensitive to the cost of their products. But customers see price as only one component of the cost they incur when dealing with their suppliers. Other supplier-driven costs range from ordering, scheduling delivery, and paying for the materials; to receiving, inspecting, handling, and storing the materials; to the scrap, rework, and obsolescence caused by the materials; and schedule disruptions (expediting and value of lost output) from incorrect deliveries. An excellent supplier may charge a higher unit price for products than other vendors but nonetheless be a lower cost supplier because it can deliver defect-free products in exactly the right quantities at exactly the right time directly to the production process and can minimize, through electronic data interchange, the administrative hassles of ordering, invoicing, and paying for materials.

INTERNAL BUSINESS PERSPECTIVE: WHAT MUST WE EXCEL AT?

Customer-based measures are important, but they must be translated into measures of what the company must do internally to meet its customers' expectations. After all, excellent customer performance derives from processes, decisions, and actions occurring throughout an organization. Managers need to focus on those critical internal operations that enable them to satisfy customer needs. The second part of the balanced scorecard gives managers that internal perspective.

The internal measures for the balanced scorecard should stem from the business processes that have the greatest impact on customer satisfaction – factors that affect cycle time, quality, employee skills, and productivity, for example. Companies should also attempt to identify and measure their company's core competencies, the critical technologies needed to ensure continued market leadership. Companies should decide what processes and competencies they must excel at and specify measures for each.

Managers at ECI determined that submicron technology capability was critical to its market position. They also decided that they had to focus on manufacturing excellence, design productivity, and new product introduction. The company developed operational measures for each of these four internal business goals.

To achieve goals on cycle time, quality, productivity, and cost, managers must devise measures that are influenced by employees' actions. Since much of the action takes place at the department and workstation levels, managers need to decompose overall cycle time, quality, product, and cost measures to local levels. That way, the measures link top management's judgment about key internal processes and competencies to the actions taken by individuals that affect overall corporate objectives. This linkage ensures that employees at lower levels in the organization have clear targets for actions, decisions, and improvement activities that will contribute to the company's overall mission.

Information systems play an invaluable role in helping managers disaggregate the summary measures. When an unexpected signal appears on the balanced scorecard, executives can query their information system to find the source of the trouble. If the aggregate measure for on-time delivery is poor, for example, executives with a good information system can quickly look behind the aggregate measure until they can identify late deliveries, day by day, by a particular plant to an individual customer.

If the information system is unresponsive, however, it can be the Achilles' heel of performance measurement. Managers at ECI are currently limited by the absence of such an operational information system. Their greatest concern is that the scorecard information is not timely; reports are generally a week behind the company's routine management meetings, and the measures have yet to be linked to measures for managers and employees at lower levels of the organization. The company is in the process of developing a more responsive information system to eliminate this constraint.

INNOVATION AND LEARNING PERSPECTIVE: CAN WE CONTINUE TO IMPROVE AND CREATE VALUE?

The customer-based and internal business process measures on the balanced scorecard identify the parameters that the company considers most important for competitive success. But the targets for success keep changing. Intense global competition requires that companies make continual improvements to their *existing* products and processes and have the ability to introduce entirely new products with expanded capabilities.

A company's ability to innovate, improve, and learn ties directly to the company's value. That is, only through the ability to launch new products, create more value for customers, and improve operating efficiencies continually can a company penetrate new markets and increase revenues and margins – in short, grow and thereby increase shareholder value.

ECI's innovation measures focus on the company's ability to develop and introduce standard products rapidly, products that the company expects will form the bulk of its future sales. Its manufacturing improvement measure focuses on new products; the goal is to achieve stability in the manufacturing of new products rather than to improve manufacturing of existing products. Like many other companies, ECI uses the percent of sales from new products as one of its innovation and improvement measures. If sales from new products is trending downward, managers can explore whether problems have arisen in new product design or new product introduction.

In addition to measures on product and process innovation, some companies overlay specific improvement goals for their existing processes. For example, Analog Devices, a Massachusetts-based manufacturer of specialized semiconductors, expects managers to improve their customer and internal business process performance continuously. The company estimates specific rates of improvement for on-time delivery, cycle time, defect rate, and yield.

Other companies, like Milliken & Co., require that managers make improvements within a specific time period. Milliken did not want its "associates" (Milliken's word for employees) to rest on their laurels after winning the Baldrige Award. Chairman and CEO Roger Milliken asked each plant to implement a "ten-four" improvement program: measures of process defects, missed deliveries, and scrap were to be reduced by a factor of ten over the next four years. These targets emphasize the role for continuous improvement in customer satisfaction and internal business processes.

FINANCIAL PERSPECTIVE: HOW DO WE LOOK TO SHAREHOLDERS?

Financial performance measures indicate whether the company's strategy, implementation, and execution are contributing to bottom-line improvement. Typical financial goals have to do with profitability, growth, and shareholder value. ECI stated its financial goals simply: to survive, to succeed, and to prosper. Survival was measured by cash flow, success by quarterly sales growth and operating income by division, and prosperity by increased market share by segment and return on equity.

But given today's business environment, should senior managers even look at the business from a financial perspective? Should they pay attention to short-term financial measures like quarterly sales and operating income?

Many have criticized financial measures because of their well-documented inadequacies, their backward-looking focus, and their inability to reflect contemporary value-creating actions. Shareholder value analysis (SVA), which forecasts future cash flows and discounts them back to a rough estimate of current value, is an attempt to make financial analysis more forward looking. But SVA still is based on cash flow rather than on the activities and processes that drive cash flow.

Some critics go much further in their indictment of financial measures. They argue that the terms of competition have changed and that traditional financial measures do not improve customer satisfaction, quality, cycle time, and employee motivation. In their view, financial performance is the result of operational actions, and financial success should be the logical consequence of doing the fundamentals well. In other words, companies should stop navigating by financial measures. By making fundamental improvements in their operations, the financial numbers will take care of themselves, the argument goes.

Assertions that financial measures are unnecessary are incorrect for at least two reasons. A well-designed financial control system can actually enhance rather than inhibit an organization's total quality management program (see Figure 17.3). More important, however, the alleged linkage between improved operating performance and financial success is actually quite tenuous and uncertain. Let us demonstrate rather than argue this point.

Over the three-year period between 1987 and 1990, a NYSE electronics company made an order-of-magnitude improvement in quality and on-time delivery performance. Outgoing defect rate dropped from 500 parts per million to 50, on-time delivery improved from 70% to 96%, and yield jumped from 26% to 51%. Did these breakthrough improvements in quality, productivity, and customer service provide substantial benefits to the company? Unfortunately not. During the same three-year period, the company's financial results showed little improvement, and its stock price plummeted to one-third of its July 1987 value. The considerable improvements in manufacturing capabilities had not been translated into increased profitability. Slow releases of new products and a failure to expand marketing to new and perhaps more demanding customers prevented the company from realizing the benefits of its manufacturing achievements. The operational achievements were real, but the company had failed to capitalize on them.

The disparity between improved operational performance and disappointing financial measures creates frustration for senior executives. This frustration is often vented at nameless analysts who allegedly cannot see past quarterly blips in financial performance to the underlying long-term values these executives sincerely believe they are creating in their organizations. But the hard truth is that if improved performance fails to be reflected in the bottom line, executives should reexamine the basic assumptions of their strategy and mission. Not all long-term strategies are profitable strategies.

Measures of customer satisfaction, internal business performance, and innovation and improvement are derived from the company's particular view

How one company used a daily financial report to improve quality

In the 1980s, a chemicals company became committed to a total quality management program and began to make extensive measurements of employee participation, statistical process control, and key quality indicators. Using computerized controls and remote data entry systems, the plant monitored more than 30,000 observations of its production processes every four hours. The department managers and operating personnel who now had access to massive amounts of real-time operational data found their monthly financial reports to be irrelevant.

But one enterprising department manager saw things differently. He created a daily income statement. Each day, he estimated the value of the output from the production process using estimated market prices and subtracted the expenses of raw materials, energy, and capital consumed in the production process. To approximate the cost of producing out-of-conformance product, he cut the revenues from off-spec output by 50% to 100%.

The daily financial report gave operators powerful feedback and motivation and guided their quality and productivity efforts. The department head understood that it is not always possible to improve quality, reduce energy consumption, and increase throughput simultaneously; tradeoffs are usually necessary. He wanted the daily financial statement to guide those tradeoffs. The difference between the input consumed and output produced indicated the success or failure of the employees' efforts on the previous day. The operators were empowered to make decisions that might improve quality, increase productivity, and reduce consumption of energy and materials.

That feedback and empowerment had visible results. When, for example, a hydrogen compressor failed, a supervisor on the midnight shift ordered an emergency repair crew into action. Previously, such a failure of a noncritical component would have been reported in the shift log, where the department manager arriving for work the following morning would have to discover it. The midnight shift supervisor knew the cost of losing the hydrogen gas and made the decision that the cost of expediting the repairs would be repaid several times over by the output produced by having the compressor back on line before morning.

The department proceeded to set quality and output records. Over time, the department manager became concerned that employees would lose interest in continually improving operations. He tightened the parameters for in-spec production and reset the prices to reflect a 25% premium for output containing only negligible fractions of impurities. The operators continued to improve the production process.

The success of the daily financial report hinged on the manager's ability to establish a financial penalty for what had previously been an intangible variable: the quality of output. With this innovation, it was easy to see where process improvements and capital investments could generate the highest returns.

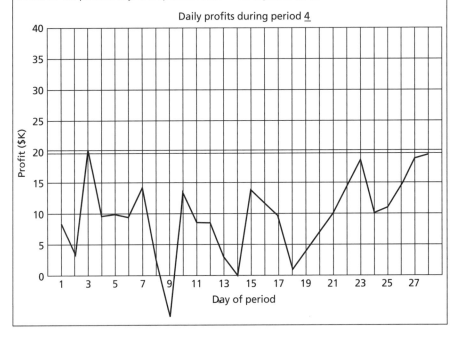

Figure 17.3 (*Source*: "Texas Eastman Company," by Robert S. Kaplan, Harvard Business School Case No. 9-190–039.)

of the world and its perspective on key success factors. But that view is not necessarily correct. Even an excellent set of balanced scorecard measures does not guarantee a winning strategy. The balanced scorecard can only translate a company's strategy into specific measurable objectives. A failure to convert improved operational performance, as measured in the scorecard, into improved financial performance should send executives back to their drawing boards to rethink the company's strategy or its implementation plans.

As one example, disappointing financial measures sometimes occur because companies don't follow up their operational improvements with another round of actions. Quality and cycle-time improvements can create excess capacity. Managers should be prepared to either put the excess capacity to work or else get rid of it. The excess capacity must be either used by boosting revenues or eliminated by reducing expenses if operational improvements are to be brought down to the bottom line.

As companies improve their quality and response time, they eliminate the need to build, inspect, and rework out-of-conformance products or to reschedule and expedite delayed orders. Eliminating these tasks means that some of the people who perform them are no longer needed. Companies are understandably reluctant to lay off employees, especially since the employees may have been the source of the ideas that produced the higher quality and reduced cycle time. Layoffs are a poor reward for past improvement and can damage the morale of remaining workers, curtailing further improvement. But companies will not realize all the financial benefits of their improvements until their employees and facilities are working to capacity – or the companies confront the pain of downsizing to eliminate the expenses of the newly created excess capacity.

If executives fully understood the consequences of their quality and cycle-time improvement programs, they might be more aggressive about using the newly created capacity. To capitalize on this self-created new capacity, however, companies must expand sales to existing customers, market existing products to entirely new customers (who are now accessible because of the improved quality and delivery performance), and increase the flow of new products to the market. These actions can generate added revenues with only modest increases in operating expenses. If marketing and sales and R&D do not generate the increased volume, the operating improvements will stand as excess capacity, redundancy, and untapped capabilities. Periodic financial statements remind executives that improved quality, response time, productivity, or new products benefit the company only when they are translated into improved sales and market share, reduced operating expenses, or higher asset turnover.

Ideally, companies should specify how improvements in quality, cycle time, quoted lead times, delivery, and new product introduction will lead to higher market share, operating margins, and asset turnover or to reduced operating expenses. The challenge is to learn how to make such explicit linkage between operations and finance. Exploring the complex dynamics will likely require simulation and cost modeling.

MEASURES THAT MOVE COMPANIES FORWARD

As companies have applied the balanced scorecard, we have begun to recognize that the scorecard represents a fundamental change in the underlying assumptions about performance measurement. As the controllers and finance vice presidents involved in the research project took the concept back to their organizations, the project participants found that they could not implement the balanced scorecard without the involvement of the senior managers who have the most complete picture of the company's vision and priorities. This was revealing because most existing performance measurement systems have been designed and overseen by financial experts. Rarely do controllers need to have senior managers so heavily involved.

Probably because traditional measurement systems have sprung from the finance function, the systems have a control bias. That is, traditional performance measurement systems specify the particular actions they want employees to take and then measure to see whether the employees have in fact taken those actions. In that way, the systems try to control behavior. Such measurement systems fit with the engineering mentality of the Industrial Age.

The balanced scorecard, on the other hand, is well suited to the kind of organization many companies are trying to become. The scorecard puts strategy and vision, not control, at the center. It establishes goals but assumes that people will adopt whatever behaviors and take whatever actions are necessary to arrive at those goals. The measures are designed to pull people toward the overall vision. Senior managers may know what the end result should be, but they cannot tell employees exactly how to achieve that result, if only because the conditions in which employees operate are constantly changing.

This new approach to performance measurement is consistent with the initiatives under way in many companies: cross-functional integration, customer-supplier partnerships, global scale, continuous improvement, and team rather than individual accountability. By combining the financial, customer, internal process and innovation, and organizational learning perspectives, the balanced scorecard helps managers understand, at least implicitly, many interrelationships. This understanding can help managers transcend traditional notions about functional barriers and ultimately lead to improved decision making and problem solving. The balanced scorecard keeps companies looking – and moving – forward instead of backward.

18

Performance Indicators
20 Early Lessons from Managerial Use

A. Likierman

As the use of performance indicators has spread throughout the UK public sector, academic writing has tended to focus on the implications and consequences. The concerns of practitioners, on the other hand, have often been centred on the technical qualities of the indicators and the costs of implementation and operation. Much less has so far been publicly discussed about the application of indicators and their effect, or what officials and managers have learned so far about devising, implementing and using them.

The early lessons outlined below are based on discussions and written feedback from over 500 middle- and senior-grade managers from all parts of the public sector. The text is illustrated by quotations from some of the written responses to requests for comments on the list, which has been tested and refined in the light of comments and suggestions from 20 groups of officials and managers over the same period. Problems of confidentiality (and potential embarrassment) mean that only some of the quotations and examples are attributed to organizations. In other cases the sector is identified, but not the organization.

A number of caveats are necessary in interpreting the list:

- First, it is intended only to be indicative and the examples to be illustrative. There has been no attempt to seek a systematic sample of organizations across the public sector and the focus has been on the non-traded part.

- Second, the general categories used to divide the 20 lessons into four groups (concept, preparation, implementation and use) are for convenience only. The boundaries are not definitive, or even easy to draw, and some of the lessons could fit into more than one category.

- Third, the focus is on managerial use. Other, wider, issues such as public accountability, equity and the allocation of funding are not covered, although the lessons from use may have implications for some of these.

- Finally, the position is changing all the time as experience is gained. So the list has to be seen as reflecting a situation in transition and one which will have to be updated in the light of developments. This last point is intended to be more than a managerial cliché, since what may be of interest is that, even taking account of the diversity of the public sector, it is the elements listed below and not others that have been seen by the managers as having priority.

The list has also been tested on groups of private sector managers. Apart from the few elements, such as accountability, which are specific to the public sector, the vast majority of the lessons were seen to apply to private sector organizations, although there was a different emphasis on which were seen as the most important.

CONCEPT

1. Include All Elements Integral to What is Being Measured

As performance indicators have been introduced, the phrase: 'What gets measured, gets done' has been increasingly heard, often with concern about the implications for what is not measured. This puts the onus on those who devise the measures to ensure that they are appropriately comprehensive. There are certainly some who are reasonably satisfied. A Chief Probation Officer judged that his report to the Probation Committee was '"good enough" to give ourselves a broad indication as to the key outcomes we are seeking' and an official in the Department of Social Security extended the principle to individuals in emphasizing that individual objectives 'should be linked to job purpose and should involve all the key areas for which a jobholder is accountable and which are within his/her control'.

The problems in this area arise when there are elements of the task which are not included in the list of measures. Thus in the Prison Service, one of the goals [*sic*] is 'helping prisoners prepare for their return to the community'. But the 1993/94 Business Plan acknowledges that the key performance indicator – the proportion of prisoners held in establishments where prisoners have the opportunity to exceed the minimum visiting requirements – measures only one aspect of the Service's performance in achieving the goal. More generally, unless the set of indicators chosen covers all elements essential to completing the task, there will be a danger that 'What gets measured, gets done' will backfire and that performance will be skewed towards what is being measured. The Chief Executive of a central government agency commented: 'An important factor in setting targets, we have found, is that the whole of resource in a particular area should be covered by targets. If an area is not so covered, there is scope for performance to be manipulated by misallocating costs to areas where no penalty is incurred to the advantage of the area where performance is measured'. This is particularly important when some aspects of an organization's operations, including quality, are difficult to measure. A civil servant noted that 'A management unit may cover not only policy work, but also routine administration of settled policies, which may be more readily susceptible to targets.

There is a danger that the targets may mislead both the staff inside and managers outside the unit to accord greater importance to the routine work'.

2. Choose a Number Appropriate to the Organization and Its Diversity

The appropriate number of indicators will be particular to the organization and its aims. It will also need to take account of the diversity of its operations. As a Health Department official observed, '...some parts of the Department's work are more susceptible to the use of performance indicators than others'. For some organizations, many indicators will be required, for others few. Too many will make it difficult to focus what is important, too few will distort action. The dangers of the latter have been exhibited to the point of parody many times – as in the preoccupation of the command economies of the former Soviet Union with output, regardless of quality or demand. Nearer home was the notorious case of a member of the Kent Constabulary who encouraged those charged with some offences to confess to others which they had not committed in order to 'improve' the clear-up rate. Certainly the Audit Commission, in consulting on Citizen's charter indicators, recognized the principle of the need to reconcile enough indicators to provide a reflection of sufficient diversity with few enough so that the 'big picture' did not get lost.

However, the concerns expressed by those contributing to this study were almost entirely on the dangers of excessive numbers. The need for sampling was emphasized by a senior health executive worried about 'the massive public sector tendency to try to measure everything all of the time' and the same sentiments were echoed by a central government agency ('performance indicators should not spawn their own cottage industry of forms and monitoring returns'); by a probation officer ('One of my fears is that we now have so much information being made available that we are unable to use most of it'); and by a local authority ('There is a tendency to have too many indicators...This tendency needs to be resisted, otherwise the indicators lose their impact and value'). From another part of the Health Service came a specific reason for parsimony: 'The fewer there are, the better, as this makes them easier to promote and explain'.

3. Provide Adequate Safeguards for 'Soft' Indicators, Particularly Quality

The difficulties of measuring certain aspects of an organization's operations means that there is a tendency for the more easily measurable to push out what is not. By extension, within what is more easily measurable, the tendency is for financial to push out non-financial indicators. Quality has proved notably difficult for organizations to measure, and great care needs to be taken to give it proper weight. A central government department emphasized the need to set and assess quality standards 'against agreed competence frameworks. This reduces subjectivity in areas where mechanically measurable criteria are absent'. However, an official in one of the armed services commented gloomily: 'We are trying to develop the more difficult "quality" PIs and are not yet in a position to offer any up for general consumption. It is possible we will never be, as the differences between organizations and the nature of services provided by them will profoundly influence their design and use of PIs'.

Quality measures may well take more time than others to develop. Social Services in Enfield have a three-year programme for implementing quality assurance, and an example of successfully completed implementation is Down and Lisburn Health and Social Services. They have developed a system of multidisciplinary quality standards for multidisciplinary staff teams. The method in the service for people over 75 was to ask key groups (including the clients) for the valued features of service and to convert these into quality standards. Process, measurement technique and required records were linked to each standard. The system has been extended to services including child health and personal social services for children aged 0 to 5. Still in the middle of the process is the Central Office of Information, which is replacing quality measures based on timeliness of delivery and conformity with specification ('both of which have been problematical') by a new indicator based on customer satisfaction. Peer review is also increasingly in evidence as a means of measuring quality. For example this has now become an essential element of the Higher Education Funding Council's periodic reviews of universities.

4. Take Account of Accountability and Politics

Since public bodies operate in a political context, care needs to be taken that the indicators reflect political constraints and pressures. The balance here is between adequate accountability and recognition of the pressures of political life. 'Data can be misused, particularly by the media' was the comment of a senior manager of a National Health Service (NHS) Trust. A consultant within public health medicine dismissed targets for perinatal and infant mortality as 'a classic example of performance indicators... which have been included for political reasons only'. The public impact of league tables in sectors such as education and local government has given rise to particular concern, and caution is also common across Whitehall about the activities of parliamentary select committees, notably the Public Accounts Committee. Whitehall departments enjoying good relationships with 'their' select committees felt themselves to be in a better position to avoid misunderstandings than those where relationships were distant. On the other hand, there can be political gains from the adoption of measures. Home Office proposals for key performance indicators for the probation service pointed out: 'you will remember that the Audit Commission has commented that a robust system of performance indicators could make a major contribution to enhancing the credibility of the probation service'.

PREPARATION

5. Devise Them with People on the Ground, Who Must Feel Ownership

'Attitudes change depending on whether you are calling for PIs or you feel they are being imposed on you' commented the finance officer of a quango, and a senior executive of a central government agency emphasized that: 'Agreeing performance indicators is a negotiating process in the broadest sense. If this is ignored it will lead to poor commitment and sense of ownership', and went on 'People must understand what is expected of them, and how this was decided. They must be allowed to contribute to the decision-making process'. The Director of Social Services of the London Borough of Hackney emphasized that in involving staff further and further down the organization: 'the process of getting them involved and thinking in terms of monitoring and evaluating is, I think, as important as the final document itself'. A regional health authority is 'currently negotiating with General Managers of DHAs and FHSAs a shared view of what is effective, appropriate and reasonable...agreement by General Managers is considered necessary in order to secure co-operation and a sense of ownership'.

It will almost always be difficult for those who are not involved in an operation to understand the potential pitfalls of implementing a new system of using indicators, and in a number of cases middle managements have effectively sabotaged imposed systems by not pointing out the pitfalls of implementation. In others, they have helped to ensure that systems are successful by closely working with those charged with implementation. In the case of the City of Sheffield, the Director of the Arts and Museums Department pointed to the case of two theatres where the move was 'from grant aid as a simple annual ritual to action with clearly designated outputs... they themselves have come up with a list of nine policy areas, to which they will be applying quantitative measures, and which will form the basis of a service level agreement between the theatres and the City Council'. For local government more generally, the finding of Palmer in this issue that a high proportion of indicators have been introduced as a result of internal management proposals bodes well for success, at least in this aspect of implementation.

6. Build in Counters to Short-term Focus

Since many indicators are set on an annual cycle, the effect of first introducing them may well be to alter the time-scale of managerial effort to a shorter term and to focus on achievement of success on a year-by-year basis. The Operations Director of the Transport Research Laboratory suggested that, as an alternative to targets which are unrealistically long term, this may not necessarily be bad in itself. However, many organizations require a long-term perspective, and this needs to be recognized in the nature of, and time-scales set for, the indicators chosen. Remaining in the transport field, short-term performance measured by the number of miles of road built may show an improvement if resources are diverted from maintenance. But, if this results in existing roads having to be expensively rebuilt because the lack of maintenance means that they can no longer be patched up, the short-term improvement will be at a considerable cost. The link can be revealed by road-condition indicators, which can be juxtaposed to measures of additions to the road stock.

7. Ensure that They Fairly Reflect the Efforts of Managers

Unless managers' efforts are fairly reflected in the indicators, they will be seen at best as not relevant, at worst as unfair and/or potentially distorting to the managerial process. This may mean thinking about indicators as applying in different ways. Thus the Central Statistical Office (CSO) noted that some performance measures successfully motivated the generality of staff by creating a sense of achievement and improvement or by directing attention to the public image. Other measures had more impact on senior managers by highlighting policy issues.

Staffordshire's Chief Probation Officer commented on one of the major difficulties in identifying true indicators of performance: 'we are not necessarily measuring the performance of our organization, but more the decisions of sentencers within the criminal justice system'. Imprecision in the measures chosen may be an indication that there is a problem. As a civil servant pointed out: 'Some objectives may be almost entirely within the control of the unit, and others lying outside its control would not be chosen for performance indicators. But many objectives lie in between … it is not easy to find a formula which fairly reflects the efforts of the unit without sliding into the subjectivity of "trying to achieve", "seeking to influence", or "facilitating others to …"'.

8. Find a Means to Cope with Uncontrollable Items and Perceived Injustices

Linked to the previous lesson, whatever the organization, there will be events which are outside the control of managers. The way the indicators are operated needs to combine the technical requirements of control with credibility to managers in recognizing the impact of such events. One way of accommodating the problem is to make the measures more sophisticated. The Employment Service (ES) at first had performance targets which did not take account of labour market conditions. 'More recently', as a section head explained, 'placing indicators have been formulated so as to be immune from external factors outside ES control. The headline unemployed placing target is based on an assumed level of vacancies; if actual vacancies differ from this assumption, the level of placings achieved can be viewed in context'. Another way of coping with uncertainty is to recognize that revisions of targets may be essential in the light of experience.

If neither of the above is possible, as Lessons 17 and 18 below indicate, the essential element in maintaining the integrity of the indicators is to ensure that the results are not misused. As a senior officer of Copeland Borough Council put it: 'We have encouraged managers not to regard indicators as necessarily reflecting their own performance. While in some cases they do, in many others there are outside influences which, at least in the short term, are outside their control. We do not want to discourage the monitoring of service standards because some of the factors are partly or completely outside the short term control of the manager.'

9. Use the Experience of Other Organizations or Other Parts of the Organization

'We have pushed for equalization of performance within the Area and as a result the worst performing offices have generally come up to the standard of the best' (Area Director, Benefits Agency). 'The need to secure effectiveness and efficiency in the contracting process (for purchaser/provider contracts) has led to sharing with General Managers a summary of all Health Authority performance in this area' (regional health authority). 'We have made significant changes in the light of our experience and that of others, particularly other local authorities' (local authority). These examples of using comparisons do not appear to be as routine as would be desirable in the public sector. Many organizations have devised and used indicators with very little reference to others within the same sector, or even within other parts of the same organization and the tendency to reinvent wheels seems to be common in public sector performance measurement. Experience on the appropriate type of indicators, or their use, may well be available elsewhere, including from comparable organizations in other countries. (Indeed, they may even be available within the UK – a central government department found comparisons between England and Wales, Scotland and Northern Ireland worthwhile in at least raising issues of the reasons for differences.) Even if no comparable organizations are available, the process of finding the reasons why no lessons can be learned has often been useful.

10. Establish Realistic Levels of Attainment Before the First Targets Are Set

If an indicator has not been used before, it is likely to be very difficult to know what level to set. Careful preparatory work is necessary to see whether a level can be found so that the indicators themselves are not brought into disrepute by being shown to be unattainable or untesting. Many managers feel very strongly on this issue and the words 'realistic' and 'achievable' occur again and again. 'One or two targets which are imposs- ible or too easy to achieve could undermine the whole system' observes the manual of Tonbridge and Malling Borough Council, and from a civil ser- vant: 'Successful performance measurement is based on setting realistic and measurable objectives which are clearly linked to the business objectives of the organization and against which assessable success criteria can be estab- lished at the outset'. If it is not possible to find a realistic level, a trial period or periods should be used to allow the appropriate levels to be established.

IMPLEMENTATION

11. Recognize that New Indicators Need Time to Develop and May Need Revision in the Light of Experience

As with any new managerial tool, performance indicators need time to develop. Even with careful preparation, it will take time to discover if there are flaws and unintended side-effects from the way the indicators have been constructed. Thus the Inspectorate of Constabulary started to develop indicators in 1983, and the matrix of 456 indicators first used to make com- parisons has been progressively refined. Revisions to central government agency framework documents also indicate the value of the learning pro- cess and in local government a district council official commented that 'our prime aim is to continuously develop the criteria for success'. In part, revision may also be due to outside circumstances – 'What we do and how we measure it is constantly changing' noted a central government agency. The British Airports Authority, when in the public sector, measured passenger service quality with two indicators, one of which was written complaints per 100,000 passengers. The two were seen to be unsatisfactory (for example, negative comments alone are not a good basis for inferring levels of qual- ity), and, over the years, a sophisticated questionnaire procedure has been instituted.

12. Link Them to Existing Systems

For a variety of reasons, including caution about whether they will be effect- ive and the difficulties of integrating them into existing information and control procedures, indicators have often been introduced into organizations in parallel to existing systems. The result has been costly in time and money and has engendered resentment among managers who have seen the new indicators as an unwelcome (and not necessarily useful) addition to their existing burdens. Early experience of performance indicators in the Health Service was blighted by their apparent irrelevance to many managers. By contrast, one local authority has linked the city council charter to annual service plans and also intends to tie it into the Citizen's Charter. In another, 'performance service contracts are now the norm for our managers and in some areas... are used for all staff. This enables us to build PIs into the fabric of the organization and, to coin the hackneyed phrase, the way we do things round here'. Three examples from very different parts of the public sector are those in Brignall's article on Solihull MBC[1]; the Lord Chancellor's Department, which has integrated circuit objectives into the planning and budgeting processes; and Liverpool's Maritime Housing Association, which has linked individual targets as part of a comprehensive review of the staff structure to the business plan.

13. They Must Be Easily Understandable by Those Whose Performance is Being Measured

In order to ensure that the indicators are trusted, the basis on which they are compiled, as well as the message from the outcomes, needs to be understood so that discussion about any action which needs to be taken is well-informed. The Employment Service Office for Scotland emphasized that 'good communications to all levels is an important element in the preparation and implementation of performance indicators', and the area director of a central government agency wrote: 'we are conscious of the need to make those measures that bit more... credible with staff and managers'.

Over-complex indicators can distance those who need to take action from the indicators. A local authority manager complained that 'the Arts Council and the Regional Arts Boards have spent a considerable amount of time attempting to develop performance indicators, many of which, in my opinion, are over-complex'. In the case of another local authority, review of the annual service plan after a year showed that 'some lessons are clear – terminology needs to be clearly understood...'.

14. While Proxies May Be Necessary, They Must Be Chosen Cautiously

Since the outcomes of many public sector activities cannot be easily measured, proxy indicators will be necessary. But unless they are chosen with care, the proxies can distort the decision-making process by emphasizing an inappropriate outcome. As a Health Department official pointed out: 'Within the Health Service, while we are always looking for outcome measures, what we have tend to be proxies for them, in some cases process measures, in others output measures – and we need to be very careful to be clear what is being measured and the extent to which it can bear further interpretation'. In a similar vein, an official of the Management Executive of the NHS in Scotland indicated the importance of moving from measurement of processes towards 'whether patients are healthier as a result of

(NHS) interventions and whether they are being dealt with in a way they are entitled to expect'. For the Driver and Vehicle Licensing Agency, speed of response and turnaround time were taken as proxies for quality. But, as the Executive Director, Operations noted, market research has indicated that speed is not regarded as the main requirement by customers and new performance measures are being devised. Even after careful review, the final result may still not be wholly satisfactory. The Director of Education for the London Borough of Croydon pointed out that 'they are often the outcome of much painstaking failure to find something better'. Finally, it is worth noting an imaginative uses of proxies by the Customs and Excise. While drug seizures make the headlines, and the value of drugs prevented from entering the country is monitored, both are acknowledged to be unrelated to the total flow. So the street price is taken as one of the proxies of success.

15. The Period of Introduction Should Be Used to Reassess Internal and External Relationships

The introduction of performance indicators can be used, and may require, changes in an organization's internal and external relationships. For example: 'The performance targets introduced when the CSO became an Executive Agency', explained the Head of the Policy Secretariat, 'have had a profound positive effect on the way we view our customers and the way they view us. Most revealing of all was the difficulty our customers had in specifying what level of performance they really wanted of us'. Internal reassessment of existing procedures should be welcomed as a manifestation of the fact that the measures are proving their worth. The Chief Executive of Hertfordshire County Council observed that 'without other management changes, for example financial devolution, the performance indicator culture will not flourish . . . PIs would merely bob along the top of the organization making the occasional appearance on the agenda of management teams'.

USE

16. The Data on Which the Results are Based Must Be Trusted

'Yes, but are the figures right?' is a constant refrain from those who take performance indicators seriously, or need to do so because their own performance is being measured. 'The reliability of available data is a considerable factor in the preparation of performance indicators' commented an official of the Department of the Environment's Property Holdings Finance Division. 'We need to be careful in the interpretation of data, particularly where there are a small number of samples' wrote an NHS Trust's personnel director, adding, in response to criticism for having too many trained district nurses at a certain grade, 'It is questionable whether the use of this tool in order to prepare league tables of providers' performance is valuable since so much of the data is unreliable'. A Chief Probation Officer indicated that some of the data 'is quite unreliable since main grade staff have yet to cotton on to the importance of filling in the forms necessary to make this information available'. Without data which is not only accurate, but trusted to be so, many of the potential benefits from introducing performance indicators may be dissipated.

17. Use the Results as Guidance, not Answers. Recognize that Interpretation is the Key to Action

The appropriate managerial response to performance measurement results is a basis for discussion among managers with a view to taking action. Results cannot, on their own, provide 'definitive' evidence of success or failure and should be used to raise questions, not to provide answers. '... it is the dialogue that arises from review that is the important message' was the advice of the Chief Executive of Arun District Council. In the case of Birmingham Social Services, questions led to a review of objectives after it was found that nursery occupancy could range from 30% to 90%. Analysis of the reasons for the range showed that the nurseries were also providing other services and that these in part depended on 'the objectives and professional leadership of local managers'. By defining objectives more clearly, there was a 15% increase in occupancy levels, despite staffing shortages. Above all, according to the Assistant Director of Social Services, the discussion about the objectives of day nurseries refocussed the tasks and 'finally led to a clear definition of a community day nursery and family centre'. More generally, the Audit Commission has long used the technique of publishing profiles of performance of specific activities as a means of encouraging discussion of the reasons for differences between organizations.

The results should always be accompanied by a commentary so that the figures can be analysed and put in context. For example one local authority includes the minimum requirement of 'An overview of the quarter... which is a brief summary of the main points of note... accompanied by some short text picking out the main points to note about the indicators and indicating action being taken'. Another, Bracknell Forest Borough Council, has comments in the reports by chief officers where appropriate, as when the improvement in turnround of building control applications was realistically explained by 'the better relationship of workload to resources that now exists compared with the peak of the 1980s' boom'. Without a commentary there is considerable danger that the figures will be misused or at least misunderstood, as when, after great efforts were made in one police force to respond to a dramatic increase in car crime, further analysis through the matrix of indicators referred to in Lesson 11 revealed Volkswagen badge stealing as the main reason for the increase.

18. Acknowledge the Importance of Feedback. Follow-up Gives Credibility; No Feedback Means Atrophy; Negative-only Feedback Encourages Game-playing

The level of outside or senior managerial attention to the results indicates how performance indicators are regarded and gives powerful messages to all those involved in preparing and using them. Figures on submission rates in higher education may once have been regarded as 'academic' but are now of enormous importance to universities since they affect future allocations of studentships. A central government department noted that for one of their sections 'the sensible setting of targets, and senior management's clear interest in their setting and monitoring, has enhanced the section's motivation'. In a central government agency the board holds quarterly performance dialogues with each regional director in preparation for a discussion with the Minister about the results.

Silence in response to results is likely to mean that the figures come to be regarded as irrelevant by those whose performance is being measured. Continued silence will mean that little trouble is taken to fix realistic target levels or respond to the results. Thus when senior officials in a government department who filled in regular annual reviews found that no action or feedback was forthcoming, first less attention was given to the results and then little importance was given to the levels of target set each year. The North East Thames Regional Health Authority, on the other hand, emphasized the importance not only of the information, but of getting it in on time 'We have initiated a system of penalty points for lateness and incompleteness of routine returns'.

If the only reaction of senior management is to emphasize the aspects of results involving failure, the message to those whose performance is being measured will swiftly be that great care is necessary to ensure that targets are set at a level that can be achieved. There is also the danger that considerable time will be spent in making sure that the figures 'look right', regardless of the underlying performance, with elaborate alibis to protect those involved. A common criticism among those subject to scrutiny by the Public Accounts Committee is that the Committee has inhibited the development of a more managerial climate by not recognizing the greater element of risk involved in the changing nature of public organizations and by continuing to focus on mistakes, rather than a balance between successes and failures.

19. Trade-offs and Complex Interactions Must Be Recognized; Not all Indicators Should Carry Equal Weight

Emphasis on one aspect of performance will almost inevitably have effects on other aspects. The use of performance indicators needs to accommodate such effects and the accompanying trade-offs. Failure to do so can result in the performance measurement system as a whole being by-passed or discredited. For example the Employment Service 'expresses three placing targets as percentages of the headline unemployed placing target. One consequence of this is that better than expected performance on the headline target can result in under achievement of the percentage subsidiary targets. This slightly paradoxical relationship needs to be clearly understood by managers in order to optimise their ability to meet all the targets and not just the headline target. Similar trade-offs exist between ES' benefit-related targets. Striving to pay people promptly may have consequences for the accuracy with which payments are made ... To concentrate single-mindedly on one indicator runs the risk of failing to achieve the other; this may represent less success than narrowly failing to achieve both'. Another agency commented on the indicators that 'their real strength lies in their overall effect which is particularly important given the highly interrelated nature of our work'. A third agency recognized the element of trade-off in ensuring that not all indicators can or should carry the same weight and altered the number of indicators after finding that the weighting towards one activity 'sent the wrong messages round the organization'. A Ministry of Defence official counselled the importance of careful interpretation: 'Apply PIs to those activities that are carrying out the most important operations and not necessarily those where it is easiest to notch up a big score'.

20. Results Must Be User-friendly and at Appropriate Levels of Aggregation and Response Time

Managers unable to understand the results of performance indicators will not be able to take appropriate action. What is done need not be very sophisticated, as indicated by a local authority's comment, 'Emphasis has been placed on good presentation, particularly the appropriate use of graphs and tables etc., so as to make information as easy to assimilate as possible'. The results also need to be presented at the right level of detail – not too aggregated to mask important trends, or too disaggregated for the manager to be overwhelmed with a mass of detail.

Since indicators may be relevant to different time-scales, the timing of results needs to reflect time-scales for decision. 'One of the biggest criticisms levelled at the Health Service Indicators over the years have been that by the time they are disseminated to the service the information is out of date and the world has moved on' commented an official. And a central government agency admitted that a yearly, national survey of customer satisfaction was 'fairly useless' because action was not possible as result – response times were too long to be meaningful, and disaggregation below national level was not possible.

The results for some indicators will need to be reviewed each month, for others the time-scale may be a year. North West Thames Regional Health Authority quotes quarterly immunization uptake rates as the relevant time-scale. For some, highly specific time-periods are relevant, for example at particular points during a contract. The London Docklands Development corporation has established a system that focuses on the elements of project management – input, time and output. Assuming that counters to short-term focus have been built in, this lesson reinforces the importance of identifying the appropriate time-scales for the indicators chosen. The managerial response to the results should also reflect the appropriate time-scales.

CONCLUSION

Consideration of the early lessons outlined above should help organizations to use performance indicators to better effect. They will not guarantee success, but failure to take them into account could mean not only a waste of managerial time and cash resources but also, potentially more serious, a distortion of managerial action. It could also mean a wasted opportunity for the use of a valuable managerial tool.

NOTES

1. See S. Brignall, 'Performance Measurement and Change in Local Government: A General Case and a Childcare Application', *Public Policy and Management* (Oct–Dec 1995).

19

A Star to Sail By?

The Economist

Were Siemens an American firm, the news that it is making the creation of value for its shareholders its top priority would be loudly applauded. But in Germany, where fans of "stakeholder capitalism" argue that their interests should be balanced with those of employees, suppliers and customers, its decision to become the first firm to adopt a measure of shareholder value known as economic value added (EVA) will provoke jeers as well as cheers.

Karl-Hermann Baumann, Siemens's chief financial officer, says that the trains-to-telecoms giant, which will switch to EVA in October, is now convinced that focusing on shareholder value is the best way to ensure its long-term prosperity. A growing number of other companies in Europe, Asia and Latin America, have reached the same conclusion – and are turning to consultants offering "performance metrics" to measure how much value is being created (or destroyed). Measures such as EVA are already well established in America, where a growing number of Wall Street stockpickers, not to mention many large companies, including Coca-Cola, Monsanto and Procter & Gamble, swear by them.

Inevitably the measures are also a big business for consultants. Stern Stewart, the New York firm that developed EVA, is the leader of the pack. But in recent years it has faced competition from the Boston Consulting Group (BCG), Braxton Associates, McKinsey and others. Many consultancies produce league tables of value added and go to increasingly absurd lengths to protect their particular "brand". As well as registering EVA as a trademark in several countries, Stern Stewart has also registered the term "EVAngelist".

Such hype is reminiscent of another management fad that swept the world and cost thousands of people their jobs – business process re-engineering. The argument about the effectiveness of re-engineering (motto: "don't automate, obliterate") still rages. On balance, it now seems that most of the firms that applied it became more efficient; but it is also clear that it was hopelessly oversold, and that it is much more use to some types of firm, or business people doing some types of thing, than it is to others. In other words, it is a useful tool, not a complete answer. Much the same seems to be true of EVA and its rivals.

ALPHABET SOUP

The notion behind the yardsticks is simple: a company creates value only if the return on its capital is greater than the opportunity cost of it, or the rate that investors could earn by investing in other securities with the same risk. Far from novel, this is one of the oldest nostrums in business. Companies have long used "hurdle" rates of return to judge individual investment projects. The new measures extend this practice to an entire business. "It's a very basic concept that big companies simply forgot over time," says Marcel Telles, the boss of Brahma, a Brazilian drinks firm that is an EVA addict.

EVA seeks to jog managers' memories by deducting from a firm's net operating profit a charge for the amount of capital it employs. If the result is positive, then the firm created value over the period in question; if the EVA is negative, it was a "value destroyer". Providing a company knows how much capital its operating units use, it can work out their EVA too. For example, if a division's capital is $100m and its cost of capital is 10%, its target rate of return will be $10m. If it earns $50m, then its EVA will be $40m. Although EVA sums involve tweaking published accounts (see Example 1 on next page), the principle is easy enough to grasp.

Other measures involve trickier calculations. A popular one is "cash flow return on investment" (CFROI), which is promoted by both BCG and HOLT Value Associates, a Chicago firm that advises fund managers and firms on questions of valuation. This is a return-on-investment measure that is adjusted to take account of the distortions that can be caused by inflation, different asset ages and lives, and different depreciation methods. Unlike EVA, which is based on adjusted accounting profit and is therefore a near-cash measure, CFROI compares a firm's cash flows with the inflation-adjusted capital used to produce them.

The problem with EVA and CFROI is that they are backward-looking measures, which tell managers nothing about how their current strategies are likely to affect the future value of their companies. So Stern Stewart has come up with a measure of overall corporate value, market value added (MVA), which takes the total capital of a firm, including equity, loans and retained earnings, and deducts this from the value of its share capital and debt. Not to be outdone, BCG has come up with a rival measure, total shareholder return (TSR), which is the change in a firm's market capitalisation over a one-year period plus dividends paid out to shareholders, expressed as a percentage of its initial value.

As well as looking at historical performance, these measures capture the market's estimates of firms' growth prospects. Stern Stewart says that there is a close correlation between EVA and MVA – if managers improve EVA, the company's MVA is highly likely to improve too. Other firms claim that their backward-looking and forward-looking measures are even more closely correlated.

Example 1 The EVA brew

Although economic value added may sound simple in theory, it can be tricky to apply in practice. Stern Stewart advises clients to make anything up to 164 changes to their accounts. The following example (see Table 19.1) shows how the same consultancy works out the 1996 EVA of South African Breweries (SAB), a company that owns hotels and shops, as well as being one of the world's biggest brewers.

First, Stern Stewart calculates SAB's "economic capital" (1). This is its equity and debt, plus adjustments for items such as cumulative goodwill associated with acquisitions. Accounting rules treat goodwill as an expense charged against profits, but Stern Stewart says that goodwill and other things such as R&D are capital investments that should produce returns in future.

Next, Stern Stewart works out how much SAB's assets earned after tax in 1996 (2). Then it calculates the company's cost of capital. The cost of its debt is simply the average interest rate that the company pays. But what about its cost of equity? To calculate this, Stern Stewart uses the capital

Table 19.1 EVAluating

South African Breweries	1996, rand, m
1. Economic capital = shareholders' equity	5,799
+ goodwill written off	1,521
+ capitalised cumulative unusual loss	930
+ deferred tax	405
+ minority interests	2,352
+ total debt	4,415
	15,422
2. Net operating profit after tax (NOPAT) = operating profit	3,406
+ interest expense	689
− unusual gain	68
− taxes	978
	3,049
3. Weighted average cost of capital (WACC)	
cost of equity	20.4%
cost of debt	10.7%
WACC =	17.5%
4. EVA = NOPAT − (capital × WACC)	
= 3,049 − (15,422 × 17.5%)	= 305m

Source: Stern Stewart

asset pricing model, which holds that a firm's cost of equity consists of a risk-free rate of return for a stockmarket plus a risk premium that reflects how volatile its share price has been relative to that market. Applied to SAB, this produces a cost of equity of 20.4%. Because SAB has more equity than debt, its weighted cost of capital is 17.5% (3).

Lastly, Stern Stewart multiplies this percentage figure by SAB's capital employed to produce a capital charge, which is then deducted from the company's profit figure. The result shows that SAB had a positive EVA of 350m rand ($81m) last year (4). Its shareholders no doubt raised their glasses to that.

CASH IS FACT, PROFIT IS OPINION

How well do these different measures perform? They are undoubtedly superior to traditional yardsticks of corporate performance, such as return on capital employed and earnings per share, which rely on accounting figures. The defect of accounting figures is that they can easily be manipulated. For example, by extending the depreciation life of assets (which improves earnings per share) or using operating leases to keep assets off a balance sheet (which boosts return on capital), firms can disguise their true financial health at the flick of a pen. Such "creative" accounting explains why changes in, say, earnings per share explain very little of the changes in firms' price-earnings ratios, a traditional gauge of corporate value.

Because they focus on cash flow, which is harder to manipulate, the new measures provide a more reliable picture of firms' performance. They also make it easier to compare them across borders. Looking at national accounts creates a severe apples-and-oranges problem, because depreciation, brand valuations and other issues are treated differently by different accounting regimes. A classic example of this was provided by Daimler-Benz, which in 1993 became the first German firm to list its stock in New York. Under German rules, it reported a $372m profit; under tougher American ones, its loss was $1.1 billion.

Little wonder that financial analysts are scrutinising the new yardsticks carefully. HOLT has signed up more than 200 fund-management firms as subscribers to its CFROI-based forecasting model, including several in Japan. And a growing number of investment banks, such as Goldman Sachs and Credit Suisse First Boston (CSFB), are using EVA to analyse equities.

Stern Stewart and other consultants claim that their metrics can be useful early warning signals. For instance, anybody monitoring IBM's EVA would have seen it decline consistently between 1984 and 1989 (see Figure 19.1). In 1988 it turned negative (ie, IBM was destroying value), even though the firm's net profit rose. However, the metric also did not predict Big Blue's turnaround in 1994.

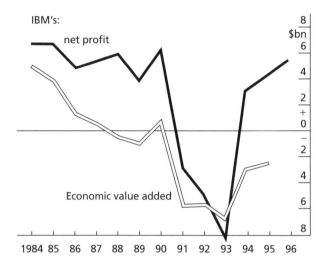

IBM's:

net profit

Economic value added

8 $bn
6
4
2 +
0
– 2
4
6
8

1984 85 86 87 88 89 90 91 92 93 94 95 96

Figure 19.1 Early warning (*Source*: Stern Stewart)

VALUE FOR MONEY?

Although EVA, CFROI and other metrics are useful as pure performance measures, consultants say they can be far more than that. Used as corporate-governance tools, they can persuade managers tempted to build huge empires at shareholders' expense to put the interests of owners first.

Firms that have taken the plunge by tying executives' share options and/ or bonuses to improvements in EVA claim that such "value-based manage-ment" strategies have had a big impact. Harnischfeger Industries, an acquis-itive Milwaukee company that makes mining equipment, paper-making machinery and overhead cranes, is one of EVA's converts. When it adopted the technique in 1993, the company was destroying some $100m of wealth a year, largely because the managers in its operations rarely thought about the cost of the capital they consumed. To make matters worse, they often exaggerated the likely returns from proposed acquisitions, forcing head office to scrutinise every deal closely. "We were the policemen," says Francis Corby, the firm's head of finance.

Now, with EVA-related bonuses at stake, both operating managers and financial ones are on the same wavelength, because nobody wants to make an acquisition whose returns will be smaller than the company's 12% cost of capital. In June Harnischfeger withdrew from a takeover battle for Giddings & Lewis, America's biggest machine-tool company, after the rival bidder, Germany's Thyssen, upped the stakes. With managers also slashing inventories abroad, helping to reduce capital employed by $300m since 1993, the company turned EVA positive last year, two years earlier than the target date it had set itself.

Table 19.2 Top ten US companies*, by market value added, 1995

	$bn
Coca-Cola	87.8
General Electric	80.8
Merck & Co	63.4
Philip Morris	51.6
Microsoft	44.9
Johnson & Johnson	42.5
AT&T	40.2
Procter & Gamble	40.0
Exxon	39.0
Wal-Mart	36.0

* Industrial and non-financial.
Source: Stern Stewart

Another way for managers to boost the new measures (and thus their bonuses) is to reduce the cost of the capital they use. Often this means reducing a firm's equity capital, because equity is often more expensive than debt. Since 1995 Brazil's Brahma has retired some $1 billion-worth of equity via a series of buybacks.

Altogether more than 300 firms worldwide have adopted EVA-based systems – which puts this method ahead of its rivals. Stern Stewart's longer track record is one reason. Brahma's Mr Telles likens choosing a metrics adviser to choosing a surgeon: "You want someone who has done a lot of operations." But EVA's biggest selling point is its relative simplicity. Rival measures, such as CFROI, are harder to explain to managers.

This simplicity, argue its rivals, comes at a cost. In a pamphlet last October, Eric Olsen of BCG argued that EVA discourages executives from making big investments because the upfront capital charge for them immediately depresses EVA. He also noted that the easiest way to boost the measure in the short run was to "milk" a business by slashing capital spending. Unchecked, this could cause a fatal spiral of under-investment. "In five years you might not have a business left," says Alistair Cox, group strategy director of Blue Circle Industries, a British manufacturer of building materials that prefers measures based on total shareholder returns.

Stern Stewart, which admits that EVA could restrict growth if used too simply, advises clients to spread out part of the capital charge associated with big projects over their expected pay-back period. And it suggests that firms allow some of a bonus awarded for beating EVA targets in one year to be clawed back if future goals are missed. In Harnischfeger's case, growth has not been a problem: sales have more than doubled since it introduced the technique.

How different are the competing products? The top-ten lists produced by the various consultancies do indeed turn up different winners and losers (see Tables 19.2–19.4). But that is largely because of the different time

Table 19.3 Top ten US* companies by "HOLT % future",† June 30th 1997

	% future
Coca-Cola	80.12
Merck & Co	67.31
Johnson & Johnson	64.93
Procter & Gamble	63.33
General Electric	59.89
3M	54.29
Hewlett-Packard	48.78
Philip Morris	42.48
Allied Signal	41.10
Wal-Mart	40.56

* Non-financial companies in Dow Jones industrial average, excludes AT&T.
† % of total market value attributed to future investments.
Source: HOLT Value Associates

Table 19.4 Top ten US companies* by TSR†, 1991–96 average

	%
3Com	92.0
Tellabs	83.6
EMC	73.9
Cisco Systems	72.7
Oracle	66.9
Dell Computer	65.6
Intel	61.1
Andrew Corp.	60.1
Citicorp	60.0
Micron Technology	59.9

* In S&P 500.
† Total shareholder return.
Source: The Boston Consulting Group

periods and samples chosen by the different consultancies. (HOLT, which uses CFROI analysis, ranks firms on a particularly complicated scale linked to the present cash value of their future investments.) Monsanto and other companies that have carefully compared EVA, CFROI and other measures say that they mostly do not turn up wildly different results. The bigger question is whether performance metrics, as a whole, carry any dangers.

In many parts of Europe and Asia, it is hard to see what harm a little bit of concentration on value can do. Siemens, where Mr Baumann admits that several of the firm's divisions currently have negative EVAs, is a case in point. In Asia, firms that have been growing, such as Singapore's SNP and Indonesia's Bakrie & Brothers, are now using similar yardsticks to re-examine their mix of businesses.

As a way of measuring things rather than reorganising them, EVA and the other tools are helpful. But there are still weaknesses. Inevitably, performance measures are a bit more useful in some industries than others. It is harder (though clearly not impossible) to find ways to calculate ratios in industries where many of the assets are intangible items such as brand names or marketing brains. Consultants have to make the similar guesstimates about the value of, say, a newspaper title to those which normal accountants are increasingly being asked to make.

Yet Stern Stewart insists that its approach works as well with service-sector companies as with manufacturing ones: it cites the example of Equifax, a credit-scoring company based in Atlanta which started using EVA in 1992 – and has saved a small fortune by selling off property and rejigging the way it collects its own debts. However, even Stern Stewart admits that two sorts of companies are not well suited to EVA-style analysis: financial institutions (which must set aside capital for regulatory reasons) and very young companies, where most of the revenue calculations would have to be guesswork.

There is a wider criticism to be made. In a recent exchange in *Fortune* magazine, Gary Hamel, a respected management writer, pointed out that the efficient use of capital is not the be-all and end-all for successful companies. Strategy and innovation, he says, count for more. It is indeed hard to imagine EVA having told Bill Gates anything useful when he started Microsoft, or when he decided to embrace the Internet last year. A stock analyst who bets on a company because he thinks the chairman is a genius may do better than the one looking for a positive CFROI.

Already, some companies are introducing yet another technique – "balanced scorecards". These try to mitigate the drawbacks of making purely numerical estimates of a firm's performance. Originally developed by David Norton, a consultant, and Robert Kaplan, an accounting professor at Harvard Business School, these models combine financial scores with measures of less tangible assets such as customer satisfaction and loyalty, and a firm's ability to nurture the skills of its employees.

The metrics merchants think that such an approach is wrong-headed. A profusion of different measures can cause more problems than they solve. It helps to have a clear focus. But then the balanced scorecard – no less than EVA – is just another form of corporate thermometer. As Siemens would concede, it is useful to know just how sick you are; but what matters is whether you get better.

Section 6

Who Should Benefit?

20

Stakeholder Capitalism

W. Hutton

Keynes famously called for the socialisation of investment at the end of his *General Theory,* and many critics of the British financial system have echoed that call. But the task is a more subtle one, if the object of the exercise is to keep the merits of private ownership while reshaping the way it works. Thus the great challenge of the twentieth century, after the experience of both state socialism and of unfettered free markets, is to create a new financial architecture in which private decisions produce a less degenerate capitalism. The triple requirement is to broaden the area of stake-holding in companies and institutions, so creating a greater bias to longterm commitment from owners; to extend the supply of cheap, longterm debt; and to decentralise decision-making. The financial system, in short, needs to be comprehensively republicanised.

The first breach would be made by establishing a republican-style central bank which understood that its role was to recast the financial system as a servant of business rather than as its master. Financial freedom would no longer be taken as axiomatically good but as a privilege which has to be earned, and which carries obligations. As matters stand the current Bank of England is a permanent obstacle to financial reform: a precondition for any wider reconstruction of the financial system is a transformation of its constitution, mission and values.

The Bank's structure would match the new federal structure of the state. As the country began to be organised politically around its constituent regions, nations and cities, there would be a framework of regional public banks reporting to the Central Bank, whose chief executives would be appointed by the elected parliaments of the appropriate region. They would sit on the governing board of the Bank, replacing the current Court (which is staffed by placemen of the rentier state) and deliberate over monetary policy and the wider reform of the financial system. The extent to which the Bank had the final word over interest rates or the extent to which it fell to the Chancellor of the Exchequer could be decided after the new arrangements had bedded down for at least one complete economic cycle and the character of the Bank became clearer. If it became a social partner in the republican sense, running monetary policy impartially with a democratic awareness of the trade-offs between lost output and lower inflation, the presumption would be that it would gain independence along US lines. With new constitutional arrangements there would, finally, be a way of ensuring its democratic accountability.

In its conduct of monetary policy the Bank would be armed with a more complete array of financial instruments than short-term interest rates. Instead of conceding the financial institutions' argument that their balance sheets are their own concern and that the only legitimate tool of policy is the price of money, the Bank would have the power to influence directly the structure and profitability of banking business in pursuit of its wider public objectives. It would, for example, reintroduce reserve requirements to support its interest rate policy, and it would follow the Bundesbank and the Federal Reserve by regulating the markets in a wider public interest than that defined by the markets themselves.

One of the Bank's chief preoccupations would be to lower the cost of capital in Britain – the combination of servicing of bank debt and shareholders' funds – and to lengthen the payback periods that companies set for their investment projects. This is the core of the British supply-side problem and the single most important explanation for indifferent levels of investment. British companies need to borrow more longterm debt and lower their target rates of return from new investment. The Bank's objective, along with a reformed Treasury, must be to construct a financial system in which this can take place; the first time the British authorities will have played such a role since the Industrial Revolution.

In order for companies to borrow more, the banks have to lend funds that companies can afford to service. In the same way that purchasing a house on a three-year mortgage with a 20 per cent interest rate would mean that fewer houses would be bought, so very few companies can sustain high investment with three-year paybacks and 20 per cent nominal returns. The first task, then, is to change the conditions that give British clearing banks their short-term, anti-industrial lending policies.

But for the banks to lend longer term, they themselves need less demanding financial criteria because longterm loans are less profitable for them than short-term revolving credits. They need to have their own cost of capital lowered; they need access to longterm deposits; and they need better credit assessment techniques, with incentives to develop closer relationships with their industrial customers in order better to judge the viability of their investment proposals.

Britain should copy other industrialised countries and create a public agency that will act as a financial intermediary collecting longer term deposits and channelling them to lending institutions. The Japanese use their post office network to collect longterm savings, and their great public investment banks then lend directly or in partnership with Japan's commercial banks. The US has deployed their federal housing finance intermediaries, 'Fannie Mae' (Federal National Mortgage Association) and 'Freddie Mac' (Federal Home Loan Mortgage Corporation), to encourage direct and indirect longterm finance for home purchase and new home construction; while Germany has its *Kreditanstalt für Wiederaufbau* (the KfW or Bank for Reconstruction) which makes longterm loans in partnership with the commercial banks and a network of regional development banks. The UK has nothing.[1]

What it could have are regional banks collecting longterm deposits to recycle to clearing banks and other specialist lending institutions, like a housing bank to cater for housing associations, local authorities and the construction industry. A new benchmark for longterm bank lending would be established as more longterm bank loans were made. A specialist bank lending to small and medium-sized companies could support the same drive. In order to encourage longterm lending, the reformed Central Bank could offer assistance on favourable terms in the money markets to all longterm lenders – public and commercial banks alike. This would reassure them about the liquidity risk they were running.

But the banks are not charities and to entrench this new attitude the target rate of return on their own capital will have to be lowered. The Germans have two key mechanisms. First they exploit the stakeholder culture engendered by co-operative capitalism to lower the cost of capital for all enterprises, banks included. Shares are tokens of a longterm relationship rather than a trading asset, so that dividend payments can be lower and payback periods lengthened. Second, public banks at both state and regional level are constrained in their dividend distributions; profits build up as reserves and balance sheets are strengthened which gives a stable platform from which to lend longterm at keen rates of interest.

The combination is a potent one. Borrowers' loan packages, a mix of public and private loans, are cheaper because the private and public banks themselves need to earn lower financial returns. Nor do the commercial banks complain about this 'subsidised' finance, as their counterparts in Britain might be expected to do. As they are themselves shareholders in the borrowing companies, they benefit from the impact that cheaper loan finance has on the borrowers' trading prospects.

To lower the cost of capital, British banks and their customers need more patient, committed shareholders and less of a hunger for dividends. The entire system could then move into a virtuous circle in which more long-term bank lending was validated by improved economic performance resulting from higher investment. Lowering the cost of capital would also allow the banks to invest more in internal systems for information gathering and credit assessment; these are expensive and time consuming, but would help the banks avoid the lending mistakes they made in the 1980s boom. If, at the same time, they could share in the success of the companies in which they invested the rewards for lending would be higher.

One immediate move would be to insist that banks take equity stakes in enterprises, and that banks which did not do so would rank lower in claims on firms' assets than stakeholding banks. The banks' legal capacity to take a 'floating charge' on all of a company's assets should be abolished; this makes companies the prisoners of a single bank loan, prevents them from borrowing heavily to finance investment and encourages banks to look for property collateral to support their lending rather than offering finance for specific projects. It worsens the present disastrous arm's-length arrangements. A proper system of loan guarantees, run by a public institution, should be set up, allowing small firms in particular to borrow more aggressively. If these measures were combined with a legal requirement to regionalise the operations of the clearing banks, they would add up to a novel and important contribution to the creation of a British *Mittelstand* sector. Britain's small and medium-sized companies are damaged most by their inability to sustain high levels of longterm debt.

Perhaps, in the short run, bank dividends should be regulated and banks encouraged to build up cheaper internal reserves of capital. Banks will complain bitterly about any infringement of their 'freedom', but since the state is required to bail them out if they get into financial difficulties and to carry the wider social costs of their anti-industrial lending policies, such an initiative would create a proper symmetry of obligations.

The most important factor in reducing the cost of capital for banks and business generally is shareholder commitment. This should be fostered by exploiting the proposed new system of corporate governance and the role of non-executive directors, for banks and business alike. Groups of core institutional shareholders might be formed who would be represented on company and bank boards by non-executive directors with their own, information-gathering secretariats. Voting rights might be limited only to those shareholders who are represented on company boards, thus legally linking ownership with obligations to commitment. It might even be useful to split the functions of the supervisory and executive boards, as in Germany, with representatives of the core voting shareholders joining the supervisory board. They would engage in an ongoing dialogue with management about business strategy, with share options and bonuses only exercisable after a specified minimum period – say ten years' service – and with tax incentives for those who exercised options later. The current incentives for paper entrepreneurship, unlocking so-called shareholder value by asset manipulation and so boosting executives' share options, would be reduced. There would be a penal short-term capital gains tax for shareholders who took early profits, tapering to near zero for longterm shareholders. This would encourage shareholders to value future returns more highly than they do and so help companies to extend their payback periods.

This would only work if takeovers were made harder to mount. The tightening of lax accounting standards, setting new upper limits for advisers' fees (in particular removing their tax-deductibility) and allowing firms a 'public-interest' defence against hostile takeovers would all help. In addition the current obligation for any single shareholder to make a full bid if more than 30 per cent of the company is owned could be dropped. Large single shareholders can be sources of much needed stability. Although current doctrine is that effective stewardship of company assets requires the fear of takeover, this militates against the construction of longterm relationships within the company. Much of the so-called 'shareholder value' that is 'unlocked' by takeover amounts to no more than unravelling co-operative and committed relationships, which are priced above market-clearing levels, and reorganising them in a strictly price-mediated relationship. This lowers the company's variable costs which, taken together with the accountants' treatment of the financing costs of takeover, appears to make the acquisition profitable. But accounting fiddles are no route to industrial success, as Britain has discovered.

The approach to takeovers highlights another aspect of a properly constitutional democratic state – the role of audit. Without impartially prepared accounts that follow a transparent set of rules, the balance sheets and profits of firms are the playthings of private boards and their accountants. In their increasing anxiety to win business, accountants have been willing to bend accounting conventions to meet the short-term requirements of boards – so that accounts no longer offer a proper measure of company worth, failing to allow comparison of performance over time or with other firms. Corporate taxation becomes the quixotic result of whatever accounting standards are adopted, allowing boards in effect to choose their level of taxation. Audit needs to be regulated in the public interest, and auditors licensed like banks before they can go into business.

In the search for fees and commissions, investment and merchant banks have become ever more imaginative in their invention of financial assets that can be bought and sold, ranging from the sale of company bank debt to instruments that protect against future share price movements – with the Bank of England indulging the whole exercise as evidence of financial innovation. But this makes the system increasingly unstable, without increasing investment and innovation in the real economy. The system must be forced to exercise greater prudence and the financial institutions' balance sheets must be more strictly monitored. A balance needs to be struck between market contracts that protect against risk, and marketisation that destabilises longterm relationships between finance and industry.

The emergence of giant financial institutions, in particular pension funds, and their growing desire to hold company equity, paying dividends, has been one of the biggest motors of short-termism. Government and company bonds, of course, pay fixed rates of interest. Equity has offered a measure of protection against inflation, with profits and dividends tending to rise at least in line with inflation; but it has also been attractive because dividends have risen significantly in real terms. As a result pension funds hold 85 per cent of their assets in company shares, bringing their total holdings of shares to 40 per cent of the value quoted on the London Stock Exchange.

Dividends are meant to fluctuate with profits but pension funds, with their longterm liabilities to their pensioners, cannot afford such fluctuation. For them, dividends need to be as secure as fixed-interest investments with the extra bonus that they always rise – and companies are now yoked to this demand from their principal shareholders with all the adverse consequences. Pension funds and insurance companies have become classic absentee landlords, exerting power without responsibility and making exacting demands upon companies without recognising their reciprocal obligation as owners.

Some funds have begun to exercise responsibilities, questioning some of the more outrageous executive pay deals, but typically the British savings institution is a supine accomplice of the board – happy to go along with corporate strategy as long as the financial returns are high. Their power to affect the course of whole industries is extraordinary. For example, Mercury Asset Management, one of the largest City investment managers, settled the fate of London Weekend Television in its fight for independence from Granada and so set in train the spate of takeovers and mergers in the independent TV sector. Should one person in one investment management group have such power? Should the sole criterion for such decisions be the maximisation of short-term value for the funds which he or she manages? Although the funds will resist the limitations on their freedom that new proposals on takeovers and their participation in corporate governance would imply, in fact they need to be relieved of such awesome responsibilities – or at least be forced to treat them as would properly informed shareholders rather than institutional rentiers.

However, the power of pension funds and institutional saving has not grown in a vacuum; it is the direct consequence, as we have seen, of the explosion of home-ownership and the private provision for old age, with the state progressively abdicating its responsibilities in the name of 'choice' and 'self-reliance'. Pension fund contributions, the underlying fund and the final payment are all free of tax. The private has been privileged at least in part because of Britain's weaknesses in providing a solid state pension. That would demand a binding contract between the generations, but in Britain such contracts are expressed through Parliament whose guiding principle is that it cannot bind successors – a principle faithfully followed when the Conservatives carelessly debauched the SERPS scheme. Any inter-generational contract cannot be trusted – and the same is true for the provision of social housing.

As a result people have exploited tax privileges and protected themselves with private and occupational pensions, while even those for whom home-ownership is unsuitable have been forced to join the stampede into owner occupation, increasingly financed with an endowment insurance policy to pay off the mortgage. The consequence has been a flood of institutional savings, an acute demand for dividends and the foreshortening of investment time-horizons. These savings, if the wider financial system had been reformed to accommodate their new power and demands, could have been and still can be a fruitful source of finance for investment. Instead they have become destabilising.

NOTE

1. Only the Agricultural Mortgage Corporation continues to play a public part, albeit small.

21

Islamic Banking
An Overview

S. A. Arar

It gives me great honour and pleasure to be asked to write an article on Islamic banking, because Islam is my religion, and it is part of my belief to share this knowledge with those who seek it. Furthermore, this paper grants me a great opportunity to address as many people as possible about the positive aspects that Islam, as an economic system, can provide to aid and improve the international economic and financial systems, along with implementing new banking concepts based on Islamic economic legislation (Shari'a).

Shari'a represents the rules of God. It forms a comprehensive plan for life. Islamic economics, with such a divine source, are not man-made, but are believed to be a way of worshipping God. They came as a revelation from God to the prophet Mohamed (peace be upon him). To the Muslim, Shari'a becomes a part of daily worship, with an objective to carry out economic activities in a fair manner, governed by noble and unchangeable values.

The Quran (the Holy Book of Islam) and the Sunnah (Ways of the Prophet) are the sources of the Shari'a as practised for fourteen centuries. Nevertheless, the Quran bears more weight than the Sunnah in setting the primary guidelines for Shari'a. The source of the Islamic economic system is based on divine revelations, a feature non-existent in any other economic system. Also, there are other sources for the Shari'a such as Ijmaa (matters agreed upon by top Islamic scholars). Ijmaa, concluded by humans, was approved earlier by the Prophet, and as such is believed to have been approved by God.

Islam stands for universality, therefore Islamic banking and financial institutions, by their ideology, are universal institutions. There is no question of nationality or locality in Islam (mankind is but a single nation).[1] To the outsider, Islam is often viewed as prohibiting followers from doing this or that. On the contrary, Islam is a positive religion, differentiating between right and wrong, and individual's rights and dues. Islamic economic teachings forbid only negative and destructive activities such as gambling, monopoly, usury, cheating and deception, extortion, injustice, deceiving the gullible, selling items you do not own and making false markets. However, the main focus of Islamic economic thought is in prohibiting usury (known today as interest) and selling short. Islamic economics does not contradict other cultures and religions and in no way tries to reflect the weaknesses of other economic systems irrespective of their religious or personal sources. On the contrary, it only aims to bring human principles and a religious context by outlawing usury. To prevent injustice, Islam identifies and separates the lawful from the prohibited.

The prohibition of interest is the centre of Islamic economics. However, this prohibition is not new in human history. Judaism, Christianity as well as leading philosophers rejected usury. Aristotle rejected it on the grounds that money is sterile. Cato even compared it with homicide. In 340 BC, the Lex Genucia prohibited interest in the Republic of Rome. In Judaism, interest was considered an unfriendly and unfair act: He that hath not given this money upon usury; nor taken reward against the innocent; he that doeth these things shall never fall.[2] The moral teachings of Jesus in this direction are clear and unqualified: Love your enemies and do good, lend, expect nothing in return.[3] In the eighth century Charlemagne made usury a criminal offence.

Interest provides the incentive for accumulation of money and making more and more of it without the need to sink it in exchange for commercial activities, which has harmful social implications. The prohibition of interest (usury then) in Islam is absolute. A number of Quranic verses reflect the severity of the admonition to those who disobey the divine injunctions to the effect:

> '... they say trading is only like usury, but God has permitted trade and forbidden usury'.[4]

> 'Relinquish what remains of usury, if you are believers. But, if you do not, then be appraised of war from God and his Messenger, and if you repent, you shall have your capital. Wrong not and you shall not be wronged'.[5]

MAN AS VICEGERENT

'I am placing on the earth my vicegerent'.[6]

Everything on this earth and beyond belongs to God. Man is declared to be his vicegerent. In that capacity, he is responsible, he has his freedom, his faculties or intellect, accountability, relations and moral existence. His moral accountability is an integral element. He is here to serve, change, recreate, rebuild, and reconstruct. All the problems of life: social, intellectual, economic, political, cultural, national, international, even sexual are elements of this new moral and ideological approach. He has been entrusted with whatever he has and whatever is there in the world, yet may operate only as a trustee, so he cannot misbehave and misuse the resources given to him on this earth or in the universe. While he is responsible for social and political justice, justice between human beings, individuals, institutions and nations, he is not to create evil on this land. The trusteeship brings the moral questions of accountability and self-accountability before humans and God.

DEFINITION OF MONEY

Based on the above, Islamic economists disputed the traditional definition of money in its entirety, i.e. it is (1) a medium of exchange, (2) a unit of value, (3) a store of value and (4) a medium of differentiated value. While the first two parts of the definition are generally acceptable, money is not thought to be a store of value, as its worth depends on the trend of prices. This is because money itself does not store but only holds a claim to some goods that it may purchase in the future. Holding money is perceived as keeping transactions in abeyance.

Money is not thought to be equivalent to a commodity for the following reasons:

- It has a technical (or artificial) property of yielding its owner real income simply by holding it, without exchanging it for other goods.

- It is liquid and has virtually no carrying or production cost and no substitute.

- Demand for money is not genuine as it is derived from demand for goods that money can buy.

- Money is exempt from the law of depreciation to which all goods are subjected.

- Money is the product of social convention, having a purchasing power derived mainly from the sovereignty over as opposed to the intrinsic value of goods.

IMPLICATIONS OF INTEREST

- Interest is not a true indicator of real generation of capital from economic activity. Interest on deposits is tantamount to arbitrarily creating new capital without a corresponding increase in the supply of goods. This interferes with market forces leading to economic anomaly. In the Islamic economic environment, new capital must be generated from real commercial – not monetary – transactions and should succeed, not precede, a commercial activity. Non-commercial financing (not backed by tangible assets) is virtually eliminated, preventing volatility and inflationary pressures while helping stabilise the value of money.

- Public sector borrowing to meet current expenditure is actually raising debt burdens for future generations to pay. When not backed by any tangible assets, public sector borrowing is considered both unjustified and unethical. Islamic systems allow only asset-backed financing. Governments therefore, can borrow to acquire physical assets so that they are forced to contain their current expenditure within the national resources available to them. Islamic asset-backed financing does not constitute a debt burden on future generations in that the debt is invariably tied to assets of value that can be sold (liquidated) to repay the debt. The prohibition of interest eliminates non-commercial borrowing for the reason that the lender has no incentive in parting with his money. On account of the constraints imposed by the system, the State is unable to raise unlimited amounts to meet current expenditure and is, at least in theory, therefore, prevented from deficit financing.

The Islamic economic system allows for the replacement of interest by a return generated from commercial activities and operations that is evaluated on completion of the transaction, not beforehand. Islamic banks are under no compulsion to provide a fixed rate to depositors, and they do not have to apply the concept of cost of funds to their clients. However, they are, of course, under pressure to produce maximum return from their investment process while safeguarding the client assets.

CHARACTERISTICS OF ISLAMIC BANKS

The following can be considered as the characteristics that distinguish Islamic banks from conventional banks:

- Completely eliminating the factor of usury (interest) from all financial dealings. Accountability to the Religious Board to ensure that its operations and assets are free of the interest factor.
- Acting as universal multi-purpose institutions embodying the functions of both commercial and investment banks.
- Directing the use of funds in a manner that it contributes essentially to the generation of economic activity that gives rise to socio-economic justice within the society by discouraging monopolies and cartels, price manipulation and concentration of wealth.
- Fulfilling a duty to the needy and the poor inspired by religious beliefs.
- Working closely with providers of funds (depositors) in the use of their funds.
- Utilising a high level of expertise and technical know-how for careful evaluation of financing and investment proposals and maintaining much closer relations and monitoring to ensure proper and optimally gainful use of funds provided.
- Enhancing the research and development process in order to develop new products within the precepts of Islamic Shari'a.

MAIN OBJECTIVES OF ISLAMIC BANKS

The main objectives of Islamic banks are as follows:

- Stewardship, mobilising surplus funds, attracting them by providing halal[7] (free of interest) yet competitive investment return.

- Channelling these funds essentially to trade or production-related activities in order that economic activities are enhanced.

- Providing financial support on an ethical and just basis ensuring that their investments do not contribute to undue concentration of wealth in a few hands but rather support value creation by offering the required level of technological expertise and management know-how.

- Providing other banking services to clients efficiently, helping them to undertake their financial dealings in conformity with Islamic Shari'a.

These processes bring into action all the factors of labour, encourage all phases of the business cycle, produce employment, generate new capital and contribute to growth. Technical expertise, rather than collateral, is the basis for finance, giving rise to the creation of new entrepreneurs and the elimination of large conglomerates.

ISLAMIC BANKS AS TRUSTEES

Unlike traditional banks whose client deposits they are borrowing, the Islamic banks are purely intermediaries, carrying out trust and advisory functions. Their client funds (except for demand deposits) are all fiduciary. While traditional banks exploit market imperfections to obtain maximum results for the benefits of their shareholders, Islamic banks maintain a greater balance between the interests of the depositors, shareholders, the users of funds and society.

ISLAMIC BANKS VS. TRADITIONAL BANKS

Due to the nature of Islamic banks, and their contractual relationship with the depositors, they are relatively less risky than traditional banks for a number of reasons:

- For an Islamic bank, deposits other than demand deposits do not count as bank liabilities. Islamic banks are therefore deemed less highly leveraged institutions than traditional banks.

- Certain concepts such as returns do not have the same significance as in the case of traditional banks, since an Islamic bank does not guarantee repayment of principal and profit.

- Depositors with an Islamic bank are deeply involved in its operations. Islamic banks are less likely to experience a run on deposits in the event of an economic upheaval or drastic change in the market conditions.

- Debt to equity and debt to assets ratio are not affected since that financing is made in the form of prepayments and not direct lending.

Meanwhile, in the case of a traditional bank the following apply:

- Liabilities are normally 12 times capital resources. Banks often use similar ratios to limit their customers' behaviour; for example, they may require customers to have a gearing ratio of less than 2.

- Whilst the liabilities of a traditional bank are short term, a good portion of its assets are longer term. Its fractional reserve policy may not always be adequate, particularly in the event of a crisis developing into a run on the bank.

- Because the bank has promised (and that means it guarantees) the return of principal plus interest at a certain future date, the client deposit becomes a loan to, or liability of, the bank. The latter takes a repayment risk, that its assets will provide full book value on the maturity dates to enable repayment. This is in addition to the normal maturity mismatch problem between the bank's assets and liabilities.

ISLAMIC BANK STRUCTURE

Islamic banks are proper organisations established in keeping with the laws, including company laws, of the state in which it operates.

Figure 21.1 shows the typical top level organisational structure of an Islamic bank.

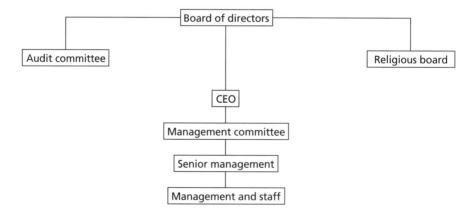

Figure 21.1 Typical organisational structure of an Islamic bank

The Religious Board of an Islamic bank is the ultimate authority with mandatory approval of all products, operations, and services and responsibilities for documentation compliance with Islamic Shari'a. All products, operations, services and documentation are submitted by the management of the bank to the Religious Board for approval before these are offered to the clients.

Table 21.1 lists financial instruments used by Islamic banks.

Table 21.1 Islamic financial instruments

Murabaha (cost plus financing)
This is a contract sale between the bank and its client for the sale of goods at a price that includes a profit margin agreed by both parties. As a financing technique it involves the purchase of goods by the bank as requested by its client. The goods are sold to the client with a mark-up. Repayment, usually in instalments, is specified in the contract.

Mudaraba (trust financing)
This is an agreement made between two parties: one provides 100 per cent of the capital for the project and another party, known as the modarib, manages the project using his entrepreneurial skills. Profits arising from the project are distributed according to a pre-determined ratio. Any losses accruing are borne by the provider of capital. The provider of capital has no control over the management of the project.

Musharaka (partnership financing)
The Islamic financing technique involves a partnership between two parties who both provide capital towards the financing of a project. Both parties share profits based on a pre-agreed ratio, but losses are shared on the basis of equity participation. Management of the project may be carried out by both the parties or by just one party. This is a very flexible partnership arrangement where the sharing of the profits and management can be negotiated and pre-agreed by all parties.

Istisna'a (manufacturing)
A contract acquisition of goods by specification or order, where the price is paid progressively in accordance with progress of a job completion. This is practised, for example, for purchases of houses to be constructed where the payments made to the developer or builder are based on the stage of work completed. In the case of Bai al Salam (described below), the full payment, is made in advance to the seller, i.e. before delivery of goods. In Islamic financing, the applications of Bai al Salam and Istisna'a are purchasing mechanisms, whereas Murabaha and Bai bithaman ajil (described below) are sales mechanisms.

Bai al Salam
Contract of sale of goods, where the price is paid in advance and the goods are delivered in the future.

Bai bithaman ajil
This contract refers to the sale of goods on a deferred payment basis. Equipment or goods (the assets), requested by the client, are bought by the bank, which subsequently sells the goods to the client at an agreed price (the sale price), that includes the bank's mark-up (profit). The client may be allowed to settle payment by instalments within a pre-agreed period, or in a lump sum. Similar to Murabaha contract, this is also a credit sale.

Bai al-dayn
The sale of a debt. To enable the sale to take place, the debts arising out of contracts of exchanges or aqad al muawadhat, such as trade financing (based on the underlying contract of Bail muajjal or bai bithaman ajil) are securitised. The securities are traded in the secondary market under the concept of bai al-dayn. Maturities of these securities evidencing bona fide commercial transactions can be traded.

Table 21.1 Cont'd

Qard ul hasan (A benevolent or good loan)
An interest-free loan given either for welfare purposes or for bridging short-term funding requirements. The borrower is required to pay back only the amount borrowed.

Ijara (Leasing)
A contract under which a bank buys and leases out, for a rental fee, equipment required by its client. The duration of the lease and rental fees are agreed in advance. Ownership of the equipment remains in the hands of the bank. The contract is a classical financial one, now in increasing use worldwide.

Ijara wa-iqtina (Lease/hire purchase)
Very similar to Ijara, except that there is a commitment from the client to buy the equipment at the end of the rental period. It is pre-agreed that at the end of the lease period the client will buy the equipment at an agreed price from the bank, with rental fees previously paid constituting part of the price.

Al-ajr
Refers to commission, fees or wages charged for services, which is the only income generated in the case of bank guarantees.

Al-rahn
An arrangement whereby a valuable asset is placed as collateral for a debt. The collateral may be disposed of in the event of a default.

Although most of these instruments are based on contracts, all commercial transactions based on the above Islamic instruments (where applicable) use letters of credit of all types (as do traditional banks). The difference is that the Islamic banks own the goods until full payment is received from the importer; meanwhile, the importer is given rights for clearing of goods or products as agreed in the contract. Another main difference between Islamic banks and traditional banks is that Islamic banks deal with goods while the latter deal with documents. In cases of default, Islamic banks are in a much better legal position to recover losses since title has not yet passed on to the importer; consequently the Bank has better control and monitoring of the credit. In the case of traditional banks, title of goods has been passed to the importer, and chances of recovery would be subject to security taken.

ACCOUNTING ISSUES

Islamic financial institutions must have fuller financial disclosure than their traditional counterparts, due to the very nature of their relationship with the depositors, which is based on profit sharing. In this regard, much effort has gone into the development of accounting standards for Islamic banks. In 1994, a group in Bahrain started to research and develop guidelines to meet the nature of Islamic banks. Today this group has succeeded in establishing a set of published accounting guidelines which have become known as the Accounting and Auditing Organisation for Islamic Financial Institutions.

Currently, a number of institutions have adopted these guidelines as their financial standards and every day more are doing so.

CHALLENGES FACING ISLAMIC BANKS

Islamic banks still have to overcome a number of issues including the following:

- Absence of a lender of last resort.
- High liquidity positions.
- Non-existence of secondary markets.
- Money markets – today they exist as commodity trading operations rather than conventional money markets.
- Product innovation under Shari'a teachings.
- Pricing yardsticks other than LIBOR. (LIBOR is only used here as an indicative price of the existing markets, and not in its true sense as a mean of interest return.)

FUTURE OF ISLAMIC BANKS

The first Islamic bank started in 1970 in Dubai, United Arab Emirates, and was known as Dubai Islamic Bank. Since then, a number of countries have allowed Islamic banks to be established. Today, Bahrain, Saudi Arabia, Malaysia and Pakistan are the main centres. Furthermore, we see increasing numbers of western banks adopting the Islamic financing concept in their operations. Citibank for example established an Islamic unit in Bahrain with a capital of USD 20 million. ABN AMRO has an Islamic desk through its affiliate Saudi Hollandi Bank. In the United Kingdom, a number of Islamic funds have been launched by brokerage and investment houses among others. Malaysia is the only country that runs a dual central bank system to govern conventional and Islamic financial institutions. Islamic financing is gaining more popularity world-wide as the documentation is simpler and it is less dependent on conventional company accounts.

Three years ago, total funds invested in Islamic products world-wide were around USD 80 billion. This has grown to around USD 150 billion today and is expected to double by the year 2000, due to the growing demand for Islamic institutions and products.

NOTES

This paper reflects the belief and opinions of the author and in no way reflects the beliefs and opinions of his employer.

1. Holy Quran 2.213.
2. Psalm 15.
3. Luke 6.35.
4. Quran 2.275.
5. Quran 2.275.
6. Quran 2.30.
7. Literally 'lawful'.

Index

Acknowledgements

The publisher wishes to thank the following who have kindly given permission for the use of copyright material.

'Estimating Expected Return' reprinted with permission from *Financial Analysts Journal*, January/February. Copyright 1995, Association for Investment Management and Research, Charlottesville, VA. All rights reserved.

'Investment Appraisal Criteria and the Impact of Low Inflation' reprinted with permission from *Quarterly Bulletin*, August 1994, 34(3). Copyright 1994 Bank of England.

'Performance Indicators: 20 Early Lessons from Managerial Use' by Andrew Likierman reprinted with permission from *Public Money & Management*, Oct–Dec. Copyright 1993 CIPFA.

'Stakeholder Capitalism', reprinted with permission from *The State We're In: Why Britain is in Crisis and How to Overcome It*, by Will Hutton. Copyright Jonathan Cape.

'New Ways with Derivatives', by S. Brady, reprinted with permission from *Corporate Finance*, June. Copyright 1996 *Corporate Finance*.

'Brand Owners Must Increase Their Focus on Value-Based Management', reprinted with permission from *Corporate Finance*, Jan. Copyright 1998 *Corporate Finance*.

'Schools Brief: Risk and Return', reprinted with permission from *The Economist*, 2 Feb. Copyright 1991 *The Economist*, London.

'Valuing Companies: A Star To Sail By', reprinted with permission from *The Economist*, 2 Aug. Copyright 1997 *The Economist*, London.

'Ring of Confidence', by G. Cooper, reprinted with permission from *Risk Magazine* 8(9). Copyright 1995, Financial Engineering Ltd.

'Creative Compliance in Financial Reporting', by A. K. Shah, reprinted with permission from *Accounting, Organizations and Society* 2(1). Copyright 1996 Elsevier Science.

'Solving the New Equity Puzzle', by P. Dechow, A. Hutton and R. Sloan, reprinted with permission from Mastering Finance Series, *Financial Times*, Summer. Copyright 1997 *Financial Times*.

'Finding The Right Measure', by T. Jackson, reprinted with permission from *Financial Times*, 23 Oct. Copyright 1996 *Financial Times*.

'Deutsche Telekom Shares Get Cautious Pricing', by W. Münchau, reprinted with permission from *Financial Times*, 18 Nov. Copyright 1996 *Financial Times*.

'Telekom Shares Surge in Buying Frenzy', by W. Münchau and A. Fisher, reprinted with permission from *Financial Times*, 19 Nov. Copyright 1996 *Financial Times*.

'Selling of Capital Investments to Top Management', by O. P. Lumijärvi, reprinted with permission from *Management Accounting Research* 2, 171–188. Copyright 1991 Harcourt Brace.

'The Options Approach to Capital Investment', by A. K. Dixit and R. S. Pindyck, reprinted with permission from *Harvard Business Review*. Copyright 1995 Harvard Business School Publishing.

'How Financial Engineering Can Advance Corporate Strategy', by P. Tufano, reprinted from *Harvard Business Review*, Jan–Feb. Copyright 1996 Harvard Business School Publishing.

'The Balance Scorecard – Measures that Drive Performance', by R. S. Kaplan and D. P. Norton, reprinted from *Harvard Business Review*, Jan–Feb. Copyright 1992 Harvard Business School Publishing.

'Operating Exposure', by D. R. Lessard and J. B. Lightstone, reproduced with permission from *Management of Currency Risk*, edited by B. Antl. Copyright 1989 Euromoney Books, tel 0171 779 8542, fax 0171 779 8541, e-mail embks@dial,pipex.com.

'The Real Power of Real Options' by K. Leslie and M. Michaels, reproduced with permission from *The McKinsey Quarterly* No 3. Copyright 1997 McKinsey & Co.

'Daimler-Benz: A US GAAP Based Stock', by D. Hawkins, reproduced with permission from *Accounting Bulletin* No. 19, 10 Oct. Copyright 1993 Merrill Lynch.

'The Search for Optimal Capital Structure', by S. C. Myers, reproduced from *The Revolution in Corporate Finance*, 2nd Edition, edited by J. M. Stern and D. H. Chew.

'Case Study: Queen Moat Houses plc', reproduced with permission from *Queen Moat Houses plc Annual Accounts*. Copyright Queen Moat Houses plc.

'The Dividend Cut "Heard 'Round the World": the Case of FPL', by D. Soter, E. Brigham and P. Evanson, reproduced with permission from *Journal of Applied Corporate Finance*, 9(1). Copyright 1996 Stern Stewart Management Services.

'The Efficient Market Theory Thrives on Criticism', by D. R. Lee and J. A Verbrugge, reproduced with permission from *Journal of Applied Corporate Finance* 9(1). Copyright 1996 Stern Stewart Management Services.

'Using Earnings and Free Cash Flow to Evaluate Corporate Performance', by R. G. Sloan reproduced with permission from *Journal of Applied Corporate Finance* 9(1). Copyright 1996 Stern Stewart Management Services.

'Rethinking Risk Management', by R. Stulz, reproduced with permission from *Journal of Applied Corporate Finance* 9(1). Copyright 1996 Stern Stewart Management Services.

'Making Accounting More International: Why, How and How Far It Will Go?', by R. Ball, reproduced with permission from *Journal of Applied Corporate Finance* 8(3). Copyright 1995 Stern Stewart Management Services.

'Modules for Standardizing the Process', by A. Steyn and A. Boessenkool, reproduced with their permission.

'The Use of Risk Analysis Techniques in Capital Investment Appraisal', by S. S. M. Ho and R. H. Pike, reproduced with permission from *Risk: Analysis, Assessment and Management*, edited by J. Ansell and F. Wharton. Copyright 1992 John Wiley & Sons.

Every effort has been made to trace and acknowledge ownership of copyright. The publishers will be glad to hear from any copyright holders whom it has not been possible to contact.